THE QUEST FOR SELF-CONTROL

The Quest
for
Self-Control

CLASSICAL PHILOSOPHIES AND
SCIENTIFIC RESEARCH

Edited by

Samuel Z. Klausner

The Free Press, *New York*
Collier-Macmillan Ltd., *London*

To Rina and Jonathan
—*a joy God has given*

PREFACE

Late nineteenth century treatises on psychology still carried chapters on will and self-control. These concepts grew out of an image of man as initiator of action. The action initiated was concrete, directly observable, and enjoyed colloquial meaning. American psychology after G. Stanley Hall and German psychology after Ach and Lewin, lost interest in concepts of will and self-control, in an image of self-directed man, and in concrete acts. The more global have been succeeded by more specific concepts such as drive and motive, voluntary and involuntary muscles, and conscious and unconscious processes. The image of the self-directed person has been replaced by a deterministic model in which behavior is a response either to environmental input or to the environment's internal representatives or the organism's own internal imperatives. Concern with the concrete person and his meaningful acts has given way to the abstraction of an "actor" and the abstract analytical variables of personality theory. Through this threefold shift in specificity of concepts, level of abstraction of the unit of study and image of man, psychology has increased its power as a generalizing science but weakened its hold on such issues as objective guilt, accountability, and human freedom. These issues are meaningful in the light of the possibility of self-control but are refractory to resolution in the deterministic frame of reference. The problem is particularly troublesome because, although psychological science has shifted to a deterministic model, other major social institutions have not. Legal, personal-social, and religious relations persist in defining man as responsible. How is psychological and sociological knowledge to be made relevant to the life of man in these institutions?

This symposium reopens the traditional question of will and self-control to explore ways of articulating twentieth century concepts with the concepts derived from a view of man as an iniator of action. Certain modern social science theorists have succeeded in articulating analytical variables and concrete behavior without reifying the former. Goldstein's concept of "self-actualization," for example, associates the abstract notion of symbolic process with the concrete realization of individual potential. Parsons treats value standards as abstract elements in a theory of culture and as bases of choice in concrete action by introducing a distinction between system levels and then examining the mechanisms by which these levels are articulated. The autonomous ego, described by Hartmann, is considered to develop in a deterministic fashion but then to become relatively independent of and to regulate the instincts from which it has arisen. The following pages add other concepts of self-control which bridge theoretical and behavioral language.

A caveat must be entered at this point in anticipation of a position which will be assumed by some reviewers. The reader should not seek a single theme in the contributions which follow. The book explores "concepts of" rather than, say, "theory of self-control." The sections are intentionally entitled "Self-Control in the Perspective of History" and "Self-Control in Psychological Perspective" and not "History of the Concept of Self-Control" and the "Psychology of Self-Control." This is a "perspectival analysis," which assembles ideas from several "universes of discourse." Its aim is to break out of the parochialism of a single discipline. The concepts of will and self-control have been the prerogative of several disciplines.

The epistemological predilections which guided the editor are those of Ernst Cassirer. Man constructs the world of culture in many symbolic forms. One does not seek the common denominator; rather, one seeks to articulate ideas from "various universes of discourse" in order to achieve an image of the essential. To anticipate the words of the concluding chapter, "Though each paper deals with some aspect of control or of stress, to review them solely in terms of those common themes would sacrifice their uniqueness on the altar of aseptic generalization. Each contribution brings its own legitimate and significant, though different, perspective to the analysis."

The first set of papers, introduced by Paul Kecskemeti, covers some classical, popular and scientific concepts which, over the centuries, have been used in discussing self-controlling behavior. The editor's introductory paper develops a typology for some of these concepts. Benjamin Nelson applies his historical erudition to trace cultural factors accounting for adherence to given conceptions of self-control. His analysis touches on classical but concentrates on medieval methods of "spiritual direction." Moses Hadas combines the sensitivity of the humanist and the precision of the classical scholar to contrast the occasions for self-control in classical Greek and in modern society.

Part Two, introduced by Richard Jung, examines the sociologists' and anthropologists' perspective on self-control. Sanford M. Dornbusch brings his experience with inspirational religious literature to analysis of the means of self-control recommended in temporary nonreligious inspirational literature. Marvin Opler combines his anthropological and social psychiatric background to draw attention to cultural contrasts in defining the control situation, and offers suggestions for those who would help people effect control in various cultural settings. Guy Swanson, in a pioneering conceptualization, uses social psychological studies of primary groups to elucidate the role played by the social matrix in the individual's efforts to control himself.

Saul Sells' introduction to Part Three outlines the psychologist's approach to the problem. Irving Janis, a student of man in disaster, explores some responses to and self-mastery in personal and communal crises. Sheldon Korchin synthesizes his experience in the study of stress behavior in discussing the organism's responses to various stressors. Howard Liddell, in his last public paper, draws upon his work in animal psychophysiology to explain the role of anticipation of danger in human self-control.

John Whitehorn, introducing Part Four, specifies the contribution of psychiatry to understanding of and to training for self-control. David McK. Rioch, with many years as a researcher in clinical settings, uniquely blends information theory and transactional conceptions to demonstrate the essentially social nature of

self-control. Martin Orne, a leading researcher in medical hypnosis, weighs the relevancy of hypnotic phenomena in general and
of self-hypnosis in particular to our problem. Kurt Goldstein, who
assumed a position of leadership in neurological research over
forty years ago with his studies of aphasia, deals with self-control
as an aspect of realizing one's potential. Self-realization involves
both the abstract attitude and encounter with the other in the
sphere of immediacy. The final chapter is the editor's attempt to
identify a few research hypotheses suggested by our contributors'
propositions.

This volume developed from work on self-management initiated by Albert D. Biderman. His keen insight and singular ability
to adopt a new perspective on an old problem were available to
the editor throughout. Robert T. Bower, the Director of the Bureau
of Social Science Research, was a constant source of encouragement in the endeavor. Especial appreciation is due to Charles E.
Hutchinson and Herman J. Sander of the Behavioral Sciences
Division of the Air Force Office of Scientific Research for their
generous administrative and substantive counsel. Earlier drafts
of these papers were presented at a Conference on Self-Control
Under Stressful Conditions held in Washington, D.C., on September
9 and 10, 1962. This Conference and preparation of the manuscript were supported by contract AF 49(638)-992 awarded by
the Air Force Office of Scientific Research to the Bureau of Social
Science Research. Much of the burden of preparing and organizing the conference was borne by Carol Bergman. The manuscripts
for the conference and for this book reflect the labor of Antonette
Simplicio, Rosa Greene, Wenonah Heyl, and June Licence.

Samuel Z. Klausner

Washington, D.C.
January 1965

CONTRIBUTORS

Sanford M. Dornbusch, Ph.D.
Professor of Sociology, Stanford University

Kurt Goldstein, M.D.
New York City

Moses Hadas, Ph.D.
Jay Professor of Greek and Chairman of the Department of Greek and Latin, Columbia University

Irving Janis, Ph.D.
Professor of Psychology, Yale University

Richard Jung, Ph.D.
Associate Professor of Sociology, Cornell University

Paul Kecskemeti, Ph.D.
Senior Research Associate, The Rand Corporation; Senior Research Fellow, Institute for the Study of Communist Problems, Columbia University

Samuel Z. Klausner, Ed.D., Ph.D.
Research Associate, Bureau of Social Science Research

Sheldon Korchin, Ph.D.
Professor of Psychology, University of California, Berkeley

Howard Liddell, Ph.D. (Deceased)
Late Professor of Psychobiology, Director of the Behavior Farm Laboratory, Cornell University

Benjamin Nelson, Ph.D.
Professor of History and Sociology, Chairman, Department of Sociology-Anthropology, State University of New York, Long Island Center, Stony Brook-Oyster Bay

Marvin K. Opler, Ph.D.
Professor of Social Psychiatry, Department of Psychiatry, University of Buffalo School of Medicine; Professor of Sociology, Graduate School of the University of Buffalo

Martin T. Orne, M.D., Ph.D.
Director, Unit for Experimental Psychiatry, The Institute of the Pennsylvania Hospital; Associate Professor of Psychiatry, University of Pennsylvania Medical School

David McK. Rioch, M.D.
Director, Division of Neuropsychiatry, Walter Reed Army Institute of Research

S. B. Sells, Ph.D.
Professor of Psychology, Texas Christian University

Guy E. Swanson, Ph.D.
Professor of Sociology, University of Michigan

John C. Whitehorn, M.D.
Professor Emeritus of Psychiatry, John Hopkins University

CONTENTS

PART
ONE
} SELF-CONTROL
IN THE
PERSPECTIVE
OF HISTORY

Introduction

"Self-control under conditions of stress" looks at first glance like a narrow, special subject—no doubt important enough in a stressful and anxiety-ridden age such as ours, but still a marginal one, relevant only to exceptional situations of a circumscribed kind.

Yet when we look at the subject more closely, we cannot help noticing its general implications. "Keeping a cool head when things go wrong," one of the typical problems related to self-control under stress, is not a matter of special technique but of the whole personality. The problem has hidden angles, as shown by a humorous sign often seen in offices: IF YOU REMAIN CALM AND COLLECTED WHEN THINGS ARE IN A TURMOIL AND EVERYBODY AROUND YOU IS FRANTIC, THEN" [in small print underneath]: "maybe you just don't understand the situation." This is a profound joke, a metaphysical joke. Reason, understanding is what you need to master life, but understanding may also make you lose your mastery. The problem of self-control and stress summons up a paradox that has to do with man's central faculty, the faculty of reason.

Thus, you must not be surprised to find that the papers to be presented at this conference range rather far. They deal with religious doctrines and philosophical systems, cultural institutions and the history of civilization, normal and abnormal psychology, and so forth—there is hardly an important aspect of man's life in society

that isn't somehow brought into the picture. Self-control under
stress, indeed, flows from, and depends upon, all these things.

To get a preliminary glimpse of the generality and complexity
of our subject, we may start by analyzing a few common locutions
related to self-control. We sometimes tell someone, maybe a child:
"You must control yourself!" Here the "self" is the *object* of control; the "yourself" is that which is to be controlled. What part or
aspect of the self is the one that has to be brought under control
here? It may be an appetite, an insistent begging for satisfaction, an
expression of hostility, of pain, or possibly, of delight; it may be
sheer exuberance, excitement, motor activity. In short, that which
is to be kept under control is the spontaneous, expressive side of
personality. And it is society which imposes this control from the
outside, through a mouthpiece who administers the exhortation.

Keeping expressive behavior under check is an important part
of socialization in every culture, but cultures differ both as to the
types of expressive behavior which they control and as to the
degree, the severity of control. Our culture puts a more severe
check upon the spontaneity and exuberance of verbal expression
than, say, the Latin American; it is more permissive toward the
outward manifestation of pain than, say, the American Indian.
Control, then, is very much a topic in the comparative analysis
of culture.

But then, the "Self" in self-control is not only that which is
to be controlled. It is, at the same time, the *subject,* the agent of
control, that which controls. This aspect of self-control comes to
the fore, for example, in the locution: "He has tremendous self-
control." Here it is still the expressive, spontaneous side of behavior which is being controlled, but control by the "self" is now
an accomplished fact. We no longer expostulate with the other
to "control himself," but admire him for doing so. There is just
a hint at limitations in this praise—it is possible to have too much
self-control, to curb spontaneous expression too much. But at any
rate, the man with self-control has demonstrated, at least, that he
is his own master.

Or is he? Is it really the case that only the recipient of the
admonition, "control yourself," is being controlled from the outside, by society, while the man with self-control actually controls
himself in autonomous fashion? It is easy to see that no such neat
contrast can be drawn here. When we say, "control yourself," we
mean that you must do the trick *yourself,* acting on behalf of
society and addressing its dictate to yourself. Control by society

or by an external authority is not incompatible with *self*-control, self-*imposed* control. It is part and parcel of it. Nobody needs, and has, as much self-control as the man completely controlled by, and dependent on, others—the slave, the prisoner. On the other hand, the man with self-control is his own master in the sense that he has taken over the controlling role from social authority: he has internalized the dictates of authority.

But is this all there is to self-control finally achieved? Is moral autonomy, for example, sheer illusion, dependence on authority masquerading as self-mastery? In this matter, I think, we must beware of neat, all-or-nothing solutions. No, the moral individual is not sovereign; he is not the sole fountainhead of his moral insights and feelings. He must have learned morality from someone. But he is also no mere "internalizer," just carrying a "superego," a precipitate of external control, within himself. Learning is not passive "internalization." It is also a creative process. All real learning is learning of a mastery. It begins with dependence and ends in freedom.

The mere curbing of expressive spontaneity is no genuine learning in this sense. The real problem of socialization is not just to check exuberance, but to regulate it so that expressive spontaneity can be preserved without disrupting society—or the subject himself. One must "control himself" in order to be able to be spontaneous without cracking, without succumbing to inner pressure.

This takes us to the other part of our topic, "stress." When self-control is achieved in the process of socialization, internal stresses are being mastered. But there are many other stresses to cope with in life, both of internal and external origin. Let us take another locution, related to severe *external* stress: "I must not lose my head now; I am lost if I do." What is to be controlled here is not the expressive, spontaneous self, nor is that which controls a proxy, an agent for society. Control here means the preservation of meaning, *Gestalt,* the integrated functioning of the organism; that which is to be kept under control is a surging chaos, formlessness, a shapeless and meaningless force that threatens to flood and disrupt the subject-in-situation as an integrated whole. The subject, threatened with disruption, responds with heightened vigilance, it becomes sheer concentrated awareness of everything, down to the smallest detail, upon which the preservation of its integrity depends.

When acute stress of this sort is too great, the integrative effort snaps, and the subject performs meaningless, inadaptive responses. It may become inarticulate, crying, acting without a goal; it may sink into torpid passivity or address itself to trivial details that it still can master (as will be shown by Professor Goldstein).

Stress, threatening to disrupt the integrity of the subject-in-situation, is not necessarily the result of an exceptional combination of circumstance. The human condition itself is inexorably generating stresses in the shape of what Jaspers called "limit situations:" illness, pain, conflict, betrayal of love, shattering of hopes, the ultimate certainty of death. Much of the meaning of human culture is summed up in a man's effort to come to terms with these chronic stresses, inherent in his condition. Here we are confronted with the protecting, preserving function of the major institutions, agencies, techniques with which many of the papers to be presented deal, ranging from yoga and Western religious beliefs and practices to academic psychotherapy on the one hand, vulgar forms of "self-help" on the other.

Contrasting with the chronic, potentially ever-present stress of the "limit situations," there is the acute stress produced by sudden disasters whose disruptive force stems from their being wholly unexpected and unassimilable. This will be discussed in Professor Janis' lecture.

As our introduction to our vast topic, you will hear Dr. Klausner present his essay, "Collocation of Concepts of Self-Control." Dr. Klausner is intimately familiar with two disparate fields of study, both of which, however, are eminently germane to our topic: religion and psychotherapy; he is engaged on a major work on the interrelation of the two fields. His paper articulates our subject in terms of objects of control (the functions that are to be controlled), the objectives to be achieved by control, the major techniques used, and examines the approach toward these problems practiced by various traditional or novel schools of thought.

When we hear of techniques of control, of social agencies helping or forcing man to control himself, the thought uppermost in our mind is that of limits set once and for all, permanent barriers raised against disruptive forces. Human reality, however, knows of no permanent barriers of this sort. It is set in the stream of history which inexorably breaks down all limits, washes away all barriers. Viewed from this angle, control is a never-ending, ever-to-be-renewed task.

In order to understand this aspect of the problem of control, we must study it in its historic setting. This will be done by Professor Nelson. His paper reveals a profound sense of history, precisely in its spiritual dimension, as a process breaking through limits and calling forth both new forms of stress and new ways of coming to terms with it. The constant urge to go beyond limits, to explore the uncharted frontier regions of human existence and experience, is particularly characteristic of the Western tradition. This is what sets the West off against other cultural areas.

Professor Nelson portrays this restless search in all its rich detail from the formative period of Western culture to its present stage. It is a complex story of never-ending tension—tension between the idea of spiritual guidance and the autonomous quest of the individual, and tension between religious and secular centers of authority. In order to understand our present situation in its historical setting, we have to see it suspended between the poles of this tension.

After this exploration of the Western background in its breadth, we come to a particular subject, the "Greek paradigm." There is a good reason for singling out the Greeks as a paradigmatic case. What happened in Greece, or rather in Athens, about 500 B.C. was a rare event, a real cultural mutation which became decisive for further cultural developments.

A cultural mutation occurs when a small, circumscribed region in a homogeneous cultural world becomes discontinuous with the surrounding area, particularly in terms of symbol systems and communication. Discontinuities in communication, esoteric cults, languages, and symbols, of course, are rather common phenomena. But the discontinuity involved in a cultural mutation is not of this sort. The new, discontinuous symbol system of the mutant culture is not the property of a secret, select circle or cult community. It is wholly public and permeates education and ordinary communication within the mutant group. The Greek word for this is *paideia:* a form of thought, feeling and symbolization, imparted by the culture, which is both public and esoteric, and sets the mutant culture off against the homogeneous "barbarian" world.

When such a mutation is successful, it radiates forth into the surrounding world and becomes the universal pattern. This is what happened with Greek *paideia* during the Hellenistic period. During the last few centuries, a similar thing happened as a result of a Western European "mutation," itself inspired by the Greek paradigm and its Hellenistic and Roman offshoots. The medieval world was still to a large extent homogeneous: it had, of course, a large variety of languages, customs, social classes, religions and political systems, but people still were able to communicate, as it were, on the same level. All basic symbols were homologous; no region was singled out as the discontinuous domain of a "higher," public-esoteric *paideia,* defining a contrast between "ins" and "outs," "Hellenes" and "barbarians." But the emergence of the Western urban paradigm was a mutation; it rendered culture discontinuous, it created a contrast between "high" civilization and barbarism or savagery. Eventually, as in the Greek case, the mutant spread over the world; the Western urban form of civilization is now becoming a universal pattern.

Professor Hadas, then, though he disclaims any special competence in matters of stress and control, has a substantial contribution to make to our topic, by showing us the background and nature of that historic mutation in which forms of cultural control and guidance fully familiar to ourselves first came to light. He needs no introduction: he is universally known as a foremost exponent of classical scholarship. As such, he inhabits two worlds. He is a member of the esoteric cult of philological erudition, a cult having its heady, secret pleasures, similar to the Epicurean "raptures without hangover" to which he will refer in his talk. But Professor Hadas is also the man of synthesis, a master of the comprehensive and large topics, as his works on Roman literature and the culture and history of late antiquity testify. He brought those crucial periods of history close to us by original insights freshly illuminating some dark corners of the human experience.

SAMUEL Z. KLAUSNER

A Collocation of Concepts of Self-Control

The study of the mechanisms through which the human is able to control his behavior brings us directly to the problem of *will*. One may state without fear of contradiction that no other psychological question has a history so fraught with errors; the actual history of the study of will is a history of mistakes, and the inventory of the contemporary psychological conceptions concerning will is a cemetery of fallacies, of loosely put questions and trivial investigations. A. R. Luria (79)* p. 397.

Introduction

The problem of self-control has remained an intransigent enigma among scholars. Some intransigencies may be traced to inflexible formulations of the question. How have our intellectual predecessors formulated the question of self-control? What answers have they tendered? We shall review the concepts found in 290 books and articles on man's ability to control his own behavior. These concepts comprise the tradition from which the contributors to this book proceed in reassessing ways of asking the question and of pursuing an answer.

The search for writings on self-control was guided by some rules of thumb which delimited, without defining, the subject. Items were selected which describe individuals or groups pressed

* Numbers in parentheses refer to the item in the bibliography.

9

by their environment or by their own inner worlds. This press would wreak change in each individual were he not to intervene behaviorally or attitudinally to prevent it. Contrariwise, items were selected which describe individuals who decide upon and effect self-change. Writings not bearing directly on self-control were admitted if it seemed possible to infer what the authors would say had they discussed self-control. Limits were set upon the means of self-control to be considered. Works dealing with the possibility of control by symbolic processes were given priority. Further, the individual was not to be expected to affect the source of the press, control the actions of other individuals, nor introduce foreign agents, such as chemicals, to change the state of his body or mind. These types of environmental manipulation, such as persuasive control of one's social setting, and changing one's physiological state, with tobacco, alcohol, or tranquilizers, are doubtless a significant means of self-control in our culture (175). Limiting inquiry to symbolic processes was a restriction on the scope of this paper rather than a judgment on the efficacy of these other means. Further, the emphasis was to be on conscious control of the self. Conscious, in this context, means that the aspect of the self which the individual controls is identical with the aspect he manifestly intends to control. He need not be aware of the mechanisms which intervene between his effort and the outcome. Without this restriction, our subject matter would be difficult to distinguish from a general theory of behavior. By and large, attention was fixed upon theoretical statements and empirical generalizations to the exclusion of primary case materials.

An exhaustive coverage of the relevant literature was not our aim. Rather, the attempt was to locate strategic or typical items in the literature of several of the intellectual traditions which have given attention to the problem of self-control. The items examined were from the traditions in Table 1.

Sociological work on social control, social philosophical works on freedom, and still other literatures have implications for self-control but were excluded by the demands of time.

Both scientific and popular literature in a given age and clime may employ the same image in asking the self-control question but might disagree on appropriate ways to seek and to validate an answer to the question. These two forms of literature will be treated together, since our task is to delineate rather than to evaluate the basic models of thought about self-control.

The attempt to sum across varied traditions encounters a terminological barrier. It would be tempting to summarize the material in psychological language. To do so, however, would be reductionist and would vitiate one of our basic purposes—to grasp and present the several thought models in the literature. Consequently, our preference is for the classical or the more nearly generic terms. Unless specifically referring to modern psychology, the term "will" is used rather than "drive" or "motive." To refer to a balancing of objects or forces, the term "harmony," rather than the more parochial "homeostasis" or "equilibrium," is used to entitle one of the sections of this review. Since the classical terminology has accreted an array of connotations, the reader should attend to the sense in which the terms appear in this paper.

The possibility of self-control rests upon the possibility of reflexive cognition. This review, therefore, begins with a short note on self-consciousness. Efforts at control generally are aimed at certain aspects of rather than at the whole self. The succeeding section outlines these aspects of self or objects of control. Certain questions follow. What is the relation between the function which exerts control and the aspects of self which are controlled? Is self-control a distinct executive function in the psyche or is it some principle of order immanent in the objects of control themselves? What are the relative merits of direct versus indirect ap-

Table 1—Number of Items from Each Intellectual Tradition Examined in the Preparation of This Chapter

	No. of Items
I. Religious and Philosophical Writings	
1. Yoga and religious mysticism.	14
2. Philosophical writings and studies of classical societies.	24
II. Psychology	
3. Personality psychology, will psychology, theories of motivation and learning.	69
4. Psychoanalysis, ego psychology and general works on psychotherapy.	64
5. Social psychology, small group studies and morale studies.	45
6. Studies of laboratory and situational stress.	23
7. Hypnosis and suggestion.	10
III. Popular	
8. Popular self-help literature, self-mastery, works on control of diet and sex.	41
Total items reviewed	290

proaches to control? What then are the mechanisms or methods by which self-control is effected? A formal typology of methods of control constitutes the major part of this review. Discussion of these issues is confined to the comments found in the literature under review. None of these issues is explored in all of its ramifications. To avoid unnecessarily burdening the reader, only a few illustrative items from the appended bibliography are cited in the text.

Self-Consciousness

Consciousness is a vehicle of perception, the subject or the "I." Self is an observed "me" among other objects, perceived and evaluated in consciousness. Self-control premises a conscious grasping and directing of the self. How, though, is consciousness thought to grasp its objects?

The self-control literature relates consciousness and its world of objects in three ways: (1) the external world, including self, is a creature of consciousness; (2) consciousness and its primary object, the self, are both products of the external world; they are created through the impact of the world, in the form of experience, on the organism; (3) consciousness is an emergent from the interaction between self and the world. These conceptions are not so much distinct positions as they are questions of an author's emphasis.

According to Kant, consciousness constructs its world with the help of experience. The "a priori" forms of consciousness shape raw experience in a cognitive mold. Hegel, conceiving of consciousness as manifested in the relation of ego to an object, agrees, in part, with the Kantian position. Consciousness could not be a product of the external world, since the latter exists only for a self-conscious subject. However, Hegel does not limit consciousness to cognitive apperception but sees it as an activity guarded by will. Consciousness is realized as the will, not cognition alone, chooses among inclinations (10). Both of these positions give priority to an innate power which constructs the world, including the self, for the individual.

A second tendency is to consider the environment as a primary source of consciousness. Freud, for example, considers consciousness as an aspect of ego evolved through experience. After being so evolved, it filters stimuli entering the self from the outer world (131). G. H. Mead combines the view that consciousness is constructive of its world with the view that consciousness is a product of the world. Environment is not totally objective. Color, for example, has meaning only for an organism equipped with vision. Consciousness, the subject or "I," observes the self or "me" as a special region of the environment. This region of self is created through internalization of certain features of the environment (199).

The third emphasis, considering consciousness as an emergent, builds on the Hegelian dialectic. There is a difference of opinion, however, regarding the elements that enter the synthesis. Marx rejects the Hegelian view of consciousness as a creature of will and the Kantian view relating it to prehension. Self-consciousness emerges from the interaction of work, or human activity, and the world (138). Darwin assents to the dialectic in principle but envisions an intra-individual conflict among expressive movements as accounting for consciousness. He uses the organism-environment dialectic to account for change in the organism or evolution (51). Tillich takes the position that self and consciousness emerge in an act of affirmation, an act executed despite anxiety (20). Similarly, Goldstein says the self is actualized in an affirmative answer to the shocks of existence (186). Sartre is not concerned about the genesis of consciousness, which he sees as a contentless activity. The engagement of this activity, however, with the world of objects creates ego or self as a transcendent object (17).

Each of these views has an implication for self-control. If consciousness is prior to and constructs the world, including the self, then control efforts would involve mental imagery to induce a personal event. Mental imagery, a content of consciousness, would be the handle for grasping consciousness and bending its power to the will. This is the approach of the mind-cure movements. If, on the other hand, consciousness results from the impact of environment on the individual, control would involve selecting an environment which would have the desired impact on the self. Setting up stimuli for the self, auto-conditioning and behavioral control by selecting desirable companions follow from this conception. If self-consciousness is conceived as an emergent of a situation of conflict, control would be a matter of engaging the threat and accepting a changed self as the result of the engagement. Training in soldier courage by mastering successively greater threats is an example of this model with the threat considered as external. If self-consciousness emerges from internal conflict, including conflict among internalized representatives of external objects, the effort might be directed to cognitively mediating the intra-psychic forces. Much recent psychotherapy rests upon this model.

Self-consciousness creates the possibility of a reflexively oriented effort. The conception of the genesis and nature of self-consciousness dictates the methods and objects of control. The next section describes those aspects of self upon which the effort of control may be exerted. A later section outlines the methods of control.

Manifest Objects of Control

Self-control connotes a more or less molar behavioral or attitudinal consequence of effort. The effort of control, however, is not directed to the whole self but to specific aspects of it. These behaviors and attitudes consciously selected for control may be termed the manifest objects of control.

The writings were classified according to their primary concern with each of four types of manifest objects of control. The control consists, in each case, of facilitating or inhibiting the action of these objects. These include the effort to control (1) overt performances by facilitating or inhibiting certain movements; (2) psychological or physiological drives of the organism by facilitating drive reduction or by enabling the person to act despite drive pressure; (3) intellectual or cognitive functions by facilitating thoughts, such as in eliminating worry or acting despite distraction; or (4) affects or emotions such as internal feeling states of elation, depression or anxiety, or organizing a cathexis or a counter-cathexis. Some authors are concerned with controlling the relation of the self to social, physical or cultural objects. This was classed along with control of the affects, since it involves the strengthening or weakening of object cathexes.

The intellectual traditions represented in the literature are not equally concerned with each manifest object of control. Table 2 provides some impression of the objects of control with which writers in each tradition are concerned. This table merely summarizes. It does not show a generalizable statistical relation between the type of literature and the manifest objects of control because the items upon which it is based are not drawn from representative samples of work in the various traditions.

Performance is of most concern to writers on yoga and personality theory. Yoga teaches physical feats such as posturing, sphincter and breath control. The interest in performance in personality literature is related, in part, to studies of the control of overt movements by will and, in part, to more recent studies on the relation of personality to task performance.

The self-help literature is particularly concerned with drive control. This may derive, in part, from moralistic attitudes toward physiological drives which are prominent in the works on diet and sex control. It may also be related to this literature's concern with task accomplishment. Much of this work is written in the tradition of ascetic Protestantism. The popular interpretation suggests that uncontrolled drives may interfere with the accomplishment of higher tasks.

Intellectual control has divergent meanings in the traditions giving it a prominent place. The stress literature analyzes intellectual acumen under difficult conditions. Subjects, for example, may attempt to solve problems while being harassed. The hypnosis and suggestion literature sees mind control as a path to total control. Psychoanalytic literature, positing an interweaving of cognitive and affective functions, considers intellectual facilitation to obtain affective control. Part of the classical and philosophical literature views the faculty of reason as the source of all self-control.

The control of affects, often formulated as anxiety control, is central in the personality, psychoanalytic and social psychological literatures. These literatures have been concerned with

Table 2—Principal Manifest Objects of Control in Works
of Various Intellectual Traditions

Intellectual Tradition	MANIFEST OBJECT OF CONTROL (PERCENTAGES)					
	Performance	Drive	Intellect	Affect	Total	N
Yoga	24	20	36	20	100	(14)
Philosophy	4	26	40	30	100	(24)
Personality	21	12	23	44	100	(69)
Psychoanalysis	6	14	38	42	100	(64)
Social Psychology	11	13	33	43	100	(45)
Stress	17	5	52	26	100	(23)
Hypnosis	10	18	45	27	100	(11)
Self-Help	5	65	19	11	100	(41)

feelings, such as depression, enthusiasm, worry or internal tensions. The self-help literature is notable for lack of interest in affective control. Despite its advice on how to stop worrying, its main thrust is to enable the person to engage the world about him.

Performance and drive involve mastering the self as it relates to the world. Intellectual and affective control are matters internal to the self. Grouping the manifest objects of control according to their external or internal orientations shows that the yoga and self-help literature aim for mastery of the self in relation to the world. Each of these traditions is concerned with the external world for a different reason. Yoga aims to free the individual from his bondage to the world. Self-help literature aims for mastery of the self as a stepping stone to mastery of the environment. Stress, psychoanalytic and hypnosis literatures concentrate on the inner self. The first two are concerned with internal strength despite a stressor environment and the last describes the self's accepting of and submitting to environmental control.

These imageries of the manifest objects of control are keys to the social philosophy associated with the intellectual traditions. The yogin's enemy is the soul's striving toward an illusory environment. The controlled self becomes an asocial self. The self-help literature affirms man's ability to translate self-mastery into environmental control. Control of self would eventuate in shaping the world to the will of man. The image in the stress, psychoanalysis and hypnosis literatures, except insofar as they are cross-fertilized by the self-help literature, is of man hoping to cope and survive while being almost overwhelmed by his environment. Self-control eventuates in a truce between self and environment. Their's is a philosophy of the steady state.

The Controlling Function

The manifest objects of control—performance, drive, intellect, and affect—are acted upon by some controlling function. The controlling function may, among other terms, be called will, drive, or reason. The objects and the function that controls them are conceptually distinguishable. Empirically, however, the distinction may not be as clear. The writings under review describe three types of relation between the controlling function and its controlled objects: the controlling function is thought of as (1) separate and different in kind from the controlled objects; (2) an object differing from the others only in its executive function; or (3) as an emergent from the patterning of the controlled objects.

A controlling function separate and different in kind from the controlled objects and which exercises a hegemony over those objects is a monarchical authority. This is the position of, for instance, faculty psychology. This conception preserves freedom for the will. The action of this separate and different controlling function is conceived in two ways: in terms of cognitive elements involved in making a decision and also as a power to effect a decision. Aristotle, in the first tradition, attributes to will the function of deciding between appetites (2). Reason assumes this role in Stoic thought (7). St. Thomas conceives of will as obeying principles different from those immanent in other aspects of an act. Part of an act belongs to nature and so follows deterministic rules. The will, however, directs the act by selecting its end. This selection is made freely. Aquinas compares this with the way the end is predetermined for the arrow by the archer while it otherwise obeys the principles of nature (18). In post-Thomistic philosophy will as drive, the notion of will as power, receives more attention. Hobbes, for example, considers it an appetite, the last appetite in deliberating (1). The notion of will as a selector has been revived in some psychoanalytic thinking. Ferenczi, for example, describes will as less like a locomotive than like a pointsman who closes off all but one path (122).

The second broad conception of the controlling function describes will as separate, but not different in kind, from the controlled. Will is a controlling motive or instinct which differs from the controlled instincts only in its executive function. This is a conception of will as a republican authority. Ebbinghaus and Bain term the will a special kind of instinct controlling other instincts. Ebbinghaus, in the tradition of will as a cognitive selector, describes the distinctive character of the controlling instinct as prescience (44). Bain, in the tradition of will as drive, describes it as a motive among other motives (43). Some psychoanalysts follow this model. Kubie, for example, conceives of tertiary or executive instincts which are otherwise similar to the instincts under control (159). Skinner's notion of a controlling response is formally similar. It is a response like any other, but is associated with the response to be controlled in such a way that it may impose a degree of physical restraint upon it (101). Lewin's concept of intention is also separate but not different from what it controls. Personality is constituted by tension or field forces organized in various ways. Intention, as an attitude which directs activity, occupies its own organized region of personality (76).

The autonomous function of the ego, as discussed by ego psychologists, stands between the notion that the controlling function is qualitatively different from the controlled and the notion that it is similar in kind to the controlled objects. The autonomous ego derives from the instincts. Through differentiation it becomes independent of them and relates to them as a regulatory factor (147). Intelligence, for example, is an aspect of ego autonomy which organizes other functions (147) including the scrutinizing of drives and defenses (162). Federn, in this tradition, combines both the selective and effective aspects of control. Will is the turning of libido cathexis, which the ego has at its disposal, to particular activities (117).

The third broad type of conception views the controlling function as a product of the organization of the elements to be controlled. This is a theory of emergence according to which will does not exist as an independent function, but comes into being when motives are organized. Will participates in a kind of primitive communism as the principle of order defining the motive pattern. Guthrie, for example, sees voluntary action and will as emergents from the juxtaposition of two incompatible acts when one is inhibited and the other realized (61). Sherrington infers will from a harmonious pattern of the moment. The fact that the pattern is harmonious means that it expresses a principle of order. Incompatible elements are automatically excluded (99). Wheeler explicitly writes of will as an emergent from the interaction or organization of elements in the situation. Will is the surplus by which the whole exceeds the mere sum of elements (107).

The theory of emergence is also stated in the reverse of the above. The elements to be controlled are conceived as emergents from, or objectifications of, will. Schopenhauer, for example, considers will as primary and the individual and world, the objects of control, as manifestations of will (1). Similarly, Rank identifies will as a primal force and the ego as its representative (166).

The type of relation thought to subsist between the controlling function and the objects of control may influence the choice of self-control method. If will is considered a distinct and specialized faculty, a monarchical authority over the objects of control, training or exercising this faculty would be a logical method. Practicing little self-disciplines, self-denials, or mortifications might strengthen the faculty. As an autonomous faculty, an increase in its strength might lead to increased self-control in all areas over which it rules. If will is considered similar in kind, but differentiated in function, from the objects to be controlled, a republican authority over otherwise equal citizens, the problem of self-control would become one of influencing the process of functional differentiation, the process by which the authority arises. This is exemplified by psychologists' concern with the experiences by which an autonomous ego develops out of the instincts. Within this conception, child training would stress development of autonomy and self-control. If will is seen as a principle of order among the elements to be controlled, a primitive communism, self-control would involve regulating the relations among the elements. This might involve introducing a kind of over-all life planning guided by principles of psychological and physical economics.

Direct Versus Indirect Approaches

The controlling effort is not necessarily exerted directly upon the ultimate object of control. An individual endeavoring to control his fear of diving might begin with an intellectual appraisal of the act or he might begin by perfecting his performance in small plunges into the water. The ultimate object, fear, is approached through control of intellect or of performances. A body of opinion in the self-control literature recommends an indirect approach. Luria, for example, states it as a fundamental law that direct attempts to control behavior always lead to negative results (79). Baudouin cites a law of reversed effort to the effect that conscious efforts to counteract a suggestion tend to intensify the suggestion (241).

Indirection requires traversing a series of intermediate steps to the goal. Its rationale may be that the element to be controlled is not the manifest one, or that control involves a factor of delay. In the first case, the manifest object of control may be recognized as a symptom. The distinction between action on a symptom and the treatment of an underlying condition is familiar in medical and psychological literature. Popular literature also advances the caveat to search out the underlying cause (283).

Reference to a time factor, the second case, is inherent in the distinction between voluntary and impulsive action. Voluntary may be defined in terms of inhibition of immediate response, some pause before action (147, 61). Control requires both effecting the pause and using the content that fills it. For example, a pause in overt intellectual activity may evoke fantasy. In psychological thinking, this fantasy may serve as a detour to the discovery of a reality relation (147, 159). Delay allows scanning and selecting among possibilities.

In either case, a series of steps mediates between the initial act and the goal of control. The series may begin with an easy step and proceed to more difficult control feats. Each preceding act triggers succeeding acts (102). Selye recommends entering a control process at an early stage. To control insomnia, for instance, he suggests refraining from excitement during the day (96). If control is indirect, it is necessary to develop self-control maps. These maps would designate the ultimate goal of control and work back through associated mechanisms to points at which one might realistically apply the initial effort. Wenger and Bagchi attribute the yogin's control of autonomically innervated functions to their use of intervening voluntary mechanisms. Control of heartbeat, for example, is achieved through striated muscle intervention (36).

Methods of Control

We have discussed a controlling function and the manifest objects of control. It was suggested above that the conception of the relation between the function and the objects would influence the method recommended for effecting control. What are the methods recommended in the writings under review?

Four images of the methods of self-control inform this literature.

1. An individual may control himself by selecting his environment. Selected stimulus input elicits the desired responses. For example, one may attend a movie in search of stimuli which evoke pleasurable responses. An alarm clock enables a person to rise at a designated hour. Because this method involves an interchange between the environment and the self-system, it will be termed the *effort to synergy.*

2. Control may mean facilitating the good and inhibiting the evil, of practicing some habits and overcoming others. This image grasps the springs of action dualistically. For example, one may attain good penmanship by practicing an appropriate style or, as some authors maintain, one may avoid salacious thoughts by developing a concern for acceptable ideas. Since control means the triumphs of one pole and the defeat of its opposite, this will be termed the *effort to conquest*.

3. Self-control may be thought of as getting in tune with nature. This involves behaving consistently with one's physical constitution or personality. For example, in playing tennis one should swing his arms in the direction of normal muscle movement and not work against the muscles. In social relations, if one dislikes an activity or a person that the values decree should be liked, one should accept his feelings as consistent with his personality predispositions and deal with them consciously. To deny them would lead to displacing the tension. This method will be called the *effort to harmony*.

4. Control may involve realizing that the threat to the self cannot be denied. One accepts the threat as part of the situation of action and acts or affirms oneself despite it. For example, a man may be afraid to risk a business investment though he must execute it to avoid financial failure. He acts in full awareness of the possibility of failure, but his act affirms him as courageous and provides the possibility of success. A social relations example would be an individual accepting a person whom he wants to accept despite a feeling of hostility toward him. These acts of control are based upon a dialectic synthesis of an impulse toward action and a threat working against action. Because the act of control resolves both poles of an ambivalence in a higher synthesis, this will be termed the *effort to transcendence*.

EFFORT TO SYNERGY

The effort to synergy involves exposing the self to inputs from some external system. The external system may be constituted by stimuli which elicit responses from the self in an automatized manner or it may consist of a social structure or set of symbols toward which the self is oriented. The initial effort, presumably accomplished voluntarily, brings the self into a relation with the outside system. If this outside system consists of stimuli to which the self has been conditioned, the responses follow a more or less deterministic pattern. If it is a social or symbol system, the self is pressed toward making additional choices regarding the legitimacy of the demands of the external system and whether to abide by these demands or endure negative sanctions from the system. A social orientation may also involve deterministic features. Each social response is a learning experience which increases the accessibility or inaccessibility of the self to further experience. According to Freud, social input changes mental structure. A mass type group experience, for example, removes the mental superstructure so that the unconscious stands exposed and one ceases to be guided by one's will (130). Participation may thus seem to lead to loss of self-control. In broader perspective, however, this is not the case. The individual initially selects the group to which he submits on the assumption that it leads him in a direction which he had previously determined to follow.

Environmental input affects the self on the basis of an existing, though latent, connection between the self and the environment. According to George H. Mead's social behaviorism, for example, the self can respond to a social relational stimulus because the self has been formed by these social relations. Its own response repertory consists of the attitudes that other selves take toward it (199). Skinner's operant conditioning model for self-control assumes a previous conditioning of the organism to the environment's stimuli. Skinner believes that one controls his own behavior precisely in the way that he would control the behavior of anyone else through the manipulation of the variables, that is, the stimuli of which the behavior is a function. An organism's behavior may be directed so as to elicit a reward from the environment. This response may reinforce that behavior and lead to seeking a further stimulus and response (101, 102).

Initially the individual scans the environment for the possible inputs to which he will attend. He is his own censor as well as selector of environmental cues. Coffin's study of suggestibility found that individuals could make themselves nonsuggestible through successful internal and external checks (180). Cantril found that persons who checked the input from the radio about the Martian invasion were less likely to act upon the idea (179).

Popular literature on sexual continence frequently suggests control through environmental input. Young men are advised not to become involved in conversations which stimulate their imagination about sex (265) and to avoid petting or brothels (276). Sexual self-control may be achieved by shifting attention to other topics. For example, it is suggested that a person keep cards in a pocket with diverting topics noted on them and examine them when aroused (277).

Social input may be conceived relationally, normatively, or affectively. Hypnotism, for example, provides a relational input.

One places oneself in a specific type of dyadic relation (248). Prior interaction with the same individual may be the basis for the input potential of the relationship. A child, for example, might reduce his sense of insecurity by seeking out his mother (172, 111). Erikson's work implies that one might control the development of his personal identity by selecting membership or reference groups during adolescence (115). Research on small groups suggests that one may select an interaction group in order to develop the self in its image (188). Social input, besides coming through interaction with group members, may come through orientation to a leader. A good leader, according to some social psychological writings, provides disciplinary inputs (214), inhibits disintegrative action, or acts as a support for an individual striving toward a goal (97). A member abdicates some of his control over his self in delegating power to a leader. However, this submission remains a self-control device as long as the authority is voluntarily delegated, or, if the authority originates with the leader, it is voluntarily accepted. Social relational inputs to control the self are also recognized in the popular literature. Choosing good companions is recommended as an aid for sex control (267). A book on weight control suggests joining a club of dieters (286). One could tell others of his intention to diet on the assumption that he would be embarrassed not to live up to the image he had presented (287). Another book, with a similar assumption, recommends against telling other women about a diet because they would be jealous and try to dissuade the dieter (288).

The actual input from the above relations may be normative or affective. Some writings, however, focus directly on the normative components of the input. Through actual group participation or by taking a group as a reference group the norms may be internalized, that is, become part of the personality so that the self acquires a predisposition to abide by them when appropriately signalled (200). For example, one who has determined to be a vegetarian may join a vegetarian society. As he internalizes the norms he becomes what he had determined to be, a more dedicated vegetarian. Other writings focus on the affective or emotionally supportive components of the input. Communal participation, for example, provides the support to keep oneself from panicking under stress (196).

Social input is generally mediated by symbols. Aside from the symbols of relationship, input may derive from more disembodied symbols such as a goal, an anticipated state of affairs, a value with special meaning for the self, or from symbols which order the environment for the self's act. The symbolic process occurs within the individual. However, insofar as goals, values, and principles of order are societally given, some aspect of the symbol is external. Their effectiveness is contingent upon the individual accepting their legitimacy. Tillich looks upon cultural inputs as an inescapable consequence of being human. Nevertheless, the individual chooses within his cultural framework (19). The goal symbols need not directly reflect ultimate goals. Bain, for example, distinguishes ends in view, which function as means, from ultimate ends (43). Orientation to a value symbol is illustrated by Hadas' description of the impact of orientation to a heroic code and to ideas of excellence upon the behavior of classical Greeks (8). Orientation to a religious symbol may involve an expectation of response. The popular literature often objectifies the notion of response in recommending a religious orientation for strengthening the will (275, 266). Schneider and Dornbusch show a general tendency of popular literature to treat the religious symbol as a means (211). A very different type of religious orientation is reflected in Underhill's description of how a mystic seeks control by relinquishing control in orienting to the divine (34).

The distinguishing mark of the effort to synergy is that self-control depends upon some input to the self from an external system. This system may be considered as a stimulus or as social relational or symbolic. The effort involved is to physically or socially position the self to receive these inputs. Though the self does not attempt to change the external system, its response to the input may have an impact on future inputs from the external system, especially when that external system is social relational.

EFFORT TO CONQUEST

The effort to conquest is a two-dimensional conception based on a polarity between what an individual wishes to do and forces frustrating his wishes. The method is either to strengthen the desired pole until it overcomes the resisting force or to weaken the negative pole until it cannot resist effectively. This strengthening or weakening may involve a calculus of values for weighing one pole against the other, methods of contemplation for the concentrating of energies toward the desired pole or against the undesired one, or methods of practicing good habits and of inhibiting or weakening bad habits.

Resolution of a motive or value conflict by weighing the positives and the negatives against each other has been a common recommendation in our culture (44). Contemplation as a self-control technique is less familiar. Contemplation may be conceived as an active and effortful way to an awareness of motives so that they can be controlled (4) or as contributing directly to self-control. For yogic contemplation, whatever ties men to this world is the evil pole to be banished. Eliade describes yogic contemplation as leading to a rebirth to a nonconditioned mode of existence (30); that is, an existence not limited to body or environment. Mental functions which interfere with freedom are tamed through breathing exercises and through mental concentration (26).

What is one to contemplate? Consistent with the two dimensional model of the effort to conquest, Patanjali yoga suggests that when undesirable habits of thought are in the mind one should meditate on the opposite (28). Selye echoes this in advocating erasing unpleasant thoughts by conscious concentration on pleasant ones (96). The idea is central to Couéism (245). Writings on self-suggestion recommend working with the positive pole alone by introducing an ideal image into the mind and then trying to realize it (25, 289, 50).

Desired behavior may be instituted through practicing it. McClelland finds this characteristic of the achieving society's attempt to develop self-reliance by encouraging boys to master something (198). The specific activity recommended may vary from mastering a technical task to engaging in morally approved behavior or living a clean life (37, 261). The diet literature frequently states its problem as replacing a bad habit with a good one (283). Physical culture is advocated for mastering sex drives (273, 262, 256).

The literature includes suggestions for inhibiting the undesired behavioral pole. This is implied when Basowitz, Persky, Korchin and Grinker attribute increased anxiety following the termination of paratroop training to the relaxation of the usual anxiety control mechanisms (217). Jolliffe analyzes eating as a conditioned reflex. Simply reducing food intake will eventually lower the need (284). Similar advice in the sex area is given by Chesser (263). Munro says building character by repressing evil is also a way toward slenderizing (285). Evil may be repressed by fear. Ross counsels boys to control masturbation by telling them that they will irritate the penis and not grow up normally (274).

The effort to conquest in its yogic form is oriented to the internal self-system. The struggle is to master the self through and as a result of relinquishing attachments to the environment. In its "active ascetic Protestant" form it involves mastery of self to enable environmental mastery.

EFFORT TO HARMONY

The effort to harmony is a striving for self-control through internal physical or psychological balance. This balance may be fomulated as getting in tune with nature, avoiding extremes or following a golden mean.

What is to be harmonized? For one thing, behavior may be harmonized with capabilities. Aristotle, for example, recommended control of self by behaving in a way appropriate to the potency in question (2). This approach has remained in popular literature which defines wisdom as adapting oneself to nature (251, 259). In the scientific literature, reference to environmental and personal order replaces the reference to the order of nature. Huizinga, for example, argues that rules of play enable an individual to come to terms symbolically with the problem of social order (189). The routine of work is said to regulate personal order (218).

Psychologists are concerned with personality as a type of "natural" order which is built into a person. Loss of control becomes identified with behavior violating the integrity of personality. Strain or anxiety is a signal warning that the balance is upset (115). The aim may be stated as remaining within the limits of natural growth (201). If one consciously employs a defense against anxiety, he should do so by following an already developed pattern (216, 161, 192). A new action should be executed in a manner consonant with prior traits (39, 148, 83) in consideration of the activity readiness of the organism (76), and consistent with preformed cognitive styles of regulation (69).

The harmony of these various elements may be achieved through an interplay of tensions or may be consequent to an all-around reduction of tension to a level of general apathy. A dynamic balance is illustrated by the Freudian notion of taming the instinct and bringing it into harmony with the ego (135). Reich describes this as libido-economic self-regulation (167). Nunberg attributes this type of harmony to the synthetic function of the ego (163). The balancing of conflicting forces may involve neutralizing a threat (141), bringing a counteractive force to bear

(105) or, as an early paper by Freud and a later one by Rank put it, balancing a will and a counter-will (127, 166). In these latter conceptions, the effort to harmony overlaps with the effort to conquest.

Harmony may also result from a reduction of tension in the direction of passive homeostasis (239). The tendency to stability referred to by Freud (136) moves toward the static equilibrium of the death instinct (110). Equilibrium attained by a severe reduction of the tension is experienced as apathy. Greenson refers to putting the mind in neutral (140).

How can one intentionally release excess tensions? Grinker and Spiegel, in their study of war neuroses, imply that this may be accomplished by acting out (142). Stouffer suggests legitimating the expression of fear to undercut the tension it would generate (213), and Ruesch notes that tension release may be triggered by laughter (94). Energies may also be released by a therapist's psychological interpretation (146). Ralph describes a form of giving interpretations to the self (165).

Mechanisms of defense restore the equilibrium of a personality subject to strain. Though these mechanisms operate unconsciously, they derive from learned behaviors. It is these behavioral analogs of the mechanisms that may be instituted consciously as a self-control device (174). For example, a drive may be undercut by selecting a substitute object for it (122, 189, 206). This type of control is explained as a result of cathecting another object with the energy pressing for expression (127, 58). Adler considers this substitute activity as compensatory (108). Redirection of energy to functionally equivalent objects is a common recommendation in the popular literature on control of sex drives (280, 278, 272, 270).

Individual conscious use of the mechanism of denial may be difficult unless the denial is socially sanctioned. Koestler observed evasiveness or vagueness as a socially approved mechanism for adjusting to a rigid Japanese society (32). Like denial, magical thinking is more effective as a defense when it is socially validated as in fairy tales. Piers and Singer relate the magic thinking characteristic of primitive omnipotence to physical courage and countering realistic fears (164).

A number of students have noted the role of a regressive defense in the management of stress. Regression involves achieving a balance at an "earlier" developmental level where the organization of energies would assumedly be less complex (226, 246).

The present personality undergoes some change to attain this type of balance. Regression may be intentionally induced through mystic exercises or in the production of art (124, 70).

Because of the consistency problem, a mechanism developed in one situation may not be adequate for, or may even hinder, adaptation in another. Selye refers to this type of disharmony as a psychological and physiological disease of adaptation which can produce rather than balance stress (96). Korchin shows how defensive behaviors may also be so inappropriate as to interfere with a task (71, 72).

Essentially, the effort to harmony is concerned with the internal aspects of self as a self-regulating system. Less attention is given the external environment than is given integrating efforts of the self under various environmental conditions.

EFFORT TO TRANSCENDENCE

The effort to transcendence involves a synthetic movement. The polarities of the effort to conquest are recognized. Instead, however, of one conquering the other, both are retained in a higher synthesis. The relation is dialectic. Control requires the active embracing of suffering or an affirmation of self despite suffering. This is not the optimism of the effort to conquest. Rather, as in Tillich's view, this is affirmation of life despite anxiety (20). Writing from the point of view of psychophysiology, Goldstein describes courage as an affirmative answer to the shocks of existence necessary for actualization of one's own nature (185). Identification with the divine is a basis of Stoic affirmation under suffering (7). Humor, according to Freud and Frankl, is an affirmation despite pain. The ego does not deny reality, but asserts its invulnerability by refusing to be hurt by the arrows of reality (133, 126). A synthesis may simultaneously realize both sides of an ambivalency. Freud explains negation in this way. In the act of denying, the repressed is taken into account (132). Similarly, gallows humor is a way of meeting a reality which is obvious and cold (203).

Mastering a painful situation may involve repeating its painful prototype. Freud, for example, describes a child dealing with a fear of losing his mother by throwing away and recovering a toy symbol of her (131, 134). Similarly, the work of mourning is accomplished by raising each memory and hypercathecting it (129). The mechanism is somewhat like what Fenichel terms the counterphobic attitude (118).

The transcendent unity may be accomplished through gaining a perspective on a situation as well as by acting in it. The final stages of yoga, dhyana and samadhi, have something of this as the yogin attains the realization of the unity of all things (27). Symbolic transcendence appears in the thinking of Luria. Lewin considers quasi-needs as regulatory mechanisms with an executive function. Luria modifies this in his concept of symbols acting as regulatory mechanisms which affect structure. They are not considered external to, but rather emerge from, the conflicting motives (79).

Metaphors for expressing the nature of the transcendence have been plentiful. The synthetic has been considered both rational and nonrational. Jung conceives of the transcendent resolution as an irrational element supravening the rational (151). The Greeks and St. Thomas believed that a rational soul held authority over desire (13, 5, 18). In a religious context, the symbolism of withdrawal and return or death and rebirth is a common metaphor of transcendent synthesis (29, 6). Psychologists, speaking of ego control as mediating a conflict between internal need and the demands of the external world, approach a conception of the ego as an emergent function (46). This is the case with those who see ego strength as a higher order regulatory principle which resolves conflict (170).

The effort to transcendence is essentially concerned with a resolution achieved internally by the self. The process, however, begins by taking the external system into account and it may end with a new action upon the external world.

Factors in the Choice of the Method of Control

It appears that each method has a particular affinity for problems connected with one or another object of control. The effort to synergy seems more likely to be applied to control overt behavior than to control affects. To improve penmanship one is more likely to engage the effort to conquest than the effort to transcendence. Each literary tradition also tends to be concerned with particular problems of control as well as with particular methods of control. Table 3 summarizes, for our sample, the relation between the literary tradition and the method of control.

Table 3—Methods of Self-Control in Various Literary Traditions

Literary Tradition	Control Methods (Percentages) EFFORT TO:					
	Synergy	Conquest	Harmony	Transcendence	Total	N
Yoga	6	56	25	13	100	(14)
Philosophy	18	14	36	32	100	(24)
Personality	14	32	43	11	100	(69)
Psychoanalysis	11	24	42	23	100	(64)
Social Psychology	24	32	32	12	100	(45)
Stress	17	22	55	6	100	(23)
Hypnosis	20	40	40	0	100	(10)
Self-Help	22	58	20	0	100	(41)

The synergic approach, with the input of external stimuli for control, does not concern the yoga and psychoanalytic writers. Though the latter theorize that individual personality is a consequence of environmental interaction and the former perceive the enemy in the desire to possess environmental objects, both view control in terms of working with strengths within the individual. Yoga overwhelmingly recommends the effort to conquest, and psychoanalysis the effort to harmony. Like yoga, the self-help literature advocates the effort to conquest. In both of these traditions the world is constituted by forces of good and evil. The former must be realized and the latter bested. Both traditions are activistic: yoga with respect to the elimination of desire, and self-help with respect to the prevention of drive expression. The nature of the problem analyzed in the stress literature, individual response to environmental stress, influences it toward the effort to harmony. These authors are concerned with the way the person maintains balance under stress. Further, they are influenced by personality theorists, who, along with psychotherapists, advocate the effort to harmony as they apply a homeostatic or equilibrium model. The effort to transcendence is absent from the self-help and hypnosis literatures and almost absent from the stress literature. Transcendence requires that pain as well as pleasure be affirmed. These three traditions aim to escape from pain or desire or even awareness. The dialectical approach of some psychoanalysts and the affirmation of suffering in classical societies prepare these traditions for a view of self-control on the basis of transcendence.

Thus, the method of self-control recommended follows from the traditions and from the problem of orientations of the various literatures. We may focus specifically on problem orientation in terms of the manifest object of control. This relation is examined, for our sample, in Table 4.

Table 4—Manifest Objects of Control According to Methods of Control

Manifest Objects of Control	Control Methods (Percentages) EFFORT TO:					
	Synergy	Conquest	Harmony	Transcendence	Total	N
Performance	11	39	11	39	100	(35)
Drive	16	50	26	8	100	(62)
Intellect	10	36	40	14	100	(94)
Affect	16	32	36	16	100	(99)

The effort to synergy is not associated with any single manifest object of control. A slight preference for synergy appears where interest is in the distribution of energies in the organism; that is, when the problem is control of drives or affects. Comparing this and the previous table, the synergic approach seems more a function of the literary tradition than of the specific manifest object of control. The effort to conquest is slightly more associated with controlling drives than with other manifest objects. This may be due to the tendency to recognize a drive by the external behavior associated with it. Having done this, it seems logical to attempt to control the drive by exerting effort on this behavior, by practicing a good habit or inhibiting a bad one. Here, too, however, the general tradition is more significant than the manifest object in determining the method. Understandably, the effort to harmony, an internally oriented approach, is not associated with performance. Performance is defined by its orientation to the world outside. The association of the effort to harmony with intellect and affect as manifest objects is consistent with our definition of the effort to harmony as concerned with the internal system. The effort to transcendence is markedly associated with performance. The image seems to be of a person acting upon the world despite pressure to the contrary from the world.

The cultural traditions underlying the various literatures are at least as, if not more, important in determining the approach to control than the concepts of the objects to be controlled. The latter are, of course, also, in some measure, culturally defined. In one setting diet control may be considered a problem of mechanically influencing the hunger drive. In another setting the question may be viewed as one of facilitating the individual's intellect so that he will know what is good for him.

Questions

This literary review leaves us with questions about self-control. The last few pages suggest that the way we conceive of self-control and what we propose to do about it are related to our cultural orientations. To what extent are the methods of control necessarily culturally bound? Must a method of control be selected in terms of its relation to other elements in a particular culture? To what extent may the methods of yoga be applied by an American population? Is the effort to transcendence limited to a highly sophisticated milieu?

The method of control advocated reflects an attitude toward personal and social change. The efforts toward synergy and toward harmony tend to be associated with adaptation and adjustment to the present reality of the self; the first because the effectiveness of environmental input depends on prior sensitization to its stimuli, and the second because the stable balance sought more often becomes a re-equilibration than a new integration at a higher level. The efforts toward conquest and toward transcendence, on the other hand, seem allied with change. Through these efforts the self emerges as something other than what it was before or assumes a new relation with its environment. An ideological element may well enter in the selection of a method of self-control.

What is the relation on the theoretical level between the typology of methods of self-control and a paradigm for social control? On the applied level, does counteracting the effects of specific types of social control require cognate types of self-control?

Is the process of control reversible once it is initiated? What is the possibility of metacontrol, of controlling the control? In the effort to synergy, for example, once a self exposes itself to stimuli, does it enter a process which it may find difficult to arrest or reverse? Once a person joins a mob to enjoy its enthusiasm, does he by relinquishing ego control, tend to slip into an irreversible situation?

What are the limits of self-control? What are the constitutional and personality conditions which limit the individual's ability to control himself? What are the limits of environmental stress under which self-control might be realistically anticipated? The more stress an individual is subjected to, the less he is able to withstand stress. It would seem, therefore, that the amount of effort required to control the self under varying degrees of stress would rise exponentially. What are the implications of this for self-control?

Each method of control described above is an ideal type. Several of the methods might be applied in any concrete situation. Similarly, the concrete object of control is not likely to be identical with one of the four pure conceptual types but to involve several of them. Given this complexity, in what combinations might the various methods and manifest objects appear? In the discussion on indirect approaches to control, reference was made to mapping the mechanisms or specifying the steps to be traversed in a control effort. Perhaps, the methods may have different applicability at different stages of the process. Might they be applied in some phased order? The contributions making up the remainder of this book will answer some of these questions and open many more questions.

BIBLIOGRAPHY

RELIGION AND PHILOSOPHY

I. Philosophical Writings and Studies of Classical Societies:

1. ALEXANDER, A. *Theories of the will in the history of philosophy*. New York: Scribner's Sons, 1890.

2. ARISTOTLE. *Metaphysics & topics*. In R. M. Hutchins (Ed.), *Great books of the Western world*. Chicago: Encyclopedia Britannica, 1962.

3. ARNOLD, E. V. *Roman stoicism*. Cambridge: Cambridge Univer. Press, 1911.

4. AVELING, F. *Personality and will*. Cambridge: Cambridge Univer. Press, 1931.

5. BENTLEY, J. E. *Philosophy: An outline—History*. Ames, Iowa: Littlefield, Adams & Co., 1954.

6. CARPENTER, E. *The art of creation: Essays on the self and its powers*. London: George Allen & Unwin, Ltd., 1904.

7. HADAS, M. *The stoic philosophy of Seneca*. New York: Doubleday & Co., Inc., 1958.

8. HADAS, M. *Humanism: The Greek ideal and its survival.* New York: Harper & Bros., 1960.

9. HASTINGS, J. (Ed.) *Encyclopedia of religion and ethics.* New York: Charles Scribner's Sons, 1911.

10. MACVANNEL, J. A. *Hegel's doctrine of the will. Contributions to philosophy, psychology and education.* V. II, New York: Columbia Univer. Press, 1896.

11. MAY, R. Historical roots of modern anxiety theories. In P. H. Hoch & J. Zubin (Eds.) *Anxiety.* New York: Grune & Stratton, 1950. Pp. 3-16.

12. MEAD, G. H. The genesis of the self and social control. *Internat. J. of Ethics,* 1925, 35(3), 251-277.

13. MURRAY, G. *The four stages of Greek religion.* New York: Columbia Univer. Press, 1912.

14. MURRAY, G. *The stoic philosophy.* New York: G. P. Putnam's Sons, 1915.

15. RANKIN, K. W. *Choice and chance.* Oxford: Basil Blackwell, 1961.

16. RUNES, D. D. (Ed.) *Dictionary of philosophy.* Ames, Iowa: Littlefield, Adams & Co., 1955.

17. SARTRE, J. P. *The transcendence of the ego: An existentialist theory of consciousness.* R. Kirkpatrick & F. Williams (Trans.) New York: Noonday Press, 1957.

18. THOMAS AQUINAS, SAINT. *Summa theologica.* In R. M. Hutchins (Ed.) *Great books of the Western world.* Chicago: Encyclopedia Britannica, 1962.

19. TILLICH, P. Anxiety reducing agencies in our culture. In P. H. Hoch and J. Zubin (Eds.) *Anxiety.* New York: Grune & Stratton, 1950. Pp. 1-26.

20. TILLICH, P. *The courage to be.* New Haven: Yale Univer. Press. 1952.

21. TOLSTOY, L. *The law of love and the law of violence.* New York: Rudolph Field, 1948.

22. TOYNBEE, A. J. *A study of history.* Vol. V. New York: Oxford Univer. Press, 1939.

23. Univer. of California. *Conference:* Seminars, Symposia and Other Post-Graduate Activities in Medicine & Allied Fields: Selections from Panels at the Symposium Man & Civilization: Control of the Mind, Freeing the Mind, Understanding and Controlling the Mind, Horizons of Psychopharmacology. National & International Conferences, Science Information Bureau, 2(4), 1961.

24. WELLS, HONORIA M. *The phenomenology of acts of choice: an analysis of volitional consciousness.* Cambridge: Cambridge Univer. Press, 1927.

II. Yoga and Religious Mysticism:

25. BAGCHI, B. K. Mental hygiene and the Hindu doctrine of relaxation. *Ment. Hyg.,* 1936, 20, 424-440.

A COLLOCATION OF CONCEPTS OF SELF-CONTROL   35

26. BEHANAN, K. T. *Yoga: a scientific evaluation.* New York: Macmillan, 1937.

27. BROMAGE, B. *Tibetan yoga.* London: The Aquarian Press, 1952.

28. COSTER, GERALDINE. *Yoga and Eastern psychology.* London: Oxford Univer. Press, 1934.

29. ELIADE, MIRCEA. *Birth and rebirth: the religious meanings of Initiation in human culture.* New York: Harper & Bros., 1958.

30. ELIADE, MIRCEA. *Yoga: immortality and freedom.* Vol. LVI Bollingen Series, Pantheon Books, 1958.

31. JACOBS, H. *Western psychotherapy and Hindu Sadhanna.* London: Allen & Unwin, Ltd., 1961.

32. KOESTLER, A. *The lotus and the robot.* London: Hutchinson & Co., 1960.

33. SCHOLEM, G. G. *Major trends in Jewish mysticism.* New York: Schocken Books, 1961.

34. UNDERHILL, EVELYN. *The essentials of mysticism and other essays.* London: J. M. Dent & Sons, 1920.

35. WENGER, M. A., & BAGCHI, B. K. Studies of autonomic functions in practitioners of yoga in India. *Behav. Sci.,* 1961, 6(4), 312-323.

36. WENGER, M. A., BAGCHI, B. K., & ANAND, B. K. Experiments in India on "voluntary" control of the heart and pulse. *Circulation,* 1961, 24(6), 1319-1325.

37. WERNER, YOGI H., & WERNER, Apprentice Yogi C. *Self-mastery through self-taught yoga.* New York: Greenwich Book Pub., 1960.

38. WOOD, E. *Great systems of yoga.* New York: Philos. Lib., 1954.

PSYCHOLOGY

III. Personality Psychology, Will Psychology,
Theories of Motivation and Learning:

39. ALLPORT, G. M., BRUNER, J. S., & JANDORF, E. M. Personality under social catastrophe: ninety life-histories of the Nazi revolution. In C. Kluckholn, & H. A. Murray (Eds.) *Personality in nature, society, and culture.* New York: Alfred A. Knopf, 1948. Pp. 347-367.

40. ARNOLD, MAGDA B. A study of tension in relation to breakdown. *J. gen. Psychol.,* 1942, 26, 315-346.

41. ATKINSON, J. W. Motivational determinants of risk-taking behavior. *Psychol. Rev.,* 1957, 64, 359-372.

42. AVELING, F. Emotion, conation and will. *International symposium on Feelings and Emotions: The Wittenberg Symposium.* Worcester, Mass: Clark Univer. Press, 1928, 49-57.

43. BAIN, A. *The emotions and the will.* London: John W. Parker & Son, 1859.

44. BARRETT, E. B. *Motive-force and motivational-tracks.* London: Longmans, Green & Co., 1911.

45. BITTERMAN, M. E. & KNIFFEN, C. W. Manifest anxiety and perceptual defense. *J. abnorm. soc. Psychol.*, 1953, 48, 248-252.

46. BLOCK, J., & BLOCK, JEANNE. An investigation of the relationship between intolerance of ambiguity and ethnocentrism. *J. Pers.*, 1950, 19, 303-312.

47. BRIDGES, J. W. An experimental study of decision types and their mental correlates. *Psychol. Rev.*, 1914, 17(1).

48. BROVERMAN, D. M. Dimensions of cognitive style. *J. Pers.*, 1960, 28(2), 167-185.

49. Character education inquiry. *Studies in deceit.* Vol. 1. *Studies in the nature of character.* New York: Macmillan, 1928.

50. CREIGHTON, J. E. *The will: its structure and mode of action.* Ithica: Andrus & Church, 1898.

51. DARWIN, C. *The expression of the emotions in man and animals.* New York: D. Appleton & Co., 1899.

52. DIAMOND, B. L., & ROSS, ALICE. Emotional adjustment of newly blinded soldiers. *Amer. J. Psychiat.*, 1945, 102, 367-371.

53. DOBZHANSKY, T., & MONTAGU, M. F. A. Natural selection and the mental capacities of mankind. *Science*, 1946, 105, 587-590.

54. DOLLARD, J., DOOB, L. W., MILLER, N. E., MOWRER, O. H., & SEARS, R. R. *Frustration and aggression.* New Haven: Yale Univer. Press, 1939.

55. DOWNEY, JUNE E. *The will temperament and its testing.* Yonkers-On-Hudson, N. Y.: World Book Co., 1923.

56. DRAYER, C. S. Psychological factors and problems. *Annals of the Amer. Acad. polit. & soc. Sci.*, 1957, 309, 151-159.

57. ELIOT, T. D. Of the shadow of death. *Annals of the Amer. Acad. of pol. & soc. Sci.*, 1943, 229, 87-99.

58. ENGLISH, H. P. Symbolic versus functional equivalents in the neurosis of deprivation. *J. abnorm. soc. Psychol.*, 1937, 32, 392-394.

59. FRANK, J. D. Emotional reactions of American soldiers to an unfamiliar disease. *Amer. J. Psychiat.*, 1946, 102(5), 631-640.

60. GURIN, G., VEROFF, J., & FELD, SHEILA. *Americans view their mental health.* New York: Basic Books Co., 1960.

61. GUTHRIE, E. R. The self and voluntary action. In *The psychology of human conflict.* New York: Harper & Bros., 1938. Pp. 163-189.

62. HEATH, D. H. Individual anxiety thresholds and their effect on intellectual performance. *J. abnorm. soc. Psychol.*, 1956, 52(3), 403-408.

63. HUMPHREY, G. *Directed thinking.* New York: Dodd, Mead & Co., 1948.

64. JANIS, I. L., & FESHBACH, S. Personality differences associated with responsiveness to fear-arousing communications. *J. Pers.*, 1954, 23, 154-166.

65. JACQUES-DALCROZE, E. *Eurythmics, art & education.* F. Rothwell (Trans.) London: Chatto & Windus, 1930.

66. JERSILD, A. T., & HOLMES, F. B. Methods of overcoming children's fears. *J. Psychol.*, 1935-36, 1, 75-104.

67. KESSEN, W., & MANDLER, G. Anxiety, pain and the inhibition of distress. *Psychol. Rev.*, 1961, 68(6), 396-404.

68. KLAGES, L. *The science of character.* W. H. Johnston (Trans.) London: Allen & Unwin, Ltd., 1929.

69. KLEIN, G. S., & SALOMON, ANN. Cognitive style and regulation of need. *Amer. Psychologist*, 1952, 7(7), 321-322.

70. KOHUT, H. Observations on the psychological functions of music. *J. Amer. Psychoanalytic Assoc.*, 1957, 5(3), 389-407.

71. KORCHIN, S. J., & SEYMOUR, L. Anxiety and verbal learning. *J. abnorm. soc. Psychol.*, 1957, 54(2), 234-240.

72. KORCHIN, S. J., & HERZ, M. Differential effects of "Shame" and "disintegrative threats" on emotional and adrenocortical functioning. *A.M.A. Arch. Gen. Psychiat.*, 1960, 2, 640-651.

73. KRETSCHMER, E. *Physique and character.* New York: Harcourt Brace & Co., 1926.

74. KUNTZ, L. F. *Education of the will in the light of modern research.* Washington, D.C.: Catholic Univ., 1927.

75. LAMBEK, C. *An analysis of volitional life.* London: Williams & Norgate, 1947.

76. LEWIN, K. Intention, will, and need. In D. Rapaport (Ed.) *Organization & pathology of thought.* New York: Columbia Univer. Press, 1951. Pp. 95-154.

77. LIDDELL, H. S. The role of vigilance in the development of animal neurosis. In P. H. Hoch & J. Zubin (Eds.) *Anxiety.* New York: Grune & Stratton, 1950. Pp. 182-196.

78. LIDDELL, H. S. *Emotional hazards in animals and man.* Springfield, Ill.: Charles C. Thomas, 1956.

79. LURIA, A. R. *The nature of human conflicts.* New York: Grove Press, 1960.

80. MAUDSLEY, H. *Body and will.* New York: D. Appleton & Co., 1884.

81. McNEEL, MAJOR B. H., & DANCEY, T. E. The personality of the successful soldier. *Amer. J. Psychiat.*, 1945, 102, 337-342.

82. MENNINGER, W. C. Psychological reactions in an emergency (Flood). *Amer. J. Psychiat.*, 1952, 109, 128-130.

83. MERCIER, MARIE H., & DESPERT, J. LOUISE. Psychological effects of the war on French children. *Psychom. Med.*, 1943, 5(3), 266-272.

84. MILLER, D. R., & SWANSON, G. E. *Inner conflict and defense.* New York: Henry Holt & Co., 1960.

85. NOBLE, D., ROUDEBUSH, MARION E., & PRICE, D. Studies of Korean war casualties, part I: Psychiatric manifestations in wounded men. *Amer. J. Psychiat.*, 1952, 108, 495-499.

86. OSS Assessment Staff. *Assessment of men: Selection of per-*

sonnel for the Office of Strategic Services. New York: Rinehart & Co., 1948.

87. PAYOT, J. *The education of the will.* E. J. Smith (Trans.) New York: Funk & Wagnalls, 1909.

88. PRIBRAM, K. H. Cerebral mechanisms and decisions processes. Report on Contract DA 49 007 MD 763, Department of the Army, 1959.

89. PRUGH, D. G., *et al.* A study of the emotional reactions of children and families to hospitalization and illness. *Amer. J. Orthopsychiat.,* 1953, 23, 70-106.

90. RENNIE, T. A. C. Anxiety states: Their recognition and management. In *Medical clinics of North America.* 1948. Pp. 597-608.

91. RICHTER, C. P. Total self-regulatory functions in animals and human beings. In *The Harvey lectures.* Lancaster, Penn.: The Science Press Printing Co., 1943.

92. ROSEN, V. The role of denial in acute postoperative affective reactions following removal of body parts. *Psychosomatic Medicine,* 1950, 12(6), 356-392.

93. ROSS, S., KRUGMAN, A. D., LYERLY, S. B. & GLYDE, D. J. Drugs and placebos: A model design. *Psychol. Rep.,* 1962, 10, 383-392.

94. RUESCH, J., & PRESTWOOD, A. R. Anxiety: Its initiation, communication, and interpersonal management. *A.M.A. Archives of Neurology and Psychiatry,* 1949, 62(5), 527-550.

95. SANDER, R. Emergency behavior. In P. H. Hoch & J. Zubin (Eds.) *Anxiety.* New York: Grune & Stratton, 1950, Pp. 150. 150-175.

96. SELYE, H. *The stress of life.* New York: McGraw Hill Book Co., 1956.

97. SHAFFER, L. F. Fear and courage in aerial combat. *J. consult. Psychol.,* 1947, 11, 137-143.

98. SHERIF, M., & CANTRIL, H. *The psychology of ego involvements: Social attitudes and identifications.* New York: John Wiley & Sons, 1947.

99. SHERRINGTON, SIR C. *Man and his nature.* London: Cambridge Univer. Press, 1940.

100. SCHILDER, P., & WECHSLER, D. The attitudes of children toward death. *J. genet. Psychol.,* 1934, 45, 406-451.

101. SKINNER, B. F. *Science and human behavior.* New York: Macmillan, 1953.

102. SKINNER, B. F. *Verbal behavior.* New York: Appleton-Century-Crofts, 1957.

103. STOKES, A. B. War strains and mental health. *J. Nervous & Mental Disease,* 1945, 101, 215-219.

104. TERRY, J. S. Training the emotions. *International Symposium on Feeling and Emotions: The Wittenberg Symposium.* Worcester, Mass.: Clark Univer. Press, 1928, 400-417.

105. WERNER, H., & WAPNER, S. Changes in psychological distance under conditions of danger. *J. Pers.,* 1955, 24(2), 153-167.
106. WERTHEIMER, M. *Productive thinking.* New York: Harper & Brothers, 1959.
107. WHEELER, W. M. *Essays in philosophical biology.* Cambridge, Mass.: Harvard Uinver. Press, 1939.

IV. Psychoanalysis, Ego Psychology and Psychotherapy:

108. ADLER, A. Feelings and emotions from the standpoint of individual psychology. *International Symposium on Feeling and Emotions: The Wittenberg Symposium.* Worcester, Mass.; Clark Univer. Press, 1928, 316-321.
109. ALEXANDER, F. On the psychodynamics of regressive phenomena in panic states. *Psychoanalysis and the social sciences IV.* New York: Int. Univer. Press, 1955. Pp. 104-110.
110. BROMBERG, W., & SCHILDER, P. Death and dying. *Psychoanalytic Rev.,* 1933, 20(2), 133-185.
111. CHESSICK, R. D. The sense of reality, time and creative inspiration. *Amer. Imago,* 1957, 14, 318-330.
112. CLAPAREDE, E. Recognition and "me-ness." In D. Rapaport (Ed.) *Organization & pathology of thought.* New York: Columbia Univer. Press, 1951. Pp. 58-76.
113. CORIAT, I. H. Dental anxiety: Fear of going to the dentist. *Psychoanalytic Rev.,* 1946, 33(3), 365-367.
114. DOOLEY, LUCILE. The concept of time in defense of ego-integrity. *Psychiatry,* 1941, 4, 13-23.
115. ERIKSON, E. H. Ego development and historical change. In *The Psychoanalytic Study of the Child.* Vol. II. New York: Int. Univer. Press, 1947, Pp. 359-395.
116. ERICKSON, E. H. *Young man Luther.* New York: W. W. Norton, 1958.
117. FEDERN, P. *Ego psychology and the psychoses.* New York: Basic Books Co., 1952.
118. FENICHEL, O. The counter phobic attitude. *Int. J. Psychoanalysis.* 1939, 20, 263-274.
119. FENICHEL, O. Psychoanalytic remarks on Fromm's book "Escape From Freedom." *The Psychoanalytic Rev.,* 1944, 31, 133-152.
120. FENICHEL, O. On the psychology of boredom. In *Organization and pathology of thought.* D. Rapaport (Ed.) New York: Columbia Univer. Press, 1951. Pp. 349-361.
121. FERENCZI, S. Two types of war neurosis. In *Further contributions to the theory and technique of psycho-analysis.* Jane I. Suttie (Trans.) London: Hogarth Press, 1926. Pp. 124-142.
122. FERENCZI, S. The psyche as an inhibiting organ. In *Further contributions to the theory and technique of psycho-analysis.* New York: Boni & Liverwright, 1927. Pp. 379-383.

123. FERENCZI, S. Stages in the development of the sense of reality. In *Sex in psychoanalysis*. E. Jones (Trans.) New York: Basic Books Co., 1950. Pp. 213-239.

124. FINGARETTE, H. The ego and the mystic selflessness. *Psychoanal. and the Psychoanal. Rev.*, 1958, 45, 5-40.

125. FLUGEL, F. C. *Man, morals and society*. London: Duckworth, 1945.

126. FRANKL, V. E. *From death camp to existentialism*. Boston: Beacon Press, 1959.

127. FREUD, S. Hypnotism and suggestion (1888) *Collected papers* Vol. V. London: Hogarth Press, 1950. Pp. 11-26.

128. FREUD, S. A case of successful treatment by hypnotism (1893) *Collected papers* Vol. V. London: Hogarth Press, 1950. Pp. 33-46.

129. FREUD, S. Mourning and melancholia (1917) *Collected papers* Vol. VIII. London: Hogarth Press, 1950. Pp. 152-172.

130. FREUD, S. *Group psychology and the analysis of the ego*. London: Int. Psychoanal. Press, 1922.

131. FREUD, S. *Beyond the pleasure principle*. New York: Boni and Liverwright, 1924.

132. FREUD, S. Negation (1925) *Collected papers* Vol. V. London: Hogarth Press, 1950. Pp. 181-185.

133. FREUD, S. Humor (1928) *Collected papers* Vol. V. London: Hogarth Press, 1950. Pp. 215-221.

134. FREUD, S. *The problem of anxiety*. New York: The Psychoanalytic Quarterly Press, 1936.

135. FREUD, S. Analysis terminable and interminable (1937) *Collected papers* Vol. V. London: Hogarth Press, 1950. Pp. 316-357.

136. FREUD, S. The economic problem in masochism (1946) *Collected papers*. London: Hogarth Press, 1950. Pp. 255-268.

137. FRIEMAN, P. Some aspects of concentration camp psychology. *Amer. J. Psychiat.*, 1949. 105(8), 601-605.

138. FROMM, E. *Marx's concept of man*. New York: Frederick Ungar Pub. Co., 1961.

139. GLOVER, E. Notes on the psychological effects of war conditions on the civilian population. *Int. J. Psycho-Anal.*, 1941, 22(2), 32-146.

140. GREENSON, R. R. The psychology of apathy. *Psychoanal. Quarterly*, 1949, 18(3), 290-302.

141. GRINKER, R. R., & SPIEGEL, J. P. *Men under stress*. Philadelphia: Blakiston, 1945.

142. GRINKER, R. R., & SPIEGEL, J. P. *War neuroses*. Philadelphia: Blakiston, 1945.

143. HARTMANN, H. Psychoanalysis and the concept of h h. *Int. J. Psycho-Anal.*, 1939, 20(3, 4), 308-321.

144. HARTMANN, H. On rational and irrational action. *Psycho-*

anal. and the Social Sciences. Vol. I. New York: Int. Univer. Press, 1947. Pp. 359-394.

145. HARTMANN, H. Comments on the psychoanalytic theory of the ego. *The Psychoanalytic Study of the Child.* Vol. 5. Anna Freud (Ed.) New York: Int. Univer. Press, 1950. Pp. 74-96.

146. HARTMANN, H. Technical implications of ego psychology. *Psychoanal. Quarterly,* 1951, 20(1), 31-43.

147. HARTMANN, H. *Ego psychology and the problem of adaptation.* D. Rapaport (Ed.) New York: Int. Univer. Press, 1951.

148. HENDRICK, I. Ego development and certain character problems. *Psychoanal. Quarterly,* 1936, 5, 320-346.

149. HENDRICK, I. Work and the pleasure principle. *Psychoanal. Quarterly,* 1943, 12, 311-329.

150. HORNEY, KAREN. *Our inner conflicts.* New York: W. W. Norton, 1945.

151. JUNG, C. G. *The integration of the personality.* New York: Farrar & Rinehart, 1939.

152. KARDINER, A., & SPIEGEL, H. *War stress and neurotic illness.* New York: Paul E. Hoeber, 1947.

153. KLEIN, MELANIE. On the theory of anxiety and guilt. In *Developments in Psychoanalysis.* Joan Riviere (Ed.) London: Hogarth Press, 1952. Pp. 271-291.

154. KRIS, E. The psychology of caricature. *Int. J. Psycho-Anal.,* 1936, 17, 285-303.

155. KRIS, E. On inspiration. *Int. J. Psycho-Anal.,* 1939, 20, 377-389.

156. KRIS, E. Danger and morale. *Amer. J. Orthopsychiat.,* 1944, 14, 47-155.

157. KRIS, E. *Psychoanalytic explorations in art.* New York: Int. Univer. Press, 1952.

158. KUBIE, L. S. The ontogeny of anxiety. *Psycho-Anal, Rev.* 1941, 28, 78-85.

159. KUBIE, L. S. Instincts and homeostasis. *Psychosom. Med.,* 1948, 10, 15-30.

160. LEWIN, B. D. *The psychoanalysis of elation.* New York: W. W. Norton, 1950.

161. LINDEMANN. E. Symptomatology and management of acute grief. *Amer. J. Psychiat.,* 1944, 101(2), 141-148.

162. LOEWENSTEIN, R. M. Some remarks on defences, autonomous ego and psycho-analytic technique. *Int. J. Psycho-Anal.,* 1954, 35(2), 188-193.

163. NUNBERG, H. The synthetic function of the ego. In *Practice and theory of psychoanalysis.* No. 74. Nervous and mental disease monographs. New York: Coolidge Foundation, 1948. Pp. 120-136.

164. PIERS, I., & SINGER, M. *Shame and guilt.* Springfield, Ill.: Charles C. Thomas, 1953.

42   SAMUEL Z. KLAUSNER

165. RALPH, J. *Self-analysis made simple: A guide to contentment.* New York: Dial Press, 1949.
166. RANK, O. *Will therapy and truth and reality.* New York: Alfred A. Knopf, 1945.
167. REICH, W. *Character-analysis.* T. P. Wolfe (Trans.) (3rd ed.) New York: Orgone Inst. Press, 1949.
168. ROSENBERG, ELIZABETH. Anxiety and the capacity to bear it. *Int. J. Psycho-Anal.,* 1949, 30(1), 1-12.
169. SULLIVAN, H. S. Psychiatric aspects of morale. *Amer. J. Sociol.,* 1941, 47(3), 277-301.
170. WAELDER, R. The problem of freedom in psycho-analysis and the problem of reality-testing. *Int. J. Psycho-Anal.,* 1936, 17, 89-108.
171. WEGROCKI, H. J. Anxiety and plane fright. *Psychoanal. Rev.,* 1946, 33(1), 1-36.

V. Social Psychology, Small Group Studies and Morale Studies:

172. ARSENIAN, JEAN M. Young children in an insecure situation. *J. abnorm. soc. Psychol.,* 1943, 38(2), 225-249.
173. ASCH, S. E. *Studies of independence and conformity.* Washington, D. C.: American Psychological Association, 1958, 70(9).
174. BIDERMAN, A. D. Concepts of self-management and social control mechanisms in captivity situations. Paper read at Meetings of the Amer. Sociol. Ass., St. Louis, August, 1961.
175. BIDERMAN, A. D., & ZIMMER, H. *The manipulation of human behavior.* New York: John Wiley & Sons, 1961.
176. BLOCH, H. A. Towards the development of a sociology of literary and art forms. *Amer. Sociol. Rev.,* 1943, 8, 313-320.
177. BRETT, G. S. Historical development of the theory of emotions. *International Symposium on Feeling and Emotions: The Wittenberg Symposium.* Worcester, Mass.: Clark Univer. Press, 1928, 388-397.
178. CANTRIL, H. Causes and control of riots and panic. *Public Opinion Quarterly,* 1943, 7, 669-679.
179. CANTRIL, H., *et al. The invasion from Mars.* Princeton, N. J.: Princeton Univer. Press, 1940.
180. COFFIN, T. E. *Some conditions of suggestion and suggestibility: A study of certain attitudinal and situational factors influencing the process of suggestion.* Evanston, Ill.: American Psychological Association, 1941, 53(4).
181. CRONBACH, L. J. *Exploring the wartime morale of high-school youth.* Applied Psychology Monographs, I. Stanford, Calif.: Stanford Univer. Press, 1943.
182. DRAYER, C. S. Relation of military and civilian psychiatry in crisis situations. *Amer. J. Psychiat.,* 1953, 109, 259-261.
183. ESTORICH, E. Morale in contemporary England. *Amer. J. Sociol.,* 1941, 47(3), 462-471.

184. GARDNER, E. F., & THOMPSON, G. G. *Social relations and morale in small groups.* New York: Appleton-Century-Crofts, 1956.
185. GOLDSTEIN, K. *The organism.* New York: American Book Co., 1939.
186. GOLDSTEIN, K. *Human nature in the light of psychopathology.* Cambridge, Mass.: Harvard Univer. Press, 1940.
187. GOTSHALK, D. W. *Art and the social order.* Chicago: Univer. of Chicago Press, 1947.
188. HOMANS, G. C. *The human group.* New York: Harcourt Brace, 1950.
189. HUIZINGA, J. *Homo ludens: A study of the play element in culture.* Boston: Beacon Press, 1960.
190. JANIS, I. L. & FESHBACH, S. Effects of fear arousing communications. *J. abnorm. soc. Psychol.,* 1953, 48(1), 78-92.
191. KERINS, F. F. *The social role of self-control.* Washington, D. C.: Catholic Univer. of America Press, 1943.
192. LAZARUS, R. S., & NOCHOLAS, L. The consistency of psychological defenses against threat. *J. abnorm. soc. Psychol.,* 1953, 48, 495-499.
193. LEWIN, K. *Field theory in social science.* New York: Harpers, 1951.
194. LOWENTHAL, L. *Literature, popular culture, and society.* Englewood Cliffs, N. J.: Prentice Hall, a Spectrum Book, 1961.
195. MACCURDY, J. T. *The structure of morale.* London: Cambridge Univer. Press, 1943.
196. MARTIN, A. R. The prevention of panic. *Mental Hygiene,* 1942, 26, 546-553.
197. McCLELLAND, D. C., ATKINSON, J. W., CLARK, R. A., & LOWELL, E. L. *The achievement motive.* New York: Appleton-Century-Crofts, 1953.
198. McCLELLAND, D. C. *The achieving society.* Princeton, N. J.: D. Van Nostrand Co., 1961.
199. MEAD, G. H. *Mind, self and society.* Chicago: Univer. of Chicago Press, 1934.
200. MERTON, R. K. *Social theory and social structure.* Glencoe, Ill.: The Free Press, 1957.
201. MORENO, J. L. *Who shall survive?* Boston: Beacon Press, 1953.
202. MUKERJEE, R. *The social function of art.* New York: Philosophical Library, 1954.
203. OBRDLIK, A. J. Gallows humor. *Amer. J. Sociol.,* 1942, 47, 709-716.
204. OPLER, M. K. (Ed.) *Culture and mental health.* New York: Macmillan, 1959.
205. PARSONS, T. The superego and the theory of social systems. *Psychiat.,* 1952, 15(1), 15-24.

206. PIAGET, J. *Play, dreams and imitation in childhood.* London: Wm. Heinemann Ltd., 1951.

207. PRINCE, S. H. *Catastrophe and social change.* Unpublished doctoral dissertation. Columbia Univer., 1920.

208. PRINS, S. A. Psychological aspects of an escape from occupied territory. *Br. J. Medical Psychol.,* 1947, 21(1), 30-37.

209. RIESMAN, D., GLAZER, N., & DENNEY, R. *The lonely crowd.* New York: Doubleday Anchor Book, 1953.

210. ROKEACH, M. *The open and closed mind.* New York: Basic Books. Inc., 1960.

211. SCHNEIDER, L., & DORNBUSCH, S. M. *Popular religion.* Chicago: Univer. of Chicago Press, 1958.

212. STOUFFER, S. A. *et al. The American soldier: Adjustment during army life,* Vol. I, Princeton, N. J.: Princeton Univer. Press, 1949.

213. STOUFFER, S. A. *et al. The American soldier: Combat and its aftermath,* Vol. II, Princeton, N. J.: Princeton Univer. Press, 1949.

214. STRAUSS, A. L. The literature on panic. *J. abnorm. soc. Psychol.,* 1944, 39(3), 319-328.

215. WATSON, B. A. Art and communication. *Sociol. and soc. res.,* 1958, 43, 28-33.

216. WOLFENSTEIN, M. *Disaster.* Glencoe, Ill.: The Free Press, 1957.

VI. Studies on Laboratory and Situational Stress:

217. BASOWITZ, H., PERSKY, H., KORCHIN, S. J., & GRINKER, R. R. *Anxiety and stress: An interdisciplinary study of a life situation.* New York: McGraw Hill Book Co., 1955.

218. BASSAN, M. E. Some factors found valuable in maintaining morale on a small combatant ship. *Bull. of Menninger Clin.,* 1946, 11(6), 33-42.

219. BEIER, E. G. *The effect of induced anxiety on flexibility of intellectual functioning.* Washington: Amer. Psychol. Ass., 1952.

220. COWEN, E. L. Stress reduction and problem-solving rigidity. *J. consult. Psychol.,* 1952, 16, 425-428.

221. COWEN, E. L., & BEIER, E. G. The influence of "threat-expectancy" on perception. *J. Pers.,* 1950, 19, 85-94.

222. DEESE, J., LAZARUS, R. S., & KEENAN, J. Anxiety, anxiety reduction, and stress in learning. *J exp. Psychol.,* 1953, 46, 55-61.

223. GREGG, R. B. *The power of non-violence.* Philadelphia: Lippincott, 1934.

224. GLASS, A. J. The problem of stress in the combat zone. *Symposium on Stress.* Division of Medical Sciences, National Research Council and the Army Medical Service Graduate School, Walter Reed Army Medical Center, 1953. Pp. 90-102.

225. HAGGARD, E. A. Some conditions determining adjustment during and readjustment following experimentally induced stress. In

J. B. Tomkins (Ed.), *Contemporary psychopathology*. Cambridge, Mass: Harvard Univer. Press, 1943.

226. HAMBURG, D. A. Psychological adaptive processes in life threatening injuries. In *Symposium on Stress*. Division of Medical Sciences, National Research Council and the Army Medical Service Graduate School, Walter Reed Army Medical Center, 1953. Pp. 222-235.

227. HAMBURG, D. A. HAMBURG, BEATRIX, & DEGEZA, S. Adaptive problems and mechanism in severely burned patients. *Psychiatry*, 1953, 16(1), 1-20.

228. KORCHIN, S. J. *The experimental study of anxiety*. Symposium on Motivation and Emotion. Copenhagen, 1961.

229. KORCHIN, S. J., & HEATH, HELEN. Somatic experience in the anxiety state: Some sex and personality correlates of "autonomic feedback." *J. consult. Psychol.*, 1961, 25(5) 398-404.

230. LANZETTA, J. T. Group behavior under stress. *Hum. Relat.*, 1955, 8(1) 29-52.

231. LAZARUS, R. S., & SPIESMAN, J. G. A research case history dealing with psychological stress. *J. Psychol. Stud.*, 1960, 11, 167-194.

232. LAZARUS, R. S., & RIESS, W. F. Clinical psychology and the research problems of stress and adaptation. *Progress in clinical psychology*, Vol. IV. New York: Grune & Stratton, 1960. Pp. 32-45.

233. LIEBMAN, S. (Ed.) *Stress situations*. Philadelphia: Lippincott, 1955.

234. MALMO, R. B. Physiologic study of symptom mechanisms in psychiatric patients under stress. *Psychosom. Med.*, 1949., 11, 25-29.

235. POSTMAN, L., & BRUNER, J. S. Perception under stress. *Psychol. Rev.*, 1948, 55, 314-323.

236. SELYE, H. *The story of the adaptation syndrome*. Montreal: Acta, Inc. Medical Pub., 1952.

237. SPIEGEL, J. P. Psychological transactions in situations of acute stress. *Symposium on Stress*. Division of Medical Sciences, National Research Council and the Army Medical Service Graduate School, Walter Reed Army Medical Center, 1953. Pp. 103-115.

238. WHITEHORN, J. C. Introduction and survey of the problems of stress. Symposium on Stress. Division of Medical Sciences, National Research Council and the Army Medical Service Graduate School, Walter Reed Army Medical Center, 1953. Pp. 2-7.

239. WOLFF, H. G. *Stress & disease*. Springfield, Ill.: Charles C. Thomas, 1953.

VII. Hypnosis and Suggestion:

240. ARONS, H. *Handbook of self-hypnosis*. Irvington, N. J.: Power Pub., 1959.

241. BAUDOUIN, C. *Suggestion and autosuggestion*. New York: Dodd, Mead and Co., 1921.

242. BRENMAN, MARGARET. Experiments in the hypnotic produc-

tion of antisocial and self-injurious behavior. *Psychiatry,* 1942, 5(1), 49-61.
244. COUÉ, E. *Self-mastery by conscious auto-suggestion.* Cincinnati: Kantaire Pub. Co., 1923.
245. COUÉ, E., & ORTON, J. L. *Conscious autosuggestion.* New York: D. Appleton & Co., 1924.
246. GILL, M. M. Spontaneous regression on the induction of hypnosis. *Bull. of Menninger Clin.,* 1948, 12(2), 41-48.
247. GILL, M. M., & BRENMAN, MARGARET. *Hypnosis and related states.* New York: Int. Univ. Press, 1959.
248. WEITZENHOFFER, A. M. *Hypnotism: An objective study in suggestibility.* New York: John Wiley & Sons, 1953.
249. WINBIGLER, C. F. *Suggestion.* Braddock Heights, Md.: Psycho-Therapeutic Pub. Co., 1914.

POPULAR LITERATURE

VIII. Popular Self Help Literature, Self Mastery and Especially Works on Control of Diet and of Sex:

A. GENERAL SELF-HELP

250. DEAMUDE, J. R. *Self mastery.* Cleveland, Ohio: Author, (3rd Ed.) 1922.
251. DRESSER, H. W. *A book of secrets.* New York: G. P. Putnam's Sons, 1902.
252. ERWOOD, W. J. *Chips from the rocks of truth.* La Crosse, Wis.: Author, 1903.
253. HABAS, R. A. *The art of self-control.* New York: Reynal & Hitchcock, 1941.
254. HAMILTON, D. H. *Autology: An inductive system of mental science.* Boston: Lee & Shepard, 1873.
255. JACKS, L. P. *Ethical factors of the present crisis.* Baltimore: Williams & Wilkins Co., 1934.
256. JORDAN, W. G. *The kingship of self-control.* New York: Fleming H. Revell Co., 1899.
257. NOYES, R. K. *On the self curability of disease.* Lynn, Mass.: Author, 1880.
258. VARNUM, H. & HERON, HENRIETTA. *Character.* Cincinnati: The Standard Pub. Co., 1926.
259. WILLIAMS, B. B. *Primal man: and the science of self control, psychology and mesmerism.* Meadville, Penn.: Tribune Pub. Co., 1887.

B. SEX

260. BAILEY, J. R. *More light on a dark subject.* Ashland, Wis.: Chequamegan Press, 1903.
261. BROWN, W. H. *The sex life of boys and young men.* Cincinnati: The Standard Pub. Co., 1917.

262. BUSCHKE, A., & JACOBSOHN, F. *Sex habits*. New York: Emerson Books, 1948.

263. CHESSER, E. *Grow up and live*. Armondsworth, Middlesex: Penguin Books, 1949.

364. DAVIS, MAXINE. *Sex and the adolescent*. New York: Dial Press, 1958.

265. DERSTINE, C. F. *Manual of sex education*. Grand Rapids, Mich.: Zondervan Pub. House, 1943.

266. DERSTINE, C. F. *Paths to beautiful womanhood*. Grand Rapids, Mich.: Zondervan Pub. House, 1944.

267. DICK, J. M. *A confidential talk with the boys of America*. Boston: Author, 1892.

268. FRANK, R. *Personal counsel*. New York: Informative Books, 1946.

269. GRAHAM, S. *A lecture to young men on chastity*. Boston: C. H. Peirce, 1848.

270. LAWTON, S. U., & ARCHER, J. *Sexual conduct of the teenager*. New York: Spectrolux Corp., 1951.

271. MACFADDEN, B. *Man's sex life*. New York: Author, 1935.

272. MEAGHER, J. F. W. *A study of masturbation and its reputed sequelae*. New York: W. Wood & Co., 1924.

273. Physical Culture Consultants. *Sex weaknesses*. Sausalito, Cal.: Author, 1927.

274. ROSS, J. G. *Personal hygiene for every man and boy*. Hollywood, Cal.: Social Guidance Enterprises, 1948.

275. SEELEY, B. *Christian social hygiene*. Portland, Ore.: Author, 1919.

276. SCOTT, G. R. *Sex problems and dangers*. London: Torchstream Books, 1948.

277. SHEPHERS, E. R. *True manhood*. (4th Ed.) Chicago: Sanitary Pub. Co., 1888.

278. Society of Sanitary and Moral Prophylaxis. *The young man's problems*. Educational Pamph. 1, New York: Author, 1912.

279. TAPP, S. C., & GREEN, H. L. *Mother nature's way to health*. Kansas City, Mo.: The Christian Purity and Health League, 1930.

280. TREVOR, C. T. *Sex and the athlete*. London: The Mitre Press: 1946.

C. DIET:

281. BELL, R. A. *Get yourself in shape*. Oklahoma City, Okla.: Author, 1928.

282. BOOHER, J. M. *Scientific weight control*. Chicago: Continental Scale Works, 1925.

283. FRIEDEL, H. *You can be thin!* New York: Caxton House, 1948.

284. JOLLIFFE, N. *Reduce and stay reduced*. New York: Simon & Schuster, 1952.

285. MUNRO, D. C. *Slenderizing for new beauty*. New York: Bartholomew House, 1953.

286. PIERCE, DEBORAH. *I prayed myself slim*. New York: The Citadel Press, 1960.

287. ROBINS, JOAN. *Common-sense slimming*. London: Odhams Press, Ltd., 1952.

288. SYLVIA OF HOLLYWOOD. *"No more alibis!"* Chicago: Photoplay Pub. Co., 1935.

289. WINSLOW, T. S. *Think yourself slim*. New York: Abelard Press, 1951.

290. WOLBERG, L. R. *The psychology of eating*. New York: Robert McBride & Co., 1936.

BENJAMIN NELSON

Self-Images and Systems of Spiritual Direction in the History of European Civilization

I. Introduction

In the midst of their incessant stresses and perplexities, men have everywhere struggled to win relief from the pangs of indifferent Fortune. Resources without number have been pressed into service in the effort to still the agonies of their spirits and, indeed, to gain lasting assurance of justification in their own eyes and in the eyes of their Divine Rulers. Among the most important of these resources have been the symbolic designs through which they have learned to express and enact meanings: images of the cosmos and universal destiny; schemes of group and personal identity; systems of self-culture and spiritual direction. It is of these last-mentioned patterns that the present essay mainly speaks.

Although we cannot now—and may, indeed, never be able to —say exactly how well the diverse systems of mental healing fulfilled the hopes and needs of the different peoples they were intended to serve, we may venture a number of preliminary observations.

At the core of all the different systems, there is discoverable a set of common concerns and procedures (Dill 1904, Eliade

1960, Harrison 1912, Linton 1956, McNeill 1951, Opler 1959, Pettazoni 1929).[1] Nonetheless, each system of mental healing has its own metaphysical commitments; its own way of classifying the various sorts of passions and infirmities which men experience; its own roster of accredited dispensers and techniques of cures (Dodds 1951, Eliade 1959, Zilboorg 1941).

Rather than attempt to elaborate cross-cultural comparisons of these varied institutions at this juncture (Eaton and Weil 1955, Field 1961, Opler 1959, Sachs 1941, Wallace 1959), I would simply begin by noting that the stresses and burdens we are called upon to bear seem to us today to stem from a variety of sources. We are prone to distinguish the following sorts of suffering.

1. Those felt to be universal experiences of every biological organism. For example: hunger, pain, sexual desire, illness, onset of death.

2. Those ascribed to the workings of central institutional structures (the economic, social, political, legal organizations). For example: poverty, status inferiority, political insignificance.

3. Those which are felt to be interpersonal in nature and which are generally charged to the malice or ignorance of other persons—injustice, deception, treachery, privation, enforced isolation, enforced contact, loss of trust, punishment, etc.

4. Those generally ascribed to the incursions of the unconscious in the intrapsychic sphere. For example: anxiety, shame, guilt, obsessiveness, loneliness, inability to love, inability to work, feelings of meaninglessness, persecutory fantasies, convictions of omnipotence, homicidal impulses, incestuous desires, etc.

The operations of psychoanalysis may be cited as a preliminary illustration at this point. When compared with the other familiar systems, it does not in the first instance concentrate on reinforcing abilities to tolerate sufferings located in the first two categories above. There are surely many Yoga (Evans-Wentz 1949, Eliade 1958) exercises which prepare one more directly (and effectively) than does psychoanalysis to tolerate hunger, pain, privation, disease, sexual desire. Psychoanalysis seems to concentrate on developing the power to bear burdens located in the two latter categories (the interpersonal and the intrapsychic spheres). Throughout the entire Freudian schema, emphasis is placed on coping with frustrations and anxieties arising from unconscious repressions of impulses to perform forbidden acts in relation to inappropriate objects, notably the members of one's own family. For Freud, experiences in the earliest years of life in the bosom of one's family are the paradigms (Coleman and Nelson 1957) of all subsequent development: they are discovered to influence the shape and character of all successive extrafamilial adult contacts even in the seemingly most rational impersonal environments.

Freud also places great emphasis on the therapeutic importance of a maximum power to know and acknowledge one's own fantasies. Acceptance of one's inner demons is one matter, says Freud; uncontrollable compulsions to act on their every call is another. Here he breaks with those previous traditions which assimilated evil thoughts to crimes.

The implications of Freudian psychoanalysis for the distribution of values located in the second category cannot be stated unequivocally. Freud does not summon men to address themselves directly to the collective remaking of their institutions by planned political action. For this reason, social and political critics (Brown 1959, Rieff 1959, La Piere 1959) have often accused Freudians of conservative and even reactionary leanings. Yet a more disinterested view will suggest that a particular affinity for Freudian views will be found among the mobile metropolitan populations of the advanced industrial societies, which strongly emphasize the consensualistic motifs in their universalistic creeds (Kardiner 1957). It may also be noted that official Communist criticisms of Freudian psychoanalysis emphasize its objectionable stresses on individualism, as evidenced in its encouragement of personal pursuit of current gratification in disregard of eventual realization of society's collective goals (Laqueur and Lichtheim 1958). Yet the incessant charges that, as opposed to the creative "freedom" ascribed to man in Soviet psychology and philosophy, "bourgeois" psychoanalysis and sociology promote "idealistic fatalism" (Bauer 1952), confirm substantial evidence from other quarters that the Soviet leaders have no desire to spread favorable attitudes to the sorts of *analysis,* whether in psychological or sociological spheres, which are favorably regarded in the so-called "Free World" (Nelson 1962c).

These preliminary references to psychoanalysis should suffice to indicate that there is no one superior medicine for every occasion. Every scheme of training has its built-in defects. We never acquire capacities without becoming unfitted for some other task. This holds as true for psychoanalysis as for any other system of self-direction.

Evidence gathered from prisoners of war and concentration

camps (Beck and Godin 1951, Bettelheim 1943, Schein and others 1961, Lifton 1961) seems to indicate that three groups fared unusually well in maintaining their equilibrium in extreme situations: fervent devotees of sectarian movements, such as Jehovah's Witnesses; specialized intellectuals, notably mathematicians (Weissberg 1951), practiced in detaching themselves from external circumstances; criminal psychopaths impervious to dominant moral codes. None of these groups characteristically frequent psychoanalysts.

Indeed, we would be remiss if we failed to recognize the extent to which the accredited healers of a given society come to act as a privileged group offering their services on their own terms. The history of conflicts within and among different groups of directors needs to be seen as an illustration of the perennial conflict of mediatorial elites (Nelson 1962a). It is, therefore, not surprising that accredited healers have seemed from time to time to be more concerned to reinforce their status-income-and-power claims than to expand the ability of their charges to direct themselves under stress.

II. Culture and Identity

Vigorous discussions over the past decades by Kluckhohn (1952), Kroeber (1952, 1958), Parsons (1957, 1958), Hallowell (1959) and others emphasize the need for renewed exploration of the concepts and contents of culture. Luckily, one-sided reductionist accounts of culture as projective responses to the social relations of production or the mothering patterns are passing out of fashion in favor of approaches doing greater justice to the regulative functions of culture. There is a fresh readiness to defer the fixing of causal explanations until due attention has been paid to the horizons opened by other perspectives, which I trust presently to describe elsewhere under the names of the intentionalistic, cognitive, and the configurative approaches (Nelson, in progress).

Four among the numerous connected ways of interpreting the more or less articulated structures of "universes of meaning" more familiarly known as "symbolic forms" (Cassirer 1953-57, Benedict 1934, Langer 1942) which culture comprises seem especially relevant to the present purpose. Among the myriad ways in which cultures may be observed to act, I shall focus, therefore, only on the following perspectives:

1. Culture as a *Dramatic Design,* serving to redeem time from the sense of flux by investing passage and process with the appearance of aim, purpose, and historical form.

2. Culture as *Defensive System,* comprising an array of beliefs and attitudes which help to defend us against vexing doubts, anxieties and aggressions.

3. Culture as a *Directive System,* that is, as complexes of instructions charging us to perceive, feel, think and perform in desired ways.

4. Culture as a *Symbol Economy,* that is, a value enterprise organization whose primary resources and net outcomes are symbols of varied worths. Society is here perceived to constitute a network of allocative institutions which produce and distribute an inevitably scarce supply of coveted symbols.

Reserving the last mentioned approach for the closing pages, I shall briefly characterize the first three perspectives in turn— I make no claim that I escape overlap.

DRAMATIC DESIGN

Culture always cries out to be regarded as symbolic form translating experience as *dramatic design.* Depending upon one's perspective, mood, or philosophic tradition, the design is either celebrated as the ultimate revelation underlying all appearance or exposed as sheer convention barely concealing the void of chance. On this view, culture in the sense of form is man's supreme, albeit most ambiguous, discovery. Were it not for the intervention of human concern, the flux of nature and time would seem without distinction or direction. Events intrinsically empty of meaning or at best agonizingly equivocal in implication achieve the status of a representative symbol; come, indeed, to constitute a higher Truth through the human device of Postulation and the human production of consensus induced by postulation (Nelson 1963b).

To study culture in this spirit is to study the complex processes connected with the invention, attribution, coordination, and action of meaning. In the Beginning was the Word (Burke 1954, 1960) and by the power of the Word, the chaos of Existence is converted into a cosmos of culture. Forever after, Nature is left to imitate Art and Illusion to define Reality.

This sense of culture as form has been expressed in radically different ways. On the one hand, there have been Plato, Kant, Hegel, Cassirer (1953-57), Huizinga (1924), Santayana (1905-06, 1922), Whitehead (1933), Suzanne Langer (1942). On the

other, there have been the Occamists, the young Hegelians (Loewith 1941), Kierkegaard and the Existentialists, the *Philosophy
of "As If"* (1911), Pirandello, Sartre (1953), the contemporary
leaders of the Theatre of the Absurd (Esslin 1961, Nelson
1963b). Very recently a fresh effort has been made to do justice
both to the natural origin and the ideal possibilities of this two-
sided "precarious vision" (Berger 1961, Becker 1962, Burke
1954).

DEFENSIVE SYSTEM

The second way of talking about culture—listed above as *2.*—
owes its recent accent to Freud (1930) and Malinowski (Parsons
1957), who tended to emphasize the defensive function of all
cultural elements. On this view, we never truly understand what
any cultural element comes to mean until we recognize the way
in which it serves psychic—whether or not unconscious—ends
within the specified bio-social framework (Lasswell 1932). Every
sphere of culture proves to contribute to the commanding task
of making men more at home in the only world they inhabit.
The anxieties, fears, aggressions generated within individuals and
societies are perceived to be mitigated by culture's protective
forms.

Although I have spoken above of the Freudian tinge of this
approach, I ought, in fact, to say that the intimations of this view
may be found among the spokesmen of the so-called Existentialist tradition—St. Augustine, the French moralists, Pascal,
Kierkegaard, Heidegger, Ludwig Binswanger and others (Bochenski 1947, Heineman 1958, Kaufmann 1956, Nelson 1961b,
Nelson 1963c, Passmore 1957).

DIRECTIVE SYSTEM

Culture may surely be construed as a repertoire of cues,
nonverbal as well as verbal, a "directive system" intended to move
individuals and groups to perform in accordance with desired
norms. At least six classes of cues may be discriminated. For the
sake of economy of diction, I use Latin gerunds to name them:

a. Percipienda cues—this first and most embracing class of
cues comprises directives which charge us to perceive any possible object, person, or occasion in one or another way.

b. Sentienda cues—this second set of cues directs us to have
one or another feeling in relation to any possible person, object,

event or situation. (After extended analysis it has seemed prudent to consider the *sentienda* cues as a second category rather than as a subclass of the *percipienda*.)

c. *Agenda* cues—this third set of cues charges us to perform or not to perform one or another act on sanction of penalty or promise of reward.

d. *Credenda* cues—are those signals or symbols which tell us what or how we ought to believe or not to believe.

e. *Miranda* cues—are those directives which define what or whom we ought to hold in awe, what or whom we ought to marvel at (Otto 1923).

f. *Emulanda* cues—this sixth set of cues influences us to emulate persons or imitate behavior of those presented to us as role-models, social paradigms, or cynosures.

It hardly needs saying that (*1*) these six classes of cues are directed at us by agents of induction variously located throughout the complex of linked social systems: the family system, the educational system, the religious system, the political system, etc.; (*2*) the opportunities for discontinuities and contradictions in the communication of cues are endless (Benedict 1938); (*3*) the effect of these signals is notably influenced by the context, style, mood of the communication.

I forbear at this time from a fuller elaboration of this particular schema, which was suggested to me by a section in Charles Merriam's neglected book on *Political Power* (1934). I would merely observe here that specialists in the systems of spiritual direction are called in when subjects go aground in internalizing and institutionalizing (Parsons and others, 1961) these cues and other experiences into workable relations to "realities." The possibilities of mishap are countless, varying from one society to another. The cues of any class or all six classes of cues may be experienced as intolerably stable or unstable, intolerably incongruous with the subject's sense of experience (Nelson 1961a). The agents of induction may be felt to be arbitrary in their provision of rewards and penalties. The task of the spiritual directors is made especially difficult when a state of normlessness (*anomie*) or crises of meaning and identity prevails (Durkheim 1893, 1897, Wheelis 1958, Erikson 1959).

As the sympathetic reader will readily sense, the tell-tale terms in our last sentence have returned us to our original starting point. The remaining sections of our paper will lightly survey representative aspects of the self-images and systems of spiritual direction which have evolved in the history of civilization. The following plan describes our prospective itinerary:

III: "Occident" and "Orient": Some Similarities and Differences.[2]

IV: Socrates, the Stoics, St. Augustine.

V: The Middle Ages: Conscience, Casuistry, and the Cure of Souls.

VI: The Transmoral Conscience: From Luther to Freud.

VII: Psychoanalysis and 20th Century Culture.

Throughout we shall be concerned to observe the ways in which acts and attitudes are defined, meanings ascribed, identities attained, anxieties allayed. Do we need to add that we make no pretence to completeness of coverage?[3]

III. Occident and Orient

It will not do, as Rudolf Otto has so brilliantly shown in his *Mysticism, East and West* (1932), to fall into the error of supposing that the images of the soul's illness and recovery vary entirely with changes of time and place. All mysticisms, he observes, have certain elements in common along with their differences. On close textual comparison, Śankara and Meister Eckhart often seem to be speaking the same idiom.

A similar observation applies to the innumerable writings on mental hygiene which succeed one another in the history of mankind (Jung 1938). It is surprising to note how many important assumptions they seem to share with respect to:

1. the origin of what we may be allowed to regard as the nuclear traumas of mankind;

2. the characteristics of what are here being called "the madnesses" of men;

3. the methods proposed for the overcoming of these madnesses;

4. the roles accorded to or claimed by spiritual directors or masters.

Yet we would be remiss if, in our concern to establish certain underlying unities of expression and attitude, we failed to observe very notable differences. By comparison to Śankara, Eckhart is inextricably Western, indeed in Otto's terms, Gothic and Faustian. Otto writes:

His [Eckhart's] mysticism is quiveringly *alive* and of powerful vitality, and therefore far removed from "Abstraction." It is therefore also very far from Sankara and Indian mysticism, and the reason for that difference lies in the foundation from which it rises (1957 ed., p. 168).

That is indeed numinous rapture. At the same time it is subtly different from that of Sankara. This difference moreover is connected with what we have already described as the Gothic element in Eckhart's conception of God in contrast to Sankara's static Indian conception of Brahman. This distinction between the Gods occurs again in the emotions with which they are sought, striven after, experienced. For Sankara when the soul (ātman) has "come come" to the eternal Being (Átman) it is there, it has arrived (āpta), it is at rest and fully content (sānta). But Eckhart is, in truth, never "there," never in a final static rest . . . (1957 ed., p. 185).

Similarly, if one were asked to sum up in a phrase how Hindu and Western Christian schemas of spiritual direction differ, one might venture to say that classical Oriental methods (notably Hindu and Buddhist) seem to be directed at the overcoming of the anguish of the individuated ego undergoing pain and privation in a remorseless world incapable of being notably ameliorated, to say nothing of being redeemed (Weber 1915). Ultimate hope is placed in the escape from this burden by the return to the primal, undifferentiated ground where all oppositions vanish.

The Western Christian image of man's Fall from Grace (Williams 1927) begins with the same sequence: the original unity; the nuclear trauma; the loss of paradise; the separation from the source of all goodness, truth and virtue; the haunting sense of alienation and estrangement. As in the East, alienation exhibits itself intermittently as:

1. over-attachment to irrelevant ideas and values which will be of no account in regard to man's eternal life;

2. under-attachment to the unfailing source of joy or peace;

3. infestation of one's spirit and the world by alien powers and noxious thoughts.

But here the accent dramatically changes and the difference from the East emerges. In contrast to a number of the ancient Oriental schemas and their neo-Gnostic (Grant 1961, Jonas 1958, 1960, Voegelin 1952, Cohn 1957, Nelson 1951) expressions at explosive junctures in Western history, the world is described as good, the creation of a *good* God (Trémontant 1955). The value of the individual soul receives the strongest confirmation. The method of mitigating estrangements and madnesses are in the first place "a way *back*" to the primal undifferentiated ground.

And then once more the new elements assert themselves strongly. The way back assumes the character of a "way forward," forward to the struggle for mastery of self and the world (Weber 1915).

Oriental schemas of self-direction are, in the ultimate sense, acosmic. The immense machinery set into play to liberate us from attachments to the world of passing illusions have as their primary purpose the overcoming of any sense of apartness from the One, which is all-encompassing and unchanging. Western teachings, even when they sound alike or are influenced by the Oriental works, preserve their peculiar flavor. They are, in the end, activistic. (Professor Otto's translators have written "actualistic," which seems to me not quite what is needed to express the situation.) To be sure, acosmism is a recurrent motif in all schemas of self-direction, as it is a phase in every pilgrimage of the spirit, but quietism has never managed to assert itself as a dominant doctrine in the West (Nelson 1951).

It is instructive, in this connection, to study the details of the controversy over Quietism and Disinterested Love connected with Fénélon and Madame Guyon. Quietism was eventually condemned as a heresy for it appeared to contradict the commandment to love one's neighbor as one loved oneself. Holy egoism, the prescribed sacred love of oneself, was too strong in the Western world to be dislodged by Quietism (Brémond 1928, Kirk 1937). Mystical individualism feeds into the instrumental activism of the modern era (Weber 1904-05).

Eastern treatises on the direction of self and others are likely to contain extremely detailed prescriptions and recommendations for the achievement of desired effects. One has only to look into any of the countless Yogi manuals (Eliade 1960), the Tibetan *Book of the Dead* (Evans-Wentz 1949), the Zen treatises (Suzuki 1956), and other works of spiritual hygiene (Jung 1938). The methods to be employed range from auto-hypnotic trances to extremely intricate sets of physical exercises intended to demolish what are sometimes called the "body armor" or the somatic resistance. There is relatively little of this in the West.

Could one reason for the contrast be the limitations placed on magic and the magical viewpoint in Western thought (Weber 1917-19)? Perhaps Western postclassical, Judaeo-Christian culture is simply more generally philosophical and psychological. In truth, we have no explanation. We simply have a fact. The Western treatises go on the assumption that the "way back," which is also the "way forward," involves the journey through the "clouds of unknowing," in search of the new self.

Now and then a particular master or theorist will recommend procedures which have the ring of auto-hypnosis. Thus, for example, in the *Spiritual Exercises* of St. Ignatius Loyola (d. 1556), we have an extraordinarily systematic arrangement of meditations which are aimed to lead the believer to arrive at an ultimate and irrevocable decision to be a soldier in the ranks of the good Lord and an enemy to death of the Devil and all his works. The exercises of Loyola involve repeated reflection with the mind's eye on the terrors of hell, on the sufferings of Jesus on the Cross, on the fires of purgatory, on the dread of damnation (Fueloep-Miller 1956). All else is to be eliminated from awareness in order that the experience of horror might be complete and the need for redemption might be experienced in the depths. It is no secret that Muslim elements have been detected in the extraordinary symbolism of Loyola.

In closing this section, one is again compelled to cite Otto:

If we turn again to Sankara, we can measure in full the distance between the two masters. Sankara knows the ātman in us, but this ātman is not the soul in the Christian and Eckhartian sense: it is not "soul" as identical with "Gemuet," infinitely rich in life and depth, a place of ever fuller experience and possession, an "inward man" with the characteristics of the biblical conception of this word. Least of all is his ātman, "soul" in the sense of religious conscience, which "hungers and thirsts after righteousness," and for which "to be" is to be righteous with the very righteousness of God. Sankara's mysticism is certainly mysticism of the ātman, but it is not soul-mysticism as *Gemuetsmystik*. Least of all is it a mystical form of justification and sanctification as Eckhart's is through and through (1957 ed., p. 206).

Eckhart thus becomes necessarily what Sankara could never be: the profound discoverer of the rich indwelling life of the "soul" and a leader and physician of "souls," using that word in a sense which is only possible on a Christian basis. Upon Indian soil there could never have developed this inward unceasing preoccupation with the soul's life as a life of Gemuet and of conscience, and therewith the "cura animarum" in the sense which is characteristic of, and essential to, Christianity from the earliest days. It is upon this calling as a *curator animarum* (shepherd of souls) that finally everything which Eckhart has said or done as a preacher, as a simple Christian or as profound Mystic, depends (1957 ed., p. 215).

And now to Greece and Rome.

IV.   Socrates, the Stoics,
St. Augustine

Thanks to Professor Hadas and the Conference program
chairman, I am relieved of the heavy responsibility of dealing
with the intricate developments in the sphere of spiritual direction
in classical antiquity. The few remarks I will permit myself in
this connection bear upon one issue of particular interest to the
argument of this paper, the recurrent rivalries among different
sorts of spiritual directors throughout the history of the West.

I have elsewhere sought to show that from the time of Socrates
to our own day, philosophy and psychiatry have been in a relation of antagonistic cooperation. Philosophers (for example, Epicurus, Descartes) have been as prone to proliferate psychiatries
as mental healers (for example, Jung, Binswanger) have been
to proffer philosophies (Nelson 1962c). These crossings of the
never well-defined twilight zones inevitably occur in times of
troubles when men grope for help from every source. At such
times, philosophy accentuates its concern with spiritual direction,
presenting itself as the true hygiene of the straying mind. Logic
and physics are treated as simply the first steps in the way to
therapy. Ethics becomes the quest for consolation (Dill 1904).

The different faces of philosophy (Cushman 1958, Nock
1933: 164-86)—science, self-examination, therapeutic conquest
of ignorance, consolation—are all mirrored in the life and thought
of Socrates. An increasing stress upon the cathartic function of
philosophy as a purgative and therapy is apparent in the Hellenistic schools, in the Epicurians, Cyrenaics, Cynics, Skeptics, Stoics
(Arnold 1911, Lovejoy and others 1935, Murray 1925).

Through philosophy we win our way to a holy apathy and
detachment; a relief from the pains afflicting anyone who sets his
heart upon unattainable ends or evanescent pleasures. The task
of philosophy is to present an unassailable truth free from illusion or blandishment. The Stoics bid men to live in accordance
with nature and to conquer every impulse which divided them
from natural law. The Cynics emphasized release from attachment to complex products and mode of satisfaction. Innumerable
stories of Diogenes the Cynic connect happiness with the abandonment of vain imagining and futile pretence (Lovejoy and
others 1935). The Skeptics also viewed philosophy as the criticism of illusion. Their minute examination of the traps of logic

and epistemology were intended to free men from subordination to painful superstition from which they could win no joy. The stress on the therapeutic role of suspension of belief recurs all through the Skeptical tradition and is perhaps seen most clearly in the writings of Sextus Empiricus (d. *ca.* 250 A.D. tr. 1933).

One of the clearest ways of seeing the distinction between classical and patristic Christian approaches to the direction of self and mind is by comparing two sets of meditations—the *Meditations* of Marcus Aurelius and the *Confessions* (or Meditations) of St. Augustine (Dill 1904). Marcus Aurelius strives to present himself as philosopher King, a perfect Stoic. The net effect he seeks to convey is that he is possessed of an indomitable will to free himself of every infirmity and defect through his own exertions. Everywhere he looks, he sees shortcoming, pettiness and a failure to express the world spirit in action. His meditations are aimed to purge himself of every least unworthiness (Dill 1904, Oates 1940).

St. Augustine sounds a different note. He talks frankly of his boyish sins and manly passions; he humbly admits his metaphysical bewilderment and his recurring fear of meaninglessness. Feeling himself adrift at sea, he does not fear to avow his need for faith, hope, and love (Burnaby 1938, Dill 1898, O'Meara 1954, Gilson 1960).

The contrast between the Roman Emperor and the Christian Bishop has always seemed to me to have peculiar relevance for the understanding of the fluctuating sensibility of our own time.

V. The Middle Ages: Conscience, Casuistry and Cure of Souls

A paradigm familiar to contemporary social scientists may help to express many central convictions of the medieval Christian consciousness. Freely adapting for our purposes a schema originally devised to classify the determinants of culture and personality, we may say that the Church viewed mankind and the world as follows:

Every man was in certain respects
1. like all other men,
2. like some other men,
3. like no other man.

(How odd the forthcoming details will sound to those who recall the expansions in the original essay (1948) by Clyde Kluckhohn and Henry A. Murray!)

1. *Every man is like all other men* in certain critical respects. All men are assumed to be sons of God. As such they share in the possession of reason and are answerable to God for the right use of reason. Thus all men are obliged to obey the moral law made available to them by the Law of Nature (Gierke 1900). As spiritual brothers, all men are obligated to the requirements of brotherhood (Nelson 1949).

2. *Every man is like some other men* in the sense that they form historically separate communities within the universal brotherhood. Only Christians have received Christ and the New Testament. All Christians—and only they—are bound to preserve the true Faith, to obey the precepts of the Church and the Canon Law (Kirk 1925).

Yet Christians differ among themselves in many ways, most obviously estate and vocations. Warriors, peasants and monks have distinct "callings." Only the monks are called the "religious"; obey the counsels as well as the precepts; observe a rule; live by the triple vow of poverty, chastity, and obedience; may expect to qualify for the status of perfection (Weber 1904-05, Nelson 1949).

3. *In the ultimate sense, no two men are alike.* Each is a unique person immediately responsible to God for the welfare of his soul and the well-being of his brother.

Who has not heard of the fateful medieval integration of the beliefs and sentiments stated in this paradigm? The extraordinary stress on the responsibility of each individual for the activity of his will and the state of his soul attained its height in the High and Later Middle Ages (Kirk 1927). Three sets of ideas and institutions—none entirely new in human history—were now fused into a single structure of spiritual direction never before (some will say never since) matched in complexity (Lea 1896, Nelson 1951c, Nelson 1963a). I refer to the beliefs and cultural arrangements embracing the determination of the individual *conscience* (Kirk 1927); the realization of the dictates of conscience in the perplexing cases or alternatives in the here and now (called *casuistry*) (Lea 1896, Nelson 1963a); the management of errant, perplexed, and obsessively scrupulous consciences (McNeill 1951), the so-called *cura animarum* (care or cure of souls). All three of these bodies of ideas are found in many parts of the world—surely they were previously known in one or another way to the peoples of the ancient Orient, and, above all, to the Greeks and Romans (Thamin 1884)—but never before the Middle Ages nor after have they been so systematically elaborated in thought or so closely connected in practice. In the Middle Ages this imposing institution in its more generally known form came to be called the Forum of Conscience and the Tribunal of the Soul. It is this court which was later to become the source of the Jurisdiction of the Chancellor, "a Judge of Conscience," The Keeper of the King's Conscience, in Equity (Fifoot 1949: 301-07, 321-29; Vinogradoff 1928).

Actually, conscience was the center of two related but separated institutions of spiritual direction to which different sorts of persons repaired for different reasons. Every Christian without exception was answerable to the Forum of Conscience for the sins he had committed and for the state of his soul. In this tribunal the presiding officer performed a complex of functions. He was a confessor, hearing or eliciting admissions; a judge, fitting the penalty to the crime; a physician, providing solace to the sinner without traducing the rights of God; a priest, mediating God's grace in the sacrament (Vacandard 1908).

In addition and beyond this path to perfection was another avenue for the more ardent wayfarers, those who thirsted to experience true illumination and mystical union with God. Only these were expected to engage in the *systematic* practice of meditation (Phillips 1955). Under ordinary circumstances, the deliberate quest of illumination was pursued exclusively only by the so-called "religious"—monks and nuns—who strove to attain the status of perfection. The rich tradition of mystical itineraries is chiefly a monastic one until the Fourteenth century, when pious men and women sought to achieve the status of perfection without wholly abandoning the world (Egenter 1928). The significance of this desire of laymen, especially those of the Low Countries and the Rhineland (Seesholtz 1934, Clark 1949) to practice innerworldly asceticism, albeit under priestly direction, will not be lost on readers of Weber (1904-05).

As must be apparent, the ruling perspectives of the two institutions of conscience were quite different. The outlook of the Forum of Conscience was predominantly legal or forensic; the sovereign end of the practice of meditation was the shedding of the old Adam, the total rebirth of the soul. In this endeavor the purgation of conscience was only the first step on the ladder. The consummation devoutly hoped for was the mystical embrace of Christ with the illumined spark of the soul.

Let us now deal with each of these institutions in turn.

Interestingly, it is the Twelfth and Thirteenth Centuries—the era of the Crusades, of Western recovery of the Mediterranean, of expanded urban liberties and mass social heresies, of vernacular literature and the new Universities (Haskins 1939, Herr 1961)— which witnessed the extraordinary advance of the new logic of conscience and the emergence of a new system of administration of the cure of souls (Lottin 1942-60). This fact alone should suffice to warn us against the naive assumption that the idea of conscience could not appear until the Reformation because of the oppressions of the Medieval Church. It was Abelard (d. 1142) who revolutionized the dialectic of moral agency and decision. The titles of his major works—*Sic et Non* (*Yes and No*), *Ethica seu Scito te Ipsum* (*Ethics or Know Thyself*)—powerfully dramatize his dual effort: to develop the implications of the new moral sense, to apply reason in harmonizing the ambiguities of tradition (Abelard tr. 1935, Sikes 1932). Like Luther after him—the contrast is as compelling as the comparison—Abelard was strongly attracted to St. Paul. The dictum *Quod non ex fide peccatum est* (Rom. XIV) suddenly seemed to require a complete reinvigoration of the human will and, therefore, an exhaustive analysis of the shades and grades of evidence, opinion, knowledge, commitment. (Luther, by contrast to Abelard, drew the opposite lesson from the *Epistle to the Romans*. He became the champion of the "serf will" and the foremost enemy of a casuistry of intention.)

Long before Aquinas, authoritative medieval theologians and jurists were construing conscience as the *proximate* (not the *remote*) rule of right reason. Specialized treatises tracing the obligations of conscience in the here and now, spelling out how individuals were obligated to act in every case they encountered in the conduct of their lives, began to appear. In these works, conscience extended into every sphere of action, ranging over the whole moral life of man from the making of contracts to the making of war (Kirk 1927). After 1215, when annual confession became the obligation of all Christians, these treatises became the guides to Christian souls everywhere. The influence of handbooks on conscience survives wherever Catholic religious life is practiced.

Only one sphere, strictly speaking, was beyond conscience in the Middle Ages—the sphere of Revealed Faith. Two positions, which seem contradictory to the illumined conscience of later days, were vigorously affirmed by all the scholastic moralists:

1. everyone was under the strictest obligation to act in accordance with the findings of his convinced conscience;

2. a convinced conscience (*conscientia certa*) was not necessarily a right conscience (*conscientia recta*). Not the individual conscience but Eternal Revelation, the natural law, the canon law and other binding rules were the ultimate imperatives of the individual conscience.

The transvaluation of the value of conscience, its detachment from the practical life of man and its expansion into and confinement to the sphere of Faith did not occur until the Reformation (Nelson 1951c). The story of the storms which culminated in this situation will be discussed in our next section on Protestantism. Here we will look more closely at the development of the meditative tradition. It was within this institution that there emerged the notion of an illumined transmoral conscience (Tillich 1945) which was to prove the undoing of the Forum of Conscience and the source of the ideas of Inner Light (Burrage 1912, Woodhouse 1951) and of the Enlightenment Concept of Reason (Crocker 1959, Hazard 1953, Sampson 1956).

There is a vast literature reporting early Christian and medieval efforts to experience the vision of God and enjoy Him in mystical union. Thanks to Dean Inge (1899), Father Pourrat (1922), Evelyn Underhill (1933), Henri Brémond (1928), Bishop Kenneth Kirk, and others, we are now able to trace the development of the philosophies and techniques of meditation in the successive works of such celebrated masters of the contemplative life as the pseudo-Dionysius the Areopagite (*ca.* 500), Johannes Climacus (d. 649), Richard (d. 1173) and Hugo (d. 1141) of St. Victor, St. Bernard of Clairvaux (d. 1153), St. Bonaventura (d. 1274), Meister Eckhart (d. 1327), Thomas à Kempis (d. 1471), the anonymous author of the *Theologia deutsch* (*ca.* 1350), which left its mark on Luther.

With endless variation of images, these authors explore the spiritual ills of men, the arduous pilgrimages which need to be undergone if peace is to be won for the soul, the indispensable role of masters in the achievement of what we would call cures and insight. The psychological and religious dimensions of these works are suggested by their eloquent titles, for example: *The*

Celestial Hierarchy, The Mind's Itinerary into God, The Cloud of Unknowing, The God of Love, The Imitation of Christ, The Spiritual Exercises.

Each phase of the spiritual pilgrimage is minutely examined in the light of the individual author's experience and conviction. Thus Johannes Climacus, the Byzantine author of the *Ladder of Divine Ascent,* is singularly revealing on the subjects of gluttony, shameful fantasies, and the value of subordinating one's will to the master under all circumstances. St. Bernard (d. 1153) is supremely eloquent on the mystical love of Christ.

It is St. Bonaventura, the noted 13th Century Franciscan thinker, who provides the systematic psychological and theological analysis which helped to codify the distinctive convictions and procedures of the meditative tradition (Phillips 1955). The titles of two of St. Bonaventura's works express his central perspectives:

1. The Threefold Way—In this extraordinarily influential work, Bonaventura systematically sets forth the triple way of the contemplative life: the *purgative* way, the *illuminative* way, and the *perfective* or *unitive* way.

2. The Mind's Itinerary into God—This work, explains a recent editor,

. . . is addressed to those who are ready to answer the divine call to live the mystical life and to taste of God's sweetness in ecstatic union (Bonaventura, 1956, p. 19).

The purgative act is practiced in meditation, prayer, and contemplation. Purgative meditation has as its main object, self-examination; its main purpose is to bring to bitter consciousness the soul's moral disorder and the grave danger which it entails, thus achieving a complete detachment from all sinful inclination. Purgative prayer transforms meditation into weeping and deploring sin and into asking for mercy; its main affections are pain, shame, and fear. Purgative contemplation, finally, leads the soul from shame to fear, from fear to pain, then to imploring prayer, to rigor and severity, and finally to ardor which culminates in the desire for martyrdom, the ultimate purification of love, and makes the soul rest and fall asleep in mystical peace under the shadow of Christ.

On the illuminative way, the soul is mainly concerned with a penetration into truth. The illuminative act is likewise practiced in meditation, in prayer (which is less clearly expressed by Saint Bonaventura), and in contemplation. Illuminative meditation turns the ray of intelligence to the multitude of sins forgiven by God's mercy, broadens it then to show all the benefits of God, natural and supernatural, and finally turns it back to the Giver of all of them, Who has still greater rewards awaiting the soul in heaven. Illuminative prayer, according to

Saint Bonaventura, has, it seems, as its main task to ask for mercy
and help in union with the Holy Spirit, groaning in us by an ardent
desire, in union with Christ by trusting hope, and in union with the
Saints by their intercession. Illuminative contemplation finally leads to
the splendor of truth by imitating Christ, or to be more exact, by an
impregnation of our mind with the passion of Christ, and that again
in seven steps: first there is a humble submission of reason to a God
who was crucified, followed by deep compassion, admiration, grateful
devotion, the putting on the form of the suffering of Christ, and finally,
the ardent embrace of the Cross, in which and through which the
splendor of truth will dawn.

On the perfective or unitive way, the soul is mainly concerned with
charity. It is the perfective act that is now practiced in meditation, in
prayer, and in contemplation. In meditation the spark of wisdom must
be kept aloof from all attachment to creatures, must be enkindled by
turning to the love of the Bridegroom, and must be elevated beyond the
senses, the imagination, and the understanding into a blaze of desire
for the Bridegroom who is absolutely desirable. In perfective prayer the
soul is prostrated in adoration and deep reverence, in benevolence and
complacence, becoming one with God in the fire of love. Here Saint
Bonaventura adds the six degrees of the love of God. In perfective contemplation the soul again reaches the sweetness of love in seven degrees: vigilance for the coming of the Bridegroom is first; then confidence in Him; third, a deep longing for Him; fourth, a rising beyond
oneself to the height of the Bridegroom; fifth, complacence that dwells
on the comeliness of the Bridegroom; sixth, joy in the abundance of
the Bridegroom; seventh, a union of the soul with the Bridegroom in
the sweetness of love (Bonaventura, 1956, p. 20-22).

We must not allow Bonaventura's theological language and
homoerotic symbolism to drive us into minimizing his psychological insights and philosophical ingenuity. His exhaustive investigating of the "threefold way" can be examined with profit by
contemporary psychiatrists. His depiction of the *Mind's Itinerary*
and the "reduction" of the arts to theology are important steps on
the way to modern thought. It is in a way accidental that Meister
Eckhart rather than the Seraphic Doctor, as Bonaventura was
called, had so profound an influence on the backgrounds of the
Protestant Reformation. Both men elaborated the image of the
soul's rebirth as a result of mystical union with God, which eventually undermined the forensic institutionalizations of thought and
sentiment. Medieval illuminism provided inspiration to Luther,
the revolutionary sectarians, the English dissenters, the American
Quakers, the myriad Continental Romantics whose voices sound in
the philosophy and literature of the last two centuries.

The illuminist philosophies which had bloomed in the meditative tradition were to attain their fullest flowering in radical Protestant cultures and their transcendental offshoots: inner light mysticism, Enlightenment rationalism, the sundry romanticisms of the 19th and 20th centuries, including Existentialism (Nelson 1961b). Each step along the way was a blow on behalf of the liberation of conscience until at the end, the wholly unencumbered conscience was itself called into question by the union of utilitarianism, Darwinism, historicism, and Freudianism (Nelson 1951c). The religion of the inner light had eventuated in the dwarfing of the moral conscience. The 20th century has been marching under the banner of "Beyond Conscience" (T. V. Smith 1934).[4]

The evolution contrasts markedly with Post-Tridentine patterns of development in the Catholic culture-areas. Surprising as it may seem to many, the bounds of "liberty of conscience" underwent audacious expansion among the probabilist theologians and jurists of the 16th and 17th centuries (Pascal 1656-57, ed. 1920, Doellinger-Reusch 1889, Lea 1890). Paradoxically, here, it was eventual success of the innovating Jesuit program for the "liberty of opinion" in the face of ardent opposition of Port-Royal, Pascal, the conservative Dominicans and the Popes them-selves which preserved the unique medieval orchestration of con-science, casuistry and the cure of souls (Kirk 1927).

Overlooking critical structural contrasts, a recent writer, Professor George Mosse (1957) of the University of Wisconsin, has insisted upon the identity of outlook across the barriers of the Reformation. The Puritans of New and Old England, alike, he contends—such men as William Perkins (d. 1602), William Ames (d. 1633), John Winthrop (d. 1649)—were hardly different from the Jesuits in their blend of piety, worldly prudence, policy and probabilist casuistry. Indeed, he insists, the great Puritan divines and statesmen were committed in principle, if not in name, to the program of *raison d'état* of Machiavelli (d. 1527) and Botero (1540-1617).

I reserve for the following section (and other writings in progress) the proofs of my view that these equations of Catholic and Protestant outlooks rest on faulty observation of surface resemblances. As I see it, the distinctively Roman Catholic and Protestant culture-areas have generally related to the moral and social ambiguities of the modern and contemporary eras in notably different ways (Groethuysen 1927-30).

These differences can—I am persuaded—be explained in significant measure by the different courses followed by the Roman Catholic and Protestant communities in the struggles over freedom of conscience and opinion in the 16th and 17th centuries.

Again we have run ahead of our story. We turn now to Luther and the Reformation.

VI. The Transmoral Conscience: From Luther to Freud

The Protestant Reformation begins a vast new experiment in the culture of the self and the systems of self-direction. The important details of the early history of these developments are not yet even now agreed upon by impartial scholars, and there is the sharpest difference of opinion as to the original associations and contemporary outcomes of the teachings of Luther and Calvin. Our own day has witnessed marked changes in the style of interpreting the meanings of the Reformation (Bainton 1956, Holl 1961). It is no longer possible to say, as used to be claimed, that thanks to Luther's renewal of Christian liberty, the free man possessed of his own free conscience was now released from the fetters of medieval priestcraft and the superstitious doctrine of the efficacy of works. Everyone now knows that Luther was not an enlightener in the manner of Diderot and Voltaire, even of Kant (Bainton 1951). Yet, it does not seem sensible to regard the Reformation as simply a reactionary throwback to the Middle Ages. To call it an "escape from freedom," the seed bed of Nazi totalitarianism, as Erich Fromm did (1941) is to regard the cultural circumstances from a hopelessly alien perspective.

More recent characterizations of the era by David Riesman (1950) and Erik Erikson (1958) represent an improvement in the social psychological studies of the relevance of Protestantism for the culture of character. Riesman and his collaborators relate the Reformation to the changeover from the traditional to the inner-directed social character, touching hardly at all on the unfolding of historical circumstance and teachings. Erikson interprets Luther's triumph over his agonies of conscience as a decisive episode in the forging of a new cultural identity. In truth, we are hardly beyond the infancy of our understanding of the inner history of conscience, character and culture in the modern world.

The exact influence of Luther on the notions of self and spiritual direction is no easy matter to state. The following must be counted among the decisive facts:

1. In his early years as a reformer, especially in his pre-Reformation treatises of 1520 and his appearance at the Diet of Worms, 1521, Luther assumed the posture of the Liberator of Conscience (Bainton 1950, Boehmer 1924). His condemnation of the medieval religion of works culminated in the burning of the Corpus of the canon law (*Corpus juris canonici*) and the so-called angelic *Summa* on the cases of conscience by Angelus Carletus de Clavasio. Luther thus publicly signalized his aversion to the medieval organization of the moral and religious life, above all to the triune integrations of conscience, casuistry and the cure of souls.

2. Once Luther had proclaimed the Gospel meanings of justification "by faith alone" and true—lifelong—repentance, mandatory annual confession, and the fourfold role of the priest in the administration of the sacrament of penance were without foundation (Hardeland 1898, McNeill 1951).

3. Gone too was the basis of the medieval concept of the moral conscience and the moral effort through casuistry to make conscience operative in the world. Luther's strongly anti-Pelagian theology ruled out the concept of the attainment of Christian perfection (Nygren 1953) through the imitation of Christ, the ultimate paradigm (Nelson 1949, Appendix). The Reformation from the time of Luther was set against the medieval system of spiritual direction.

As against these stresses of Luther, we have to recall others which present Luther in a very different guise:

a. Luther recoiled in horror from the conclusions drawn from his teachings on conscience by the left-wing supporters of his movement. In his withdrawal, he relapsed into the medieval truism that *conscientia* (conscience) was meaningless without *scientia* (knowledge), *Gewissen* was folly without *Wissen* (Castellio, 1935). This endorsement of medieval intellectualism was a blow against the unrestricted emancipation of the conscience from superpersonal norms. It also allowed the continuance of persecutions for conscience, although now under the charge of blasphemy.

b. Luther's attack on casuistry was coupled with a proclamation of unqualified temporal authority in the political sphere. Conscience was now increasingly confined to the religious realm.

Inner freedom and outer bondage tended to occupy entirely separate domains in Luther's stark dualism (Trinkaus 1955). It was this less familiar side of St. Paul's influence which gave lay rulers a control over men they had not had in medieval civilization (Troeltsch 1911).

Again and again, efforts have been made in the long history of Protestantism to restore analogues of the medieval framework free of the alleged medieval excesses or corruptions. These results have always been unavailing. Confession, casuistry, moral and religious counsel, organized spiritual direction have lacked for fundamental support within the framework of Protestantism (McNeill 1951, Nelson 1963a, Troeltsch 1912). The individual in Protestant cultures has the choice and the obligation of doing God's will without the aid or regulation of learned casuists, counsellors, and confessors.

According to Weber (1904-05), Groethuysen (1927-30), and others, a fundamental reorientation of the social and cultural patterns of the Western world could not occur until the medieval administration of self and spiritual direction fell before the onslaughts of Luther, Calvin and their followers. So long as a distinction was made between the special calling of monks who lived "outside the world," systematically observing a rule in their pursuit of the status of perfection and everyone else *in* the world, who lived irregularly, without benefit of a rule, in the midst of continued temptation; so long was there a brake on the incentive of ordinary men and women to forge integrated characters with a full sense of responsibility. The Protestant notion of a disciplined character nourished by a resolute conscience replaced the medieval sense of life as a round of sin and penance (Groethuysen 1927-30).

This aspect of the influence of the Reformation has been the subject of continuous debate by sociologists, historians, and culturally inclined psychologists. Recently there has been a shift in the focus of discussion. Interest has lately been centering on the alleged disappearance under our very eyes of the inner directed Protestant ethic in favor of a so-called "social ethic" as a result of the spread of the power of the large-scale organization in the institutional structure of the United States. The limitations of this paper do not permit a full-scale review of the evidence in these pages. One observation may be allowed however: current discussions both of the origin and demise of the Protestant Ethic generally neglect to distinguish between the many dimensions of the problem. At no time has Protestantism been lacking for a collective church ethic. The connections between the contemporary organizational ethic and the normative patterns and life style of the Protestant church have been overlooked in the recent characterizations of Riesman, W. H. Whyte (1957), and others.

Many of the most impressive institutional consequences of the Protestant variants of conscience, character, and culture have yet to be appreciated in their full implication. A selected number of episodes will be briefly mentioned in the following paragraphs:

Perhaps the most important development in the Protestant era recalls the struggles and wanderings of the dissenting groups that came from England, Holland and Germany to the United States where the notion of the inner light was to have its foremost influence. The nonconformist illuminist sectarians effected a transvaluation of the value of conscience by subordinating the moral conscience in the medieval sense to the inner light (Burrage 1912, Cohn 1961, Woodhouse 1951). Neo-Platonic illuminism which had been so significant in the medieval practice of meditation decisively triumphed over medieval rationalism which nourished the medieval administration of the moral self and the form of conscience. The important link between late medieval mysticism and Protestant illuminism was the concept of the spark or witness of God (Hof 1952) in the soul (*scintilla animae, syneidesis*). Modern rationalism of the Enlightenment variety owes more than most men know to Platonic and neo-Platonic mysticism. The shift from the religious to a more secular orientation occurs as early as the seventeenth century (Cragg 1950, Tawney 1926). Once the move had been made to the new notion of inner light by the dissenting groups of the seventeenth century (Solt 1959, Woodhouse 1951), the medieval orchestration of conscience, casuistry and the cure of souls was undone.

Over the centuries, Protestantism has seemed to vacillate between rationalism and fundamentalism (Troeltsch 1911, H. R. Niebuhr 1957). Although these two have been at swords point a thousand times since the onset of the Protestant Reformation, they do not seem entirely dissimilar from the point of view of the medieval concept of conscience. Rationalism is illuminism detached from its mystical source and symbolism. Forgotten is the image of the rebirth of Christ in the soul, leaving the sober afterglow of a reason freed of irrational constraints and declaring the truth by the sole authority of its inner light. Fundamentalism is biblicism, the desperate effort to maintain a fixed point of authority against the threat of the dissolution of landmarks by the work of reason. Both rationalism and biblicism have little need for the learned doctors of theology and canon laws, the learned directors of the soul who crowd the medieval scene.

Romanticism is illuminism in a new guise. It is the deification of the individual (and collective) ego (Santayana 1916) and the apotheosis of the unconscious forces which have been discovered to be the ego's foundation and underside. Romanticism joins all other variants of illuminism by rejecting the contextual integration of conscience, and casuistry, and the cure of souls. Romanticism makes the emancipated feelings the sovereign legislator for each man and for all mankind; directly applies these feelings to the complicated circumstances of the daily life resolving the riddles of tangled interest by reference to the command of love and the dictate of will; relieves itself of the need for spiritual counsel by treating explosive impulse as ultimate norm. The most impressive and fashionable expression of contemporary Romanticism is Existentialism. Reducing the matter to a simplified equation for our present purposes, we may say that Contemporary Existentialism seems to be Romanticism triply armed by three of the most forbidding constructions of modern thought: Husserl's constitutive phenomenology, Heidegger's neo-Gnostic fundamental ontology, and Kierkegaard's neo-orthodox theology of crisis (Nelson 1961b).

The nineteenth century witnessed the near demise of the older arrangements of conscience, casuistry and the cure of souls, and the surge forward of a series of surrogate religions. One of the most powerful among these new religions may be described as the *religion of the transcendental self, the transmoral self beyond conscience* (Tillich 1945). Its myriad expressions are elaborated in all the masterpieces of art, literature, philosophy, and even science. Perhaps the most revealing expressions are the intense and stark journeys into the interior which began with Rousseau, Goethe, and Fichte. Every last corner of the phenomenology of existence and spirit is probed in the pages of such philosophers and literary explorers as Hegel, Kierkegaard, Nietzsche, Baudelaire Rimbaud, Conrad, Mann, and Joyce. We are in great need of a thoughtful full-length study of the spritual itineraries (Hopper 1947, 1957) during the last two centuries from the point of view suggested in this paper. Without this, we can hardly hope to understand our own times (Balakian 1947, Heller 1957, Praz 1951, Raymond 1950, Sypher 1962). If we would appreciate what Freud and psychoanalysis mean in our present era we need to know *to what degree Freud is the heir of the religion of the transcendental self, to what degree he is its undertaker.* I have elsewhere suggested that a key to this riddle lies locked in Freud's 'Divine Comedy' which he called by the name, *The Interpretation of Dreams* (Nelson 1957). The following lines from a previous essay of mine suggest half of the answer:

[When the *Interpretation of Dreams* was ended], there was little life left in the gallery of guises—Byronism, Promethianism, Parnassianism, dandyism, diabolism, pietism, scientism, moralism and so many others—assumed by the philosophies and substitute religions of the modern era (1957, Perface).

It seems appropriate to close this section of our paper with some reflections on two historical paradoxes marking the relations of Protestantism, the major source of the religion of the self, and psychoanalysis, whose cultural implications are even at this moment being violently disputed.

1. Psychoanalysis did not originate in Protestant settings. It emerged in Catholic Vienna and its pioneer was a Jew.

2. The highest development of psychoanalysis to date has occurred in Protestant America.

So far as the present writer knows, nobody has yet thought to wonder about the first paradox. I take the liberty of putting my suspicions in the form of questions. Is it possible that the limitations upon the confessional in Protestant lands were too great to admit the growth of organized spiritual direction? Protestant culture tended to produce individuals who understood their responsibility and wills in ways that inhibited recourse to others. Jews and Catholics have never shared the Protestant religion of self-reliance.

How then explain the second paradox? Our most interesting hypothesis on this score has been provided by a French publicist, Raoul de Roussy de Sales (1938). It was precisely, claims this author, because of what we are calling "instrumental activism" in American Puritanism that once it was decided to organize the overcoming of neurosis, no cultural limits were placed upon the achievement of a liberation from sin and guilt in relation to the superego. It was precisely sectarian Protestantism which encouraged the conviction that world and self could be permanently purged of imperfection and confusion. Nowhere else has there been so much conviction in the positive power of unashamed love and self-expression. The social constraints upon the triumph of any such notions on the Continent have always been very notable. America is a country in which, in Max Weber's language (1904-05), the psyche was to receive its most comprehensive rationalization. If time allowed it would be interesting to trace out the ways in which the social democratic outlooks so clearly noted by de Tocqueville in the 1830's (Lipset and Lowenthal 1961), contributed to the permeation of American culture by psychiatric and psychoanalytic ideas.

If in one critical respect Protestant antipathy to spiritual direction set up barriers to the promotion of psychoanalysis, in another it provided the patterns for the relation of therapist and patient. The weakening of the separate priestly class implied that the relationship of spiritual direction lasted only so long as the client was unable to act on his own with responsibility. This emphasis is a Protestant element within psychoanalysis. From the beginning Freud emphasized that the goal of treatment was the achievement of autonomy on the part of the patient, the ability to regulate his own life by norms of his own devising. Freud was in many ways closer to Kant than to Nietzsche.

It is now time to consider the relations of psychoanalysis to 20th century culture.

VII. Psychoanalysis and 20th Century Culture

A new era in the history of spiritual direction begins with Freud. Our knowledge of the formative phases in this development has now been vastly extended thanks to the recovery during the last 15 years of important documents and unpublished manuscripts. The following sources are especially revealing: Freud's intimate letters to his friend and mentor, Dr. Wilhelm Fliess (Freud 1887-1902); the surprising *Project for a Scientific Psychology* (1895); the candid letter of Breuer on his collaboration with Freud (Cranefield 1958). These new materials carry us far beyond the indications published in Freud's Clark University. Lectures of 1909 (Freud 1910), *On the History of the Psychoanalytic Movement* (1914), *An Autobiographical Study* (1925), and occasional biographical papers.

The turning points in the crystallization of psychoanalytic methods of treatment may be sketched as follows:

1. While still a relatively young man, Freud had the good

fortune to be associated with the experienced Viennese internist, Dr. Joseph Breuer, who, as we now know, had a highly developed theory of aetiology and cure of mental disorders. In Breuer's view, hysterical disturbances resulted from undergoing of traumatic experiences which left painful memory traces in a state of hypnoidal suspension. Through the application of hypnotism, the patient achieved the ability to recall the traumatic episodes. The recall was accompanied by the fresh experience and cathartic abreaction of suppressed affects and noxious ideas (Breuer and Freud 1895).

Too many contemporary writers have spoken of the break between the two men purely in terms of their different estimates of the role of sexual factors in the aetiology of neurosis (Sullivan 1959, Nelson 1959). As Freud tells the story, his first decisive technical departure from Breuer was the abandonment of hypnosis in favor of unrestricted and undirected free association.

2. Another critical moment in Freud's development is associated with his departure from the teachings of Charcot and Janet on the subject of aetiology of hysteria. Whereas the French school spoke in terms of congenital failures in the capacity for psychosynthesis, Freud (1910) insisted on stressing the role of unconscious repression of conflicted affect. The implications of this shift for the concepts of therapy can hardly be exaggerated. Freud was thus launched on the road to construing analysis as a relationship of antagonistic cooperation between therapist and patient. Analysis was, above all, the struggle against the resistances which crystallized in the transference relationship.

(It may be remarked parenthetically here that Freud failed to give due weight in this period of his development to the valuable contribution embodied in the Charcot-Janet position. How *are* psychosynthesis and executive integration of the ego effected? How, indeed, does the individual under the stress of massive doses of heterogeneous and inconsistent stimuli manage to achieve a stable identity? Fortunately, this way of conceptualizing the problem was not to disappear into the mists. Owing to the influence of Janet and Emile Durkheim on a number of notable writers, notably Elton Mayo, an important social-psychological and psychiatric theory of malintegration developed in the United States.)[5]

3. Freud reports that the decisive steps in the separation of psychoanalysis from previous therapies occurred as a result of his efforts to understand his own feelings in the course of (a) his

friendship and correspondence with Wilhelm Fliess, and (b) his intensified professional relations with private patients. We are indebted to Kris, Erikson (1957), Jones (1953-57), James Strachey (Freud 1900), and others for important studies of these years.

It will not hurt to repeat here:

It was the need to understand his own feelings, above all, which led Freud to the decisive findings of early psychoanalysis. Psychoanalysis in all its senses—an approach to the general theory of human behavior, a method of clinical research, a technique of treatment (Erikson 1957)—came to fruition in the course of his own self-analysis (1895-99).

Thanks to Strachey's variorum edition of *The Interpretation of Dreams,* we can now trace the steps in Freud's momentous journey within. Freud was by no means the first person to undertake this painful pilgrimage. In addition to the philosophers and theologians noted earlier in this paper, one would need to mention such intrepid searchers as Goethe, Kierkegaard, Amiel, Rimbaud, Dostoyevski, Strindberg, Nietzsche (Heller (1957, Hopper 1957). Freud's distinction consists in the fact that he devised a prosaically scientific way of charting the depths he had explored. Neither villifying nor deifying the inner demons he had uncovered, Freud doggedly sought to map and explain the workings of the unconscious in man's passage through life (Nelson 1957).

Contented that he had penetrated the riddle of dreams, Freud spent the next six years (1900-05) chiefly in surveying two other domains still shrouded in darkness; the action of the unconscious in the psychopathology of everyday life (Freud 1901), the itinerary of the "libido" in the child's psycho-sexual maturation in the setting of the family culture (Freud 1905).

The principal cornerstones, as Freud conceived them—*The Interpretation of Dreams* (1900) and his *Three Essays on the Theory of Sexuality* (1905)—had now been set in the edifice.

4. Freud explains elsewhere that he was spurred on to develop psychoanalysis as a distinctive set of procedures in the hope of improving upon available methods of therapy, notably the electrotherapy of Erb, the relaxation therapy of Weir Mitchell and the rational therapy of Dubois (Freud 1914). His own approach, psychoanalysis, was in use many years before he began to set down his thoughts about therapy. Though the word psychoanalysis was used for the first time in 1896 (Freud 1951), his major papers on technique did not begin to appear until the

years 1910-15 (Freud S.E. 12). The ensuing discussion of psychoanalytic technique takes its point of departure from these papers.

The exact connections of psychoanalysis with our theme will not be grasped unless we look with a fresh eye at the distinguishing features of the so-called "classical psychoanalytic treatment." This is more easily said than done. Familiar professional manuals rarely explain with sufficient detail and discrimination what implications are to be drawn from the collections of stipulations and procedures presented as "basic psychoanalytic technique" (Menninger 1958). For the present purpose, I shall place the distinguishing features of classical psychoanalytic treatment under two headings, comprising *ten articles:* Part I, *The Analytic Contract,* entered into by patient and doctor, comprising *five* sets of conditions which the patient agrees to observe and *two* conditions which the doctor accepts; Part II, *Analytic Techniques, three* articles naming critical aspects of the procedures agreed upon by qualified practitioners.

In my view, the seven articles in Part I are not in themselves *techniques* of treatment, as they are so often said to be, but rather the conditions precedent or the *mise-en-scène* of treatment. Part II represents minimal agreements as to technique among persons engaged in the practice of psychoanalysis. The least well understood, and, indeed, the most controversial article is no. 6, on "interpretation' 'which is hardly ever defined even in the specialized papers:

Part I contains the following seven articles:

1. The patient agrees to come for treatment at stated times, a fixed number of times per week (six, five, or fewer).

2. The patient agrees to pay a fixed fee in an agreed upon manner at stated times.

3. The patient agrees to adopt a reclining position with the analyst out of sight behind the couch.

4. The patient agrees to desist from "acting out" in the course of treatment.

5. The patient agrees to report his thoughts and feelings without restriction or censorship. This is the so-called "cardinal rule" of psychoanalysis.

6. The analyst agrees to analyze the patient, that is to communicate to the patient "interpretations" by which the patient gains "insight" into his problems.

7. The analyst (implicitly) agrees to terminate the treatment when the patient's condition has been sufficiently improved or been removed.

Part II involves the following three understandings agreed upon by analysts:

8. To the greatest extent possible, in the manner of a surgeon, the analyst is to maintain an attitude of strict neutrality and impenetrability to the patient.

9. Properly speaking, psychoanalysis is analysis of the resistance to cure.

10. In the course of treatment, the resistances concentrate in the transference resistance or neurosis. Therefore, psychoanalysis is the analysis of the transference neurosis.

It is not possible here to deal with more than a few of the issues relevant to the ten articles. I shall especially stress the *cultural* implications of the cardinal rule on free association (art. 5); the limitations of the analyst's role to "interpretation"; the significance of the emphasis on the analysis of the transference resistance; and the value commitments underlying all 10 articles. I shall also ask what important considerations of a cultural nature are "bracketed" (temporarily treated as out of bounds) by classical psychoanalysis. What cultural consequences follow from this methodic suspension?

As Freud tells the story, the advantages of "free associations" were first brought home to him by evidence that Breuer's patient, Anna O., appeared to improve notably when she was freely allowed to practice what she called her "chimney sweeping" (Freud 1910). Freud's dislike of hypnotism and his awareness that hypnotherapy had restricted usefulness led him to prefer "free associations" as a device for gathering information (Freud 1910).

We have only to look closely at the analytic interview against the background of its cultural and social contexts to perceive many functions of free association not emphasized by Freud. The patient encouraged to associate freely is in effect being advised that the analytic session may be regarded as an opportunity to try his wings on the ocean of his unconscious with full assurance that the analyst will buoy him up if he threatens to sink or drift. Since it is uncontrolled fantasy the patient fears, the supervised practice of free association is a way of developing greater ease in the management of one's own inner demons. In this way, the patient acquires enhanced ability to fight off the frightening feelings and thoughts—the shame, guilt, disbelief, anxiety, panic—occurring in the wake of the stream of associations.

As analysts well know, the ability to be relatively uninhibited in associating increases in the course of the analysis. It is both the effect and the proof of the patient's expanded power to tolerate his wildest fantasies. Supervised association in the analyst's office performs the function of trial exercises of "regression in the service of the ego" (Kris 1952).

One may observe parenthetically that great creative artists have long understood the necessity of enlarging the horizons of awareness by deliberate regressions. An extraordinary anthology of passages on the avenues to expanded consciousness could be gathered from the writings of such notable figures as Goethe, Byron, Stendhal, Rimbaud, Kierkegaard, Joseph Conrad, Joyce, Nietzsche, Gide, D. H. Lawrence, Mann, and the playwrights currently associated with the so-called Theatre of the Absurd (Esslin 1961, Nelson 1962e, Nelson 1963).

An especially memorable passage will be found in an auto-biographical statement by Conrad:

Remember that death is not the most pathetic—the most poignant thing,—and you must treat events only as illustrative of human sensation,—as the outward sign of inward feelings,—of live feelings,—which alone are truly pathetic and interesting. . . . That much is clear to me. Well, that imagination (I wish I had it) should be used to create human souls: to disclose human hearts,—and not to create events that are properly speaking *accidents* only. To accomplish it you must cultivate your poetic faculty,—you must give yourself every sensation, every thought, every image,—mercilessly, without reserve and without remorse: you must search the darkest corners of your heart, the most remote recesses of your brain,—you must search them for the image, for the glamour, for the right expression. And you must do it sincerely, at any cost: you must do it so that at the end of your day's work you should feel exhausted, emptied of every sensation and every thought, with a blank mind and an aching heart, with the notion that there is nothing,—nothing left in you. To me it seems that it is the only way to achieve true distinction—even to go some way towards it (Letter of Oct. 28, 1895 to Edward Noble in Conrad 1951, 731-33).

In the consistent opinion of artists and their publics, the greatest figures in the history of literature have been those who have had the courage to plunge into the whirlpools of the unconscious in order to discover truths that have been repressed and denied.

The psychoanalytic conception of the relations of master-client is markedly different from the earlier conceptions of this relationship. Innumerable writers before Freud recognized the importance of the emotional connection which he was to call transference. None thought to say that in the treatment proper all other symptoms tended to collapse into the transference neurosis; that as helpful as transference was in promoting therapy the transference was the foremost *resistance* to cure; that cure was not effected unless the transference, *negative* as well as positive, was "worked through."

Psychoanalysis is the first schema of direction of souls in the West which conceives transference in this many-sided way. All earlier methods emphasized the religious duty to strive for a permanently positive transference and allowed no place for the possibility of a negative transference. The new conception of transference implies a new conception of society and self. Freud himself hedged a bit on the matter of the negative transference. His reluctance to become involved in the treatment of the narcissistic neuroses and the psychoses may be explained in part by his unwillingness to become involved in the stormiest tempests of the negative transference.

The exaggerated emphasis on the loving relation of therapist and patient in recent days may well be a mark of the discomforts associated with the challenges of Freud's universalistic consensualism. In this respect, interpersonal psychiatry and existential psychoanalysis allow for regressions from the Freudian position. This is especially evident in the existentialist's neglect of negative transference. Considerable insight into the importance of provoking the negative transference may be found in several schools of Zen Buddhism (Senzaki and McCandless 1961).

Universalistic consensualism is the central value on which Freud built his system of psychoanalysis. Anything which restrained the equal freedom of both parties militated against a therapeutic analysis. For this reason he insisted on the equal observance by therapist and patient, alike, of the formal stipulations of the analytic contract. Freud was the first great director of souls who recognized the threats to liberty built into the strongly emotional connections of master and disciple. His exceptional care about the establishment of fees, hours of appointment, etc., subserved this central function (Menninger 1958).

Easily the best way to discover the strains and gaps which developed in the Freudian system is to study the succession of

crises in the psychoanalytic movement (Munroe 1955). Ernest
Jones and Erich Fromm (1959) notwithstanding, all error was
not on one side, nor all truth on the other. Nor is it sensible to
argue that every act of dissent was a blow for liberty and every
defense of the Establishment a justification of intellectual obscur-
antism. In fact, there is much to be learned about all the principles
and doctrinal questions concerned by viewing the history from
the perspective of the changing polemical contexts.

Each decade since the origin of psychoanalysis produced its
own crises. We may confine ourselves here to referring to the
central points at issue in the differences with Adler, Jung, Ferenczi,
and Rank in the second and third decades of the present century.
To speak of this in turn:

Underlying the separation from Adler was the fact that Freud
had allowed his distinctive stress on the dominion of the unconscious to becloud the role of the ego. Adler pressed so hard on
this front that he soon found himself in a camp of his own (Freud
1914, Colby 1951). For the abandoned unconscious, Adler
(1939) eventually substituted the notion of conscious identification with the "social interest" (*Gemeinschaftsgefuehl*). Adler's
emphasis on the ego was not without influence on Freud's later
restoration of an ego psychology *within psychoanalysis* (Ansbacher
1956).

Jung pointed to a more serious gap in the Freudian schema.
He was the first psychiatrist to recognize the magnitude of the
spiritual crisis which marked the dissolution of traditional religion
in the 19th and 20th centuries (Jung 1933). His insistence on the
symbolic archetypes in the collective unconscous (Jung 1912, rev.
1952) grew out of a desire to provide guidance to lost spirits who
were unable to find meaning in existence without the aid of a
metaphysical involvement. The wild exaggerations which came
to characterize Jung's work do not vitiate his frequently profound
insights. Freud's theories of man and culture did require enrich-
ment.

The psychoanalytic crises of the '20's are not so well remembered today as are the crises of 1912-13. In many ways, however,
the crisis of the '20's left a deeper mark on the subsequent
development of psychoanalysis as a therapeutic system than did
the more widely publicized deviations of Adler and Jung. Here
the issues developed out of a dissatisfaction with the inhibiting
biases of ultra-Freudian theories of aetiology, dynamics, and
technique. Ferenczi and Rank both sought to move psycho-

analysis toward a greater emphasis on the pre-Oedipal sources of neurosis. Both were deeply stirred by the influence of object-relations in mental development. Each in his own way was convinced that Freud's approved techniques of treatment were unsuitable for the sorts of cases—so-called "borderlines"—increasingly coming into treatment in their day (Bromberg 1959, Munroe 1955, Jones 1957).

Regrettably, Freud's polemics against the excesses of Rank and Ferenczi drove object-relations theory and treatment technique into a corner from which, surely in orthodox circles, they do not truly dare to emerge even today.

Robert Waelder's recent codification of what he calls basic psychoanalytic theory provides an especially revealing illustration of the severity of the orthodox reaction against the alleged insurgence of a new therapeutic irrationalism (Waelder 1961). He refuses to mention any deviations from the so-called model techniques which have developed in the last three decades on the grounds that all of them are merely restatements of the excesses of Rank and Ferenczi. Instead he calls upon his colleagues to pursue the study of psychoanalysis as a basic science. Only by such efforts can psychoanalysis hope to discover a way of ending emotional and mental disorder. In the name of the pure science of psychoanalysis and, presumably, the ultimate drug, Waelder turns his back on the possibility of responsible innovation in psychotherapy.

The situation at present may be described as follows:

1. Freudian psychoanalysis has made great inroads into clinical psychiatry at the medical schools and at many important major psychiatric faculties and mental hospitals (Lewin and Ross 1960).

2. To the informed, these external successes do not obscure the fact that orthodox analysis has been undergoing a loss of vitality at its own core (Alexander 1961). The efforts of Hartmann (1958) and others (Rappaport 1960) to build a bridge between psychoanalysis and general psychology by developing a general theory of ego development and function have been resulting in notable shifts in Freud's fundamental orientation. The loss of vitality is particularly evident in the unreadiness of classical theory to keep pace with progress in the sphere of technique. Eissler (1953) has sought to make room for deviant procedures by permitting what he calls "parameters of deviation from the model technique" on the understanding that these deviations will be liquidated at the earliest possible opportunity in favor of the pure psychoanalysis. The outcome of this scholastic compromise recalls the circumstances of astronomy before Copernicus and Galileo. The multiplication of "epicycles" (*read* "parameters of deviation") is allowed to proceed indefinitely in order to preserve the model theory (Ptolemaic theory, "pure psychoanalysis"), in the face of the "irregularities" of the current data and the "premature" demands for a more comprehensive codification of established findings (Coleman and Nelson 1957).

Experimental psychiatry has been making new headway in the development of chemotherapy. As usual, utopian claims (Dubos 1961) are made by sanguine publicists.

Among the most perceptive practitioners there is increasing sensitivity to the new challenges presented to the therapist by the deepening crisis in our cultural situation (Alexander 1961). Classical psychoanalysis has yet to adjust to the fact that great numbers of men and women are unable to discover meaning in their lives and times (Wheelis 1958).

The slowness of orthodox analysis to relate to the deepened crisis has provided an opportunity for dubious faiths newly borrowed from the Continent. The various forms of existential analysis (*Daseinsanalyse,* American existential and onto-analysis) are not really new systems of relieving individual souls so much as surrogate religions in the guise of clinical psychiatries and philosophical anthropologies (Nelson 1961b). The willingness of all but a few leaders of these movements to continue obsolescent techniques of treatment is a mark of the insignificance of the role of psychotherapy in existential analysis (Boss 1957, May and others 1958, Rogers 1961). The bitter indictments of Western science and the striking congeniality to neo-Gnostic, theosophic, and Eastern mystical strains of thought in the newer existential psychiatries represent a high point in the advance of the "transmoral conscience" at the expense of the remaining hopes for a fresh integration—purged of the traditional excesses—of conscience, casuistry and the cure of souls.

It remains to be seen how well distinctively Western orientations will fare in the stressful years ahead.

Epilogue

Nature and nurture, alike, equip individuals variously to promote their ends in the worlds they inhabit. If, then, we wish to estimate, perhaps even to predict, their powers to respond to the challenges of their several environments, we must include reference to the many disparate factors likely to be relevant in their varied life situations. The physical coordinates are the easiest to study: How well do different organisms tolerate changes of different sorts in the atmosphere they are asked to inhabit? In what patterns are physiological and neural mechanisms linked in the processes of adaptation to bear stress (Selye 1956)?

Soon we find ourselves spurred to introduce reference to "nonphysical"—social, cultural, interpersonal, and intrapsychic— aspects of the field. How differently matters appear when we trouble to ask: when does a perceptual stimulus, indifferent or innocent to one, become a catastrophic psychic stress to another? How do different cultural schemes define stresses and responses? How do individuals variously estimate the relative shares of stress meted out to them (Merton and Kitt 1950, Merton 1957, Merton and others 1957)? In what ways are subjects affected by the situational and interpersonal contexts of the stresses they are bound to undergo—the times at which, the places in which, the persons in whose company, the authorities at whose instance, they undergo stress.

We will not go far in discovering how well an individual will probably do, given a battery of stress challenges of different sources—a psychometrician might be disposed to call this his Adjusted Multiple Stress Potential (AMSP) or Quotient (AMSQ) —by cleaving to a purely physicalistic conception of response to stress (Selye 1956). All measurements of human capacity must reflect rather than ignore the distinctively symbolic character of human existence. The so-called behavioral sciences have no way of escaping the cultural dimensions of human behavior.

The time has now come to say some parting words about the workings of the allocative institutions we have referred to above under the head of Cultures as Symbol Economies:

Every social system necessarily engages in the production and distribution of coveted symbols. Available resources are assigned to competing uses with a view to maximizing desired value outcomes, which, inevitably, remain in scarce supply relative to effective demand. Within this framework, systems of spiritual direction emerge, which acquire great influence in determining the abilities of people to bear the passions and infirmities societies and systems define as stressful. The capacity of an individual to perform constructively in the midst of stress is a function of the society's success in maintaining a favorable balance of the supply of symbolic (and other) resources at its disposal.

Mental healers perform critically important functions in the symbol economies of societies. They invent, distribute, and consume significant symbols. Along with other cadres engaged in whatever measure in spiritual direction, they play strategically ambivalent roles in framing definitions of the social, cultural, and personal states of affairs. At different times, as I have elsewhere sought to show (Nelson 1962b), mental healers have acted, in the language of W. Robertson Smith (1889) as prophets and priests; in the language of Arthur Koestler (1945), as yogis and commissars. We are, in truth, in dire need of fresh research and insight on these fateful matters.

The future of self is extremely obscure in the present historical interim. Depending on their political and philosophical commitments, groups and individuals are describing the self as culture's foremost achievement, mind's vilest metaphysical illusion or society's most noxious disease.

It is still too early to tell how well the Western sense of self will fare in the galactic era ahead. There are powerful forces working at cross purposes in this regard. Whatever the outcome, spiritual directors and systems of direction will continue to play strategic roles in defining stressful situations and aiding men to cope with them. Original nature is too fitful in expression and incoherent in aim to serve Everyman as a trusty guide. So long as each of us is required to be symbolically endorsed by others; so long as all aspire to taste vindication in however vague a sense, we search for our meaning in a design not of our own devising (Nelson 1963b).

The emotional illnesses of men will change their shapes; the techniques of psychological cure will adopt new strategies; mental healers and spiritual directors will claim and be accorded new roles. Selves may light up the skies or they may disappear behind the clouds. But of one thing we may be sure:

Conscience, Casuistry, and Cure of Souls—Madnesses, Methods, and Masters—these and other of man's puzzling cultural inventions serving now as solvents, now as sources of stress— will be with us to the end, so long as human society endures. Better to face this prospect squarely than to waste ourselves in vain attempts to "escape from the gloomy actual" by entering upon "the quest of oblivion, sought in the delusion of ideal harmony" (Huizinga 1924, Nelson 1957b)!

BIBLIOGRAPHY

ABELARD, PETER. *Abelard's Christian ethics.* J. Ramsey McCallum (Trans. and Ed.) Oxford: Blackwell, 1955.

ADAMS, JAMES L. (Ed.) *The Protestant era.* Cf. below, P. Tillich (1948).

ADLER, ALFRED. *Social interest: a challenge to mankind.* J. Linton and R. Vaughan (Trans.) New York: G. P. Putnam, 1939.

ALEXANDER, FRANZ. *The western mind in transition.* New York: Random House, 1960.

ALEXANDER, FRANZ. *The scope of psychoanalysis 1921-1961: selected papers of* . . . . New York: Basic Books, 1961.

ALEXANDER, FRANZ. Buddhist training as an artificial catatonia. In *selected papers of* . . . . (1961), 74-89(a).

ALLPORT, GORDON. *Personality and social encounter.* Boston: Beacon Press, 1960.

AMES, WILLIAM. *De conscientia et eius iure, vel casibus, libri quinque.* Amsterdam, 1631.

ANON. *The cloud of unknowing.* Ira Progoff (Ed. with Intro.) New York: Julian Press, 1957.

ANON. (A Friend of God). *The book of the poor in spirit.* C. F. Kelley (Trans. with Intro.) New York: Harper, no date.

ANON. *Theologia germanica.* (*ca.* 1350) S. Winkworth (Trans.) Boston: J. P. Jewett, 1856.

ANSBACHER, H. & ANSBACHER, R. *The individual psychology of Alfred Adler.* New York: Basic Books, 1956.

ARNOLD, E. V. *Roman stoicism.* Cambridge: Cambridge Univer. Press, 1911.

AUDEN, W. H. *The enchafèd flood.* New York: Random House, 1950.

BABBITT, IRVING. *Rousseau and romanticism.* New York: Houghton Mifflin, 1919 (paper bound ed. 1961).

BAINTON, ROLAND H. The struggle for religious liberty. In *Church History*, X (June 1941). Pp. 95-124.

BAINTON, ROLAND H. *Here I stand: a life of Martin Luther.* New York: Abingdon-Cokesbury Press, 1950.

BAINTON, ROLAND H. *The travail of religious liberty.* New York: Harper Torchbooks, 1958. (1st ed. 1951).

BAINTON, ROLAND H. *The Reformation of the sixteenth century.* Boston: Beacon Press, 1952.

BAINTON, ROLAND H. *The age of the Reformation.* Princeton, N.J.: Van Nostrand, 1956.

BAINTON, ROLAND H. *Collected papers in church history: early and medieval Christianity.* Series I. Boston: Beacon Press, 1962.

BAKER, G. W. and CHAPMAN, D. W. (Eds.) *Man and society in disaster.* New York: Basic Books, 1962.

BALAKIAN, ANNA. *The literary origins of Surrealism.* New York: King's Crown Press, 1947.

BAUER, RAYMOND. *The new man in soviet psychology.* Cambridge: Harvard Univer. Press, 1952.

BAXTER, RICHARD. *Chapters from a Christian directory.* Jeanette Tawney (Ed.) London: G. Bell, 1925.

BECK, F. & GODIN, W. *The Russian purge and extraction of confession.* E. Mosbacher and D. Porter (Trans.) London & New York: Hurst & Blackett, 1951.

BECKER, ERNEST. *The birth and death of meaning.* New York: Free Press, 1962.

BENEDICT, RUTH. *Patterns of culture.* New York: Mentor Books, 1960. (1st. ed. 1934).

BENEDICT, RUTH. Continuities and discontinuities in cultural conditioning. In *Psychiatry,* 1938, I.

BERGER, PETER. *The precarious vision.* New York: Doubleday, 1961.

BETTELHEIM, BRUNO. Individual and mass behavior in extreme situations. *J. of Abn. and Social Psychology,* 1943, 38, 417-52.

BINSWANGER, LUDWIG. *Drei Formen missglueckten Daseins.* Tuebingen: Max Niemeyer, 1956.

BINSWANGER, LUDWIG. *Schizophrenie.* Pfullingen: Guenther Neske, 1957.

BOCHENSKI, I. M. *Contemporary philosophy.* D. Nicholl and K. Aschenbrenner (Trans.) Berkeley: Univer. of Calif. Press, 1956. (2nd rev. German ed. 1947).

BOEHMER, HEINRICH. *Martin Luther: road to Reformation.* J. W. Doberstein & T. G. Tappert (Trans.) New York: Meridian, 1961. (1st ed. 1924).

BOEHNER, PHILOTHEUS. *Medieval logic: an outline of its development from 1250 to ca. 1400.* Univer. of Manchester Press, 1952.

BOISEN, ANTON I. *The exploration of the inner world.* New York: Harper Torchbooks, 1962. (1st ed. 1936).

BONAVENTURA, SAINT (d. 1274). *On the reduction of the arts to theology.* Sister E. T. Healy (Trans.) N.Y.: The Franciscan Institute, St. Bonaventure College, 1939.

BONAVENTURA, SAINT (d. 1274). *Itinerarium mentis in Deum.* Ph. Boehner (Trans. with Intro. and Comm.), N.Y.: The Franciscan Institute, St. Bonaventure College, 1956.

BOSS, MEDARD. *Psychoanalyse und Daseinsanalytik.* Bern: Hans Huber, 1957.

BRÉMOND, HENRI. *A literary history of religious thought in France from the Wars of Religion down to our times.* K. L. Montgomery (Trans.) New York: Macmillan, 1928.

BREUER, JOSEF & FREUD, SIGMUND. *Studies on hysteria.* J. Strachey & A. Freud (Trans. and Eds.) New York: Basic Books, 1957. (1st German ed. 1895).

BROMBERG, WALTER. *The mind of man.* New York: Harper Torchbooks, 1959.

BROWN, NORMAN O. *Life against death.* Middletown, Conn.: Wesleyan Univer. Press, 1959.

BUBER, MARTIN. *Eclipse of God.* M. Friedman & others (Trans.) New York: Harper, 1952.

BUBER, MARTIN. *Between man and man.* R. G. Smith (Trans.) Boston: Beacon Press, 1955.

BURKE, KENNETH. *Permanence and change.* Los Altos, Cal.: Hermes Pub., 1954. (1st ed. 1935).

BURKE, KENNETH. *The rhetoric of religion: studies in logology.* Boston: Beacon Press, 1961.

BURNABY, JOHN. *Amor Dei.* London: Hodder and Stoughton, 1938.

BURRAGE, CHAMPLIN. *The early English dissenters in the light of recent research.* . . . Cambridge: Cambridge Univer. Press, 1912. 2 Vols.

BUTLER, DOM C. *Western mysticism.* London: Constable, 1922.

CASSIRER, ERNEST. *The philosophy of symbolic form.* 3 vols. R. Manheim (Trans.) New Haven: Yale Univer. Press, 1953-57.

CASSIRER, E., KRISTELLER, P. O., & RANDALL, J. H. (Eds.) *The Renaissance philosophy of man.* Chicago: Univer. of Chicago Press, 1948.

CASTELLIO, SEBASTIAN. *Concerning heretics.* Roland Bainton (Trans. and Ed.) New York: Columbia Univer. Press, 1935.

CLARK, JAMES M. *The great German mystics: Eckhart, Tauler and Suso.* Oxford: Blackwell, 1949.

CLIMACUS, SAINT JOHN (d. 649). *The ladder of divine ascent.* Archimandrite L. Moore (Trans.) New York: Harper, no date.

COHN, NORMAN. *The pursuit of the millennium.* New York: Harper Torchbooks, 1961. (1st ed. 1957).

COLBY, KENNETH M. On the disagreement between Freud and Adler. *Amer. Image,* 1951, 8, 229-38.

COLEMAN, MARIE L. & NELSON, BENJAMIN. Paradigmatic psychotherapy in borderline treatment. *Psychoanalysis,* 1957, 5(3), 28-44. *Cf.* Nelson, M. C. (1962).

COLIE, ROSALIE L. *Light and enlightenment.* Cambridge, Eng.: University Press, 1957.

CONRAD, JOSEPH. *The portable Conrad.* M. D. Zabel (Ed.) New York: Viking, 1954.

CRAGG, GERALD R. *From Puritanism to the Age of Reason: a study of changes in religious thought within the Church of England, 1660-1770.* Cambridge: Cambridge Univer. Press, 1950.

CRAGG, GERALD R. *The Church and the Age of Reason 1648-1789*. Harmondsworth: Penguin Books, 1960.

CRANEFIELD, P. F. Joseph Breuer's evaluation of his contribution to psycho-analysis. *Int. J. of Psa.*, 1958 Sept.-Oct., 319-322.

CROCKER, LESTER G. *An age of crisis: man and world in eighteenth-century French thought*. Baltimore: Johns Hopkins Press, 1959.

CUSHMAN, ROBERT E. *Therapeia: Plato's conception of philosophy*. Chapel Hill: Univer. of North Carolina Press, 1958.

DEMAN, TH. Probabilisme. *Dict. de théologie catholique*, 1936, 13, 417-619.

DE ROUGEMONT, DENIS. *Love in the western world*. M. Belgion (Trans.) New York: Pantheon Books, 1956.

DILL, SIR SAMUEL. *Roman society in the last century of the Western Empire*. New York: Meridian, 1957. (1st ed. 1898).

DILL, SIR SAMUEL. *Roman society from Nero to Marcus Aurelius*. New York: Meridian, 1956 (1st ed. 1904).

DIONYSUS THE AREOPAGITE (*ca.* 500). *On the celestial hierarchy*. Rev. John Parker (Trans.) London: Skeffington, 1894.

DODDS, E. R. *The Greeks and the irrational*. Berkeley: Univer. of California Press, 1951.

DOELLINGER, I. VON & REUSCH, H. *Geschichte der Moralstreitigkeiten in der roemisch-katholischen Kirche seit dem 16ten Jahrhundert* . . . . Nordlingen, 1889. 2 vols.

DOWEY, EDWARD A. (JR.) *The knowledge of God in Calvin's theology*. New York: Columbia Univer. Press, 1952.

DUBOS, RENÉ. *The dreams of reason, science and utopia*. New York: Columbia Univer. Press, 1961.

DUMOULIN, H. *Zen: Geschichte und Gestalt*. Bern: Francke Verlag, 1959.

DURKHEIM, EMILE. *On the division of labor in society*. G. Simpson (Trans.) New York: Macmillan, 1933. (1st French ed. 1893).

DURKHEIM, EMILE. *Suicide*. G. Spaulding (Trans.) Glencoe, Ill.: Free Press, 1951. (1st French ed. 1897).

EATON, J. & WEIL, R. J. *Culture and mental disorders*. Glencoe, Ill.: Free Press, 1955.

ECKHART, M. (d. 1327). *Meister Eckhart: a modern translation*. R. Blakney (Trans.) New York: Harper Torchbooks, 1957.

ECKHART, M. *An introduction to the study of his works with an anthology of his sermons*. James M. Clark. (Trans. and Ed.) London: Thomas Nelson, 1957.

EGENTER, R. *Gottesfreundschaft: Die Lehre von der Gottesfreundschaft in der Scholastik und Mystik des 12. und 13. Jahrhunderts*. Augsberg: 1928.

EISSLER, K. R. The effect of the structure of the ego in the psychoanalytic technique. *J. Amer. Psychoanalytic Ass.*, 1953, 1(1), 104-43.

ELIADE, M. *Yoga: immortality and freedom.* New York: Pantheon, 1958.

ELIADE, M. *Cosmos and history: the myth of the eternal return.* New York: Harper Torchbooks, 1959.

ELIADE, M. *Myths, dreams, and mysteries.* P. Mairet (Trans.) New York: Harper, 1960.

ERIKSON, E. The first psychoanalyst. In B. Nelson (Ed.) *Freud and the Twentieth Century.* New York: Meridian, 1957. Pp. 79-101.

ERIKSON, E. *Young man Luther.* New York: Norton, 1958.

ERIKSON, E. *Identity and the life cycle.* New York: Intn'l Univers. Press (Psychological Issues), 1959.

ESSLIN, M. *The theatre of the absurd.* New York: Anchor, 1961.

EVANS-WENTZ, W. Y. *The Tibetan book of the dead.* London: Oxford Univer. Press, 1949.

FELDMAN, GENE & GARTENBERG, MAX. *The beat generation and the angry young men.* New York: Dell, 1959.

FIELD, M. J. *Search for security.* Evanston, Ill.: Northwestern Univer. Press, 1960.

FIFOOT, C. H. S. *History and sources of the common law: tort and contract.* London: Stevens, 1949.

FINGARETTE, H. *The self in transformation.* New York: Basic Books, 1963.

FLEW, R. N. *The idea of perfection in Christian theology.* London: Oxford Univer. Press, 1934.

FOWLIE, W. *Age of Surrealism.* Bloomington: Indiana Univer. Press, 1950.

FREUD, S. (C.P.) *Collected papers.* J. Riviere & J. Strachey (Eds.) New York: Intn'l Psychoanalytic Press, 1924-50. 5 Vols.

FREUD, S. (S.E.) *The standard edition of the complete psychoanalytic works of Sigmund Freud.* J. Strachey and others (Eds.) London: Hogarth Press and Institute of Psychoanalysis, 1953, in progress. 24 Vols.

FREUD, S. (1887-1902) *The origins of psychoanalysis: letters to Wilhelm Fliess, drafts and notes.* M. Bonaparte, A. Freud and E. Kris (Eds.) (E. Kris, Intro.) London: Imago Pub. Co., 1954.

FREUD, S. *Studies on hysteria,* 1895.

FREUD, S. *The interpretation of dreams,* 1900.

FREUD, S. *Psychopathology of everyday life,* 1901.

FREUD, S. *Three essays on the theory of sexuality,* 1905.

FREUD, S. *Five lectures on psychoanalysis,* 1910 [1909].

FREUD, S. *Papers on technique,* 1911-15. (S.E. 12).

FREUD, S. *On the history of the psycho-analytic movement,* 1914. (S.E. 14).

FREUD, S. *An autobiographical study,* 1925. (S.E. 20).

FROMM, ERICH. *Escape from freedom.* New York: Farrar & Rinehart, 1941.

FROMM, E. *Sigmund Freud's mission*. New York: Harper, 1959.
FROMM, E., SUZUKI, D. T., & DE MARTINO, R. *Zen Buddhism and psychoanalysis*. New York: Harper, 1960.
FUELOEP-MILLER, R. *The power and the secret of the Jesuits*. F. S. Flint and D. F. Tait (Trans.) New York: George Braziller, 1956.
GIERKE, O. VON. *The political theory of the Middle Age*. F. C. Maitland (Trans. with an Intro.) Cambridge: Cambridge Univer. Press, 1900.
GILSON, E. *The philosophy of St. Bonaventure*. Dom Illtyd (Trans.) New York: Sheed & Ward, 1938.
GILSON, E. *History of Christian philosophy in the Middle Ages*. New York: Random House, 1955.
GILSON, E. *The Christian philosophy of St. Augustine*. L. E. M. Lynch (Trans.) New York: Random House, 1960.
GRANT, R. M. (Ed.) *Gnosticism*. New York: Harper, 1961.
GROETHUYSEN, B. *Die Entstehung der buergerlichen Welt-und Lebensanschauung in Frankreich*. Halle: Niemeyer, 1927-30. 2 vols.
HALLOWELL, A. I. *Culture and experience*. Philadelphia: Univer. of Pennsylvania Press, 1959.
HARDELAND, A. *Geschichte der speciellen Seelsorge, in der vorreformatorischen Kirche und in der Kirche der Reformation*. Berlin: Reuther & Reichard, 1897-98.
HARNACK, A. VON. *History of dogma*. (Trans. from 3rd German ed.) London: Williams & Norgate, 1897. 7 Vols.
HARRISON, JANE E. *Epilegomena to the study of Greek religion* and *Themis: A study of the social origins of Greek religion*. New Hyde Park, N. Y.: Univer. Books, 1962.
HARTMANN, H. *Ego psychology and the problem of adaptation*. D. Rapaport (Trans.) New York: Intn'l Univers. Press, 1958.
HASKINS, C. H. *The Renaissance of the 12th century*. New York: Meridian, 1961. (Prev. ed. 1939).
HAZARD, P. *The European mind 1680-1715*. J. L. May (Trans.) London: Hollis & Carter, 1953.
HEER, F. *The medieval world: Europe 1100-1350*. J. Sondheimer (Trans.) Cleveland: World, 1961.
HEGEL, G. W. F. *Phenomenology of the mind*. J. B. Baille (Trans. with an Intro.) New York: Macmillan, 1955.
HEIDEGGER, MARTIN. *Being and time*. J. Macquarrie & E. Robinson (Trans.) New York: Harper, 1962. (1st ed. 1927).
HEILER, FRIEDRICH. *Prayer: a study in the history and psychology of religion*. S. McComb (Trans. and Ed.) New York: Oxford Univer. Press, 1932.
HEILER, F. Contemplation in Christian mysticism. In *Papers from the Eranos Yearbooks*. J. Campbell (Ed.) (1960)4, 186-238.
HEINEMANN, F. H. *Existentialism and the modern predicament*. New York: Harper Torchbooks, 1958.

HELLER, E. *The disinherited mind: essays in modern German literature and thought.* New York: Farrar, Straus & Cudahy, 1957.

HILTNER, S. (Ed.) Rogers and Niebuhr. *Pastoral psychology.* 9[(85) special number], 1958.

HILTON, W. (d. 1396). *The scale of perfection.* (Newly ed. from ms. sources with an Intro. by E. Underhill.) London: John M. Watkins. 1948. (1st ed. 1923).

HOF, H. *Scintilla Animae: Eine Studie zu einem Grundbegriff in Meister Eckharts Philosophie.* Bonn: Peter Hanstein Verlag, 1952.

HOLL, K. *The cultural significance of the Reformation.* New York: Meridian, 1961.

HOPPER, S. R. *The crisis of faith.* London: Hodder & Stoughton, 1947.

HOPPER, S. R. (Ed.) *Spiritual problems in contemporary literature.* New York: Harper Torchbooks, 1957. Esp. 153-73.

HUIZINGA, JAN. *The waning of the Middle Ages.* New York: Longmans, Green, 1924. (1st ed. 1919).

HUXLEY, A. *The perennial philosophy.* New York: Harper, 1944.

INGE, W. R. *Christian mysticism.* New York: Scribner's, 1899.

JAMES, W. *The varieties of religious experience.* J. Barzun (Foreword) New York: Mentor, 1958. (1st ed. 1901-2).

JASPERS, K. *The great philosophers.* H. Arendt (Ed.) R. Manheim (Trans.) New York: Harcourt, Brace & World, 1962. (1st ed. 1957).

JOHN OF THE CROSS, SAINT (d. 1591). *The complete works of St. John of the Cross.* E. A. Peers (Ed. and Trans.) London: Burnes, Oates & Washbourne, 1934-35. 3 Vols.

JONAS, H. *The Gnostic religion.* Boston: Beacon, 1958.

JONAS, H. Gnosticism and modern Nihilism. *Social Research,* 1960, 19(4), 430-452. (1st German ed. 1952).

JONES, E. *The life and work of Sigmund Freud.* New York: Basic Books, 1953-57. 3 Vols.

JUNG, C. G. *Symbols of transformation.* R. F. C. Hull (Trans.) New York: Harper Torchbooks, 1962 (1st German ed. 1912, rev. ed. 1952) 2 Vols.

JUNG, C. G. *Modern man in search of a soul.* New York: Harvest Books, no date. (1st ed. 1931).

JUNG, C. G. *Psychology and religion: west and east.* R. F. C. Hull (Trans.) New York: Pantheon (Bollingen series xx), 1938.

JUNG, C. G. *The undiscovered self.* R. F. C. Hull (Trans.) Boston: Little, Brown, 1958.

KARDINER, A. Freud: the man I knew, the scientist and his influence. In B. Nelson (Ed.) *Freud and the Twentieth Century.* New York: Meridian, 1957.

KAUFMANN, W. A. (Ed.) *Existentialism from Dostoevsky to Sartre.* New York: Meridian, 1956.

KEMPIS, T. à (d. 1471). *The imitation of Christ.* Vol. 6 of *The works of Thomas à Kempis.* London: Kegan Paul, Trench, Trubner, 1905-08.

KIERKEGAARD, S. *The point of view for my work as an author.* W. Lowrie (Trans.) Benjamin Nelson (Ed. with a Preface) New York: Harper Torchbooks, 1962. (1st Danish ed. 1859).

KIERKEGAARD, S. *Fear and Trembling, The Sickness unto death.* Robert Payne (Trans.) New York: Doubleday Anchor, 1954.

KIRK, K. E. *Ignorance, faith and conformity.* London: Longmans, Green, 1933. (1st ed.) 1925).

KIRK, K. E. *Conscience and its problems: an introduction to casuistry.* London: Longmans, Green, 1927.

KIRK, K. E. *The vision of God: the Christian doctrine of the SUMMUM BONUM.* Bampton Lectures 1928. London: Longman's, Green, 1937.

KLUCKHOHN, C. & KROEBER, A. L. *The nature of culture.* Chicago, Ill.: Chicago Univ. Press 1952 (a).

KLUCKHOHN, C. & MURRAY, H. A. *Personality in nature, society and culture.* New York: Alfred A. Knopf, 1948.

KNOX, R. *Enthusiasm.* New York: Oxford Univer. Press, 1950.

KOESTLER, A. *The yogi and the commissar.* New York: Macmillan, 1945.

KOESTLER, A. *The lotus and the robot.* New York: Macmillan, 1961.

KRIS, E. *Psychoanalytical explorations in art.* New York: Basic Books, 1952.

KRISTELLER, P. O. *Studies in Renaissance thought and letters.* Rome: Storia e Litteratura, 1956.

KROEBER, A. L. *The nature of culture.* Chicago, Ill.: Univer. of Chicago Press, 1952a.

KROEBER, A. L. & KLUCKHOHN, C. *Culture: a critical review of concepts and definitions.* Cambridge: Harvard Univer., Peabody Museum series of Archaeology and Ethnology Papers. 47(1), 1952(b).

KROEBER, A. L. & PARSONS, T. The concepts of culture and of social system. *Amer. Soc. Rev.,* 1958, 23(5), 582-83.

LAING, R. D. *The divided self.* Chicago: Quadrangle, 1960.

LANGER, SUZANNE. *Philosophy in a new key.* Cambridge: Harvard Univer. Press, 1942.

LAPIERE, R. *The Freudian ethic: an analysis of the subversion of American character.* New York: Duell, Sloan & Pearce, 1959.

LAQUEUR, W. & LICHTHEIM, G. *The Soviet cultural scene 1956-1957.* London: Atlantic Books, 1958.

LASSWELL, H. The triple-appeal principle. *Amer. J. Soc.,* Jan. 1932, 523-38. Anthol. in B. Nelson and others (Eds.) (1953), Bk. I, 253-60.

LEIBRECHT, W. (Ed.) *Religion and culture: essays in honor of Paul Tillich.* New York: Harper, 1959.

LEWIN, B. & ROSS, HELEN. *Psychoanalytic education in the United States.* New York: Norton, 1960.

LIFTON, R. J. *Thought reform and the psychology of totalism: a study of "brainwashing" in China.* New York: Norton, 1961.

LINTON, R. *Culture and mental disorders.* G. Devereux (Ed.) Springfield, Ill.: Charles C. Thomas, 1956.

LIPSET, S. M. & LOWENTHAL, L. (Eds.) *Culture and social character: the work of David Riesman in review.* Glencoe, Ill.: Free Press. 1961.

LOEWITH, K. *Von Hegel bis Nietzsche.* New York: Europa Verlag, 1941.

LOTTIN, DOM O. *Psychologie et morale au douzième et treizième siecle.* Louvain: Abbaye du Mont César, 1942-60, 6 Vols.

LOVEJOY, A. O. *Essays in the history of ideas.* New York: George Braziller, 1955.

LOVEJOY, A. O. *The reason, the understanding and the time.* Baltimore, Johns Hopkins Press, 1961.

LOVEJOY, A. O., CHINARD, G., BOAS, G., & CRANE, R. S. (Eds.) *A documentary history of primitivism and related ideas.* Baltimore, Johns Hopkins Press, 1935. Vol. I.

LOYOLA, IGNATIUS (d. 1556). *Spiritual exercises.* W. H. Longridge (4th ed.) London: A. R. Mowbray, 1950.

MACQUARRIE, J. *Twentieth-century religious thought.* New York: Harper & Row, 1963. (In *The Library of Religion and Culture.* General Editor: B. Nelson).

MALINOWSKI, B. *Sex, culture, and myth.* New York: Harcourt, Brace & World, 1962.

MARSHALL, S. L. A. *Men against fire.* New York: Wm. Morrow, 1953.

MAY, ROLLO, ANGEL, ERNEST & ELLENBERGER, HENRI F. (Eds.) *Existence.* New York: Basic Books, 1958.

MAYO, E. *The social problems of an industrial civilization.* Cambridge, Mass.: Harvard Univer. Graduate School of Business Administration, 1945.

MAYO, E. *The psychology of Pierre Janet.* London: Routledge & Kegan Paul, 1952.

MCNEILL, J. *A history of the cure of souls.* New York: Harper, 1951.

MENNINGER, K. *Theory of psychoanalytic technique.* New York: Basic Books, 1958.

MERRIAM, CH. *Political power.* New York: McGraw-Hill, 1934.

MERTON, ROBERT K. *Social theory and social structure.* Glencoe, Ill.: Free Press, 1957.

MERTON, R. K. & KITT, ALICE C. Contributions to the theory of reference group behavior. In R. K. Merton & P. Lazarsfeld (Eds.)

Continuities in social research: studies in the scope and methods of "the American soldier." Glencoe, Ill.: Free Press, 1950, Pp. 40-105.

MERTON, R. K., BROOM, L., & COTTRELL, L. S. (Eds.) *Sociology today.* New York: Basic Books, 1959.

MILLER, D. R. & SWANSON, GUY E. *Inner conflict and defense.* New York: Henry Holt, 1960.

MOODY, E. A. *The logic of William of Occam.* New York: Sheed & Ward, 1935.

MOSSE, G. L. *The holy pretence.* Oxford: Blackwell, 1957.

MOWRER, O. H. *The crisis in psychiatry and religion.* Princeton: D. Van Nostrand, 1961.

MUNROE, RUTH L. *Schools of psychoanalytic thought.* New York: Dryden Press, 1955.

MURRAY, GILBERT. *Five stages of Greek religion.* Oxford: Clarendon Press, 1925.

NELSON, B. *The idea of usury: from tribal brotherhood to universal otherhood.* Princeton: Princeton Univer. Press (History of Ideas Series, no. 3), 1949.

NELSON, B. and others. *Conflict in the social order.* Minneapolis: Centennial Lecture Series, Mimeographed, 1951(a).

NELSON, B. and others. *Value conflicts, moral judgments and contemporary philosophies of education.* Minneapolis: The Philosophy of Education Society, Mimeographed, 1951(b).

NELSON, B. The moralities of thought and the logics of action. In Nelson [1951(b)] Minneapolis: Mimeographed. Separate copy available on request. 1951(c).

NELSON, B. Actors, Directors, Roles, Cues, Meanings, Identities: Further Thoughts on "Anomie." *Psychoanalytic Review* 51(1), *Spring* 1964, pp. 135-60. Cited above as B. Nelson, 1963(c).

NELSON, B., CALHOUN, D. W., NAFTALIN, A. SIBLEY, M. Q., & PAPANDREOU, A. G. (Eds.) *An introduction to social science: personality—work—community.* (3rd rev. ed.) New York: J. B. Lippincott, 1961. (1st ed. 1953).

NELSON, B. The future of illusions. *Psychoanalysis,* 1954, 2. In rev. form in *Man in contemporary society* Contemporary Civilization Staff (Eds.) New York: Columbia Univer. Press, 1956, II, 958-79.

NELSON, B. and others (Eds.) *Essays in medieval life and thought.* New York: Columbia Univer. Press, 1955. With J. H. Mundy and R. W. Emery.

NELSON, B. (Ed.) *Freud and the twentieth century.* (with Intro.) London: Allen & Unwin, 1958. New York: Meridian, 1957(a).

NELSON, B. and others (Eds.) *Psychoanalysis and the future.* In collaboration with the board of editors of *Psychoanalysis.* New York: Nat'l Psychological Ass. for Psychoanalysis, 1957(b).

NELSON, B. and COLEMAN, MARIE L. Paradigmatic psychotherapy in borderline treatment. *Psychoanalysis,* 1957(c), 5(3), 28-44. Reprinted in M. C. Nelson, *Paradigmatic approaches to psychoanalysis: four papers.* New York: Dep't of Psychology, Stuyvesant Polyclinic, 1962-63. Pp. 3-16.

NELSON, B. (Ed.) *Sigmund Freud: on creativity and the unconscious.* (with Intro. and Annotations.) New York: Harper Torchbooks, 1958(a).

NELSON, B. Questions on existential psychotherapy. *Psychoanal. and the Psychoanalytic Rev.,* 1958(b), 45(4), 77-78.

NELSON, B. Social science, utopian myths and the oedipus complex. *Psychoanal. and the Psychoanalytic Rev.,* 1958(c), 45(1-2), 120-126.

NELSON, B. & TRINKAUS, C. (Eds.) *Jacob Burckhardt: Civilization of the Renaissance in Italy.* (With Intro. and Notes) New York: Harper Torchbooks, 1958(d) 2 Vols.

NELSON, B. The great divide. *Psychoanal. and the Psychoanalytic Rev.,* 1959, 46(2), 66-68.

NELSON, B. Contemporary politics and the shadow of de Sade. *Psychoanal. and the Psychoanalytic Rev.,* 1960(b), 47(3), 43-51.

NELSON, B. *Social structure, cultural process, personality system: boundary paradigms.* Mimeographed. Copy on request, 1961(a).

NELSON, B. Phenomenological psychiatry and American existential analysis: a 'progress' report. *Psychoanal. and the Psychoanalytic Rev.,* 1961(b), 48(4), 4-23.

NELSON, B. (Ed.) *Psychoanalysis and the social-cultural sciences: contemporary perspectives.* New York: Special number of *Psychoanal. and the Psychoanalytic Rev.,* 1962(a), 49(2).

NELSON, B. Sociology and psychoanalysis on trial: an epilogue. *Psychoanal. and the Psychoanalytic Rev.,* 1962(b), 49(2), 144-160.

NELSON, B. Faces of 20th century analysis: psycho-; linguistic; semantic; phenomenological; *Daseins;* existential, (onto-); etc. *Amer. Behavioral Scientist,* 1962(c), 16-18.

NELSON, B. Comment on E. Grant's "Hypotheses in late medieval and early modern physics." *Daedalus,* 1962(d), 91(3), 613-616.

NELSON, B. (Ed.) *Søren Kierkegaard, the point of view for my work as an author: a report to history.* (With Preface) New York: Harper Torchbooks, 1962(e).

NELSON, B. Casuistry. *Encyclopaedia Brittanica.* 1963(a).

NELSON, B. (Jean Genet's) *The Balcony* and Parisian existentialism. *Tulane Drama Review.* Spring issue, 1963(b).

NELSON, B. Meaning systems and crises of identity: paradigms. Paper delivered in symposium of "The structure of meaning systems." *AAAS,* Section H (Anthropology). Philadelphia: December 30, 1962. Forthcoming pub. 1963(c).

NELSON, B. The social sciences and the humanities: boundary disputes and treaty proposals. In progress.

NELSON, MARIE COLEMAN. *Paradigmatic approaches to psycho-*

analysis: four papers. New York: Dep't of Psychology of the Stuyvesant Polyclinic (Reports in Medical and Clinical Psychology.), 1962.

NIEBUHR, H. R. *Social sources of denominationalism.* New York: Meridian, 1957.

NOCK, A. D. *Conversion: the old and the new in religion from Alexander the Great to Augustine of Hippo.* Oxford: Clarendon Press, 1933.

NYGREN, A. *Agape and eros.* P. S. Watson (Trans.) Philadelphia: Westminster Press, 1953. (1st eds. 1932-39).

OATES, W. J. (Ed.) *The Stoic and Epicurean philosophers: the complete extant writings of Epicurus, Epictetus, Lucretius, Marcus Aurelius.* New York: Random House, 1940.

OCKHAM, WILLIAM of (d. 1349). *Philosophical writings.* Philotheus Boehner (Ed. and Trans.) London: Thomas Nelson, 1957.

O'MEARA, J. J. *The young Augustine.* New York: Longmans, Green, 1954.

OPLER, M. K. (Ed.) *Culture and mental health.* New York: Macmillan, 1959.

OPLER, M. K. Cultural definitions of illness. Conference on medicine and anthropology. Arden House, Harriman, New York, November 17-20, 1961. In press.

OTTO, R. *The idea of the holy.* J. W. Harvey (Trans.) London: Oxford Univer. Press, 1950. (1st ed. 1923).

OTTO, R. *Mysticism, east and west: a comparative analysis of the nature of mysticism.* B. L. Bracey & R. C. Payne (Trans.) New York: Meridian, 1957. (1st ed. 1932).

PARSONS, T. Malinowski's theory of the social systems. In R. Firth (Ed.) *Man and culture: an evaluation of the work of Malinowski.* London: Routledge and Kegan Paul, 1957.

PARSONS, T. & KROEBER. The concepts of culture and of social system. *Amer. Soc. Review.*, 1958, 23(5), 582-583.

PARSONS, T., SHILS, E., NAEGELE, K. D. & PITTS, J. (Eds.) *Theories of society.* New York: Free Press, 1961. 2 Vols.

PASCAL, B. *Les lettres provinciales.* H. F. Stewart (Ed.) Manchester Univer. Press, 1951. (1st ed. 1920).

PASSMORE, J. *A hundred years of philosophy.* New York: Macmillan, 1957.

PETTAZZONI, R. *La confessione dei peccati.* Bologna: Nicola Zanichelli, 1929.

PHILLIPS, D. The way to religious perfection according to St. Bonaventura's "De Triplice Via." In B. Nelson and others (Eds.) *Essays in medieval life and thought,* 1955, 31-58.

POURRAT, P. *Christian spirituality.* New York: O. J. Kennedy, 1922.

PRATT, J. Motivation and learning in medieval writings. *American Psychologist,* 1962, 17(7), 496-500.

PRAZ, M. *The romantic agony*. Angus Davidson (Trans.) New York: Meridian, 1956.

PROGOFF, I. *The death and rebirth of psychology*. New York: Julian Press, 1956.

PUMPIAN-MINDLIN, E, HILGARD, E. R., & KUBIE, L. S. *Psychoanalysis as science*. New York: Basic Books, 1952.

RAPAPORT, D. *The structure of psychoanalytic theory*. New York: Int'l. Univer. Press, 1960.

RAYMOND, M. *From Baudelaire to surrealism*. New York: Wittenborn, Schultz, 1950. (1st ed. 1947).

RICHARD OF SAINT-VICTOR (d. 1173). *Selected writings*. Claire Kirchberger (Trans. with an Intro.) New York: Harper, no date.

RIEFF, P. *Freud: the mind of the moralist*. New York: Viking, 1959.

RIESMAN, D., DENNEY, R., & GLAZER, N. *The lonely crowd*. New Haven: Yale Univer. Press, 1950.

ROUSSY DE SALES, R. DE. Love in America. *Atlantic Monthly*, 1938, 161, 645-51. Anthologized in B. Nelson and others (Eds.) (1953), Bk. I, 329-32.

RUYSBROECK, J. VAN (1293-1381). *Adornment of the spiritual marriage*. C. A. Wynschenck (Trans.) London: J. M. Dent, 1916.

SACHS, W. *Black Hamlet*. Boston: Little, Brown, 1947.

SAMPSON, R. V. *Progress in the age of reason*. London: Wm. Heinemann, 1956.

SANTAYANA, G. *Egotism in German philosophy*. London: J. M. Dent, 1916.

SANTAYANA, G. *The life of reason*. 5 Vols. New York: Collier Books, 1962. (1st ed. 1905-06).

SANTAYANA, G. *Soliloquies in England*. New York: Scribner's, 1922.

SARTRE, J. P. *Existential psychoanalysis*. H. Barnes (Trans. with an Intro.) New York: Philosophical Library, 1953.

SCHAAR, J. H. *Escape from authority: the perspectives of Erich Fromm*. New York: Basic Books, 1961.

SCHEIN, E. H., SCHNEIER, I., & BARKER C. H. *Coercive persuasion*. New York: Norton, 1961.

SCHELER, M. *On the eternal in man*. B. Noble (Trans.) New York: Harper, 1960.

SEESHOLTZ, ANNA GROH. *Friends of God*. New York: Columbia Univer. Press, 1934.

SELYE, H. *The stress of life*. New York: McGraw-Hill, 1956.

SENZAKI, N. & MCCANDLESS, R. S. (Eds. and Trans.) *The iron flute*. Rutland, Vt.: Charles E. Tuttle, 1961.

SEXTUS EMPIRICUS. *Works*. R. B. Bury (Trans.) New York: Putnam (Loeb Classics), 1933. 4 Vols.

SHATTUCK, R. *The Banquet years: the origins of the avant-garde in France 1885 to World War I.* New York: Anchor Books, 1961.

SIKES, J. G. *Peter Abailard.* Cambridge: Cambridge Univer. Press, 1932.

SMITH, T. V. *Beyond conscience.* New York: Whittlesey House, 1934.

SMITH, W. R. *The religion of the Semites.* New York: Meridian, 1961. (1st ed. 1889).

SOLT, L. F. *Saints in arms: Puritanism and democracy in Cromwell's army.* Stanford, Cal.: Stanford Univer. Press, 1959.

STEIN, M., VIDICH, A. J., & WHITE, D. M. *Identity and anxiety: survival of the person in mass society.* New York: Free Press, 1960.

SULLIVAN, J. From Breuer to Freud. *Psychoanalysis and the Psychoanalytic Review,* 1959, 46(2), 69-90.

SUSO, H. (d. 1366), *Little book of eternal wisdom and little book of truth.* James M. Clark (Trans. with an Intro. and Notes) London: Faber & Faber, 1953.

SUZUKI, D. T. *Zen Buddhism.* W. Barrett (Ed.) Garden City, N.Y.: Doubleday Anchor, 1956.

SUZUKI, D. T. *Mysticism: Christian and Buddhist.* New York: Harper, 1957.

TAWNEY, R. H. *Religion and the rise of capitalism.* New York: Harcourt, Brace, 1926.

THAMIN, R. *Un problème moral dans l'antiquité: étude sur la casuistique stoicienne.* Paris: Librarie Hachette, 1884.

TILLICH, P. Conscience in Western thought and the idea of a transmoral conscience. *Crozer Quarterly,* 1945, 22, 289-300. Reprinted in P. Tillich (1948).

TILLICH, P. *The Protestant era.* James L. Adams (Ed.) Chicago: Chicago Univer. Press, 1948.

TILLICH, P. *The religious situation.* H. R. Niebuhr (Trans.) New York: Meridian, 1959. (1st ed. 1956).

TILLICH, P. *Theology of culture.* New York: Oxford Univer. Press, 1959.

TRÉMONTANT, C. *Etudes de métaphysique biblique.* Paris: J. Gabalde, 1955.

TRINKAUS, C. *Adversity's noblemen: the Italian humanists on happiness.* New York: Columbia Univer. Press, 1940.

TRINKAUS, C. The religious foundations of Luther's social views. In B. Nelson and others (Eds.) 1955, 71-90.

TROELTSCH, E. *The social teaching of the Christian churches.* 2 Vols. Olive Wyon (Trans.) H. R. Niebuhr (Intro.) New York: Harper Torchbooks, 1960. (1st ed. 1911).

TROELTSCH. *Protestantism and progress.* W. Montgomery (Trans.) Boston: Beacon Press, 1958. (1st ed. 1912).

UNDERHILL, EVELYN. *Mysticism*. London: Methuen, 1914.

UNDERHILL, EVELYN. *The golden sequence: a fourfold study of the spiritual life*. New York: Harper Torchbooks, 1960 (1st ed. 1933).

VACANDARD, E. Confession, ii: Du 1er au xi^{ime} siècle. In A. Vacant & E. Mangenot. *Dictionnaire de théologie catholique*. Vol. III, Paris: Gabriel Beauchesne, 1908.

VAIHINGER, H. *The philosophy of 'as if'*. C. K. Ogden (Trans.) London: Routledge & Kegan Paul, 1952. (1st German ed. 1911).

VAN DER LOEUW, G. *Religion in essence and manifestation*. J. E. Turner (Trans.) New York: Macmillan, 1938. New York: Harper Torchbooks, 1963. 2 Vols.

VINOGRADOFF, PAUL. Reason and conscience in the 16th century. In *Collected Papers* II, Oxford: Clarendon Press, 1928.

VOEGELIN, ERICH. *The new science of politics*. Chicago: Univer. of Chicago Press, 1952.

WACH, J. *The sociology of religion*. Chicago: Univer. of Chicago Press, 1944.

WACH, J. *Types of religious experience Christian and non-Christian*. Chicago: Univer. of Chicago Press, 1951.

WACH, J. *The comparative study of religions*. J. M. Kitagawa (Ed. with an Intro.) New York: Columbia Univer. Press, 1958.

WAELDER, R. *Basic theory of psychoanalysis*. New York: Intn'l. Univer. Press, 1961.

WALLACE, A. F. C. The institutionalization of cathartic and control strategies in Iroquois religious psychotherapy. In M. K. Opler (Ed.) *Culture and Mental Health*, 1959, 63-96.

WEBER, M. *Gesammelte Aufsaetze zur Religionssoziologie*. (Henceforth given as *GAzR*.) Tuebingen: J. C. B. Mohr (Paul Siebeck), 1st ed. 1920-21. Latest reprinted ed. 1963. 3 vols. Includes works originally written in 1904-5, 1915-19 and cited here in translations of 1930, 1946, 1950, 1951, 1952. Dates given after titles are times of original writing. The pages of the German originals in the *GAzR* are given in parentheses.

WEBER, M. *From Max Weber: essays in sociology*. H. H. Gerth & C. W. Mills (Trans, Ed. with an Intro.) New York: Oxford Univer. Press, 1946.

WEBER, M. *The Protestant ethic and the spirit of capitalism*. 1904-5. Talcott Parsons (Trans.); R. H. Tawney (Intro.) New York: Scribner's, 1930. (*GAzR*, I, 17-206.)

WEBER, M. The social psychology of the world religions. Tr. in H. H. Gerth and C. W. Mills (Eds.) 1946, 267-301. (*GAzR*, I, 237-75.)

WEBER, M. Religious rejections of the world and their directions, 1915. Tr. in H. H. Gerth and C. W. Mills (Eds.) 1946, 323-359. (*GAzR*, I, 536-73.)

WEBER, M. *The religion of China*. 1916-17(a). H. H. Gerth (Trans., Ed. with an Intro.) Glencoe, Ill.: Free Press, 1951. (*GAzR*, I, 276-536.)

WEBER, M. *The Hindu social system*. 1916-17(b). H. H. Gerth & Don Martindale (Trans. and Eds.) Glencoe, Ill.: Free Press, 1950. (*GAzR*, II, 1-133.)

WEBER, M. *Ancient Judaism*. 1917-19. H. H. Gerth & Don Martindale (Trans. and Eds.) Glencoe, Ill.: Free Press, 1952. (*GAzR*, III, 1-442.)

WEBER, M. Vorbemerkung, 1920. Constitutes introduction to the 3 Volumes of the *GAzR*. Trans. in Weber, *The Protestant Ethic* (1930), 13-31.

WEBER, M. *The sociology of religion*, 1911-12. E. Fischoff (Trans.); Talcott Parsons (Intro.) Boston: Beacon Press, 1962. Originally published in Weber's *Wirtschaft und Gesellschaft*. Tuebingen: J. C. B. Mohr (Paul Siebeck), in rev. ed. J. Winckelmann, I (1956), 245-381. Original ed. 1922.

WEINBERG, J. *Nicholas of Autrecourt*. Princeton, N.J.: Princeton Univer. Press, 1948.

WEISSBERG, A. *The accused*. E. Fitzgerald (Trans.) New York: Simon & Shuster, 1951.

WHEELIS, A. *The quest for identity*. New York: Norton, 1958.

WHITEHEAD, A. N. *Adventures of ideas*. New York: Macmillan, 1956.

WHYTE, W. H. *The organization man*. Garden City, N.Y.: Doubleday, 1957.

WILLIAMS, N. P. *The idea of the fall and original sin*. Oxford: Oxford Univer. Press, 1927.

WOOD, T. *English casuistical divinity in the 17th century*. London: S.P.C.K., 1952.

WOODHOUSE, A. S. O. (Ed.) *Puritanism and liberty: being the Army Debates (1647-9) from the Clarke Manuscripts with supplementary documents*. A. D. Lindsay (Foreword) Chicago: Univer. of Chicago Press, 1951.

ZAEHNER, R. C. *Mysticism—sacred and profane*. New York: Oxford Univer. Press, 1961.

ZILBOORG, GREGORY & HENRY, GEORGE W. *A history of medical psychology*. New York: Norton, 1941.

NOTES

1. Slight modifications of the usual patterns of citation have been introduced whenever the interest of clarity dictated, in the hope of avoiding confusion as to relevant historical contexts. Thus, numerals contained within parentheses do

not always represent the dates of current editions of published works. The first mentions of premodern authors are generally accompanied by indications of the year of their death, e.g. (Saint Bonaventura d. 1274). Original dates of publications are provided in the citations of a number of modern writers, e.g. (Emile Durkheim, 1893). Many scholars have remarked that unsuspecting readers may be easily led astray by the odd concatenations which frequently result from conventional forms of citation, e.g. (Saint Thomas Aquinas 1962, Max Weber 1957). A recent paper on medieval writings in the *American Psychologist* (Pratt 1962) is a choice illustration of this difficulty.

2. Thus to mention one prominent example: the Italian Renaissance receives little mention in the following pages. The chief reason for this neglect is that we are still largely in the dark about the ruling self-concepts and schemas of spiritual regulation in this vastly over-interpreted but under-researched era: Cassirer and others 1948, Kristeller 1961, Trinkaus 1940, Nelson and Trinkaus 1958d. (The same cautions clearly apply to the state of our current knowledge of Eastern systems of spiritual direction. An earnest attempt to go beyond traditional stereotypes is made by Herbert Fingarette in a work now going through the press.)

3. The terms "Occident," "Orient," "East," and "West," as used in the present pages, are largely metaphorical in character. They are not meant to imply archtypal unities of differences, but simply clusters of stresses in as yet too ill-defined culture-areas, in which marked diversities become more evident the more carefully we study the data. New results along these lines are currently being promised by an active University of Illinois group (Miron, Archer, and others) applying Osgood's "semantic differential" tests to selected societies.

4. The absence of any historical examination of Riesman's evidences in the recent full-length review of his work by S. M. Lipset, Leo Lowenthal, and others (1961), is only one symptom of the present state of the problem. Even more revealing is the lack of any history of the idea of conscience since the time of Abelard. The present writer hopes to improve this situation before the present decade is ended.

5. Strangely, this thread of influence emerges in only an intermittent and vague way in Mayo's booklet on Janet (Mayo 1952, pp. v, 120-21). See, however, Mayo (1945). Additional clues will be found in an essay now being readied for publication by the present writer (1963e).

Material relevant to the theme of this essay will also be found in two other recently published papers of the present writer:

Nelson, B. Hesse and Jung: Two Newly Recovered Letters. *Psychoanalytic Review*, 50(3), Fall 1964, 11-16.

Nelson, B. Sartre, Genet Freud. *Ibid.*, 155-71.

Self-Control: The Greek Paradigm

I must begin by explaining how a student of Greek antiquity with no competence in the specialized disciplines and techniques relevant to the problem before this meeting can presume to participate in its deliberations. The Greeks did in fact lay the foundations for European outlooks. They not only invented virtually all our literary forms, determined the modes and substance of our philosophic discourse, shaped our canons of taste, but through these innovations they established our general unspoken premises for relations between man and man and external authority. It may therefore be useful to examine this outlook on a given problem where these premises are involved, not only as a specimen among other specimens afforded by intelligent and articulate groups, but, more important, as a foundation which enables us to assess the deviations from the plumb which the upper stories of our structure exhibit.

Our conclusions cannot be scientifically reliable because we cannot procure the precise and complete statistics which sociology demands, nor can we properly bring the psychologist's techniques to bear. Our data all derive from literature—not realistic reportage but a highly stylized and self-conscious formal literature, where what we get is not what actual people said and thought, but the frank distillations of a poet, according to his own conceptions and insights, of what his subjects' behavior might signify. The most

that we can say is that the poets did not, after all, work in a
vacuum and that the modes of conduct they set forth were at least
recognizable to their audiences.

At many points, relevant to the general area of our inquiry,
modes of behavior which the Greeks seem never to have questioned are at polar opposites from the code which controls
modern behavior. Specifically, a mighty warrior like Achilles can
weep freely and publicly under stress where his modern analogue
would be expected to grit his teeth and hold his chin up. He can
mope in his tent in the hour of battle where his modern analogue
would be jailed as a deserter or referred to a psychiatrist. To
satisfy his personal honor he can pray that his own side be
defeated, where his modern analogue would be shot for treason.

Another mighty warrior, like Ajax, can exhibit the grossest
brutality to his associates and dependents and yet be deemed
worthy of heroization. Zeus can tell Hera, who is purposely seeking to distract him, that he desires her more than he had desired
a long series of other females (whom he catalogues) and then
say, despite his epic grandeur, Come to bed. Historical characters, among them the brilliant generals Themistocles and
Alcibiades, can go over to the enemy side for private interest,
and no one shouts traitor. Amongst ourselves a man might wish
to behave in these unhallowed ways, might even be convinced
that it would be right for him to do so, but be deterred by the
exigencies of our different code. The deterrence, the frustration of
being prevented from doing what one wishes and privately thinks
legitimate, is a basic cause of stress. In certan centuries between
the Greeks and ourselves when the codes were accepted fully and
without question obedience need not have entailed psychological
frustration. It is when the ultimate validity of the exigent code
comes to be questioned that a disrupting rift appears, so that we
must pretend that the specious currency of what Samuel Butler
called the musical banks is of equal value with the hard money of
the real banks, and behave as though what Eric Fromm distinguishes as the ritual and the operative parts of a code imposed
upon us had equal validity.

What is there in the Greek view which freed men, or some
men, of the consequences of such a rift? What significant deviations
from the Greek foundations made the kinds of behavior I have
mentioned wicked? How did it happen that certain natural reactions, what we might almost call reflexes, came to be curbed, that
mere assertion was glorified as authoritarian faith and what phi-

losophers call the Law of Contradiction fell into abeyance, that sentimentality replaced hard reason?

The first and most obvious answer is of course religion: whereas classical antiquity was pagan, medieval Europe was Christian, and that fact alone is deemed sufficient to account for all differences between the two periods. And if we are inclined to regard the medieval world as inferior we have in support Gibbon's conclusion that it was Christianity and barbarism which brought about the fall of ancient civilization. But the matter is not so simple. What Gibbon was thinking of, and what is germane in our present context, is not so much the particular unpagan teachings of Christianity nor even its otherworldliness but its claim of sole and exclusive validity. But claims to exclusive validity were being put forward in the late Hellenistic age, when kings usurped the prerogatives of gods and philosophy became the exegesis of texts regarded as authoritative rather than uninhibited quest for truth. The most telling claim to exclusive validity, because it was accompanied by power to enforce the claim, was part of the official program of pre-Christian Rome.

It is the rise of Roman power rather than the advent of Christianity (which then adopted the Roman program) that marks the subordination of the individual to a larger, ideally a universal, community and which imposed a superficial uniformity. It is now that constrained obedience to the merely ritual part of the code produces stresses which tax individual personalities. The response of stoicism, which was the paramount philosophy in Rome, is significant. Stresses, or what they called perturbations, are not to be acknowledged or combatted but classified as "things indifferent" and disregarded.

The transformation from the Greek outlook receives striking illustration in the Aeneid, which was written as a kind of scripture for Augustus' cult of Rome, intended to inculcate submission to the authoritarianism which Augustus promulgated. Where Achilles is a thoroughly bad citizen by our traditional gauge, Aeneas is the perfect European hero. He is concerned not for himself but for his divinely ordained mission of bringing his people to their promised land, establishing their religion, starting them on their career as apostles of order and enlightenment over the whole world. Where the Greek hero is almost obsessed with his own individuality the Roman is expected to find complete fulfillment in serving and being absorbed by the infinitely more important cause. Individuality does sometimes emerge and produce stress, but then the Roman is praised for disregarding it. Aeneas does sometimes grow weary and chafe; he would much like to settle down in Carthage with Dido, who would be an agreeable and comfortable wife. But he is reminded of his mission by a divine messenger. Schoolboys think he is a cad for deserting the lady; it is significant that it is precisely when he seems most the personal cad that the poet chooses to give him the epithet *pius*.

What Augustus and his ministers had done was to make of Roman patriotism a cult, demanding and inclusive. Other cults, so long as they did not serve as seedbeds for political subversiveness, were not molested; but to the degree that the cult of Rome took precedence over all others and was coterminous with the oikoumene it can fairly be regarded as sole and exclusive. If Christianity, then, was not the initial catalyst for transforming the world, religion in a real sense was, and it therefore behooves us to look at the aspects of Greek religion which made untrammeled expression of individuality possible.

The most obvious and the most meaningful characteristic of Greek religion is that it is a true polytheism, with even the lesser figures in the theogony exercising sovereignty. The conception and its implications are not easy for us to grasp. So fully conditioned are we by all our literature and all our habits of thought that "religion" means to us "monotheism"; our own beliefs are irrelevant, for what the atheist disbelieves is one god, not many. Polytheism cannot be exclusive or authoritarian for the individual may, indeed must, exercise his choice among disparate and equally valid sanctions. Nor did the gods belong to a single company, like the Olympians who dominate the literature. There were besides the less attractive chthonic deities, who antedate the coming of the Greeks, and there were the Orphics, who looked forward to a blissful afterlife and who constituted something like a church.

But the important thing is that there was no church in any real sense. There was no revelation or sacred book, no dogma and no claim to infallibility, no priestly caste. The various strands of religion functioned side by side. With the arrival of the Olympians the chthonic powers were not anathematized, as Canaanite worship was upon the advent of Judaism or Judaism on the advent of Christianity. The chthonic beliefs, with their emphasis on blood and kinship and ritual purifications, continued, if in sublimated form, along with other strands. Because there was coexistence not only among deities but among classes of deities, the range of individual freedom was almost unlimited.

That is why there can be no Christian epic or tragedy in the Greek sense of epic or tragedy. Where black and white are authoritatively defined the choices are prescribed. There is no particular merit in choosing the white, and only a villain would choose the black. If a man is behaving according to prescription and is not self-impelled he cannot properly be an epic hero. If a man chooses a course plainly and authoritatively labelled bad he is not a tragic hero, but a sinful fool. In classical Greece there could be several disparate rights simultaneously, each with its valid sanction: hence, strictly speaking, there can be no villains.

It is the consciousness of villainy, of having transgressed a prescribed and acknowledged code, even when the transgression is not apprehended, or perhaps particularly when it is not apprehended, that produces the element of stress. But when a man consciously transgresses one valid sanction to follow another, then the unpleasant consequences which the disregard of the rejected sanction may entail are not spiritually oppressive for the sufferer does not look upon himself as the victim of unreasonable persecution.

If we reduce to familiar rational terms the conflict between Olympian and chthonian sanctions presented in mythologic terms in such Aeschylean plays as *Suppliants* or *Eumenides,* we get something like this. A man with no money in his pocket conceives an intense craving for luscious fruit in a market stall. If he takes the fruit he will be in trouble with the police, who represent Apolline requirements of order and respect for property rights. If he does not he may be in trouble with his psychiatrist, who represents the irrational but none the less valid requirements of the chthonic powers. But the decision is his, and he cannot rebel at an eventuality inherent in his nature. The other choice would have entailed its own penalty.

Nature, as distinguished from convention, becomes the explicit criterion for all values in the rational formulation of the Sophists. Every phenomenon and every institution we encounter is what it is either by *physis* (nature) or by *nomos* (law or convention). If it is so by nature we can only accommodate ourselves to it, but without feeling that we are the objects of malevolence or injustice. If it is so by convention, then we remember that it was first instituted by men for expediency's sake, and when it is no longer expedient it not only may but should be altered. Are foreigners inferior to Greeks, slaves to freemen, women to men, commoners to the nobility, by nature or convention? If by convention then subversion of traditional institutions, including political and religious, is not wickedness. For convention no external authority is recognized, for, in the words of Protagoras, man is the measure of all things.

The implications of the doctrine of man the measure, which is surely the crystallization of classical humanism and the thing which most vividly sets the Greeks apart from their successors, can best be illustrated by the celebrated Melian dialogue, at the end of the fifth book of Thucydides' history. During the Peloponnesian War the islanders of Melos, who were racially akin to the Spartans, wished to remain neutral, but Athenian policy dictated that they should become part of the Athenian empire. The Melians begin their argument by saying that high-handedness will stain the Athenians' reputation for equity, and the Athenians answer that this is a problem for themselves to decide. The Melians then say that they can only point out that the gods will not like what the Athenians are doing. To this the Athenians reply: "Of men we know, and of the gods surmise, that they rule where they can and yield when they must. This is the law of nature; we did not introduce it." Considerations other than the law of nature, which is red in tooth and claw, are irrelevant. If we are shocked, as Thucydides apparently was, at the high-handedness of the Athenians, we can at least reflect that theirs was the last empire which did not feel constrained to cover greed with hypocrisy. Beginning with the Romans empires have felt obliged to proclaim that they were generously carrying the white man's burden.

"Of the gods we surmise" deserves comment. Protagoras' man the measure is not, as has often been alleged, a program of atheism. Of the gods he did not speak, he said, because he could not know. So far from being atheistic, then, this conception of the divine— that it is not subject to our understanding and does not demand our approval—may be loftier than the view which claims full knowledge of the ways of the gods, is ready to reward them with hymns of praise for doing what men think they should and is puzzled and hurt (and it is this which causes stress) when they inexplicably fail to do what men think they should. I do not wish here to trace the influence of this view upon subsequent theologies, but merely to illustrate its implications. I should mention the schools, mainly Arabic, which held that *any* predication concerning deity is arrogant blasphemy, that it is fully as wicked to say that God is good as to say that he is evil or redheaded or wears a long beard. The upshot of this mode of thought is the dictum of the unorthodox but essentially devout Spinoza; man should love God with no expectation of being loved in return.

In this view the realm of the divine and the realm of the human are distinct. The gods behave as it behooves gods to behave, and man must behave as it behooves man to behave; he must give expression to his own humanity, not seek to assimilate himself to an ideal (which he cannot in any case know) outside humanity. There is no sense of inadequacy *vis-a-vis* an extra-human ideal, no feeling of unjust persecution, no sense of sin.

It must be emphasized that this view of the separateness of the realms of the divine and the human was never the sole and perhaps not even the dominant view among the Greeks. All of Plato (but we do not know how large his following was) proves the contrary. But it is the view which sets the Greeks apart from ourselves, and may well explain why they were relieved from, or better never burdened with, pressures which have burdened us. It is a view which runs in a steady current from Homer to the rise of Rome and Christianity; the Epicureans, who are the most outspoken advocates of the self-sufficiency of individual man, only rationalized and systematized what is implicit in Homer. It will be useful to glance at several stages of the current in its strength, and then notice the causes and effects of its disappearance.

Critics with different theological premises dismiss Homer's gods, who appear on every page, as merely literary ornament. They are indubitably real, but in a separate realm, and feel no special responsibility to man. Apollo can say, when he is tempted to intervene in the fighting, Why soil my hands with these creatures of a day? Ajax prays only for light to return, when a cloud has obscured his vision; the fighting he will take care of himself. When a deity does help his protégé it is not by importing some force from without but by enabling the warrior's own faculties to function at their most efficient. A father sending his son out into the world enjoins him: Always be best, always be ahead of all others. The measure of excellence is what a man can achieve, with his hands and his words. He will be prudent in his relations to the gods as he is prudent with regard to the potentially dangerous manifestations of fire or gravity. But his goal is the glory he achieves by his own efforts, not by obedience to the gods, and his reward is not otherworldly but the survival of reputation, which is the greatest of all goods.

Homer was the one book all Greek boys learned, and its code was therefore accepted with as little question as we accept the facts of the multiplication table. That, I think, is the explanation for the Athenians' relentless drive to excellence in all departments and for the quality of their production in arts and crafts. A man composed music or wrote tragedy not merely for self-expression or profit, but as an entry in a contest and his main objective was honor. Even the potters who fashioned the cheapest kinds of household wares took pains to sign their work. The agonistic element in public life, the drive to assert individuality, is a convenient gauge for measuring the current of humanism. In non-Greek contexts there was no such insistence on recording names. In the Apocrypha which is preserved in Greek, we have two books of the Maccabees. The first is a translation from a Semitic language and anonymous; the second, an abridgement of a Greek work, bears the name of Jason of Cyrene as author.

The contrast I have drawn between Achilles and Aeneas shows the direction Rome was taking, and it is true that as time goes on we have fewer names recorded. Any Athenian could say who designed the Parthenon and who executed its sculpture; the builders of the great cathedrals were content to be anonymous. And the most striking manifestation of the renaissance is the re-emergence of signatures. Artists are again eager to sign their work, biographies come back into vogue, and books are written to glorify the dignity of man.

A telling indication of the importance of the individual, his freedom from ordinary constraints, and the implications of this freedom for society is the institution of heroization. A hero in the Greek sense is not merely a leading figure in a literary work but, technically, any deceased person who has been deemed worthy of a cult, which is to say, of receiving offerings of flowers or wine on his special anniversary. Originally the hero was doubtlessly a ghost, and the offerings were intended to appease him and so prevent him from doing harm.

In the developed Greek view the hero was a man whose career had somehow extended the boundaries of what is possible for man and so had enriched the common life. And the offerings were intended not to appease him but to serve the people for whom his career was meaningful—as we eat cherry pies and chocolate hatchets to serve ourselves, not our first president. Because the institution of heroization bears a superficial resemblance to that of beatification and canonization it is instructive to notice the essential difference. A man approaches sainthood in the degree that he suppresses the impulses of ordinary humanity and assimilates himself to a pattern outside humanity. A man becomes a hero in the degree that he emphasizes his human attributes.

All the Greek heroes we know best are prickly, often unconventional characters, but it is not to be expected that men with sufficient drive to deserve heroization will also be model citizens. The coin cannot be split, and if we wish the obverse we must take the reverse in the bargain. This is illustrated by Achilles and illustrated even more specifically by the Ajax of Sophocles. Ajax is a brute, obsessed with self and cruel to his dependents. But Ajax is the only man who can stem a Trojan advance single-handed, and if we want such a hero we must take his roughness into the bargain. No namby-pamby could have stopped the Trojans.

Oedipus may be a better case, because his story is so widely known and so often misread. The conventional interpretation makes Sophocles' play into an edifying moral lesson: Oedipus had killed his father and married his mother and therefore received proper punishment. If the reader is inclined to protest that the punishment is monstrously disproportionate because Oedipus clearly did not know what he was doing and would never have committed his crimes if he had known, the conventional response is that his hasty temper and self-righteousness constitute a moral flaw which merited the punishment. But the punishment is still disproportionate.

Actually what happens to Oedipus has nothing to do with his crimes and every sensitive reader feels that despite the terrible outcome he emerges a true hero. His greatness lies in his unflagging pursuit of truth, and his faults are the inseparable concomitants of his virtues: It takes a hasty and self-righteous man to persist in the pursuit after it has become manifestly unsafe to do so. Oedipus is a hero because he has done well what it becomes a man to do. When a man who has done what it becomes a man to do and is nevertheless struck down by forces outside his knowledge and control, we have tragedy.

If we must find a villain in the piece it would perforce be Apollo; but Apollo is no villain because he is a god, and therefore presumed to operate by different standards than man's. Other plays of Sophocles also amount to demonstration that some great figure who was accepted as hero did in fact merit that status; his heroes are all headstrong men and women. If we demur at the evidence of the Sophists, whom conservative authors like Aristophanes and Plato condemn for their radicalism, we must observe that Sophocles was much beloved, extremely popular, and had a reputation for piety.

If Sophocles represents the notion of heroic humanism, Euripides shapes many of his plays on the armature of the *physis-nomos* dichotomy. One after another of his plays shows the unfortunate results of accepting *nomos* as if it were *physis*. The *Medea,* which is probably the most familiar, is, besides other things an exposé of masculine smugness *vis-à-vis* women and of Greek smugness *vis-à-vis* foreigners. Disabilities imposed on women and foreigners are justified, Euripides suggests, on a false belief in their "natural" inferiority, and it is because they are wrongly treated as inferiors that tragic consequences ensue. Medea passionately taxes Jason with ingratitude for deserting her, and Jason blandly replies that he owes her nothing because (a) it is expected that women will sacrifice their all for men, and (b) the enlightenment of Greece and the advantages of notoriety in a civilized country are more than adequate compensation for Medea's loss of royal status. Medea's slaughter of her children is not approved, but we are given to see how the injustice she was exposed to because of mistaking mere *nomos* for *physis* drove her to the deed. *Physis* alone makes life difficult enough, Euripides implies; why multiply the difficulty by treating convention as if it were as inexorable as nature? It is evidence of the wide acceptance of the *nomos-physis* dichotomy that conservatives who justified the disabilities imposed on certain classes did so, as Plato and Aristotle both did, on the ground that "slaves are inferior by *nature."*

I pass now to the Epicureans, who are the latest, most systematic, and most uncompromising exponents of the doctrine of separation between the world of man and the world of the gods. Accepting the doctrine of the pre-Socratic atomists, the Epicureans maintained that the world and everything in it was composed exclusively of fortuitous concatenations of atoms. There is no room for non-material interventions. Since death is simply a dispersion of atoms, there can be no consciousness and no punishments after death. Gods are completely indifferent to man, and spend their time enjoying their own divine picnics: what advantage in being gods if they must keep book on the doings of mankind?

The end of life is pleasure, which is defined as absence of pain. But it is a travesty of Epicureanism to say that it taught "Eat, drink and be merry, for tomorrow you may die." Pleasures were chosen according to the calculus of hedonism, which is to say, the pleasure must be measured against the pain it might entail.

There is no "Thou shalt not" to prevent a man from drinking a whole quart of gin if he so chooses, but if he knows his arithmetic he will refrain because the hangover will produce more pain than the drinking produces pleasure. Actually, the orgies in which the Epicureans indulged in their garden had to do largely with geometry, which entails the least hangover.

The Epicureans were humanists in more senses than one. They were much concerned with education, as *the* essentially human enterprise, and their use of text-books, even graded ones, shows their democratic bent. Learning is not a mystery reserved for the privileged but is accessible to all who are willing and able to partake of it. Where others held that human society represented a progressive degeneration from a perfect age of gold down through ages of silver, bronze, and iron, the Epicureans held that man had progressed from primitivism to ever-increasing complexity and sophistication, each change being directed solely by expediency. Men came together to form societies for better protection against wild beasts, they specialized functions in order to obtain abundance and ease.

But though they recognized no external authority for political institutions or class distinctions, yet, for the sake of avoiding inner and outer frictions, the Epicureans accommodated themselves to the usages of their environments, even to the point of participating in religious observances. For centuries Epicureanism continued as a popular sect; it succumbed at last to the determined opposition of Rome and Christianity. The intensity of the propaganda against Epicureanism shows that it was a formidable enemy —and shows also how the humanist program was eventually eroded.

The primary reasons for the opposition were of course doctrinal: No institution which declared itself based upon revelation and divine providence could tolerate a system which denied the possibility of revelation and providence. But even aside from doctrinal considerations, to certain temperaments and at certain conjunctures of history the starkness of the separation between the human and the divine could be very disturbing. Men yearn for what modern preachers call the "friend behind the phenomena," and feel naked and helpless when their own limitations are not enlarged by aid from without. They long for a protective sheath of softness and gentleness, and make of these qualities cardinal virtues, of which the antithesis is brutishness and heartlessness. But is the cultivation of the gentler virtues consistent with man's native endowment, or is it rather a willful denial of what might almost be called automatic reflexes? Are charity and hope a feasible program?

The classical Greeks apparently thought they were not. Hesiod's *Works and Days,* which is our earliest Greek book devoted to moral instruction, tells us that one good turn does deserve another but one bad turn deserves as many as you can get in. The attitude to hope is very instructive. When her importunate curiosity drove Pandora to open her box, in Hesiod's version of the fall, it proved to contain all the various calamities and disasters which afflict mankind. These all flew out of the box, and left only hope clinging to the rim. But what was hope doing in a box reserved for calamities?

The answer must be that hope is not a good thing. To accept as a likely eventuality an outcome we have no rational grounds for expecting is not healthy, and hope is therefore a drug for sick minds. So it appears to be in the related story of Prometheus, set forth in Aeschylus' play of that name. There Prometheus lists his benefactions to mankind—fire, tools, housing, clothing, which made human life more comfortable; agriculture, navigation, and other arts, which enriched life; drugs which enabled man to survive sickness; and finally hope, which apparently is the ultimate drug for situations which are otherwise intolerable. The rational and realistic mind sees hope for what it is; it becomes glorified only in the age which Gilbert Murray has aptly described as The Failure of Nerve. Sentimentality, under which hope is subsumed, is always suspect. It is characteristic of the gloomy chthonian view as clear reason is characteristic of the Olympian. The same Prometheus whom Shelley's adaptation and other modern interpretations admire as a glorious rebel against tyranny is, in a true reading of the Aeschylean play, a meddling do-gooder who tries to wreck a rational plan.

When Zeus came new to his task (the Greeks never thought of him as Creator; he came to his sovereignty in time, and hence would in time be superseded) he found mankind a weak and miserable lot, able to drag along only by Prometheus' crutches and bandages and drugs and finally hope. It was Zeus' plan to abolish the race which had to be cossetted and lied to, and replace it with a superior breed. For us it is naturally difficult to conceive of such a plan and impossible to approve of it; but if we can separate ourselves from our skins we might understand that, fom Zeus' rational point of view, the plan might have merits. But

Prometheus, who belonged to the chthonic order, operated not by reason but by sentimentality. To us his efforts on our behalf cannot be other than sympathetic, but like the meddling of all sentimental do-gooders they are not only softheaded but arrogant. Men must be allowed to work their fate out by behaving well as becomes men to behave and leave the gods to behave as becomes gods to behave.

This is not to imply that the operative power of sentimentality was ignored—any more than the rationalist Thucydides ignored the operative power of belief in omens and oracles. The Furies may be wrong in holding that a son's murder of his mother is the most heinous of all crimes, and Apollo right in holding it no different than the murder of any other elderly female, but in spite of logic sentimentality does make the crime seem more outrageous. This the Olympians know, and so instead of merely suppressing the Furies they seek to sublimate them to a socially useful function and to put them under rational control. They were never wholly sublimated, of course, and even in the most enlightened period by no means all the Greeks wished them to be. In the end the sentimentalist urge outlived the rationalist, as it has done in other periods after a rationalist "enlightenment." A significant aspect of the Greek experience is that outlooks so disparate could exist amicably side by side; the devout did not call the wrath of heaven down upon the worldlings, and the rationalists could acknowledge the claims of sentiment. Because neither claimed sole and exclusive possession of truth each could both learn from and fructify the other.

From Homer through the Epicureans, then, the significant and persistent strand in the Greek outlook is the self-sufficient independence of the individual, based upon the premise that the realms of the human and the divine are distinct from one another. The Homeric warrior went in to battle without looking back over his shoulder; he knew that he would either win glory for himself or yield it to his opponent. What was decreed for him by a power outside himself he could not alter and need not bother to understand; he was definitely captain of his soul, but made no pretense of being master of his fate. So the hero of tragedy knew that he must behave well as a man; the disasters that might befall him had no relationship with his own excellence. Essentially the same attitude was rationalized in the Sophistic enlightenment. The imperatives of society are based only on conventions shaped by men, and therefore ephemeral and relativistic; what belongs to the realm of nature, on the other hand, is outside man's control and therefore outside his responsibility. And the Epicureans, finally, taught how the conviction of man's essential independence could contribute to a self-sufficient serenity. Unpleasantnesses from the world without do not impinge upon this serenity, for they signify no more than a tale told by an idiot.

Even if the oversimplification I have attempted has validity —you will understand that my own colleagues would find it questionable—I realize that its value is mainly historical. At best, from the point of view of our immediate concern, it points to one factor which may contribute to our own stresses. There are of course other and perhaps weightier factors, and in any case patterns which may have proved effective in one world cannot be transferred bodily to another. What I have tried is not to suggest a program but to contribute to understanding.

SELF-CONTROL IN A SOCIOLOGICAL PERSPECTIVE

RICHARD JUNG

Introduction

Each of the three social scientists,
whose chapters follow, has examined the general problem of
"Self-Control Under Stressful Conditions" from a particular social
or cultural perspective. Instead of attempting to list the various
social and cultural perspectives from which this problem may be
investigated, this introduction considers a prior step, i.e., the
formulation of the problem to be investigated.

The focal problem of this Symposium lies somewhere within
the intersection of two domains of inquiry. One has been referred
to by the terms "stress" or "stressful conditions," the other characterized by the terms "control" or, more generally, "regulation."
To formulate the problem would require the definitions of the
two domains and of their intersection, first in general terms and
then in social and cultural terms. Limitations of space, however,
will allow only an outline of one method of formulating the "stress"
domain. The main intent is to explore the feasibility, the advantages, and the difficulties of such a formulation.

A domain of scientific inquiry is objectively defined by a
fundamental substantive problem, and by the methodological and
theoretical problems related to it. These paramount problems are
appropriately stated in the most abstract and general basic terms
available. Terms (concepts) peculiar to the domain of inquiry are
defined subsequently, in an attempt to solve the domain-defining
problems.

The "stress" domain of scientific inquiry is defined by the

same fundamental substantive, methodological, and theoretical problems, whether the systems studied are solids, organisms, or collectivities.

The two related *substantive* problems are: (*1*) knowing the deformation of the surface (shape) of an object, what is the distribution of forces within it? (*2*) knowing the distribution of forces acting on the surface of an object "loads," i.e., what is (*a*) the resultant deformation of its surface, or (*b*) the distribution of forces within it?

The basic *methodological* problems are: (*1*) how to observe the actual forces within an intact object without interfering; (*2*) how to describe adequately the characteristics of the object that are relevant to, but independent of, its actual deformation or subjection to a load; and (*3*) how to measure, independently of each other, the loads and the deformation of surfaces.

The basic *theoretical* problem arises because a deterministic explanation or prediction of the behavior of objects under load is often impossible. (It would require knowledge of the initial state of infinitely many variables, and the solution of an infinite set of simultaneous equations.) Instead, deductive inference from data obtained by a case-historical method of analysis becomes necessary. (A mathematical deductive system that is applicable to this problem is the integro-differential calculus.)

The *conceptual* apparatus originally developed by physicists to study the above problems in solids and fluids is also fully relevant to the study of these problems in organisms and collectivities. Once their physical meaning and their logical status are fully appreciated, the concepts evoke immediate intuitive meanings and denotative instances from psychology, sociology and economics. This is not only the case for the distinctions between strain and stress, between loads as forces (vectors) and strain and stress as force-fields (tensors), and between elastic, plastic, and rupture types of behavior, but also for many other concepts, such as "softening up," "fatigue," or "work hardening."

The *criteria of classification* of bodies are based on the values of additional variables and relations, which determine or characterize their behavior under various loads. Among the criteria that appear equally suitable for the classification of organisms and collectivities in this context are: (*a*) the characteristic values of their elastic limits, yield points, and breaking points; (*b*) the various coefficients expressing their resistance to deformation and their restoring tendencies as functions of type and magnitude of load, the extent of the already realized deformation, and the duration of application of load; (c) description of their anisotropy, i.e., distribution of the above characteristics relative to different directions within the body; and (d) description of their heterogeneity, i.e., distribution of the above characteristics with respect to different locations within the body.

These concepts and principles of classification also seem capable of distinguishing differences between the behavior of solids and organisms under load into those that are only a matter of degree and complexity, and those that appear to be fundamental. Among the differences that seem fundamental and that can be expressed and explained precisely and elegantly within the general formulation, are:

1. The apparent *hyperelasticity* of organisms under certain kinds of loads. Matter in its elastic range is only partly successful in resisting deformation, and, at most, only nearly restores original shape. Organisms, however, often appear to over-restore their form, sometimes even while the load is still being applied. This results in secondary deformations and gives rise to various cycles of successive deformations. Among the many examples that suggest themselves, perhaps the process described by Selye as "diseases of adaptation" is most striking.

2. The apparent *hyperplasticity* of organisms and collectivities. In the plastic range, matter flows only while a sufficient load is applied, and freezes into a permanent deformation once the load is removed. Organisms and collectivities, however, often continue to flow and deform even after the load has been removed. This general type of behavior receives various interpretations in the behavioral sciences, among which the ideas of internalization and institutionalization of external forces may be mentioned.

3. Both types of behavior are explainable by a fundamental *dichogeneity* which seems characteristic of organisms and collectivities. Two media with basically different elastic, plastic, and rupture properties are coupled together into one system. The first medium functions as an information-control subsystem, the other as an energy-response-amplification subsystem. The interaction of the two subsystems makes a joint over-compensating response possible. A minimal load is sufficient to deform the information-control subsystem. Its response activates the energy subsystem, which provides the amplification of the total response. In the case

of hyperplasticity, a plastic deformation of the information-control subsystem governs the hyperplastic flow of the energy-response subsystem.

Problems concerning not only mechanical, but also electrical and chemical forces can be formulated and solved in this framework. Can the same framework be more than a language for a systematic general discussion of the problem and a scheme for collation of essentially qualitative information when it comes to "psychological" and "ecological" forces? The answer depends on our ability to define the nature of these forces, and then identify individual forces in terms required by the conceptual scheme referred to on the preceding pages. Since the scheme presents a format for the isolation, identification, and specification of forces, it should make the task easier than if it were approached as an unfocused general problem.

One approach to this task, that would appear compatible both with the general framework and with the state of conceptualization in the behavioral sciences, involves the following initial steps: (1) The interpretation of the behavior of the organism as a set of transactions (exchanges) with its environment. (2) The interpretation of exchanges as forces, whatever the items exchanged, be they objects, energies, information, relations, or anything else. (3) The segregation into one general class of all items of transaction that carry a peculiarly ecological, rather than chemical, mechanical, or other significance. (4) The allocation of the items in this class into mutually exclusive categories. (5) Proceeding subsequently on the hypothesis that the class exhausts the universe of ecological forces, and that each category describes a qualitatively different ecological force (transaction).

These qualitatively different ecological forces or types of transactions become the *principal frame of reference for any* further analysis of the behavior of organisms.

The next conceptual task would be to classify any environment into sectors. A *sector* of an environment is the total concrete environment described and analyzed solely as a device producing and emitting a particular kind of ecological force, or commodity. The process of abstraction is similar to the one used in sociology, when a "situation" is defined as the environment analyzed solely in terms of its relevance to a particular norm (or set of norms) held by an actor. Incidentally, a given sector becomes a "strainful situation" for a given organism if and only if the output of the sector acts as a load on the organism.

The organism would be likewise described in terms of an ecological surface, with different *transactional planes* perpendicular to the orientation of the different ecological forces. Components of strain and stress could be then identified as forces acting perpendicularly on the different transactional planes of the organism. The components of strain experienced by the organism would be given a positive sign and called transactional surfeits, if an item were added in the transaction; a negative sign and called transactional deficits, if an item were lost in the transaction.

A conceptual scheme developed along these lines would be as suitable for a description of the sectors of environments and the transactional planes of organisms in absolute terms, as for a description of strainful situations, loads, strain, and stress relative to the transactional condition of a given organism.

The purpose of these remarks was to explore, within given limitations of knowledge and space, to what extent the use of the general formulation of a problem, common to several other sciences, could advance the understanding of the same problem in the social sciences, and what minimal requirements would have to be fulfilled by the social sciences before the potentialities of the formulation could be exploited further.

There is neither intent nor occasion here to attempt the conceptualization that seems indicated. Yet it would be desirable to review the current state of conceptualization of the behavior of organisms under ecological loads, as it is reflected in the works of behavioral scientists, philosophers, and artists. There is scattered throughout these works an impressive amount of unevenly developed, often primitive, frequently inconsistent, but occasionally nevertheless strategic and profound meanings, distinctions, and formulations. The over-all impression is that preliminary meanings have already been established for most of the required concepts, and that a sufficient number of qualitatively different ecological forces has already been tentatively identified to provide the foundation for a systematic attempt to conceptualize the domain of behavior of organisms under ecological loads.

SANFORD M. DORNBUSCH

Popular Psychology:
A Content Analysis of
Contemporary Inspirational
Nonreligious Books

This paper is an initial attempt to
determine the prevalent themes of the contemporary popular
inspirational literature. These works are often poorly written and
commercial in purpose, so that one might wonder whether they
are worth serious attention. In my opinion, the fact that they
exist and are bought in large quantities is sufficient justification
for treating them as a "quick and dirty" method for learning
about the psychology of Everyman. Because of the necessary
ambiguities of the process of communication, the content analyst
cannot assume that he is studying the thinking of the reading
public, a middle class segment of the American population.
Rather, one studies what writers write and uses it as a biased index
of what readers read. Content analysis of literature is not a
substitute for interviewing a population, but it can be a source
for preliminary checking of hunches.

A point of departure for this study is the preliminary draft
by Samuel Z. Klausner, "A Collocation of Concepts of Self-Control." As part of his analysis of the self-help literature, he studied

10 general self-help books, as well as a large number of works oriented toward control of dietary and sexual problems. The latest copyright on any of the general self-help works was 1941, with 1902-1903 as the median date of publication. In this paper we have an extensive replication of Dr. Klausner's pioneering analysis. It is an *extensive* replication, because:

1. I have sought more recent works currently available in bookstores and in the many outlets which purvey paperback books. Every book in my sample was written after World War II or has been recently published as a paperback. Differences in our findings may be the product of this 50 year difference, with all the possibilities of major changes in American values.

2. This analysis is limited to general self-help books, eliminating works which emphasize sex, diet, or religion. The exclusion of religious volumes is designed to prevent overlap with an earlier work by Schneider and Dornbusch, *POPULAR RELIGION* (Chicago: University of Chicago Press, 1958). The elimination of works on diet and sex is a major shift, to determine whether Dr. Klausner's findings persist for general self-help literature.

3. Another source of variation in results is the shifting of the content analysis code to include additional material.

During the summer of 1962, the books considered for inclusion in the new sample were on sale in Rochester, New York; Ithaca, New York; and Syracuse, New York. For the first two cities, every outlet for books and paperbacks, whether new or used, was visited. Forty-nine books were found, and they may be considered representative of currently available general self-help literature.

Within the set of 49 volumes, which are all addressed directly to the reader for his action towards self-improvement, I then sought to develop a subset which would be more homogeneous with respect to audience and object. The intent was to have books oriented toward American adults which stressed self-help in general, rather than any specific theme. To this end, the following negative criteria were used to produce a more homogeneous set of works. These criteria were employed during a perusal of the contents of each of the works. Appendix B lists the works eliminated. The negative criteria were:

1. The work was not written by Americans.
2. The book was written by more than two authors.
3. The book is oriented toward women.
4. The work is addressed to adolescents or to the aged.

5. The emphasis is upon manipulation of others as an object in itself rather than toward change of the self.

6. The book does not make frequent suggestions that the reader perform specific actions.

7. The book is a popularized text on elementary psychology or psychoanalysis or psychiatry.

8. The book seeks to teach self-analysis in a psychoanalytic sense.

9. The single major theme is control of fatigue.

10. The single major theme is creativity.

11. The book is concerned with a single performance activity, such as public speaking or salesmanship.

12. The author already has a book in our sample (random choice).

Appendix A lists the remaining 15 works which were content-analyzed. The additional criteria used to select the subset do not produce a biased sample, but rather the sample is representative of a narrower universe of works in this period. The small number of elements in the sample must, of course, make the reader cautious in accepting the findings of this paper. At best, this is a first approximation to the results of a larger and more intensive analysis.

The coding categories are reproduced in Appendix C. They are the product of three sources:

1. Implicit or explicit categories in Dr. Klausner's collocation.

2. The category scheme used in *Popular Religion*.

3. Categories especially created for the purposes of this study.

The numerical code is a modification of the global coding recommended in *Popular Religion,* pp. 166-167. The reader notes the first instance of the appearance of a particular theme. There may be more than one theme in a page or paragraph. The first appearance of a theme is recorded, but no further data are required until the complete book has been read. Then the coder records the relative importance of each theme in this volume on a four point scale:

0   Absent
1   Some attention to this theme
2   Considerable attention to this theme
3   Major theme of this volume

The books were read in random order so that changes in the coding behavior of the reader would not be associated with any specific type of volume. Reliability tests showed a lack of reliability in coding if the requirement was identical coding of each category. There was 70 per cent agreement among two coders if the criterion was agreed presence of theme, lumping together 1, 2, and 3 on the scale. The highest reliability, 75 per cent agreement, was found when categories coded 2 or 3 by one reader were compared to 2 or 3 ratings by the other reader. This level of reliability is quite high, and it would soar over 90 per cent were we to include agreement on the absence of a theme. Therefore, this paper relates themes only to books for which they are coded 2 or 3, unless otherwise noted.

Methods of Self-Control

The authors of these works have a problem: How to assist persons in an imperfect world where the ends of action are neither certain nor universally desired. Faced with the need to motivate the reader to act and to give him some feeling of confidence in his action, the response of the organism is emphasized. In the terminology of Hadas' paper, the stress is on *nomos*. If techniques of self-hypnosis or self-suggestion were scientifically understood and popularly diffused, then these authors would have a shared body of methods to endorse. But Orne notes the lack of research in this area in his paper, and the result is seen in the variety of combinations of methods which are recommended by these authors. Even with Klausner's abstract categorization, there is little unity.

The most common method can be labeled "positive thinking." It is central to nine of these self-help books. IA_1 (affirm the positive), IA_{1a} (imagine the end result and it will move events in the desired direction), IA_2 (deny the negative), and IA_3 (deny the negative by affirming the positive) are all elements of this approach, which may be peculiarly consonant with American values of optimism and progress. The response of the organism to the environment is used to structure the world in accordance with a theme of uplift. Yet positive thinking alone is seldom employed. Let us suggest the confusion as to appropriate methods for self-help by listing authors in terms of the types of methods they stress.

Positive thinking—Lurton, Schindler, Chase
Positive thinking plus IA_{1b} (control sub-conscious or unconscious processes in the desired direction)—Maltz, Bristol

Positive thinking plus control of subconscious plus IC (engaging the threat and accepting a changed self as the result)—Powers, Albert

Positive thinking plus engaging the threat plus ID (cognitively mediating intra-psychic forces)—Terhune

Positive thinking plus control of subconscious plus cognitive mediation plus IB (selecting an environment which would have the desired impact on the self)—Hill

Control of subconscious, plus engaging the threat plus cognitive mediation—Hart

Control of subconscious plus selection of the environment plus cognitive mediation—Fink

Engaging the threat plus cognitive mediation—Bisch, Ray

Engaging the threat—Carnegie, Reilly

This list illustrates the surprising heterogeneity of methods of control employed in what appears to be a unitary self-help orientation. Approaches range from the kitchen sink of Hill to the single-mindedness of Carnegie and Reilly.

It is easy to look at the positive-thinking notion as a childish American attempt to impose the search for happiness as a perceptual category upon the unyielding objects of man's environment. I have been surprised to note that the seemingly obvious connection between emphasis upon positive thinking and low intellectual quality simply does not hold. Among the more reasonable and realistic works are those of Schindler and Terhune, two of the four psychiatrists, and they both stress positive thinking as a method of changing the self. The relation of positive thinking to the structure of self-help is certainly more complicated than expected.

As is pointed out by Klausner, the emphasis upon the individual's response to the world may be a function of a general approach which treats the organism rather than the environment. Associated with positive thinking as a recommended method for the readers are three examples of positive thinking by the authors. Thus, five out of nine positive-thinking authors ask the reader to set his aspirations very high (VIII F), while only one out of the remaining six authors requests that the reader set a high level of aspiration.

The confidence of the author (his positive thinking?) is also shown by the belief of six of the nine positive-thinking authors that their advice always is effective if followed (IXA, IXB). Only two of the six remaining negative-thinkers about positive-thinking assure the reader of guaranteed effectiveness.

We find that the positive thinkers are again positive in promising happiness to all who follow the prescribed regimen (VA4). Six out of the nine positively oriented works give this theme considerable attention, while only two out of the remaining six emphasize this theme. We may analyze the data from another standpoint. A somewhat negative theme states that both happiness and unhappiness are to be expected even by a diligent reader (VC). Using a less restrictive criterion, noting any case (1, 2, or 3) in which the author observes the non-Pollyanna qualities of a human environment, we can count the books that give a single mention to this category. Three of the nine positive-thinking books mention such unhappiness, while three of the six remaining works also note that unhappiness is a possibility. The relationship here is slight, but in the proper direction. One interesting aspect of this finding is the lack of a stronger relationship. Positive-thinking is a method; happiness is a goal; and one can stress positive-thinking as a useful technique without necessarily promising achievement of happiness.

We can also learn from this analysis by noting the least used method of self-control, the selection of an environment to have a desired impact on the self. The other categories of methods are closely related to emphases of contemporary American values. Engaging the threat is analogous to activism, positive-thinking to optimism, and cognitive mediation and control of subconscious represent a new attention to psychological and psychiatric conceptions of internal dynamics. Concern with the social environment, despite the efforts of social psychologists and sociologists, has not yet affected the naive psychology of the layman.

Magic

Categories IVB4, IVB5, IVC4, and IVC5 can provide an operational definition of magic. They portray thought as both affecting and forecasting physical and social events, both as instrumental and clairvoyant. In a world in which we all share many superstitions and prejudices, it is a pleasure to be able to state objectively that three of these works are high in their orientation toward magical processes, without worrying about biases influencing the researcher. The works of Bristol, Hill, and Chase clearly differ from the other works by emphasizing unknowable extra-sensory processes. Perhaps they are right, but there is no harm in my labeling them as different in kind. These three works are remarkably consistent. They exhort the reader to have a very high level of aspiration, three out of three stressing this theme, while only three of the remaining 12 works do so. If we look at VIIIC, which relates aspirations to individual capabilities, none of these authors stress that theme, while six of the remaining 12 books employ it. Finally, if we combine VIIIC and VIIID, so that aspirations are related to capabilities or to both capabilities and the environmental situation, we continue to find that the three magical works set no limit for their readers' guidance, while eight of the remaining 12 do ask for some reality testing.

Manifest Objects of Control

Klausner has stated that, "The self-help literature is particularly concerned with drive control. This may derive, in part, from its moralistic attitude toward physiological drives and, in part, from this literature's concern with task accomplishment. The popular interpretation suggests that uncontrolled drives interfere with the accomplishment of higher tasks. Books on diet and sex control within the self-help literature inflate the drive category."

The content analysis performed here supports only the *caveat* in Dr. Klausner's last sentence. The modern self-help literature is not concerned with drive control (IIB). The control of physiological or psychological drives is a theme in only five of the 15 works. Three of these five are written by psychiatrists in the sample. Ray, taking an Adlerian view, joins the psychiatrists, while Hill is the only representative of popular moralistic concern. Hill sees sex as necessarily sublimated in order to accomplish the higher ends of life, such as earning money. Therefore, two-thirds of our works do not stress drive control, and the "popular" moral concern is found only in one work. Of course, this may represent a change over a half-century.

If drive control is not central to this literature, then what are the manifest objects of control? Three of the works stress performance (IIA), 10 emphasize intellectual or cognitive functions (IIC), and 14 stress the control of emotion or affect (IID). The only exception is Powers, who is almost completely concerned with intellectual functions as a means toward achieving success.

In our content-analysis, the control of affect or emotion is broken down to include as an additional set of categories the relation of self to social objects (IID1), physical objects (IID2), or cultural objects (IID3). Twelve of the 14 works in this area stress control of emotion *per se,* while Bristol and Reilly only consider affective relations of the self to these objects. It may be expressive of a shift toward other-directedness or emphasis on social interaction that every one of these 14 works gives considerable attention to the relation of the self to other persons. Two works relate the self to physical objects and are magical in their orientation. The four which emphasize relations to cultural objects are discussing such diverse phenomena as money, conformity, and religious orientations.

Types of Effort

Klausner's finding of an association between the self-help literature and conquest (IIIB) is confirmed for the later sample. Fourteen out of 15 works stress this theme. Klausner is also correct for the recent books in his belief that the self-help literature is not oriented toward harmony (IIIC) or transcendence (IIID). Only the work of two of our four psychiatrists use these themes. (Klausner has noted a relationship between psychoanalysis and the emphasis upon transcendence and harmony.) Bisch strongly endorses both and Terhune seeks to promote the effort toward harmony. Nine of the 15 books have not a single mention of these notions.

Klausner has stated that the synergic approach is stressed in the self-help literature. It is a powerful theme in this sample only for Hill and Terhune. But before scrapping Klausner's belief, we should note that the theme appears at least once in 11 out of the 15 books.

In his collocation Dr. Klausner links the effort to conquer with the attempt to control physiological and psychological drives. In this sample, as noted above, 14 of our 15 works use conquest as a central type of effort. It is of interest that Bisch, one of only five authors who emphasize drive control, does not stress conquest. He appeals for efforts toward harmony and transcendence.

It is possible that the association reported by Dr. Klausner is based on a general tendency of self-help literature *per se.* The sample he used included many works on diet and sex, which would emphasize drive control, and it is conceivable that a general tendency of all self-help literature might be perceived as relating to drive control itself. Dr. Klausner could settle this issue by cross-classifying his sample into diet, sex, and general self-help works, and then relating types of effort to manifest objects of control.

Summary

This paper reports an extensive replication of Dr. Klausner's analysis of the self-help literature. The tentative findings indicate that the self-help works range from sheer magic to reasoned products of human experience. With this somewhat more homogeneous and later sample of books, it was possible to analyze the data in terms of Dr. Klausner's theoretical orientation. The findings support the fruitfulness of his classification scheme. It is clear that analysis of inspirational works can provide a foundation for the study of societal assumptions about the individual's relation to himself and his world.

APPENDIX A

WORKS CONTENT-ANALYZED

ALBERT, DORA, *You're Better than You Think*. Englewood Cliffs, New Jersey: Prentice-Hall, 1957. (Hardcover)

BISCH, L. E., B.A., M.D., Ph.D., *Cure Your Nerves Yourself: How Understanding Yourself Can Bring Peace of Mind*. Greenwich, Conn.: Fawcett Publications, revised 1957. (Paperback)

BRISTOL, C. M., *The Magic of Believing*. New York: Prentice Hall, 1948. (Hardcover)

CARNEGIE, D., *How to Stop Worrying and Start Living*. New York Pocket Books, 1961; earlier published by Simon and Schuster, 1948. (Paperback)

CHASE, JO ANNE (as told to Constance Moon), *You Can Change Your Life Through Psychic Power*. New York: Permabooks, 1960. (Paperback)

FINK, D. H., M.D., *Release From Nervous Tension*. New York: Simon & Schuster, Revised Edition, 1953. (Hardcover)

HART, H., Ph.D., *Autoconditioning: The New Way to a Successful Life*. Englewood Cliffs, New Jersey: Prentice-Hall, 1956. (Hardcover)

HILL, N., *Think and Grow Rich.* Greenwich, Conn.: Fawcett Publications, Revised Edition 1960; earlier edition, 1937. (Paperback)

LURTON, D., *The Power of Positive Living.* Greenwich, Conn.: Fawcett Publications, no date, originally New York: McGraw-Hill Book Co., 1950. (Paperback)

MALTZ, M., M.D., *Psycho-Cybernetics: A New Way to Get More Living Out of Life.* Englewood Cliffs, New Jersey: Prentice-Hall, 1960. (Hardcover)

POWERS, M., *Dynamic Thinking: The Technique for Achieving Self-Confidence and Success.* Hollywood, California: Wilshire Book Co., 1955. (Paperback)

RAY, MARIE BEYNON, *The Importance of Feeling Inferior.* New York: Ace Books, 1957. (Paperback)

REILLY, W. J., Ph.D., *How to Get What You Want Out of Life.* Englewood Cliffs, New Jersey: Prentice-Hall, 1957. (Hardcover)

SCHINDLER, J. A., M.D., *How to Live 365 Days a Year.* New York: Prentice-Hall, 1954. (Hardcover)

TERHUNE, W. B., M.D., *Emotional Problems and What You Can Do About Them.* New York: William Morrow & Co., 1955. (Paperback.)

APPENDIX B

WORKS NOW ON SALE BUT EXCLUDED FROM
CONTENT-ANALYSIS SAMPLE

BANKS, M., *How To Live With Yourself.* New York: Prentice-Hall, 1951.

BERGLER, E., M.D., *Tensions Can Be Reduced to Nuisances: A Technique for Not-Too-Neurotic People.* New York: Collier Books, 1962; earlier Liveright, 1960.

BINSTOCK, L., *The Road to Successful Living.* New York: Simon and Schuster, 1958.

BISCH, B. A., M.D., Ph.D., *Be Glad You're Neurotic.* New York: McGraw-Hill Book Company, Second Revised Edition, 1946.

CARNEGIE, D., *How to Develop Self-Confidence and Influence People by Public Speaking.* New York: Pocket Books, 1956, revised from *Public Speaking and Influencing Men in Business.* Association Press, 1926.

CARNEGIE, D., *How to Win Friends and Influence People.* New York: Pocket Books, 1959; earlier published by Simon and Schuster, 1936.

CARNEGIE, MRS. DALE, *How to Help Your Husband Get Ahead.* New York: Pyramid Books, 1957; originally 1953.

CHAPPELL, M. N., *Worry and Its Control.* New York: Collier Books, 1949.

COUE, EMILE and C. H. BROOKS, *Better and Better Every Day.* New York: Barnes & Noble, 1961.

DAVIS, MAXINE, *Get the Most out of Your Best Years.* New York: Permabooks, 1962; originally by Dial Press, 1960.

DIMNET, E., *The Art of Thinking.* Greenwich, Conn.: Fawcett Publications (printed in 1962); earlier published by Simon & Schuster, 1928.

DUVALL, S. M., S.T.M., Ph.D., *The Art and Skill of Getting Along With People.* Englewood Cliffs, New Jersey: Prentice-Hall, 1961.

GIBLIN, L., *How to Have Confidence and Power in Dealing With People.* Englewood Cliffs, New Jersey: Prentice-Hall, 1956.

GRACIAN, B., *The Art of Worldly Wisdom.* New York: Frederick Ungar Publishing Co., originally 1892; no date for this printing.

KRAINES, S. H., M.D., and E. S. THETFORD, *Live and Help Live.* New York: Macmillan Company, 1951.

LACKNER, S., DR., *Discover Your Self: A Practical Guide to Auto-analysis.* Greenwich, Conn.: Fawcett Publications, 1956.

LAIRD, D. A., Ph.D., Sc.D., *Increasing Personal Efficiency.* New York: Harper and Brothers, 1953.

LEES, HANNAH, *Help Your Husband Stay Alive.* New York: Collier Books, 1962; originally 1957.

LINDGREN, H. C., *How to Live with Yourself and Like It.* Greenwich, Conn.: Fawcett Publications, 1958; earlier published 1953 by Hermitage House.

LUCAS, F. L., *The Art of Living.* New York: Macmillan, 1961; earlier copyright 1959.

MAGER, N. H. and S. K., Editors, *A Guide to Better Living.* New York: Permabooks, 1959; earlier published by Affiliated Publishers, 1957.

MANGAN, J. T., *The Knack of Selling Yourself.* New York: Grosset & Dunlap, 1947.

OSBORN, A., *Your Creative Power.* New York: Dell Publishing Co., 1961; earlier published by Charles Scribner's Sons.

OVERSTREET, B. W., *Understanding Fear in Ourselves and Others.* New York: Collier Books, 1962; earlier Harper and Brothers, 1951.

OVERSTREET, H. A., *About Ourselves: Psychology for Normal People.* New York: W. W. Norton, 1927.

OVERSTREET, H. A., *The Mature Mind.* New York: W. W. Norton & Company, 1949.

OVERSTREET, H. and B., *The Mind Alive.* New York: W. W. Norton & Company, 1954.

PALMER, S. *Understanding Other People.* Greenwich, Conn.: Fawcett Publications, 1959; earlier published by Thomas Y. Crowell, 1955.

RUSSELL, B., *The Conquest of Happiness.* Avon Book; originally 1930, Horace Liveright Co.

SEABURG, D., *Keep Your Wits*. New York: Whittlesey House, 1935.

SHERMAN, H., *Your Key to Happiness*. New York: Fawcett Publications, 1956; earlier published by G. P. Putnam & Sons, 1935, 1943, 1944.

SMITH, ETHEL SARBIN, *The Dynamics of Aging*. New York: W. W. Norton & Company, 1956.

SPERLING, P., DR., *How to Make Psychology Work for You*. Greenwich, Conn.: Fawcett Publications, 1957.

VERMES, H. G., *Senior Citizen's Guide to Better Living*. New York: Key Publishing, 1959.

APPENDIX C

CODING CATEGORIES

I. Methods of self-control
- A. Mental imagery to grasp consciousness and bend its power to the will
  1. Affirm the positive
     a. Imagine the end-result
     b. Control sub-conscious or unconscious processes in the desired direction
  2. Deny the negative
  3. Deny the negative by affirming the positive
- B. Selecting an environment which would have the desired impact on the self
- C. Engaging the threat and accepting a changed self as the result
- D. Cognitively mediating intra-psychic forces

II. Manifest objects of control
- A. Control overt performances by facilitating or inhibiting certain movements
- B. Control physiological or psychological drives by drive reduction or acting despite drive pressure
- C. Control intellectual or cognitive functions by facilitating thought or inhibiting troublesome thoughts
- D. Control affect or emotions, such as internal feeling states
  1. Control relation of self to social objects
  2. Control relation of self to physical objects
  3. Control relation of self to cultural objects

III. Types of effort
- A. Synergy
  1. Physically position the self to receive inputs from external

systems, whether considered as stimuli, social relations, or symbolic

2. Socially position the self to receive inputs from external systems, whether considered as stimuli, social relations, or symbolic

B. Conquest
1. Strengthening or weakening forces by a calculus of values
2. Strengthening or weakening forces by concentration of energies
3. Strengthening or weakening forces by practicing good habits and inhibiting bad habits

C. Harmony—internal physical or psychological balance, integrating self under various environmental conditions

D. Transcendence—internal dialectic synthesis which takes external systems into account

IV. *Thought and reality*
A. Matter is illusion
B. Matter is real but subservient to thought
1. Absence of thought allows no influence from matter
2. The cast of thought, positive or negative, decides the nature of the influence from matter
3. The thought itself, by a form of the self-fulfilling prophecy, will affect outcomes
4. Thought affects physical events by some extra-sensory process
5. Thoughts can foretell future physical states
C. Social relations are real but subservient to thought
1. Absence of thought allows no influence from social relations
2. The cast of thought, positive or negative, decides the nature of the social influence
3. The thought itself, by a form of the self-fulfilling prophecy, will affect outcomes
4. Thought affects social interaction by some extra-sensory process
5. Thoughts can foretell future social relationships
D. Matter is not subservient to thought
E. Social relations are not subservient to thought

V. *Happiness and Unhappiness*
A. Happiness
1. Happiness cannot be expected by any man
2. Happiness cannot be expected by most men
3. Happiness can be expected by most men who act in accordance with advice given in this book

4. Happiness can be expected by all men who act in accordance with advice given in this book

B. Unhappiness
   1. Unhappiness has divine significance
   2. Unhappiness is a sign of environmental obstacles
   3. Unhappiness is a sign of personal deficiencies
   4. Unhappiness is a product of environmental obstacles and personal deficiencies
   5. Unhappiness should be avoided and fought

C. Both happiness and unhappiness can be expected by all men who act in accordance with advice given in this book

VI. *Sources of advice*
   A. Personal experiences of the author
      1. In business
      2. In clinical practice
   B. Personal experiences of others
      1. Successful businessmen
      2. Scientists
         a. Natural scientists
         b. Behavioral scientists
         c. Clinicians
      3. Religious leaders
      4. Philosophers
      5. Heroes of sports and entertainment
      6. Other famous persons (government, exploration, art)
      7. Ordinary people
   C. Religious authority
      1. Christian
      2. Hebrew
      3. Other religious groups
      4. Non-institutional religion
   D. Scientific authority
      1. Natural science
      2. Behavioral scientists and clinicians
         a. Psychiatry and psychoanalysis
         b. Psychology
         c. Physicians
         d. Sociology
         e. Anthropology
         f. Other behavioral sciences

VII. *Functions of God and religion*
   A. God as Universal Mind or Infinite Intelligence, providing a storehouse of solutions to problems
   B. God as giver of great potential to each man
   C. God as healer, forgiver, and helper

VIII. Levels of aspiration
  A. Be satisfied with the status quo
  B. Set aspiration level moderately higher than current state
  C. Set aspiration level according to individual capability
  D. Set aspiration level according to individual capabilities and environmental situation
  E. Do not expect to achieve perfection
  F. Set a very high level of aspiration

IX. Certainty of improvement if advice is followed
  A. Advice, if taken, will always produce an improved state
  B. Improvement is certain, but not immediate, requiring continued effort
  C. Most persons will show improvement
  D. Some persons will show improvement
  E. Improvement may occur and no harm is possible

MARVIN K. OPLER

Social Identity
and Self-Control

Introduction: The Problem
of Classification

A plan of research in any field of science must depend, in the last analysis, upon the phenomena being investigated. By this we mean that if psychopathological states are the concern of social psychiatry—as they are the concern of any branch of psychiatry—we must begin with the character of such states at least insofar as present-day psychiatry understands them.

It has been argued that "what is normal," or some relativistic concept of normality, lies at the root of such questions since conduct and behavior vary noticeably from one community to another. A few decades ago, Ruth Benedict stated that the "normals" of one culture might seem to be the "abnormals" of another, that is, their behavior would seem strange in alien cultural contexts. This passing and plausible observation had added to it the astonishing corollary that out-and-out abnormals of one cultural context could "fit in" somewhere else, something which the author had occasion to test, and which he found to be incredibly naive, in studies among Northwest Coast Indian schizophrenics, found together with Eskimo and White psychotics in the Morningside Clinic and Hospital, a federal institution in Oregon. Illness, in short, represents impairments in functioning destructive of any individual's integration in his adaptation to *any* context or to his adjustment in any scene. The accurate point, from culture to culture, is not that such deviancy can find a haven elsewhere, but that it is etiologically traceable to *stresses implicit in a social and cultural background.*

In contrast with this last point, psychiatry has its time-honored classifications of mental disorders which date back to the last century with little modification. These categories are based, not upon etiology nor upon dynamics, but upon clusters of symptoms. The fact that many such symptoms, like hallucinations, feelings of depersonalization, etc., are found cross-culturally argues of course for the existence of general illness classification (the schizophrenias, neuroses, and the like). At the same time, the overlapping of many elements such as "asocial withdrawal," "restlessness," "sexual identification problem," or their incorporation into illness states of varying degrees of seriousness, links up very well with what we know of culturally varying types within such single or generic classifications like the schizophrenias. Both sets of facts denote or point to a necessity for new, etiological classifications within the more generalized rubrics.

If this is so, most studies of generic categories like schizophrenias, alcoholism, character disorder, etc., have been, statistically speaking, studies of apples and oranges which do not sort out the predominant, descriptive and independent variables which cut most deeply. Social psychiatry has exactly these etiological interests for it is concerned *ab initio* with the impact of culture, social environment and family type upon the developing personality. It can reach this goal only if it maintains a focus upon both facets of the problem: the incidence *and* the variations of psychiatric disorders. Both of these foci are important at the same time. There is a growing faith among social psychiatry personnel that all is well if the study is one of incidence of psychiatric disorders *in general.* Having participated in the Midtown Study in New York, where we sought the prevalence, treated and untreated, of mental ills throughout a whole population, the author can note that even criteria like "impairment in life functioning," together with symptoms, do not describe wholly the degrees of adjustment, adaptation, or the measure of seriousness of an illness. A psychiatrist knows this insofar as he knows the history of a case in its total setting. The quality of knowing is pre-eminently important. In our opinion, there is no good substitute for studies in depth of the individual in settings of family and sociocultural environment; and these are the methods used both by anthropology and social psychiatry. In measuring degrees of seriousness of an illness, one requires in psychiatry, as in other branches of medicine, some knowledge of the total case, of prognostic indicators, of personality assets and liabilities in a known family and community environment—in short, a wide variety of information involving etiology and dynamics.

Earlier Approaches to Disease Classification

Of all the fields of knowledge, man's discovery of himself has come most recently in human history. First, in the heliocentric and planetry motion theories of Galileo and Copernicus, came man's discovery of the heavens. Then with Lyell, the earth sciences were solidly established. The acceptance of Darwin's discoveries completed the gains made in the 19th Century. Freud, of course, followed in the 20th Century.

In conceptions of health and illness, likewise, the cosmic and astrological theories precede the earthly ones. Plato, for example, spoke of disharmony and disproportion of four universal or cosmic elements, earth and water or fire and air. He thus projected illness out into an anonymous universe with which the sick were simply out of step or out of tune. Stoics, like Buddhists elsewhere, believed suffering was just a matter of individual judgment and urged calm detachment in the face of pain. A Hippocratic version of disease made it more a part of human existence, but restricted illness to its own sphere in life processes in order to study its various manifestations. Not till Galen was the challenge uttered, "Man is a whole with his environment." But to the Paris Medical Faculty in the Middle Ages, this could mean merely noxious agents in earthly environment such as "atmospheric causes" of the Black Death, or the Italian peasant's *mala aria* (literally "evil air") in a miasmic theory of diseases (1, 2).

From cosmic theories to those of gross and earthly noxious agents, one goes from fate or fatalism to that long advance in theory that at least places man in his earthly environment. Yet the earthly theories of noxious agents, propounded during long centuries of an age of agriculture, retained their own brand of fatalism implicit in man's dependence upon such gross forces of nature as wind and weather. When atmospheric and miasmic theories become converted to theories of internal juices ("humors"), doctrines of internal assault held sway. Not till micro-organic life was understood, with Koch and Pasteur, could the theories of internal assault be refined. Later Claude Bernard, Walter B. Cannon and Sigmund Freud demonstrated the essential unity or integration of the human being, physiologically and psychologically. With this step, the door was opened to awareness that human values, emotional attitudes and habits played their role in the disease process. A sociologist like Talcott Parsons could search for roots of various psychological patterns and influences within human societies and their social processes. A psychiatrist like Kardiner could speak of different kinds of social emotions as being patterned in social structure. Anthropologists could investigate these patterns for clues as to their origin in cultural experience (3).

Cultural Process
Versus Cultural Stereotype

Following Darwin, evolutionary schemes applied to culture offered a way of explaining or analyzing, rather than merely describing, man's world (4). Some of these early doctrines of cultural evolution stressed a simultaneous progression from simpler to complex forms in both biological and cultural realms. The task Herbert Spencer assigned himself, of defining a universal law of progress, expressed in his *First Principles,* emphasized simultaneous biological, psychological and cultural developments, making the former the precondition for the latter. Others like Lewis Morgan in the United States, wavered between ideas of biological evolution governing the slow progress through stages of cultural development, and his much more greatly emphasized and contrary idea that technical progress influenced both cultural evolution and the developing "germs of thought" even affecting factors such as brain weight. These confusions in the often conflicting theories of Spencer, Morgan, McLennan, Tyler or Westermarck meant there was much unfinished business in 19th Century anthropology. It led American anthropologists of the 20th Century, following Franz Boas and Robert Lowie, to fall back on descriptions of particular cultures and on regional descriptive classifications rather than attempt formulations of general cultural processes. This last movement was more reminiscent of a Lamarckian description and classification than of a Darwinian analysis of process (5).

Much of the Spencerian type of theory of a simultaneous evolution on all levels, biological, psychic and cultural inevitably stressed inadequacies of early man, nonliterate cultures, and of so-called, contemporary "primitives." In anti-racist American anthropology, this early evoked, as in Franz Boas' book, *The Mind of Primitive Man,* a cogent defense on psychological and cultural grounds of any *Homo sapiens* on all continents and in every world area. Henceforth, in the leading position of American anthropology, mental processes were linked firmly with cultural ones, "race" was demolished as an explanation of culture, and psychological stereotypes could no longer stand for either cultural development or particular cultural systems.

The search for given cultural patterns, and awareness of their variety and difference, led in due course to revivals of more psychological descriptions of them, as in Ruth Benedict's *Patterns of Culture.* While descriptions of particular cultures in terms of pattern or personality type multiplied, the central problems of how personality or pattern originated were not always convincingly analyzed. The Benedict position, for example, involved a circularity between pattern and personality which was hardly an explanation. Subsequent zonal theories of a Freudian basic personality patterning were so limited in their range of description of possible behavior in a given culture as to lead to rebuttals to the effect that these elements or aspects did not encompass either the personality range in a Freudian sense or the behavioral range in the culture at all (6). It appeared in the simpler accounts, that the racial stereotypes of the 19th Century were rapidly being replaced by personality stereotypes of the first half of the 20th. For one thing, the statistical frequencies of various illnesses, or of personality types and problems, had to be better known. For another, it was necessary to study in greater depth than hitherto the development of personalities in well understood cultural settings inasmuch as human reactive and adjustment systems were, in all probability, not simple closed systems of adaptation, but complex, open and integrative systems in which much more than one organic locus or set of personality characteristics operated at a time.

In addition to this complexity, in which one organ system or another could substitute in taking the brunt of strain, and in which personality had to be viewed as a more or less precarious balance, there was the question of universal cultural values, or human values as such, which might be operative irrespective of particular boundaries. All cultures, as a general phenomenon, were instrumentalities in providing some control over nature and adaptation to environment. All, therefore, contained such modalities as economic systems, or the organized provisioning of food, shelter, and protection within variable limits. All regulated social and sexual conduct. All contained explanatory devices in ideology, whether in myth, science or philosophy; or provided some modicum of relaxation in arts, literature and the like. These least common denominators, expressing universal values, gave some unity to culture as a generic phenomenon despite historical or evolutionary differences in the various means for their attainment. Thus, culture was a resultant of human activity and a precipitant of further social systems of action.

For this reason, adequate cultural descriptions or analyses, because of their generalized character, were not stereotypes in the sense that racial or psychological characterizations of whole peoples were. They corrected the Tweedledum and Tweedledee theories that all persons had exactly the same ideological or psychological characteristics. At the same time, the whole realm of systems of meaning, patterns of emotional response, and effects of culture on personality could be searched as part of the study of cultural process.

Illness and the
Socio-Cultural Process

We have seen that one aim of anthropological research was not simplistic description of stereotypes, but rather research into the processes of cultural growth in which one aspect is the dynamic relationship between culture, on the one hand, and statistical frequencies of personality types within cultural boundaries on the other. A research model for this inquiry must contain persons some of whom represent the culture at its best, and some at its worst. Thus an interest in illness, from this vantage point, hardly implies that the most positive and creative aspects of the culture are exemplified by one illness type or by illness types found in it in general. Yet the description of a culture includes its disorders and their frequencies of occurrence, since illness is never a private problem either in origin or in effects. Parsons has noted the ability of illness to disrupt the smooth functioning of social systems and the stylized methods used in cultural systems for dealing with these effects (7).

In respect to more scientific controls, it was not until man's protective and reactive functions were revealed by Cannon and by Freud that the control and prevention of disease was effectively extended beyond those illnesses having a specific, isolated pathogenic agent. J. L. Halliday, in his book, *Psychosocial Medicine,* has therefore defined illness generally as the reactions or responses of an individual to those forces encountered as he functions and develops in time (8).

However, with humans, we are all too prone to assume that these responses are the isolated reactions of individual organisms. Since culture itself is a human agency or organization of instrumentalities for adjusting and adapting to nature, its functions do not cease with the illness process. We can report that individual reactions are mediated by a whole system of values, attitudes and behaviors which are not exclusively possessed by any one person in a culture. By furnishing guidelines to behavior, culture over generations enters into the illness process (9).

Cross-cultural comparative studies indicate that even such ills as heart disease, hardening of the arteries, or the human organism's vulnerability to intestinal amoeba are anything but inevitable and invariable organ reactions. F. S. C. Northrup reports a Latin American country in his experience with a pleasant lack of our efficient conceptions of time; they also had a pleasant rarity of our heart disease or arteriosclerotic conditions among the elderly. In Burma and Thailand, American health teams and technical aids must be eternally vigilant about water supply and its amoebic hazards. But the village populations, even down to the smallest children, seem relatively immune to many of these conditions either through natural selection over time, or through the immunity built up from the earliest years. On the broadest, world-wide basis, the physical anthropologists, Coon, Garn and Birdsell have shown how certain body builds such as the Eskimo pyknik or barrel-shape, even down to small noses and fat cheeks, are fitted to circumpolar survival, whereas the tall, asthenic build and aquiline features of Sahara dwellers are better adapted to the heat they must endure (10). Alfred Hess' studies of diet deficiency diseases could be adduced for a modern, urban example of environmental effects (11). Certainly, the individual and his environment are not mutually exclusive systems.

While most organisms react directly to inborn, organic potentials and outer stimuli, humans are both more sensitive reacting systems, and more complex self-regulating systems. One of Cannon's most interesting papers concerned schizophrenic fear reactions in different nonliterate cultures resulting from the breaking of social group taboos. The guilty individuals, or those victims impressed by the taboos and their magical death sanctions, literally wasted away and died (12). Any psychiatrist can think of similar modern occasions where unmet or extravagant emotional needs of one or more parents were fulfilled at the expense of the child. Robert Lindner's *Rebel Without a Cause* was such a case, though a less seriously damaged one (13). It is significant that Lindner states in the first two pages of his book that psychopathic behavior is relative to, or stems from, the culture in which it develops. His patient's illness is measurable only by the prevailing ethic or morality. He concludes that any prevailing psychopathology or any illness is relative to the culture in which it flourishes.

Not only do psychological and physiological processes integrate or interweave in the individual, but community pathology may reflect these precarious balances on a statistical level. Illnesses like certain forms of diabetes were prevalent, for whatever reasons, in Italian and Jewish populations. Alcoholism is relatively common among Irish, but rare among urban Chinese (14). Beyond this, there are community reactions to health programs in which conceptions of illness play a role. Dr. John Cassel reports the difficulties of promoting milk or egg consumption or restrictions of grazing lands among Zulus where cattle are important in ancestor worship and connected with ideas of proper conduct. Parallel difficulties were encountered among sheep-herding Navajos of the American Southwest because of attachments to a mobile existence and the importance of tangible property in sheep. In the same volume, published by the Russell Sage Foundation, Drs. John and Elaine Cumming reveal social attitudes and beliefs about mental illness in a Canadian town, where the community, no more rationally than Zulus or Navajos, solved the problem by segregating those ill in a class apart and refusing to think of such illness as a community problem. Lyle Saunders and Julian Samora consider the failure of a health association plan among 7,000 Spanish Americans of rural Colorado through neglect of local leadership practices and long established individualized or more intimate approaches to those ill (15).

More optimistically, we recall the tremendous success of Japanese American community hospitals in Relocation Centers where Japanese American physicians and hospital committees mobilized to serve medical needs of barracks towns of 10,000 or more people.

Here efficient organization developed almost spontaneously to insure health safeguards in a totally insecure population for whom other forms of security—economic, social and political—had virtually disappeared. In addition to effective hospital organization, the drive towards health revived a parallel and additional "safeguard" in ancient and folk methods of healing along with various magical means of coping with disaster none of which prevailed later in the mainstream of American life (16).

There can be no doubt, then, that all peoples value health, though their conception as to what good health is or how to obtain it varies with ethnic groups, generation levels and social classes. Action programs, aimed at health improvement or illness prevention, must start with existing health practices and behavior noting the integration of these elements in the general cultural system, and the functions they perform for those who practice them. In this light, a knowledge of a community and its people is as indispensable in health programs as a knowledge of the epidemiology of the area and the appropriate medical techniques.

In 1945, Dr. H. B. Richardson reported the results of a two-year study of the concept of the family as a unit of practice. The concerted efforts of general practitioner, psychiatrist, nursing and social work personnel, combined as a team, were assessed. The evidence was convincing that such an approach led to better diagnosis and treatment, less pressure on existing clinical facilities and faster progress towards medically sound solutions. Unfortunately, such teams are complicated in structure and most readily available, if at all, in institutional settings. Even so, education of such teams for community operation requires an understanding of cultural backgrounds in a community. Earlier, in 1940, Dr. Leona Baumgartner suggested that an understanding of the cultural backgrounds of various ethnic groups provided an implementation of more effective health programs (17).

Ethnic Variations in Concepts of Health and Illness: A Case Study

Lyle Saunders has illustrated the importance of providing medical advice in a way that is certainly acceptable to the community for which it is intended (18). The same is true of therapeutic efforts with individuals and families. In one Italian case involving urinary disturbance in a small girl, the public health nurse reported the mother's refusal to have the child referred to a hospital clinic in the neighborhood from a child health station similarly located. After months of regretting she had divulged the matter to anyone, the mother reluctantly took the child to a neighborhood physician. Despite her devotion to the child, she could not bring herself to reveal the difficulty and seemed relieved when the child was pronounced, quite correctly, in fairly good health. During this period, she avoided the health station and refused to admit even the nurse in whom she had confided on routine call at her home. Instead she prayed for strength "to give" the little girl.

Many cultural beliefs are indicated here and we shall refer to them again in respect to a case of greater psychodynamic significance. Here the mother, a South Italian, first generation woman of rural origin merely translated cultural attitudes directly into action. For one thing, South Italians of this generation frequently have an almost reverent attitude towards anything relating in their conception to the reproductive system. This concern and respect applies equally to females as to males, but girls are especially to be protected or shielded. As Phyllis Williams indicated, they are chaperoned by own siblings and by older female relatives in the nubile years, and protected by male relatives at all times previous to marriage. When young, like the child in the illustration, they are safeguarded by mothers (19).

In addition, later matchmaking for marriages must scrutinize such matters as venereal infection, mental illness and tuberculosis, each being in the most literal sense a shameful and feared blot on family reputation. In this case, it was later learned, the mother feared her own scant and irregular menstrual periods were possibly linked with some unknown mishap under the heading of venereal infection. Or if nothing else, scant and irregular menses mean low fertility and impaired femininity in this culture, something which again it is believed may be imparted to a daughter. In some areas of South Italy, feminine boasting or shame will be exactly on such bases, and women with scant flow would wash their napkins with those better favored to increase fertility. Theodora Abel and N. F. Joffe have reported the alacrity with which such information is imparted to the young at public feminine gatherings and included in the learning of sex role at puberty; or the insignia (red kerchief) sometimes worn by peasant women at such times (20). In the particular case of the small girl, we can well imagine the shame and worry of the mother, and no less the discomfort and guilt of the child.

In the case to be outlined below, menstrual difficulties appear and disappear, but a more sustained problem relates to food intake. In regard to food, South Italians have elaborate folklore. Earl L. Koos, working with the Committee on Food Habits investigating nutrition in sociocultural groups, noted the Irish, even over generations, favored the pork-pattern or beefsteak with potato and cabbage. The Czechs adhered to a heavy meat and potato dumpling combination, and Italians to a *pasta* with red vegetables or meatsauce diet. Italo-Americans state that one of the worst aspects of a hospital stay is the paucity of Italian foods. In southern rural sections of Italy or Sicily, the producing and rearing of strong children is a matter of great importance. Red vegetables "make blood." Bread or *pasta* are natural grain foods. Fresh vegetables rather than canned ones maintain health and vigor essential for both men and women. Among the Japanese who prize vigor and potency, especially for males, there is the desirability of having pickled *daikon* (a phallic-shaped root vegetable) accompany practically every meal, both for taste and for the psychosexual reason of promoting male potency. Italians of both sexes prize proper food for similar reasons, whereas rural Puerto Ricans would merely see a reflection on the husband's potency if his wife failed to have children. Each of these geographically separated cultures tend to favor male virtues and values since the son, tilling and planting in his turn, carries on the family name and fortune. But of all three, the Italian most emphasizes relationships between food, girth and fertility, and apply these measures of sexuality equally to men and to women.

Again, while one is struck by the restraint, sobriety and dignity of many if not all Japanese social occasions, both social life and emotional expression among South Italians are pitched at a high intensity. In South Italy, social life centers in small towns that serve as the meeting ground of the surrounding locale. Robert Lowie, in his *Social Organization,* remarks on the *campanilismo* or community feeling which unites the persons within earshot of the common church bells. We can all remember *A Bell for Adano,* but few sense the importance of a central piazza flanked by this church, by a school or monastery, sometimes by an opera house, and always containing the village fountain. The scarcity of water alone would make this a pleasant place for general gatherings, but in addition no door is closed except at meal times and children rise and retire with their elders. Social life, combining young and old alike, is carried on out of doors to a considerable extent, promoting an air of intimacy and frank expression "from the heart" that few other peoples possess in similar degree.

In addition, strong ties in a padrone system or even stronger ones of family intermarriages unite people of the same locale or *paesani*. These local ingroup ties, resulting in dialect differences for the larger districts, often persisted in the street settlement patterns, by district, long after the inhabitants had migrated to this country. While second-generation districts, such as we have studied in New York, do not adhere to Williams' picture of a street for a former district, the pattern varies to one of relatives, often mothers and daughters living contiguously. The sense of intimacy, the direct expression of emotions, the high marital rates, and the wide affective extent of the family characterize the Italian individual. The family, including unmarried sons and daughters and sometimes even collateral relatives is more in evidence than the narrower family of parents and children found among Irish, English or Scottish descendants.

While in Irish families a mother or grandmother is usually the central authority in matters concerning the home and children, the Italian family recognizes the father as head or breadwinner, and the mother as the delegated, secondary authority. By the same token, the Italian mother is often closer to the children and their problems. In the first and sometimes in the second generation, the Italian mother manages the home scene on a budget provided by the husband and older unmarried sons. Women are expected to marry early. While this devotion to male needs and the production of large families have been modified in this country, there are still more male dominance and family-centered life than characterize Irish families.

In South Italy, as in Japan, parent-arranged marriages usually with the good offices of go-betweens minimized inter-family friction and embarrassment. In Italy, the prospective couple met at Sunday family conclaves and dinners, or the young man, if more impetuous, conversed through the doorway with the whole protective armament of the girl's family in solemn array. In the United States, where family honor is less a topic of local gossip, these customs wear away; but courtships and marriages are still a matter of lively family concern. While also, persons of second and third generation do not arrange home births with midwives and with 40 day house confinements as in the first generation, the women's interest in prenatal care, large babies and dietary safeguards is often promoted by a parental or grandparental generation. For the latter, heavy people are vigorous and good-natured; large babies are desired; and thin people are often ill-tempered. Elderly females of this type were only thought to be in all likelihood "witches" with the "evil eye." *Pasta,* oil and blood-making vegetables in prenatal diet link with these beliefs. To strike a compromise in inter-generation conflicts on this point, higher protein *pasta* are now manufactured commercially.

As we have seen in the opening case of this section, the birth of a malformed or stillborn child is not only a family tragedy, but it is also a sign of physical and sexual weakness and a parental disgrace. Besides large babies, which Japanese or Irish consider no great gain and perhaps even a maternal hazard, male children are preferred, a matter which is left up to personal preferences among Irish. In addition, Italians or Puerto Ricans allow a double standard to prevail in premarital or postmarital sexual conduct, enjoining chastity and submissiveness upon the subordinate distaff side while at the same time stressing male escapades and sexual impulsiveness. The Italian girl at first menses immediately assumes women's dress and household occupations. With Irish, the event frequently went unnoticed, even among women of the family, and only sacramental events like confirmation, the Eucharist, or matrimony mark social steps in maturation. Because of high rates of male and female celibacy in Irish, only a birth of a child, and its baptism, clearly denote the true assumption of the status of matron. In the mother-centered Irish home, this is a status position of enhanced authority and control. Thus, South Italians may be influenced by many folk beliefs connected with menstruation, prenatal diet, size of family and the presence or absence of male children, whereas Irish have virtually none. Not only are Italian babies swathed or bundled, but since women are thought to be vulnerable in birth or menstruation, they must be bundled to prevent a chill at such times, much as men wore a "cholera belt" or abdominal covering in colder seasons. Finally, since menstrual blood is antithetical to infants in Italian folk belief, even causing mares to abort or curing skin growths, the help of female relatives, or godmothers, is needed at such times.

Equally, studies of pain-threshold differences have stressed the low tolerance standards of Italians for whom bodily functions are so important or body image so clear that stoical equanimity is out of question. Postoperative recovery rooms, particularly where older Italian female patients are involved are frequently scenes of voluble acting out. Obstetricians have repeatedly contrasted the variance between the young Japanese-American mother who views birth almost as a battle where pain cannot be conceded and the Italo-American girl who may be somewhat more relaxed about the whole process, or more openly exultant about feminine functions, but for whom women have no part of "male fortitude" where pain may be involved.

While therefore pain, or even hypochondriachal ailments are easily ventilated by Italians, Irish will often pride themselves on taking little notice of bodily functions. Persons who do so are peevish, morose or ill-tempered. The family scene is often the last place for the ventilation of bodily concerns or over-concern. While the Irish death-wake is a community rather than a family function, the help bestowed upon a prostrate Italian family which has suffered a death (and known as *il consolo*) more usually illustrates the solidarity of the extended family group and local blood ties, as do the reciprocal gift or money donations to a family in need, known as *la pieta*.

We have outlined just enough of South Italian and Irish cultural differences to indicate variations in family size and affective extent, in sex role, in concepts of health and illness, and in certain additional details of behavior. It is helpful to turn finally to the outline of a case which dramatizes, in a married couple, significant aspects of illness better understood through a knowledge of these cultural background conditions. The case is given in bare outline to preserve anonymity.

Synopsis of the case indicates a young, second generation Italian woman suffered from menstrual difficulties, hypoglycemia and obesity, migraines and metabolic upsets, all restricted to certain life periods in which particular life crises occurred. Each difficulty had its transient hysteriform character. Her Irish husband's difficulties were somatized only in acute ulcer conditions, of which the type will not be indicated in any revealing detail. Suffice it to say that his illness improved as hers worsened, and that the contrary was also the case.

It is not necessary to indicate the number of children of this marriage, except to state that at the wife's insistence the family was a large one. Her own parents were of South Italian extraction and her own family of origin contained only one female sibling. At the time of study, she was in treatment for both hysterical and hypoglycemic conditions, exacerbated by the pattern of obesity and one of night eating. As we shall see, her own ailments and her husband's represented in the main a microcosm of the clash of two cultural backgrounds, or better the stress systems of the two backgrounds exemplified in each case. Therefore, in the clash of personalities and in the balance of their difficulties, neither could improve singly without a worsening of the condition in the partner.

Just as menstruation was a focal point of her difficulties, so the birth of each child was a tempestuous event, followed in one instance by illness. The children's birth weights were uniformly excessive. Concern about their weight and subsequent health led in each case to excessive weight gains in the mother, each gain to be retained and added to during the next pregnancy. As a young girl, even in post-adolescence, she describes herself as slim and pretty, as her mother had been. Following the last birth, and her husband's mounting disinterest in the children, her feminine assertiveness was signalized by profuse, extended and painful menstruation brought to his attention as an instance of her self-sacrificing motherhood. When this symptom failed to stir sympathy, it disappeared as dramatically as it had occurred.

The patient gave a history of having always rebelled, as some second-generation Italian girls do, against the authoritarian nature of her father's household. Yet there were no overtones. Feelings towards the father were extremely ambivalent. He was not only authoritarian; he was decisive, assertive and distinctly attractive. These characteristics, all good ones by Italian norms, had been freely exhibited in the home scene, in at least two occupational successes, and in other sudden impulsive decisions which proved successful. Her father's equally unguarded rejection of her in favor of a sister first unleashed hysterical tendencies. When the sister displaced her as to a certain occupational preference, or was overly protective in the chaperoning duenna role, the patient fulfilled all the cultural expectations concerning the solidarity of sisters, was self-effacing about the occupational aspirations and developed emotional tension symptoms. For the first time, night feeding patterns were used as an oral substitution for withheld affection. That self-esteem had suffered was indicated by other evidences of habit deterioration in dress and grooming. Headaches occurred in periods of tension.

Courtship, even without the family's usual interested participation in this culture, was an asymptomatic period. Marriage was viewed as a triumphal moment. Pregnancies were desired, but

with each and the home conflicts engendered in her own household, migraines recurred. During pregnancies, nausea and the old
tensions could only be checked by excessive night feedings. On the
other hand, the husband's ulcers became worse when her headaches subsided. When her migraines and night feeding patterns
were worse, his ulcers were better.

Her drive towards marital status, the sanctioned adult status
in this culture, was a more aggressive and self-conscious attempt
than is true of most Italo-American girls. In addition to the
normative desire to marry, she parried paternal rejection by
determining to avoid getting a husband of Italian antecedents.
Her position, a stereotyping one, was that their authoritarianism
and selfishness were to be avoided. (We are reminded, parenthetically, that Chinese girls in Hawaii rarely marry into Japanese
households, and give both male authoritarianism and mother-in-
law domination as the reasons for this avoidance; Romanzo Adams
and others have indicated that attractions occurring between these
two large population groups are served by Japanese girls marry-
ing in far greater numbers into the less authoritarian Chinese
households where the authority is diffused or dissipated in a
wider circle of kin.) In this case, the attraction to a second generation Irish male was in large part because of his avowed opposition
to "any authoritarianism," including opposition to his own father
as well. The husband, however, had been raised to value neatness,
perfectionism and rationality at all costs. As the spouse later discovered, he was no little dominated by an Irish mother, the more
typical authoritarian pattern of the Irish household, against which
he no doubt internally rebelled. Marital conflicts led to his periodically seeking refuge in his parental home, especially when the
conflicts were bared by verbal argument.

In addition, the female patient alleged a difference between
them in degree of sexual interest and attention. Rather than analyze
this as being, in part, a cultural difference, which in this setting
required the seeking of joint psychiatric help, the Italian tendency
was to emotionalize the situation further, dramatize it in operatic
fashion, and develop "blank spells" of a hysteriform nature. In
such periods of excitation, both basal metabolism and oral intake
took sharp upswings. The husband's rationalizing reactions to
these periods of her disorder were along the line that he could
not cope with the difficulty and was free of responsibility. During
such periods his ulcer problem was quiescent. When medical
attention resulted in some gain in her facing her problem and a

loss in weight occurred, she renewed her demands for her husband's supportive sympathy and affection. His condition promptly worsened, requiring hospitalization. Again with his convalescence, her cycle began with food substitutions for inadequate affection. The greater her spontaneity and frankness, traits congenial to Italian character and temperament, the more his discomfort grew with internal bleeding as a consequence.

Of special interest in the female patient are low frustration tolerance thresholds, vivid dramatizations of her difficulties and high impulsiveness. For her to convert sex drives to feeding patterns, or to find other ready "solutions" not reported here constitute the kinds of impulsiveness and action patterns for emotional expression which are poles apart from rationalizing, perfectionistic, planful fantasy behavior more characteristic in the Irish system of defenses. Her rebellion against parental disapproval, rejection and thwarting surveillance dated back to her teens, but did not include open warfare with a sibling in the tightly organized Italian family, or assertive modes of behavior more suited to Italian males.

Her husband's attachment to his mother, and the tendency for his ulcer to bleed when he faced the realistic picture of growing family responsibility is the opposite of this picture. The lack of a stable anchor image like her father, or of impulse control mechanisms, leads to literal incorporation techniques to prevent an alleged loss of love. Meanwhile, the husband's unsuccessful attempts to make her over in a maternal image as indicated in his preference in dress and hair style are thinly veiled fantasy. Her impulses in the balance of these interpersonal transactions are periodic, negatively hostile and self-destructive. His critical and perfectionistic drives are deeply marked by inner rebellion. One is reminded, in the fantasies about independence, in the facile verbosity, in the critical attitudes and planfulness of the Irish patient that these same qualities, in a different personal setting, mark the genius of a George Bernard Shaw or James Joyce. But instead, in this man one finds, at bottom, empty dependence, rationalization and anger covering and no doubt underlying the helpless somatizations of anger. Neither tensions nor aggression— his with ulcer attacks or hers in fluctuating hysteriform illnesses represent the respective cultures in the sense of stereotype or epitomization, but both point to cultural stress systems, once the cultural system and its pitfalls are laid bare. In each case, illness is not wholly personal or exclusively cultural, but is both at the same time.

These are but two cases of the effects of culture on behavior and on health. Both, unfortunately, represent complex problems. The solutions are not wholly within the province of internal medicine, psychiatry, or social science, but require insights and knowledge from each contributing discipline. They illustrate effects of a massive system, called culture for convenience, upon the sensitive and reactive system of human personality. The latter is obviously an open system, interdependently organized with both psychological and physiological components existing in some type of balance or integration. Such complex organization of cultural, psychological and physiological elements is present in every one of us, and the requirement in health practice is to analyze adequately each component.

NOTES

1. Erwin H. Ackerknecht, *A Short History of Medicine* (New York: Ronald Press, 1955).

2. Walter Riese, *The Conception of Disease* (New York: Philosophical Library, 1953).

3. Iago Galdston (Ed.), *Beyond the Germ Theory* (New York Academy of Medicine: Health Education Council, 1954).

4. J. H. Steward, "Cultural Evolution", *Scientific American:* 194:69-80, 1956.

5. M. K. Opler, "Anthropology:" In P. L. Harriman, J. S. Roucek (Eds.), *Contemporary Social Science* (Harrisburg, Pa.: Stackpole, 1953).

6. M. K. Opler, *Culture, Psychiatry and Human Values* (Springfield, Ill.: C. C. Thomas, 1956).

7. Talcott Parsons, *The Social System* (Glencoe, Ill.: Free Press, 1951).

8. J. L. Halliday, *Psychosocial Medicine* (New York: Norton, 1948).

9. M. K. Opler, *Culture, Psychiatry and Human Values, op. cit.*

10. C. S. Coon, S. M. Garn and J. B. Birdsell, *Races* (Springfield: C. C. Thomas, 1950).

11. A. F. Hess, *Scurvy Past and Present* (Philadelphia: J. B. Lippincott Co., 1920.

12. W. B. Cannon, "Voodoo Death," *American Anthropologist:* 44: 169-81, 1942.

13. R. Lindner, *Rebel Without a Cause* (New York: Grune and Stratton, 1944).

14. Oskar Diethelm, *The Etiology of Chronic Alcoholism* (Springfield: C. C. Thomas, 1955). See study of New York Chinese by M. L. Barnett.

15. B. D. Paul (Ed), *Health, Culture and Community* (New York: Russell Sage Foundation, 1955).

16. E. R. Spicer, M. K. Opler, *et al, Impounded People* (Washington, D. C.: Government Printing Office, 1946). Compare, M. K. Opler, "Japanese Folk Beliefs and Practices," *Journal of American Folklore*, 385-397, 1950.

17. H. B. Richardson, *Patients Have Families* (New York: Commonwealth Fund, 1945).

18. Lyle Saunders, *Cultural Difference and Medical Care* (New York: Russell Sage Foundation, 1954).

19. Phyllis H. Williams, *South Italian Folkways in Europe and America* (New Haven: Yale University Press, 1938). Much of these data of Williams may be compared with recent fieldwork in New York City. Barring regional variation and generation changes, the comparisons were favorable

20. Theodora Abel and N. F. Joffe, "Cultural Backgrounds of Female Puberty," *American Journal of Psychotherapy:* 4: 90-113, 1950.

GUY E. SWANSON

The Routinization of Love: Structure and Process in Primary Relations

Whenever we search for the roots of human fulfillment or courage or creativity, we soon confront the fact of love. To be sure, the word itself appears but rarely in scientific reports; but those reports are filled with terms which catch some aspect, phase, or variety of love. We are told, for example, that the parents of psychiatrically healthy children are "nurturant" or "permissive" or "supportive" and make only "reasonable" demands of youngsters (136). Soldiers "integrated into" or "solidary with" their officers, units, or comrades display higher morale in battle (132). "Cooperation" sometimes enhances productivity (41, 78, 96). Intellectually creative adults are "secure" in their relations with others and "dedicated" to the realization of long-range objectives (103, 104). Men who withstand the rigors of imprisonment in concentration camps have a comparable dedication (20, 21) as do families which thrive despite an abrupt loss of income (4, 29, 87).

These discoveries concern only some bits and facets of love. Observations which capture more of its features relate with even greater precision to particular variations in behavior and experience. To illustrate, it has been shown that parental supportiveness is associated with the mental health of children only when the support is dependable and is directed toward promoting the child's growing independence (79). This reveals something that most people understand; that overprotection is not love, and altruism without justice may signify masochism or dominance rather than mature concern and respect.

Three contemporary efforts have inspired most scientific investigations which touch on aspects of love. Each concerns a failure, or a possible failure, of self-control under stressful conditions. The first is the effort to prevent and treat those mental disorders believed to be acquired through learning. The second is the attempt to mitigate loneliness and anxiety produced by the size, impersonality, and rapid social changes of urban societies. The third is the task of preparing soldiers and civilians against the strains of international tensions, the terror of nuclear attack, and possible "brainwashing" by an enemy's forces. Recent summaries of our knowledge concerning the first and second of these problems, and, in considerable measure, the third as well (3, 5, 7, 21, 28, 56, 69, 88, 98, 121, 136), record a large number of small but reliable associations between men's responses under stress and some feature of love or its absence to which they have been exposed. These summaries encourage the judgment that research guided by an even more comprehensive view of love's character, development and dynamics would possess a still greater power for explanation and might resolve many contradictions in present findings. My present objective is to move toward a statement of that larger view as a necessary preliminary to more effective research.

Why is it that love, loving, and being loved help us explain so much of importance in human conduct? If love enhances a man's satisfaction, personal force and social responsibility and underlies the flowering of his capacities, what are its sources and how can it be encouraged? Can one routinize the presence and potency of so subtle a relationship as love? Are the tensions and problems which often accompany love inherently uncontrollable or can they, like love's presence, be directed and modified? We must say what love means before these questions can be understood or answered.

The Meaning of Love

The objects of love are many. The occasions for love are various. The means by which love is shown are great in number.

But, within these variations, there is a common theme, an essential meaning (21, 39, 65, 67, 85, 94, 103, 104, 141, 142). At least within societies of the modern West there is general agreement about the meaning of love, and people commonly feel they can identify the genuine article from the counterfeit.

In common usage, love stands for that relationship in which people are committed knowingly, willingly, freely and responsibly to enhance the lives and growth of others in whatever ways they can. Loving is behavior which implements these commitments. If any one of the ingredients in this definition is found missing, the genuineness of the love is suspect. Thus if a person initiates this sort of association but is not committed to it, he is condemned as arousing false expectations, as "trifling with" the other's life, as being insincere and, if only by implication, committing a breach of promise (17). Again, if love is genuine it involves a somewhat conscious choice. People try to learn whether persons seeming to extend love do so knowingly, or whether they will withdraw from the relationship when they see its implications. Further, enhancement is not to be called love if it is extended unwillingly or if the enhancer's will is not free—is coerced by forces and interests he does not consider consistent with his personal desires (27, 33, 75). In addition, as Fromm (67) says, attempts at enhancement unrestrained by responsibility, by efforts to do only that for which one is competent, contain great hazards (60). They can easily become negligent, inconsiderate or thoughtless.

Genuine love is also defined as a diffuse relationship. The individual does not elect to perform one or more particular acts, but to assist, by whatever means he can, in bringing about a certain state of affairs. His commitment is fulfilled only when that state is achieved. For some commitments, such as those to promote the welfare of one's family or friends or country, no final achievement is possible.

Genuine love does not require that people be committed to enhance all aspects of each others' lives. It does require that they stand ready to do what they can with respect to those aspects of the other's concerns for which they accept responsibility. This may, for example, be the nurturance by colleagues of each other's professional growth, or the teacher's devotion to his student as student, or the support any men give each other as fellow citizens or as co-workers or as comrades in a common enterprise.

Finally, in authentic love, this generalized commitment is guided by the concern to nourish the powers, independence, and integration of the other—to promote not just that which is presently in his interest but to assist a partner in developing interests that he will find of even greater worth (59). Ideal friends wish not only that one will be what one is, but that one will become the more enriched person that one is capable of being.

The notion that partners in love must be equals has its great relevance at this point. As many successful marriages and friendships demonstrate, the participants may be quite unequal in the nature or absolute amount of their contributions to one another (76, 155). There is, however, one respect in which equality is required for the success of their relationship as love. They must be similar in the *proportion* of their requirements which are satisfied through this relationship. One of them may get far more than the other if enhancement is measured in absolute amount, but they must be equal in the *importance* for each of whatever he receives. This equivalence of *relative* reward and cost is the ultimate guarantee that each will take the relationship with equal seriousness and insures that each will respect the independence and integrity of his partners (82).

The problem of distinguishing genuine love from its counterfeits is especially difficult because some of love's several ingredients can be present without the others, and because the mixture of those which are available at a particular time is subject to great and unanticipated modifications. Farber (55) documents the independence among three of love's facets in a study of the relations of 495 husbands with their wives. He measured the extent to which each man: (*1*) sought to enhance his wife's experience (*e.g.,* was cooperative and supportive toward her), (*2*) took account of her needs and potentialities (*e.g.,* correctly interpreted her attitudes, intentions, and behavior), and (*3*) contributed responsibility to their relations with each other (*e.g.,* was resourceful in devising new and effective solutions to problematic interpersonal situations; was skillful in handling interpersonal tensions where self-esteem was threatened or challenged). There is no relationship between a man's rating on any of these measures and his scores on the others.

The difficulties of evaluating professed love are furthed increased by the subtlety of the judgments required. Reasonable accuracy in these matters reflects extensive training and high skill. By some means, much of the population acquires facility in making such judgments.

The Relevance of Love

Why is love important for so many aspects of human life and experience? Having said what love means, one can answer this further question. We must consider love's significance for the lover as well as for one who is loved.

Love's most obvious importance is for the person who receives it. It nurtures to a degree and in a fashion unique in human experience. This unusual nurturance flows from love's properties as perhaps the most elaborated instance of social interaction. By calling it "the most elaborated instance," I mean that, in love, one finds employed in consummate measure the ingredients and processes which characterize all instances of social interaction [Interestingly, the more exquisite forms of sadism seem to be among love's closer competitors for this distinction (15, 21, 58, pp. 354-358, 67, pp. 18-20 and 30-31, 69, pp. 12-48, 72, chapters 3, 4, 7, 8, and 9).]

Men can relate to each other in several ways. They can interact, for example, as do physical bodies, exerting blind force on one another. Social interaction refers to situations in which people take into account each other's knowledge, intentions, preferences, hopes, beliefs and the like. It refers, in short, to men relating to each other's minds. Social interaction can occur if people learn that they depend on one another, if they come to appreciate the essential requirements for their continued association, if they have some experiences in common which they can share, if they possess standardized symbols to serve as a medium for the expressing and sharing of experience in a form that will be understood, if they have become aware of the existence and importance of their own and each other's mental life and the conditions under which it can be influenced. These are the understandings and skills in which parents first train their children and easy competence in their use—competence employed despite great obstacles and in a wide variety of situations—is customarily taken as the mark of an individual's maturity (90). A life-time of exploration and experience seems not to exhaust the potentiality for further significant growth in such competence.

The special nurturance which love provides is its support for the individual's mental life. Loving means close attention by others to an individual's problems and potentialities. It means efforts to enhance his behavior and his powers for behaving.

Loving is thus directed toward discerning and influencing his mental life as, for example, the wisdom with which he formulates objectives, the appropriateness of his choices from among alternatives, the security with which he can venture and take risks, the effectiveness of his efforts to make restitution for errors and to find and accept forgiveness, the justness with which he evaluates failures, and the gaiety or contentment with which he celebrates a success. A loving relationship provides not just particular deeds that lead to such benefits, but whatever acts will have these results. So generalized or diffuse a commitment, requires that the person who offers love relate not merely to another's immediate behavior, but to his long-term purposes and potentialities and to changes that will occur in them. Within this generalized relationship more specialized forms of interaction can grow as the occasion may demand. They will be particular applications of love to given situations, but love is their general form and their source. In return, a loving relationship costs the loved individual the commitment to employ these resources for the maintenance and development of himself as a person—as a minded individual who interacts with the minds of others. Because love, or an association bordering on it, so often provides the infant's first social experience and because it affords general principles to be employed in developing more specialized forms of social interaction, Cooley spoke of love as the socially "primary" relation and of the groups most distinguished by it as "primary groups" (13, 25, 36, 37, 57, 119, 124).

Thinking only of receiving love, men commonly make this relationship the foundation for their pictures of utopia. But the cost of being loved can be substantial. Stagnation may prove easier than growth, wisdom may appear less desirable than immediate action, and forgiveness may prove harder to bear than the absence of love. A man may prefer to receive fear or blind admiration from others because these require no changes in him. Love, as psychotherapists and theologians insist, is work for him who receives it as well as he who provides it. Willingness to perform such work is founded on a sense of its necessity.

Although it is sensible to speak of the members of a formally organized group as loving each other, such love will not be as diffuse as that possible between particular individuals (1). This is so because the leaders or members of such a group define their responsibilities toward each other in terms of the joint enterprise in which they are engaged, not toward all enterprises in which any of them may engage as individuals. Love between individuals, interpersonal love, has the possibility of this widest of references. This may be why many writers treat it as the standard for all expressions of love.

Greater scope is not the only benefit which interpersonal love may provide. Because it can be directed to all of an individual's interests, it is of unusual importance in assisting his personal integration. Each individual is at once a particular organism, the bearer of a distinctive history from previous experiences, and the center of a unique set of present conditions. In most of his relations with other people he is expected to employ some of his skills and tastes and inhibit others. What he is obliged to do or to forego varies from one group to another and often is the subject of conflicting instructions. But the individual as a sentient being is not divisible. Organism, mind, and relations with others, even with diverse or conflicting others, are co-essential in his existence. His ability to achieve fulfillment as a single, total being requires that all his several aspects with their differing, competing requirements become organized.

The love of another person can nurture him as a distinctive individual. It can, for example, help him interpret the application of general social rules to his particular situation, needs, and deeds. This is possible not only because interpersonal love can relate to the whole of a given individual's situation, but because love is, as we have seen, the most elaborated form of the principles general to social interaction itself. The more general the principles, the greater is the range of special situations to which they may be applied and for which they may supply guidance. The most generalized principles of a fully developed social relationship are thus the ground for the integration of particular individuals with themselves and with the social order. To be fulfilled most completely as a distinctive individual in all one's particularity one must enter into the most profoundly social of relationships.

We have found that love's special importance for the person who receives it is its nurture of some large range of his interests as a minded individual, that this is perhaps true in greatest degree of interpersonal love, and that some people consider the costs of receiving love to outweigh its benefits. But what of the person who gives love? What is its importance for him? If one views man as living only for rewards, then getting love is the chief thing. It is in studies that treat man as being most fulfilled when expanding or exercising his powers that we obtain a picture of love's significance for the lover (2, 67).

Loving, say these accounts, is the expression of the highest social skill. It is the sign of real maturity, full membership in humanity. It employs most completely those talents which seem to distinguish men from all other animals and in which they most resemble God.

Loving, these writers say, deals with difficult and challenging problems forever leading men to new, stimulating experiences. For a mature person, loving is the embodiment of his essential self and he delights in both the exercise of his potency and the evidence for it. To live is to act. To act as other than what one is is frustrating. Therefore, the argument goes, mature people get their greatest fulfillment in loving. As Fromm (67) writes, the theme of maturity is "I need you because I love you," not "I love you because I need you."

To be sure, gains from auto-fulfillment are not the only importance love is said to have for lovers. He who loves is often applauded by others and this may be sufficient reward. Loving another is often the requisite for obtaining another's love, and, if so, he who wants to be loved must first love others. Finally, one may love another to end an intolerable separation or estrangement, not so much because one wants the other's love but because one wants to be with him or at peace with him and there is no relationship short of love that will bridge the gap.

However important love may be in human affairs, it certainly is not enough for man's survival or accomplishment. Health, rationality, self-government, competence in modifying the environment to serve human needs, skill in framing symbols to represent, objectify, and bring order into experience—these capacities and abilities and many others are among the essentials (60, 85). Most of them are required for love to arise and many seem to require love in order to increase their fruition.

The Routinization of Love

If, as now, love itself is our concern, we shall find several guides to relevant literature. Materials concerning the rearing of children have been collated and appraised (7, 28) as have modern investigations of such matters as interpersonal sensitivity (137), self control and social responsibility (56, 121, 136), loyalty and devotion to political systems (80, 88, 98), and the psychological characteristics of friends (47). To contribute to the synthesis of our knowledge, I shall focus primarily, though not exclusively, on problems of establishing, developing, and maintaining love in certain groups of intermediate size most of which have adults as their principal clientele. Thus, many observations I report are taken from studies of cloistered religious bodies, collective settlements, primitive societies, fraternal organizations, small groups of workers, professional organizations, therapeutic milieux, and gangs.

There are several reasons for this emphasis. I wanted, above all, to bring together observations relevant for research concerning the social organization of love—the development, routinization, and management of this consummate form of social interaction. I sought to find in patterns of social organization some sources of love and of its stability and natural history. The structure of this social organization tends to be more visible in settings somewhat larger than friendships or nuclear families because the requirement of coordinating a large number of people forces on participants a considerable degree of awareness concerning the objective they seek and the means appropriate to it. What might be a spontaneous and fleeting adjustment between friends often becomes a matter of policy and doctrine in larger groups, and, consequently, becomes apparent to an observer. (Curiously, there is only a sparse literature which considers the social organization of love in marriages or families.)

To further enlarge the chance of finding relevant material, I chose, second, to focus on relationships in which love was a salient concern. I sought, third, to study settings in which interpersonal love of wide scope might appear together with more impersonal social relations—this to increase the range of considerations under investigation. Finally, I omitted some important manifestations of love (patriotism, for example) because relatively little is known about them.

ESTABLISHMENT

Where will loving appear? How do its scope and form get established? By what means is its genuineness determined? The very definition of love suggests a part of the answers to these questions.

¶ THE OCCURRENCE OF LOVE: It seems plausible to think that loving is likely to occur when people find that they are similar in their relative need for one another to be what each potentially is, providing that this need is satisfied not by a few readily specified acts to be performed at certain times but by the performance of whatever acts may be appropriate to meet changing conditions. To forecast the occurence of love we should know the degree to which all these conditions are met.

a. DIFFUSE DEPENDENCY: Adequate evidence is lacking on all these matters, but a considerable body of observations supports the notion that a diffuse dependency is one requisite for love. Thus both Sarma (120) and Eisenstadt (51, 52) conclude independently and from cross-cultural studies that one type of highly personalized attachment, friendship, appears in the more complex societies. Both interpret the rise of friendship as signifying a relation which helps particular individuals in complex societies to thread their way among the many groups and institutions which make demands on their allegiance and which, often, set conflicting requirements for their behavior. The problem each individual faces has multiple facets which change from time to time, requiring a comparable many-sided and adaptable relationship to mediate them.

Again, the informal groups of friends and co-workers that grow spontaneously within large organizations seem to flourish in situations where people depend on each other in many important ways that are difficult to govern or specify in advance and for which no formal rules are laid down. General norms are required to guide conduct in these circumstances. One, the norm of reciprocity, is discussed by Gouldner (74) who suggests that the two social rules which define this norm are universal: (1) people should help those who have helped them, and (2) people should not injure those who have helped them. A norm of reciprocity, he continues, is necessary to control the effects of differences in men's power. Because the principle of reciprocity is very general, it can be applied to countless *ad hoc* transactions not otherwise regulated by specific status obligations. The norm also reinforces specific obligations which may be present. In all cases, it provides a basis for confidence that one's friendly overtures toward another will be returned. The ubiquity and importance of such a norm is epitomized in one account of the fleeting relations between cab drivers and their customers:

Even in an urban and highly secularized society . . . , most service relationships, be they between a professional and his client or a menial

and his patron, are characterized by certain constraints on too crass
a rendering and consuming of the service . . . (40, p. 158).

It also seems that an increase of diffuse dependencies which
are, correspondingly, hard to supervise or control provides impetus
for the spread of the "human relations" approach in bureaucratic
organizations (46, 108, pp. 30-60 and 196-213). Managers in
those settings are told they must obtain the commitment of their
more skilled personnel to the organization's interests precisely
because such persons are essential to the organization's work yet
hard to supervise. If they are not on the employer's side, they
can damage his interests and he will know it only after the damage
has occurred. The stress on love (typically phrased as supervisory
relations governed by adaptability to individual needs and by a
spirit of collaborative consultation) is openly justified as required
to obtain and retain skilled personnel because the supply is short
and such other attractions as salary and hours are relatively equal
from one organization to another.

It is impossible to examine each familiar setting in which love
flourishes to see whether a diffuse dependency preceded the occurrence of devotion and affection, but a few additional illustrations may indicate the range of affairs over which such dependency
seems to be a precondition for love: the responsibility of professional men for their clients, the devotion of a family's members
for each other's concerns, the affectionate care of a citizen for
his country. Illustrations like these which suggest that love grows
where people are broadly dependent on each other also remind
one that such dependency is, at best, a necessary, not a sufficient,
requisite for love.

b. FACILITATIVE ROLE INTERDEPENDENCE: There have been
systematic studies of five conditions which, in addition to diffuse
dependency, might relate to the appearance of love. These are:
facilitative role interdependence, trust and trustworthiness, approachability, similarity of interpersonal characteristics, and the
willingness with which people engage in a relationship. These
certainly are not independent phenomena, but an approach through
each reveals distinctive preconditions for love. We begin with an
experiment by Thomas (140).

Working with a population of 160 young women, all employees
of a large private utility, Thomas established four types of experimental situation. In each type, his subjects were told that they
were to work in "groups" on a test of General Work Intelligence.

Half of the subjects were told that they would be scored on the basis of their work as individuals; the others on the grounds of their group's performance. In turn, half the subjects in each of these two populations were placed in a situation in which every person was responsible for all aspects of the task; half in a setting in which each person was responsible for only a particular part of the enterprise.

For our interests, as for Thomas', the significant experimental variation is that in which people are scored on the basis of their joint performance *and* the task is divided up among them; thus the group's score is dependent on their cooperation and coordination rather than simply the sum of their performances as individuals. He speaks of this variation as embodying facilitative role interdependence. Comparing persons in this situation with those in the three remaining variations, Thomas found greater feelings of personal responsibility for the success of the enterprise, greater willingness to help others do their work, and a stronger attraction to the group. There was, moreover, greater speed of progress in completing the task.

Of equal importance were some negative relationships. Under facilitative role interdependence, subjects also showed greater anger toward others in their group and displayed feelings of restlessness and of being "hemmed in." Thomas, in the manner of French (63) before him, interprets these results as inherent consequences of close cooperation. He argues that the close coordination of activities gives rise to greater opportunity for people's getting in each other's way even as they facilitate one another's efforts. These frustrations provoke anger. Similarly, the close articulation of efforts affords less room for individuals to do what they might wish, when and as they might like, giving rise to the experience of being confined.

c. TRUST AND TRUSTWORTHINESS: Thomas' work generates or evokes responsible and cooperative conduct by providing a task requiring coordinated efforts for the joint attainment of a desired objective. Deutsch and his collaborators (43, 44, 45, 100, 128) have sought to define a task and other conditions that lead persons to trust one another when there are dangers of exploitation or injury from collaboration. They assume that people will trust each other if they: 1) are committed to reach some goal and failure will cost more than they want to risk in an uncertain venture, 2) need each other's help and perceive one another as able to help, 3) perceive one another as similarly dependent, and 4) are each aware that this is their joint situation. Loomis (128) found that the greater the extent to which these several conditions were present, the greater was the likelihood that pairs of experimental subjects would trust each other in a situation involving risk and that the recipient of trust would prove trustworthy. In a second experimental manipulation, Deutsch showed that individuals are more likely to trust one another if they believe the other person has nothing to gain from untrustworthy behavior and if they perceive themselves as able to exert some control over the other person's outcomes.

Deutsch (43) also sought to learn whether certain orientations of his subjects were associated with trustfulness and trustworthiness. He reports that persons rated low on the California F Scale, indicating little tendency to be domineering or submissive, tend also to be trustful. Subjects who are themselves trustful are also more likely to be worthy of trust. Of particular interest is the finding that subjects whom the experimenter assigned a role of being trustful, prove trustworthy as well. This may indicate the presence of some fundamental behavioral or social incompatability between assuming one of these orientations and not the other.

Where time and opportunities do not permit assessments of a situation and dangers from collaboration are likely, trust may nonetheless be required for work to proceed. Cohen (35) suggests that certain ritual gestures come into existence to provide rough and ready tests of trustworthiness under these conditions. The hand salute of modern armies may, he says, have appeared to indicate that the soldier approaching an officer was not concealing a knife in his palm. Knights approaching another horseman indicated trust by opening their visors and thus weakening their defenses. Cohen interprets the rituals of the manual of arms as an especially vivid and subtle test of trustworthiness. Believing that inter-status hostilities between officers and men are likely to be strong and concealed in modern military organizations, he views the rule requiring whole-hearted deference of a man toward the officer who inspects his weapon as an institutionalized denial of aggressive intent. He thinks it significant that when troops are in contact with an enemy and, presumably, their hostility is vented on the foe, officers dispense with these and related rituals. Cohen finds similar patterns in the stylized etiquette of inter-racial contacts in the American South.

d. APPROACHABILITY: There is evidence that people who want

and seek intimate relations with others tend to have them (73, 93, 153). They approach others and are approachable.

In this connection, Blau (24) has made an interesting proposal. He suggests that, "the more attractive a person's impressive qualities make him appear to the others in a group, the more reluctant will they be, at least initially, to approach him freely and to draw him into friendly social intercourse." He believes that several considerations support this position: (1) the attractive person may hurt us by rejecting our overtures; (2) his very attractiveness threatens the relative popularity of all others in the group; (3) an approach to such a person may make him still more attractive in his own eyes and those of others, thus further increasing the first two dangers. If, however, the attractive person makes himself approachable by volunteering information about personal weaknesses, or if by referring to similarities between his background and experience and those of other members, he indicates that he seeks standing as a peer, not a superior, he can be integrated into the group. As Blau summarizes:

If group members are classified on the basis of two attributes, common sense would lead us to expect that those with two positive qualities have the greatest chance of being accepted by their peers, and those with two negative qualities, the least chance. In contrast, the theory implies that the members who are positive on the more salient attribute (and hence attractive) and negative on the less salient one (and hence also approachable) are the most likely to win the acceptance of their peers. And the members who are negative on the more salient but positive on the less salient attribute are expected to be least likely to be integrated.

Blau himself was able to present only fragmentary data providing an indirect test of his proposal. Although the findings are in the direction expected, more cases, better indices, and greater control of other variables would be required to conclude that Blau's proposition had been given a fair evaluation.

In a study by Gross (77) we do, however, have data important for a simpler proposition concerning approachability.

Gross puts the matter this way:

. . . every cohesive group strikes a bargain with its members: It accepts him if he will be approachable, and he, in turn, agrees to be approachable if guaranteed that nothing he reveals will be used against him. . . .

From this reasoning, Gross concludes that social intimacy will appear only between persons who are not competitors. This condition is satisfied if there is, inherently, no competition in a relationship or if participants can artifically obliterate an existing state of competition. Examining 11 informal groups of friends (ranging from 2 to 6 members) in the head office of a wholesale manufacturing and mail-order firm, Gross found that in "every informal group, not one member was a competitor of any other member in it." (In this case he was defining competition as the performance of similar kinds of work or employment under the same supervisor.) He proposes that a necessary condition for the rise of intimate groups among competitors (*e.g.,* among manual workers in factories) is the imposition by their members of effective limits on each other's productivity, thus eliminating competition.

e. SIMILARITY OF PERSONAL CHARACTERISTICS: It has often been argued that love is most likely to arise in a population with homogeneous characteristics. The rationales to support this position are two: 1) people can relate in a diffuse and intimate manner only if they share many understandings in common and 2) people with common tastes and objectives are more likely to find one another attractive. The counter argument is that, to love one another, people must find in their fellows qualities or services they themselves lack and want and which can be acquired by association.

The largest body of systematic data invoked to support the first approach concerns mutual friends. As a recent survey of this large literature concludes (47), mutual friends are almost always shown to be alike in social attitudes, aesthetic and avocational tastes, and level of intelligence. Similar observations appear in comparisons of husbands and their wives, buttressed, in their case, by great homogeneity of demographic characteristics. Moving to much larger social units, we have Angell's (5) discovery that, in American cities of more than 100,000 population, homogeneity of the citizens with respect to social class, race, and ethnic origin is positively associated with their rate, *per capita,* of contributions to community welfare and negatively with the rate of crime.

Winch (155), on the other hand, has published a pioneering investigation which purports to show that members of a married pair, whatever their homogeneity in values, ability, and social background, are likely to be opposite but complementary in temperament and in the character of their participation in interpersonal relations. He proposes, in short, that husbands and wives tend to be alike in objectives and abilities, but to differ in their characteristic contributions toward utilizing those abilities and achieving those goals. Data obtained from 24 married couples, all students at Northwestern University, afford some support for his contention, especially in the finding that spouses are likely to complement each other with respect to dominance and submissiveness.

There seems, however, no gain in continuing to treat these issues in the simple terms conventionally employed. It is evident from everyday experience that "birds of a feather flock together" and that "opposites attract." (More technical formulations appear in Durkheim's discussion of mechanical and organic solidarity (48).) What needs to be done, and has not been done, is to specify the conditions under which one or both or neither are true. Winch deserves particular credit for taking the furthest step in that direction.

f. WILLINGNESS: At the beginning of our survey, we found that a criterion of genuine love was the willingness of participants to undertake it. Thibaut and Riecken (139) have isolated one important condition associated with the judgment that a man has acted of his own free will: his social status. In each of two matched laboratory experiments, they found that subjects believed that high status collaborators acted as they did from personal desires; low status collaborators in response to external pressures. (The "collaborators" were, in fact, confederates of the experimenter and their interaction with the subjects was carefully standardized to make them alike except for certain alleged background factors such as having graduated from a high school of high or low prestige.)

The investigators report a second finding of interest. Some subjects saw the low status collaborator as acting freely; some viewed the high status collaborator as coerced by events. If one controls for the collaborators' status, he discovers that, from the beginning of the experiment, subjects like, admire, and accept a man that they believe is acting of his own free will; and they like him even more at the end of their work together.

¶ SEARCH AND SELECTION: If people happen to be thrown together with others who are attractive and approachable, or engaged with them in facilitative interaction so safeguarded that trustfulness is justified and willingness evident, love may flourish without much further effort. It often happens, however, that individuals must seek out the love or the beloved they need. This may entail a long search and difficult choices, depending on the alternatives available and the character of a person's desires.

A search of this kind by a thoughtful girl, hiding with her family and some neighbors from German persecution, is the principal theme of Anne Frank's diary (61). Her experience is especially revealing, not because her hopes or desires were unusual, but because the persons who might have helped with them were drastically limited in number and, for various reasons, unsuited to the task.

Anne was on the verge of adolescence. She also was unusually perceptive of meanings in human relations. She wanted to explore the values around which a worthy adult life might be organized. She wanted to evaluate and control her own selfishness, her disgust with the compromised standards of adults, her ambivalence toward her mother, and her varied feelings about sexuality. She wanted to express and clarify sentiments that were variously bizarre, grandiose, highly idealistic, superficial, earthy, or harsh. Trying to establish an appropriate friendship with each of the others in hiding with her, she slowly came to realize that each had interests or responsibilities that made him unsuitable. Anne was already at odds with her mother. The adults in neighboring families were insensitive and egocentric. Margot, her older sister, proved helpful for a time, but, as their relation deepened, broke it off to protect her specially favored place in their mother's esteem. Peter, the adolescent son of a neighbor's family, was more concerned with endearments and sexual explorations than serious discussions of Anne's inner self. Finally there was her perceptive and loving father. It seemed for a long time that here was the friend she sought. Then Albert Frank's responsibilities to his wife and older daughter (and his duty as a parent who corrected, disciplined, and taught Anne) precluded his becoming her intimate friend, her coconspirator, and someone who could freely exchange fantasies, ambitions, and dislikes.

Everyone around Anne was capable of love and was, in fact, giving it, seeking it, and receiving it. But none of them could provide love for the purposes Anne required, legitimate though those objectives were, without seriously compromising other important obligations.

The friend Anne sought, and might well have found in some other girl of her age had she lived under normal conditions, would have been a person highly gratified by Anne's being all her many selves, a person without conflicting commitments. This friend would almost certainly have been somewhat removed from Anne's ordinary round of life; not her superior or subordinate, her competitor or someone mutually responsible with her for some common enterprise. That friend would be a person whom she could neither threaten nor fail by being herself.

A search for someone who can give the love one needs is a part of dating and courtship, of the choice of an advisor, counselor, clergyman, therapist, or faith, of affiliation with voluntary associations, an employing company, and with political figures and parties. Aristotle's (6) judgment that persons capable of skillful, complete love are rare, corresponds to what is known concerning the distribution of such component skills as empathy, ego-strength, insight, self-discipline, and devotion to the welfare of others. It is not the whole story.

To nourish a man adequately in one respect commonly prevents our aiding him in others. To support his most penetrating explorations of self requires a suitable social role as well as interpersonal competence, and this role may prevent the offering of other kinds of love. For example, Albert Frank could not have supported Anne in such a venture and also provided her with the fatherly care she required. There is, in short, no perfect lover, no complete friend, and persons who supply a man with one kind of love should often be socially removed from those who supply other kinds.

As a consequence, most people obtain love from a variety of sources for a variety of purposes. This means that, other things being equal, the number and diversity of a man's social contacts increase the likelihood of his getting the love he desires.

Such contacts are not distributed at random in the population. Membership in formal, voluntary groups such as churches, unions, fraternal organizations, sports clubs, and neighborhood associations is strongly and positively related to socio-economic position (9, 62, 118, 123, 152, 157). One large scale investigation found that, with the population's demographic characteristics and the distance of their residence from the city's center controlled, such membership is greater in the city than in its suburbs (159).

Although the relationship is not as spectacular, such informal associations as those with friends, co-workers, relatives, and neighbors are often reported to be positively and significantly associated with socio-economic status (9, 18, 126, 127). With status controlled, these informal contacts have been found in positive association with number of memberships in formal organizations (9, 152). The number and/or intensity of such contacts is further related to longer residence in one's present neighborhood (109, 127), belonging to a large family (109), being married but without children or being the parent of more than one child (123), having experienced regular advances in one general type of occupation (141), being identified with the community (54), being a woman (153), being young (153), living in an urban community (116), desiring upward social mobility (102), and having an income and education consistent with the prestige afforded by one's ethnic background (92). The desire for such informal contacts is associated with inhibiting or controlling one's behavior to provide satisfaction for others (66) and seems to be a generalized characteristic of individuals (73, 153).

Whether needs for love are differently satisfied as a consequence of this uneven distribution of certain potential sources, we do not know. (We also do not know the distribution within any substantial population of needs for various degrees and types of love.) If, however, one is right in thinking that the loves men need must come from specialized and separated sources, each person is left with the difficult task of integrating all these experiences into a coherent style of life. (Indeed, the specialized loves he receives may only nourish expectations and potencies that the individual cannot bring together in a mutually compatible whole. To take one example, the nurturance by colleagues of one another's professional skills and tastes may exacerbate the conflict between their careers and their roles as husbands and fathers.)

Involvement in a social order whose norms embrace the whole of the individual's life career and which provide him with criteria for the evaluation and reconciliation of his specialized experiences seems to be a precondition for his development of personal coherence (48). If no embracive normative or institutional framework is experienced as real or valid or worthy, all the specialized loves lose their meaning and worth (48, 141). Then, in Sartre's words, man's condition is one of anguish. There is no information about the frequency with which given individuals experience this kind of despair during their careers or its incidence or intensity in any society. Some psychotherapists and social observers believe it is on the rise in post-industrial societies and efforts to cope with its presence are the great objective of a new school of practitioners, the existential psychotherapists (105).

As the person in need seeks love, many people, often the

same ones, search for someone they may love. The task is to establish the relevance of others' needs for one's love and their capacity to accept and use it.

It is frequent in such assessments that love must be given before its relevance can be fully judged. If the subjects have little present capacity to use it, they must be able at least to receive it, and every assurance must be provided that it is given freely and for the recipients' sake to be what they are and what, in freedom and integrity, they may become. Thus it is standard practice in therapeutic institutions for badly traumatized children to provide a full larder, its contents available whenever the child wants to eat; unlocked doors that permit him to explore or withdraw as he will; extremely considerate handling of wakening and going to sleep; a tolerance for his display of symptoms limited only by the requirement that he not destroy essential property nor make physical attacks on the staff (19, 114, 115). If the child becomes incapable of handling even these limits, he is removed gently from the situation, accompanied by an adult who waits with him until he becomes calm. Simultaneously, his ability for action and decision is encouraged through enterprises such as team games and free art in which he can take some initiative without being threatened by pressures to compete or choose as an individual.

But such institutions do not take all disturbed children. They usually admit only those of at least normal intelligence and physical health, those who are neither too withdrawn or too troubled by pathological suspicion of their peers. They also seek youngsters who are similar to one another in cultural background. These restrictions assure a clientele which can learn new styles of conduct, receive and use the kind of love offered under the conditions through which it is provided, and communicate readily with each other and with the staff.

In varying degree, as fits particular situations, these four considerations—the granting of love, the acceptance of the person for what he is including his unloveable characteristics, the setting of limits within which love is exercised, and the determination of probable capacity to receive and use love for his enhancement—are employed in establishing a loving relationship. Friendships and courtships, for example, often have their rudimentary beginnings in some special kindness beyond the requirements of formal social obligation, progressing, perhaps to the sharing of small confidences and to the acceptance of joking and teasing which indicate that the other person is desired even when he proves prickly. Occasions may be created in which each can move toward greater intimacy or, gracefully, keep the relation as it is (146). All these initial steps must be taken with delicacy or too much may seem promised and graceful withdrawal made impossible.

Judgments of the quantity of love that can be accepted, even by one who needs it, pose subtle problems. An offer of great love may frighten or may raise intolerable guilt. Similarly, the support offered must be usable for the beloved's particular enterprises or it may be seen as competitive with them or as exploitative. Thus Litwak, Count, and Hayden (99) present findings which suggest that the exercise by a wife of creative social sensitivity in areas where her husband feels he should excel is associated with less satisfaction in marriage for both of them.

¶ THE SCOPE OF LOVE: The forms of love vary in their scope from the almost limitless obligations entailed in love for God or a close friend to the circumscribed commitments of a physician or attorney to his client. Wherever something of love appears, there are delicate problems of setting its scope. These problems arise because, in love, the extent of responsibility is inherently vague, and because the genuineness of professed love is so difficult to determine.

The work of love cannot go on within clearly defined boundaries. Even in the relatively limited relationship between professional and client the obligation is one of creating a general state of affairs in which growth can occur. The doctor or attorney who lacked a general understanding of his client as a person and of the man's affairs would be ill informed to render competent service. The facts most relevant for diagnosis and prescription may lie far afield from the client's "presenting symptoms" and must be sought. To permit such a search the client must trust his counselor's judgment of what is relevant and accept the obligation to give fully and accurately what information is required of him. The professional, too, is obliged to extend trust. He must respect his client's integrity and speak candidly of his judgment of the client's situation, keep in confidence the information the client provides, and be guided solely by the client's general interests. He must inform the client of considerations which that person may not have foreseen, even if these will shorten or terminate his need for professional services. Where mutual obligations are presumed to be without limit, as in a close friendship, the suggestion of reservations or boundaries threatens the relationship even more.

What, then, if the friend or client seeks to define certain vital matters as off limits or if either makes demands that go beyond the relationship's boundaries? How, short of terminating the relationship, may its necessary indeterminateness be preserved while suggesting the presence of limits?

Perhaps the most common strategy employed in our society to counter excessive expectations is tactful but persistent refusal to deal directly with those demands, not defining them as unrealistic or an imposition and not acceding to them. This appears most likely of success if accompanied by unobtrusive but clear evidence of making some special effort in matters that come legitimately within the relationship's scope.

Clark (34) describes this procedure, developed to a self-conscious technique, in the junior colleges, the so-called "open-door" colleges, where many students ill equipped for advanced studies must be given the opportunity to develop their intellectual skills at their own pace and as fully as they can in the hope of eventual success, a task in which large numbers will fail. The college counselor must keep open the door to further attempts, seeking always for some legitimate means by which the student may achieve his goals, yet must keep him aware of the real state of his present achievements. To this end, the counselor devotes endless time, effort, and ingenuity in helping a failing student overcome personal difficulties that impede his progress. The counselor always confronts him with the continuous measures of his performance, but never says directly either that the cause is hopeless or that success is likely. By thus giving of himself beyond what seem to be in the formal requirements of his office, the counselor testifies to the depth and sincerity of his commitments while defining, indirectly, the limits to their scope.

We should notice that the counselor's approach succeeds because it employs yet another criterion of love and because the environing society defines that criterion as a limit to the demands men may make on one another. Genuine love, as we saw earlier, is a commitment to nourish the powers, independence, and integration of another; to enrich another in these respects, not just to maintain him as he is. To fulfill this objective, the one who receives love must show greater potency in dealing with the environment and with himself; increased powers in defining objectives and obtaining and utilizing resources from that environment. Movement toward these accomplishments provides a standard governing lover and loved alike, limiting as well as describing their mutual responsibilities. Under this standard, the friend or parent or spouse is, like the professional, limited to practicing within his competence and governing his conduct by its relevance for enhancing the person he loves. Under the same standard, the person loved is obligated to use the support received for growth and to respect the integrity and independence of the person or institution that nourishes him (21, 112).

Because those who give love and those who receive it often violate this standard and are, themselves, unwilling or unable to implement it, or are ignorant of the consequences of its violation, a variety of sanctions are routinely employed in its support. There is always the threat, inherent in the situation, that the relationship will be broken off, or, if continued, that it will fail of its purpose and make pressing needs go unsatisfied. There are the continued costs of attending college or paying the professional or spending time with the friend which go for nothing if the relationship is unproductive. There are evaluations by supervisors, kinsmen, acquaintances, teachers, and other friends.

Where these indirect and informal sanctions fail, agencies of government or of professional groups may take formal action. The difficulty in applying formal sanctions is that they can govern successfully only the performance of reasonably specific and objective acts, not the multiplicity of subtle, almost intangible judgments and behaviors required for a life of love. Even here, however, special controls have been devised, although generally with no understanding of their real effectiveness. Catechisms, lists of questions for self-examination before confession or communion, professional seminars concerned with desirable practice, and instruction in the meaning of the ethical code governing one's occupation are routinized methods for training in love and for the reinforcement of standards learned in the past. Monastic orders have one or more officers in each chapter house required to examine and guide members at regular intervals concerning the great and small details of their conduct. Some orders also make it the responsibility of each member to provide the chapter's director with detailed reports concerning the spiritual development of their fellows. Patients in psychotherapy and prisoners in group reorientation sessions have been trained or retrained in the nuances of responsible behavior by means of a detailed examination of their successes and failures in social life (22, 147, 154).

One group of social scientists has taught decision-making committees to employ a related device when they reach an impasse

(97). The members sit back and soliloquize aloud, reflecting with great candor on their view of the difficulty including observations concerning each other's personalities and rectitude.

MAINTENANCE AND DEVELOPMENT

Once begun, love may or may not be sustained. It will not persist or grow without special effort. There are at least four activities concerning which some difficulties are likely to appear. These are: 1) efforts to differentiate this socially "primary" association from other relations in which people engage, 2) efforts to conduct necessary relations with the environment outside the primary relationship, 3) efforts to manage the internal routines of giving love and receiving it, and 4) efforts to guide individual participants' careers in love.

¶ DIFFERENTIATING A PRIMARY RELATIONSHIP FROM OTHER ASSOCIATIONS: In comradeship men are beside each other, jointly confronting their common task. In love, men are face to face, their relationship itself the focus of attention. The outer world is a source of support or interference, but not the occasion for their union. Each person attracts the other to himself, not merely to his works. The more diffuse their obligations for one another, the more are they oriented inward toward their own interaction.

All human organizations requiring large commitments from their participants try to encapsulate their members' lives, eliminating potential sources of seduction and subversion. The more intense forms of love are among these. The cloister guards its members' loyalty by removing them physically from contacts with the world outside, by absorbing all of their time in a predetermined round of life, by immersing them in a special task and language and dress (10, 31, 83, 84, 138, 156). It guards also against the development of competing loyalties within the organization (10, pp. 112-113, 31, p. 203). Close friendships may be forbidden. The new member may be required to eat, sleep, worship, and work always between the person who preceded him in membership in the order and the one who happened to follow (10).

Many other groups guard their members' love against comparable seductions whether from outside the organization or from within it. Thus law, custom, and the routines of life shield a married couple from easy opportunities for unfaithfulness. In ordinary life, as in the cloister, social restrictions on looking, listening, bodily posture, movement, dress, and speech focus conduct in approved channels and block forbidden paths. Cliques within families are discouraged by the precept that parents give equal treatment to each of their children.

College fraternities and sororities also deter the rise of special friendships and intimate cliques within their memberships. The following are excerpts from descriptions which members have written for me of fraternity practices at The University of Michigan:

It is considered poor form for one active to sit at the same table very often.

About four men are "on" a rushee the entire time he is in the house. When another active joins a group consisting of four men one active drops out and switches to an undermanned group. It is the duty of every active to meet or observe the rushee before he is bid. This system is slower in bidding than some others . . . [but it] tends to prevent a fraction of the house that has developed from perpetuating itself.

A whole society is sometimes defined as a community of intense love with the consequence that special attachments to more limited groups are discouraged. Thus, speaking of an ideal Chinese mother, the Red Flag Literary and Art Critique Group of Peking University says (101):

She loved her sons in the same way as she loved the 650 million people [of] China. . . . In the Communist society . . . maternal love . . . will be cut loose completely from the ideological influence of private ownership.

There are, however, special reasons why love is a relationship closed to influences from without. The first is that, in love, the focus of attention is on developing a relationship with one's fellow participants. This distinguishes it from any enterprise in which the objective is to modify the outer world and in which the social relationship, as such, is only a means to this external end, evaluated by its efficiency for that purpose.

Second, if love is authentic, it is aimed at the enhancement of participants relative to their own needs and potentialities. The standard of enhancement or growth is not what someone else has accomplished. The nature of the participants' needs and possibilities define the relation's productivity and their advance. To judge their growth by some other standards may be necessary, but it is not love. As a consequence, it becomes necessary to avoid situations and contacts with the outer world that might involve such judgments. Each monk is defined as striving to enlarge his own abilities to love God; not to match the abilities of someone else. Husbands and wives are encouraged to do more for each other than they have and to aim at doing all they can; not to equal the other's performance.

Again, the work of love deals with people as they really are and, to proceed, they must be free to be what they are. By definition, this means that many of the parts they play in life must be dropped (68) revealing private and central aspects of their selves. The deeper the love given and accepted, the more are people vulnerable to one another. It is inescapable that, as the popular song has it, "you always hurt the one you love." Because heightened vulnerability makes such traumatic incidents inevitable, even though quite unintended, forbearance, patience, contrition, and forgiveness are a required part of successful loving. The working through of all these relations require somewhat private surroundings.

Complementing these needs for privacy is the seemingly universal social norm that any legitimate instance of love has the right to privacy (106, 125). The state may define conversations between a professional man and his client as privileged. Spouses cannot be called to testify against each other in court. The house of a blood brother is a legitimate sanctuary for a man fleeing from tribal justice, however heinous his crime. Relatives are discouraged from prying into the affairs of a married couple; outsiders from disturbing the communion of friends. Friends and monks are forbidden to tattle about each other (31, 131, 133, 143, 149).

A peculiar feature of the economics of love also militates against its ready accessibility to outside influences. The source of gain in love is from a relation to someone else as a person. Other things equal, the degree of such intimacy between an original pair declines in the presence of a third person. The former members come under constraints to compete with each other for the newcomer's devotion and with him for each other (24). Impersonality grows.

But some primary relationships are certain to expand in membership; others are likely to do so. The common solution is to define the essential relation as that of each member to the "spirit" or "personality" or "character" of the group as a whole which is said to benefit each participant equally according to his need. New members are defined as increasing the group's resources in excess of the costs they lay upon it, thus enhancing its potential contribution to each of its members. This will often be expressed symbolically by elaborating the symbols, practices, rituals, and terms that represent the whole group and its potency. It is now the individual as a member of this increasingly complex and powerful group that is loved, not the individual as a unique person. The group, or its representative—the Pope, the General, the President, the parents, the Abbott, the chief therapist—is then said to love each member equally (64).

I have sketched four special considerations that operate to shield a primary relationship from the influence of its environing world: the focus on the development of the relationship itself, the avoidance of standards of accomplishment unrelated to the needs and potentialities of its own members, the provision of privacy in which participants need not fear to be themselves, and the protection of deep intimacy against dilution from impersonality. A fifth should be added: A primary relationship requires considerable "local autonomy" because it embodies responsible action.

Loving nurturance, we found, must be responsible. Responsible action, in turn, is impossible without the freedom to allocate resources and make choices which one is committed to pursue. Successful love is impossible without responsibility and responsibility is impossible without considerable autonomy of action.

¶ CONDUCTING NECESSARY RELATIONS WITH THE OUTER ENVIRONMENT: "Love," says Bettelheim's memorable title, "is not enough" (19). It supplies some, not all, of man's needs. Its actualization and maintenance require that skills, standards, and resources be brought from without into the loving relationship.

There is no way for lovers to avoid immersion in the world beyond their circle, no way even for their love to flourish apart from that wider environment. Love is not the whole of human life. As people devote more and more of their relationship to loving, they are ever less capable of employing it to provide other requirements for life and must obtain them elsewhere. In sum, loving is not self supporting.

As we have seen, the objective of genuine love is to increase the participants' powers as self-conscious, discriminating beings. Those powers are exercised in many enterprises in addition to love and, at least in Western thought, a primary relationship's relevance for the problems posed by that outer world is one essential test of its worth. It is, we say, unhealthy to continue a love which fails this test. Love means greater, more effective involvement in the world, not less.

Requirements for love's fruition through performance in the

world outside, have long been recognized as important safeguards against certain pathologies which otherwise would go uncorrected. It is, to take an instance, all too easy for the members of a group to fall in love with loving, making of their mutual devotion an ultimate goal and fearing to disrupt their beatific relationship by solving problems. When this occurs, difficulties and deficiencies are papered over for the sake of harmony until the point is reached at which they cannot be ignored and the group's integration cannot bear their cumulative weight.

Again, love is a diffuse relationship. Without the criteria provided by particular tasks which need attention, objective, rational standards to govern the relationship would be difficult to define and maintain, including those which test love's genuineness and appropriateness.

Then there is the dilemma that the tendencies toward privacy in any living relationship make it suspect in the larger society (70). Are the lovers developing standards that subvert other groups? Service in the outer world prevents the rise of such interpretations and affords a test, for lovers, of the likely viability of any novel standards emerging among them.

There is support for the further judgment that primary relations are undependable unless some more embracing external organization to which all participants adhere may legitimately and effectively enforce compliance with standards of love and respect (71). Blau's (23) study of a social agency provides an example. He found that the social workers most dedicated to helping their clients were least willing to allow others to provide those clients with certain special services. He also discovered, however, that the more of such especially dedicated workers there were in a given unit of the agency, the more each was willing to allow another, and more appropriate, person to provide specialized services for clients. Blau attributes this "structural effect" to the development, when several client-oriented workers interact, of norms concerning what is in the clients best interest regardless of the satisfactions afforded the individual members of the agency staff.

There also is evidence that intimate and diffuse associations in the absence of such embracive external controls are often characterized by extreme and "irrational" hatred. Thus, in those aspects of work in large organizations where men are interdependent but ungoverned by traditions or by formal rules, petty feuds and spiteful vindictiveness seem equally prevalent with spontaneous friendships. Banfield (12) found that diffuse intimacy unsupervised by larger institutional standards was accompanied by deep suspicion within and between families of an isolated village in southern Italy. Several reports have linked such close but uncontrolled associations with the prevalence of witchcraft among primitive peoples (135).

There seem to be no examples of groups devoted primarily to love which also succeeded in closing themselves off from the outer environment. Hostility from the larger social order, the groups' lack of self-sufficiency, and their internal stresses and contradictions, unmitigated by outside controls, have routinely destroyed utopian communities, isolated monasteries, romantic social movements (16), and the like.

There are, on the other hand, some conditions under which such groups can maintain their integrity while in contact with the larger society. They can operate successfully if they can obtain needed resources without participation in the outer world in ways which would vitiate their inner organization. Sometimes, as in the case of monastic orders or approved friendships, other groups freely provide the required supplies as gifts, and, apart from certain clearly delimited types of supervision (31, pp. 216-229), honor the primary group's privacy in its internal affairs. Sometimes, as in the case of juvenile gangs, necessary resources can be seized without the members' becoming involved in the production of those resources. Again, primary groups may be able to obtain support by performing for the outer world activities that are natural expressions of their members' mutual devotion—the teaching or social service of monks and nuns, the business enterprise of the Calvinist merchant, or the propaganda or intelligence activities of the dedicated communist.

If intimate and informal relations with competing external groups are inescapable, the employment of banter, irony, and polite fictions allows the association to occur while controlling its effects (30).

To use banter is to play at being hostile, distant, unfriendly, while intimating friendliness. It is a style of interaction used when two roles are presented to an individual and he decides to retain the status appropriate to both, while, as he must, acting out the role of only one. . . . the relationship with the group dominant at the occasion of interaction is retained; it is the other relationship which bears the episode of banter, as of less social significance at the time but . . . requiring safeguard for the future. . . . it is almost impossible to behave in any other way in messrooms and canteens.

There are other occasions when . . . a primary status membership of a socially dominant group is threatened by the simultaneous presentation of an alternative, secondary status membership, which on its side is not valuable enough to be safeguarded. However, simple rejection of a relationship is damaging to the primary status, implying a disregard for values which is dangerous to the esteem structure in which the primary status is located. . . . To use irony is to play at being friendly—at maintaining a member-relationship—while intimating enmity, rejection.

In addition . . . there exist . . . polite fictions. The arrangements are in general directed toward the exclusion from the terms of interaction of any status occupied by a participant which is incompatible with the establishment of the consensus necessary. . . .

¶ MANAGING INTERNAL ROUTINES: The origin and conduct of all human associations require that men be somewhat different from one another. People come together because they need each other to provide what none can supply for himself. They may have different kinds or amounts of skill or resources, but they must differ at least in that one has what the other needs and lacks.

Once together, participants must become different in certain additional respects in order to share their respective resources. As Bales (11) points out, there is some measure of specialization among men in every conversation, for, in the nature of the case, they do not repeat each other's words, but elaborate, evaluate, question, or otherwise respond to what was said. They also divide up the use of such facilities as time and space, each becoming different from the others with respect to the particular share available to him.

It is a long distance, but one without discontinuity, from these microscopic forms of social differentiation to the massive, clearly marked division of labor in complex societies. In groups of all sizes we find differentiation in its two forms—in "specialization" which refers to the *nature* or *source* of the influence that men exert, and in "stratification" comprised by variations in the *amount* of social influence.

Whether in the form of specialization or stratification, differences among men are as necessary a means for the conduct of love as for *any* other instance of social interaction. Such differences are also potentially subversive of the *particular kind* of social interaction that love represents. We have seen that loving involves a considerable equality among participants. Differentiation is a condition which commonly represents inequality. Loving is directed toward the enhancement of others. The coordination of differentiated activities may be so time-consuming that it becomes an end in itself rather than a means to love. Loving requires intimacy. Specialization and stratification generate differences in interest and commitment within a group and embody a degree of social distance among members. Because these alien forces become ever more conspicuous and significant as organizational complexity increases, they are always the subject of compensatory actions by larger groups seeking to cultivate love (123). Such actions temper social inequalities and differences, but rarely eliminate them.

One of these compensatory devices is the refusal to vest specialized activities in the individuals who perform them. Groups may, for example, employ a system of rotation such that a particular specialized task is always performed but is executed by a given individual on a temporary basis only—a system of "taking turns." Speaking of experience with this practice in a kibbutz, Spiro (129) notes that it could not be employed rigorously because only 12 to 15 persons possessed certain skills vital to the community's life. Etzioni's (53) study of collective settlements in Israel produces a similar conclusion.

Nevertheless, great and costly efforts may be made to rotate personnel through jobs. Although frequently disruptive of a house, fraternity presidents are often elected for terms of only six months and limited to one term in office. Baldwin (10) says that rotation sometimes resulted in dangerous incompetence in the cloister. When, however, a nun protested that she lacked training to act as a pharmacist, drycleaner, or cook, she was told that God would provide the strength and talent necessary.

When stratification presents a special threat, it, too, can be curbed by distinguishing between the individual and the authority he wields. Authority and control of all essential resources may be lodged in the whole group, and the leader required to consult with the group; he then seeks to express their consensus rather than to develop a personal policy. We find this practice in many primitive societies, in religious and academic bodies, and in the advice of group dynamicists that decision-making conferences restrict the power of leaders to the facilitation of procedures for making decisions while reserving all control of policy to the whole group

(31, 97, 134). Frequently, in these same settings, there is a formal rule that all decisions are tentative, subject to review and modification by the group as changing needs require.

Even more drastic measures have been taken in some primary groups. The group may delegate responsibility but not power. It is quite likely to prohibit members from obtaining special benefits for themselves or their friends from offices they hold. Thus the Mother Abbess must live as simply as any other nun and do nothing which would show favoritism or lead to her personal gratification (10, 83). Her Sisters give special deference to her office, not to the woman who occupies it. The general manager of the kibbutz is not the social superior of the cleaner of latrines (129, p. 24).

There also are some actions which embody equality and humility and which may be required of all members, however exalted their office. The Abbott and Abbess periodically move about their communities kneeling before each member and washing his feet. All staff members of therapeutic homes are expected to be available for informal, individualized relations with their patients (19). Friendly but irreverent lampooning of authority, offices, and office-holders may be a regular part of life in a kibbutz or fraternity or family. In organizations like the cloister or kibbutz where moral fervor is likely to be high, these periods are especially important safeguards against temptations to self-righteousness, pontification, cant, and perfectionism.

Finally, when possible, differentiation is avoided. The more integrated chapters of college fraternities entertain guests by means of group games rather than performances by individuals. All the members sing together or circulate around the room. Team play rather than individual competition is encouraged.

¶ GUIDING THE CAREERS OF INDIVIDUALS: All these efforts to preserve equality do not mean that there are no careers in loving, no socially acknowledged stages in an individual's developing skill, no routinized measures of his progress. Without such measures it would be difficult for him to guide his conduct, to judge his competence, and to formulate plans for future development.

There are such stages, marked with special clarity in the larger, more persistent associations devoted to love, but absent from none. Figures like the saint or the elder statesman or the beloved neighbor mark upper extremes. Increases in privileges, responsibilities, and the holding of offices occasionally indicate intermediate steps. But the marks of advancement in love stress features absent from, or less conspicuous in, other types of careers.

Growth in love is an increased immersion in, and dedication to, a relationship with others, an increased integration with others. Saints, good neighbors, and the like differ from their fellows, not in the nature of their interests, but in their embodiment of concerns shared equally by all. Nuns who specialize in obedience or poverty are not turning from other believers but are especially thorough in eliminating those aspects of their behavior which separate them from others. The Mother Superior is an administrator not primarily because she possesses skills relevant for administration, but, at least in theory, because she is more perfect in devotion than her subordinates. This type of perfection, and only it, is the legitimate basis for her greater power in the cloister, and it is power to be used for the whole cloister's benefit, not her own. Indeed, as we have seen, her way of life is otherwise to be like that of the humblest novice.

Seniority seems to be employed universally as a means for distinguishing stages in love. On the one hand it is a rough index of the number of contributions a man has made and separates those who are more experienced from others. At the same time, seniority makes these distinctions by means of a criterion, years in service, which all can achieve and which preserves equal status among age-mates by not registering differences in the character or importance of their services. Students in fraternities and sororities often receive a membership number indicating the order in which they were pledged. Members are then given their choice of rooms in accordance with length of membership. One student observes:

The use of sigma numbers is necessary in many instances other than room allocation. . . . the president couldn't settle the disputes; it would give him too much power. The chapter couldn't vote on some matters since this would . . . split the group. Also it would be too time consuming.

When the career is officially recognized, the stages are perceived in terms of years of service to the group or unusual contributions to it. Celebrations of a career may involve gifts to the institution and much will be said of the genius of the group in recruiting and training this human instrument. If gifts are given the individual himself, they are likely to be of the sort that further promote his services to the group—a new prayer book, money to support a favorite charity.

Because the objective of loving is the enhancement of another and not personal aggrandizement, the appropriate measure of success must be a man's contribution, not his own gains. One does not set out to be a saint or a great benefactor of mankind or a superb patriot and to do so would preclude achieving one's end. One would be exploiting the needs of others for personal benefit and so precluding the growth of love. One can succeed only by setting out to serve, not to gain for oneself. It would, consequently, be grossly inappropriate to recognize growth in love by a gift that would benefit the lover in particular apart from the causes to which he is devoted. The most appropriate gift will be one that furthers those causes or allows him to contribute to them more fully and effectively or that displays, by some special growth of the beloved, the efficacy of his efforts in the past. The retiring professor is suitably honored by a *festschrift* displaying his students' best talents or an endowment to support his favorite scholarly programs. The parent is honored appropriately by mementos of his children's growing competence.

Although a career in love occurs through time, the main course of that career has a markedly cyclical character. One changes by becoming more fully what one has been but never completely what one might be. The career is the elaboration and perfection of a single style of life, not the exploration of various styles. One's skills and outlook may be applied to many diverse tasks, but the general character of their objective is the same in each and the mechanisms by which their work is accomplished are essentially constant. It could scarcely be otherwise. Here, comprising this most elaborated form of social interaction, are the relationships on which all special forms of human association depend. As with any highly general principles, however varied their applications, the possibilities for employing these foundational skills are never fully exhausted, their meaning is never completely grasped, nor is the need for their exercise outgrown. There is a constant venturing forth from these principles, a continuous reference back to them for guidance, and, when one enterprise is finished, a return to them as preparation for tasks to come (11, pp. 30-84).

There are, however, other aspects of an individual's career in loving. He becomes irritated. He wants to withdraw and pursue other activities. He finds increasing involvement frightening as well as fulfillng. Social arrangements must be provided if these periods of stress are to remain within bounds.

In larger organizations it becomes necessary to insure that

love will be embodied in interpersonal relations despite the inability of participants to spend large amounts of time adapting to each other individually. Sincere expressions of repentance, restitution, forgiveness, and reconciliation cannot wait upon the gradual readjustment of personal feelings and must be routinized. Cloistered religious orders sometimes have the rule that, when two members have a falling out, the younger must apologize to the older and the older grant immediate and complete forgiveness. It also is common that the norms of such institutions define annoying habits of one's fellows as great blessings, for, in learning to love them despite those irritations, one grows more like God who can love the utterly unloveable. Some college fraternities require feuding members to work together on a project that benefits the whole group, especially a project that represents the group to the larger campus community, thus forcing them to submerge their personal differences in their common aspirations. Collective settlements occasionally give persons with persistent grievances some special responsibilities for the care of their opponents' families or livestock.

It is difficult, however, for participants in love to tolerate the withdrawal of their members because withdrawal indicates the existence of interests apart from their mutual concerns and, possibly, some reassessment of the value of those concerns. It is, in fact, typical that the more formal primary groups have a rule making continuous participation an obligation as well as a privilege and refuse readmission to a person who once rejects his membership.

Members of a kibbutz who seek more privacy are thought queer. The ultimate criterion of a good high school, kindergarten, or kibbutz is whether it is a group characterized by intimacy of interaction and by mutual concern (129, p. 30). In the older Jewish communities of eastern Europe, the *shtetls* (158, pp. 225-227):

To insist on privacy if you are not sinning is a serious misdemeanor. . . . One of the worst things you can say of a man is "he keeps it for himself" or "he hides it from others" whether "it" is money or wisdom, clothes or news.

Locked doors, isolation, avoidance of community control, arouse suspicion. . . . "Home people," . . . are free to come in whenever they like at any time of the day. . . .

Withdrawal is felt as attack, whether physical or psychological, and isolation is intolerable. "Life is with people". . . .

The freedom to observe and to pass judgment on one's fellows, the need to communicate and share events and emotions is inseparable from a strong feeling that individuals are responsible to and for each other.

The doctor's patient or lawyer's client are bound to speak openly and comprehensively of their problems; the communicant must tell all to his confessor. Spouses must not withhold from each other information relevant to their mutual love. Group dynamicists require full disclosure of relevant thoughts from participants in decision-making conferences.

Some withdrawal is permitted if it can be justified as necessary to the performance of a service for the group. Thus a novice in the cloister may be permitted to sew or launder alone where she can regain her composure. A journey alone on business allows a wife or husband to find repose. Again, claims of illness or need for extra sleep or rest or quiet are withdrawals legitimatized by the promise of renewed ability to contribute to the common enterprise.

If negative feelings can be discharged outside the primary relationship itself and in a manner that does not affect that association, all may go well. The patient complains to a friend about his therapist and to his therapist about his friend. The child discusses the limitations of parents with his playmates; of playmates with his parents.

On occasion, however, there is no opportunity to discharge such feelings outside the group. Cloistered monks and nuns must spend all their hours together. So, in some cases, must the members of small utopian communities or of groups in hiding. Certain individuals, although able to go about in the larger social world, get no relief because their problems are so specialized they would not be understood by most other people or because their difficulties relate to a secret organization.

Faced with this problem among their members, some organizations have developed a special role, that of the informal confessor. In most cases, this is a senior member of the group, but not one who holds, or is likely to hold, an office which disciplines members. These characteristics insure that he will act on behalf of the original organization, but only by means of friendly counsel. The confessor is usually bound by a vow of silence, thus assuring the dissident member that his remarks will not be revealed. Discontent can be aired, the group being represented and given a chance to respond in a non-punitive fashion, yet, simultaneously, being insulated from deviant pressures (31, p. 192, 112).

Essayists on love often remark that, among the symptoms of growing devotion, is satisfaction with silence, with merely being together though "doing nothing." They are less likely to note something that seems typical of all situations in which people are to love one another over many areas of their lives and for long periods of time. An initial period of goodwill is followed by a time of great coolness or hostility. In these periods of stress, people may hold together in stark dependency, no graces lightening the burden of their need for each other, no respite at hand in which to enjoy such fruit as their relation bears. Yet this may be as much a part of loving as the moments of gaiety or consummation. Moreover, this cycle will be repeated should they be called upon to make some further, significant increase in their commitments to each other. The sequence is familiar in the "sunshine to storm" cycle as the child moves from infancy to early childhood or from late childhood to adolescence. It is often noted in observations of courtship and marriage, of psychotherapy and of friendships. Students of occupational careers have noted it in schoolteachers and in managers of large concerns. Directors of institutions which provide long term care for children expect it of many youngsters during the first year or two under their roof.

Two interpretations of the cycle are common. First, the individual can test the trustworthiness and depth of the affection proferred him only by becoming a major liability. If that behavior is accepted, he is probably desired for what he is, not for some particular service he performs. Second, love will require him to give up behaviors he may enjoy even though they appreciably weaken his potentialities. He may need to withdraw from a relationship to assess his own willingness to make a still greater commitment to it. In this sense, a withdrawal from intimacy or even open hostility may be a necessary preparation of the ground for deeper love.

When this preparation is understood, and, perhaps, cultivated, there is a possibility of guiding its course, mitigating if not eliminating its rigors. When, after a period of passive cooperation, his patient becomes hostile, the skilled psychotherapist sees enlarged opportunities for healing. He and the patient are now deeply and honestly involved with each other, not playing parts but struggling in an authentic human relationship. They now have a chance of finding and reshaping essential features of the patient's outlook, and of the physician's as well.

Spiritual advisors recognize similar opportunities. Certain

steps in growth toward loving union with God are commonly observed, named, and managed (144). The Awakening of the Self is the joy of first recognition of God's presence and goodness. The Purgative Way is a period of self discipline to control and, more rigorously, to excise the more obvious kinds of selfishness that separate a man from his holy friend. The Illuminated Way follows upon successful purgation, as a period of serene enjoyment of God's love. For many contemplatives, whether lay or religious, this stage is the culmination. But others seek a deeper love which can be had only if the will as well as the more external aspects of behavior become consonant with God's purposes. The Dark Night of the Soul is the time of spiritual crucifixion when the man clings to his search, unable to turn back and gradually realizes that he cannot advance by his own power. Finally he asks to be accepted as he is and surrenders all pretensions to sufficiency. This can be an agony of years or decades and may still be unresolved at death. Verve and elan may vanish, spiritual dryness set in. God may seem unattainably distant or absent. The greatest temptations, the most sacrilegious of thoughts, emptiness, unrelievable heaviness or congestion, all these are common symptoms. What remains is sheer need and a final, tenacious faith which one may even pray to abandon but cannot. If acceptance finally comes, acceptance of God for what He is and one's self for what it is, there opens the Unitive Way of a self at one with God. The imagery now is of iron penetrated by the fire or the drop of water blended into the ocean. This need not mean a loss of self. In Eastern cultures such loss is common; in the West it is unorthodox, for, in the West, the holy is love, not unfeeling fate, and the union between man and God is mutual acceptance, not the soul's annihilation (32, 111).

Thus, throughout the child's socialization, the healing of sick minds, the growth of friendships and marital love, and the reaching of souls toward a divine love, problems are raised for which many lovers are unprepared. Assuming devotion to be unalloyed beatitude, they are dismayed or crushed by the obligation of the loved to grow, or, as lovers, are overwhelmed by the effort, skill, and commitment required to deal creatively with the developments they have nourished. They cannot accept dissent from their present views, even when the disagreement is directed toward helping them. They find it hard to see a conflict of responsible opinions as creative and lack skills to resolve such issues fruitfully.

Nothing is more fatal than to love or accept love beyond

one's competence, yet nothing more likely than the flourishing of love beyond those bounds. Even when loved and lover can name what they are doing, when they understand enough to seek for those hindrances to the growth that alone can relieve the tension and can take comfort in knowledge that it is love, not madness, with which they wrestle, there is no certainty that they will have the strength or competence or opportunity to realize a fortunate conclusion.

Where love is wise, informed by experience and training, it moves, but moves gradually. Where love is institutionalized, there are methods for controlling as for promoting its growth. There is a routine of work, wakening, relaxation, bathing, and sleep, there is care for diet and health, and there are opportunities for privacy, withdrawal, deviance, candor, intimate interaction, and separation (19, 31, pp. 30-43, 206).

Routine and care sustain with a minimum of novel decisions. They underscore elemental dependencies and realities, provide time and opportunities for assimilating past experiences and the testing of new approaches. If directed only to preserving relations as they are, they generate conflicting feelings of obligation and rebellion (14, 95). If directed to providing for future growth, they encourage development by affording participants with the experience of larger continuities and the fresh opportunities that a new day brings.

But routines have another, greater, significance. As we have seen, routinized, unrewarded, steady care and sacrifice characterize authentic love. They are not the only authentication of love, but they are necessary and the persistence of such care in spite of adversities can take on a heroic quality rarely matched by more spectacular sacrifices, its very cumulativeness being sufficient to provide the energies needed for fresh advances. Perhaps such care is additionally important because it affords evidence that the lover's need is also great, thus making it respectable for the beloved to accept his gifts (110, pp. 125-213).

Finally, routines require continued effort from the person seeking love. Submission to them indicates sufficiency of need and continued willingness to bear the costs of growth. It is evidence of strength to meet these requirements. Without this evidence, there is reason to doubt that love, as such, can be accepted. What is sought is, perhaps, hospitalization without therapy or, perhaps, resources to use, not for growth, but for whatever one pleases.

Like routines, periods of initiation serve to gauge the seeker's capacities and commitments. It is alien to the achievement of love that a novitiate or a series of diagnostic interviews or a courtship should be humiliating but they may be humbling experiences, and the intensity of the tests made do seem geared to the seriousness of the relationship into which people are to enter (113, 150). There also is evidence that, other things equal, the more severe the preliminary testing, the greater is the candidate's initial commitment to the relationship when he finally enters it (8). This is interpreted as meaning that, in order to reduce his conflicts over the high costs of establishing the relationship, the initiate must stress for himself the intensity of his need for it.

An Integration of
These Observations

Love, we said as our study began, is the commitment, knowingly, willingly, and responsibly to do whatever one can toward enhancing the powers, independence, and integration of another in some area of his conduct. Each of the many social arrangements we subsequently reviewed serves as a means for routinizing love— for establishing it, implementing it, or protecting it.

"Love is the commitment. . . ." We have seen that the strength of this commitment and its constancy are tested. In this survey, we found that the requirements for continuous interaction, steady support, and the passing of an initiation provided such tests. The requirement for equality of need among the participants provided a guarantee of their faithfulness.

"Love is the commitment . . . to do whatever one can. . . ." The diffuseness of love must also be established and repeatedly evaluated. Requirements for informality, personalization, and intimacy serve this purpose.

"Love is the commitment . . . to do whatever one can . . . in some area of his conduct." We found that alternating periods of harmony and conflict test the scope of love and that a variety of methods are employed to perpetuate the relationship despite these shifts in affective climate. We found also that loving cannot escape the world in which it occurs and certain devices have been found especially suited for preserving love's character even while the participants relate to the outer world as well as to each other.

Love occurs "knowingly, willingly, and responsibly." The autonomy of the lover, whether it be an individual or an organization, seems to be one guarantee that the relationship is a matter of conscious choice and is entered willingly. Autonomy is likewise necessary for that freedom to allocate resources and commit oneself to choices which distinguish responsible action. Of equal importance in promoting responsible behavior—the practice of love within one's competence—are the presence of objective norms, binding upon lover and loved alike, and the tests of love's strength and scope, each requiring a decision about competence and willingness to enlarge the relationship. Again, the demand for continuous participation insures opportunities to expend the necessary effort.

Finally, love is directed toward "enhancing the powers, independence, and integration" of another. Some of our observations have shown how this objective is kept in view; others indicate devices by which one measures or guides movement toward such a goal. In keeping this objective in focus, equality of need among the participants is once again important, in this case to prevent dominance and exploitation. So is the requirement that the quality of the beloved's performance in the outer world be employed as an objective measure of the fruitfulness of the loving relationship. The several procedures for testing the existence of interests that conflict with love's goal and for judging the ability to receive love are also relevant here.

Movement toward the goals of love is measured by the stages of loving and being loved. Many techniques discovered in our survey have arisen to promote one or more of these stages, to manage the strains they engender, and to break up resistance to further growth.

One might expect that the coherence and apparent lawfulness we observe in the social relationship called love would be reflected in systematizations of the philosophy of ethics. Ethical judgments and rules are the norms governing moral relationships which, in turn, have much in common with love. It is customary to speak of a relationship as moral to the extent that competent (responsible) persons, knowingly, freely, and willingly incur some responsibility or indebtedness toward one another in return for something of value which the others provide him. Love differs from other instances of moral association only in being especially diffuse, in having the objective of actualizing the other's potentialities as a person, and in often being directed toward the other in all his particularity. Thus, although not identical with all other moral associations, love has much in common with them and our ability to understand the logic of love would be advanced by the development of systematic principles of ethics.

Unfortunately, no well-established systematizations of ethics exist. A number of efforts to produce them have been shown untenable. The reasons for these failures need not be reviewed here, although I believe they frequently stem from internally confused and inconsistent definitions of the problem itself, from tendencies to view morality as a condition within the conduct of individuals rather than as a relationship among them, and from attempts to picture the behavior of individuals as governed solely by some variety of hedonistic principle. It is of immediate importance, however, to recognize that the present chaos in ethical theory represents a failure to systematize observations which, ethical theorists generally agree, appear to be orderly and lawful. Their dilemmas should not be taken to mean that these theorists have concluded that moral relations or their special forms, such as love, are empirically chaotic. To the contrary, contemporary efforts toward the reconstruction of ethical theory are founded explicitly on the opposite judgment (26, 27, 50, 89, 130).

The organizational pathologies to which particular approximations of love seem unusually susceptible should be understood as consequences of the special difficulty inherent in each of routinizing some aspect of love (39, 67, 94, 142). Take, for example, what C. S. Lewis calls "affection"—the loving association characterized by easy familiarity, warm comfortableness, and mutual acceptance of participants for what they are. Founded on an appreciation of people as they are at present, this relationship is threatened if they begin to change. Because affection typically appears without a very searching exploration of the equality of the participants' needs, or the responsibility of their commitment, persons become diffusely open to one another without strong safeguards against exploitation and other injury. In friendship, by contrast, equality, responsibility, and many other criteria of love are usually well-established. Typical problems here, however, are the growth of mutual enjoyment at the expense of pressing commitments in the outer world and the loss of objectivity of judgment about the relationship and each other.

BIBLIOGRAPHY

1. ALDERIDGE, G. J. Informal social relationships in a retirement community. *Marriage Fam. Living,* 1959, 21, 70-72.

2. ALLPORT, G. W. *Becoming.* New Haven: Yale University, 1955

3. ALMOND, G. A. *The appeals of communism.* Princeton: Princeton University, 1954.

4. ANGELL, R. C. *The family encounters the depression.* New York: Scribner, 1936.

5. ANGELL, R. C. The moral integration of American cities. *Amer. J. Sociol.,* 1951, 57, (2), 1-140.

6. ARISTOTLE, *The Nichomachean ethics.*

7. ARONFREED, J. *The nature, variety, and social patterning of moral responses.* (Mimeographed) Dept. of Psychology, University of Pennsylvania, 1961.

8. ARONSON, E. and MILLS, J. The effect of severity of initiation on liking for a group. *J. Abnorm. Soc. Psychol.,* 1959, 56, 177-181.

9. AXELROD, M. Urban structure and social participation. *Amer. Sociol. Rev.,* 1956, 21, 13-18.

10. BALDWIN, M. *I leap over the wall, a return to the world after twenty-eight years in a convent.* London: Hamish Hamilton, 1949.

11. BALES, R. F. *Interaction process analysis.* Cambridge: Addison-Wesley, 1950.

12. BANFIELD, E. C. *The moral basis of a backward society.* Glencoe, Ill.: The Free Press, 1958.

13. BATES, A. P. and BABCHUK, N. The primary group: a reappraisal. *Sociol. Quart.,* 1961, 2, 181-191.

14. DE BEAUVOIR, S. *Memoirs of a dutiful daughter.* (J. Kirkup, Trans.) Cleveland: World Publ. Co., 1959.

15. DE BEAUVOIR, S. Must we burn Sade? In P. Dinnage (Ed. and Trans.), *The Marquis de Sade.* New York: Grove Press, 1953. Pp. 11-82.

16. BECKER, H. *German youth, bond or free.* London: K. Paul, Trench, Trubner, 1946.

17. BECKER, H. S. Notes on the concept of commitment. *Amer. J. Sociol.,* 1960, 66, 32-40.

18. BELL, W. and BOAT, M. D. Urban neighborhoods and informal social relations. *Amer. J. Sociol.,* 1957, 62, 391-398.

19. BETTELHEIM, B. *Love is not enough: the treatment of emotionally disturbed children.* Glencoe, Ill.: The Free Press, 1950.

20. BETTELHEIM, B. Individual and mass behavior in extreme situations. In G. E. Swanson, T. M. Newcomb, and E. L. Hartley (Eds.), *Readings in social psychology.* New York: Henry Holt, 1952. Pp. 33-43.

21. BETTELHEIM, B. *The informed heart, autonomy in a mass age.* Glencoe, Ill.: The Free Press, 1960.

22. BION, W. R. *Experiences in groups.* New York: Basic Books, 1961.

23. BLAU, P. M. Structural effects. *Amer. Sociol. Rev.,* 1960, 25. 178-193.

24. BLAU, P. M. A theory of social integration. *Amer. J. Sociol.,* 1960, 65, 545-556.

25. BLUMER, H. G. Social psychology. In E. P. Schmidt (Ed.) *Man and society.* New York: Prentice-Hall, 1938. Pp. 144-198.

26. BRANDT, R. B. *Hopi ethics, a theoretical analysis.* Chicago: University of Chicago Press, 1954.

27. BRANDT, R. B. *Ethical theory, the problems of normative and critical ethics.* Englewood Cliffs, N. J.: Prentice-Hall, 1959.

28. BRONFENBRENNER, U. *The role of age, sex, class, and culture in studies of moral development.* (Mimeographed) Dept. of Psychology, Cornell University, 1961.

29. BURGESS, E. W. and LOCKE, H. J. *The family, from institution to companionship.* New York: American Book Co., 1945.

30. BURNS, T. Friends, enemies, and the polite fiction. *Amer. Sociol. Rev.,* 1953, 18, 654-662.

31. BUTLER, E. C. *Benedictine monachism: studies in Benedictine life and rule.* London: Longmans, Green and Co., 1924.

32. BUTLER, E. C. *Western mysticism.* London: Constable, 1927.

33. CAMPBELL, C. A. Is "freewill" a psuedo-problem. *Mind,* 1951, 60, 441-465.

34. CLARK, B. R. "The cooling-out" function in higher education. *Amer. J. Sociol.,* 1960, 65, 569-576.

35. COHEN, Y. A. Some aspects of ritualized behavior in interpersonal relationships. *Hum. Relat.,* 1958, 11, 195-215.

36. COOLEY, C. H. *Social organization.* New York: Scribners, 1909.

37. COOLEY, C. H. A primary culture for democracy. *Publications of the American Sociological Society,* 1918, 13, 1-10.

38. CROSSMAN, R. H. S. (Ed.) *The god that failed.* New York: Harper, 1950.

39. D'ARCY, M. C. *The mind and heart of love.* New York: Henry Holt, 1947.

40. DAVIS, F. The cabdriver and his fare: facets of a fleeting relationship. *Amer. J. Sociol.,* 1959, 65, 158-165.

41. DEUTSCH, M. An experimental study of the effects of cooperation and competition upon group processes. *Hum. Relat.,* 1949, 2, 199-232.

42. DEUTSCH, M. A theory of cooperation and competition. *Hum. Relat.,* 1949, 2, 129-152.

43. DEUTSCH, M. Trust and suspicion. *J. Conflict Resolution,* 1958, 2, 265-279.

44. DEUTSCH, M. Trust, trustworthiness, and the F scale. *J. Abnorm. Soc. Psychol.*, 1960, 61, 138-140.

45. DEUTSCH, M. The effect of threat upon interpersonal bargaining. *J. Abnorm. Soc. Psychol.*, 1960, 61, 181-189.

46. DRUCKER, P. F. *The practice of management.* New York: Harpers, 1954.

47. DU BOIS, C. A. *Studies of friendship.* (Mimeographed) Dept. of Social Relations, Harvard University, 1955.

48. DURKHEIM, E. *Suicide.* (J. A. Spaulding and G. Simpson, Trans.) Glencoe, Ill.: The Free Press, 1951.

49. DYNES, R. R. The consequences of sectarianism for social participation. *Soc. Forces*, 1957, 35, 331-334.

50. EDWARDS, P. *The logic of moral discourse.* Glencoe, Ill.: The Free Press, 1955.

51. EISENSTADT, S. N. African age groups, a comparative study. *Africa*, 1954, 24, 100-113.

52. EISENSTADT, S. N. *From generation to generation.* Glencoe, Ill.: The Free Press, 1956.

53. ETZIONI, A. The functional differentiation of elites in the kibbutz. *Amer. J. Sociol.*, 1959, 64, 476-487.

54. FANELLI, A. A. Extensiveness of communication contacts and perceptions of the community. *Amer. Sociol. Rev.*, 1956, 21, 439-445.

55. FARBER, B. Elements of competence in interpersonal relations: a factor analysis. *Sociometry*, 1962, 25, 30-47.

56. FARBER, S. M. and WILSON, R. H. L. (Eds.) *Control of the mind.* New York: McGraw-Hill, 1961.

57. FARIS, E. The primary group: essence and accident. *Amer. J. Sociol.*, 1932, 38, 41-50.

58. FENICHEL, O. *The psycho-analytic theory of neurosis.* New York: Norton, 1945.

59. FOOTE, N. Love. *Psychiat.*, 1953, 16, 245-251.

60. FOOTE, N. and COTTRELL, L. C. *Identity and interpersonal competence.* Chicago: University of Chicago, 1955.

61. FRANK, A. *The diary of a young girl.* New York: Doubleday, 1952.

62. FREEMAN, H. E., NOVAK, E., and REEDER, L. G. Correlates of membership in voluntary associations. *Amer. Sociol. Rev.*, 1957, 22, 528-533.

63. FRENCH, J. R. P. Organized and unorganized groups under fear and frustration. In K. Lewin *et al., Authority and frustration.* Iowa City, Iowa: University of Iowa, 1944. Pp. 299-308.

64. FREUD, S. *Group psychology and the analysis of the ego.* (J. Strachey, Trans.) London: Hogarth, 1922.

65. FRIEDMAN, M. S. *Martin Buber: the life of dialogue.* Chicago: University of Chicago, 1955.

66. FRIEDRICHS, R. W. Alter *versus* ego: an exploratory assessment of altruism. *Amer. Sociol. Rev.*, 1960, 25, 496-508.

67. FROMM, E. *The art of loving.* New York: Harpers, 1956.

68. GOFFMAN, E. *The presentation of self in everyday life.* Edinburgh: University of Edinburgh, 1956.

69. GOFFMAN, E. *Asylums: essays on the social situation of mental patients and other inmates.* Garden City, N. Y.: Doubleday, 1961.

70. GOODE, W. J. The theoretical importance of love. *Amer. Sociol. Rev.,* 1959, 24, 38-47.

71. GOODE, W. J. Illegitimacy, anomie, and cultural penetration. *Amer. Sociol. Rev.,* 1961, 26, 910-925.

72. GORER, G. *The life and ideas of the Marquis de Sade.* London: Peter Owen, 1953.

73. GOUGH, H. G. Predicting social participation. *J. Soc. Psychol.,* 1952, 35, 227-233.

74. GOULDNER, A. W. The norm of reciprocity: a preliminary statement. *Amer. Sociol. Rev.,* 1960, 26, 161-178.

75. GRANT, C. K. Freewill: a reply to Professor Campbell. *Mind,* 1952, 61, 381-385.

76. GROSS, E. Symbiosis and consensus as integrative factors in small groups. *Amer. Sociol. Rev.* 1956, 21, 174-179.

77. GROSS, E. Social integration and the control of competition. *Amer. J. Sociol.,* 1961, 67, 270-277.

78. HAMMOND, L. K. and GOLDMAN, M. Competition and non-competition and its relationship to individual and group productivity. *Sociometry,* 1961, 24, 46-60.

79. HARRIS, I. D. *Normal children and mothers.* Glencoe, Ill.: The Free Press, 1959.

80. HELFGOTT, M. J. *The effect of variations in mobility norms upon the legitimation of the personnel distribution by subordinate populations.* (Unpublished dissertation,) Doctoral Program in Social Psychology, The University of Michigan, 1954.

81. HOLLANDER, E. P. and WEBB, W. B. Leadership, followership, and friendship: an analysis of peer nominations. *J. Abnorm. Soc. Psychol.,* 1955, 50, 163-167.

82. HOMANS, G. C. *Social behavior: its elementary forms.* New York: Harcourt, Brace, World, 1961.

83. HULME, K. *The nun's story.* Boston: Little, Brown, 1956.

84. HYMA, A. *The brethren of the common life.* Grand Rapids, Mich.: Eerdmans, 1950.

85. JAHODA, M. *Current concepts of positive mental health.* New York: Basic Books, 1958.

86. JANDY, E. C. *Charles Horton Cooley: his life and his social theory.* New York: Dryden, 1942.

87. KOMAROVSKY, M. *The unemployed man and his family.* New York: Dryden, 1940.

88. KORNHAUSER, W. *The politics of mass society.* Glencoe, Ill.: The Free Press, 1959.

89. LADD, J. *The structure of a moral code: a philosophical analysis of ethical discourse applied to the ethics of the Navaho Indians.* Cambridge: Harvard University Press, 1959.

90. LANTZ, H. R. Number of childhood friends as reported in the life histories of a psychiatrically diagnosed group of 1,000. *Marriage Fam. Living,* 1956, 18, 107-113.

91. LAZARSFELD, P. F. and MERTON R. K. Friendship as a social process. In M. Berger (Ed.) *Freedom and control in modern society.* New York: D. Van Nostrand, 1954. Pp. 18-66.

92. LENSKI, G. E. Social participation and status crystallization. *Amer. Sociol. Rev.,* 1956, 21, 458-464.

93. LEVINE, G. N. and SUSSMANN, L. A. Social Class and sociability in fraternity pledging. *Amer. J. of Sociol.,* 1960, 65, 391-399.

94. LEWIS, O. S. *The four loves.* London: G. Bles, 1960.

95. LEWIS, O. *Children of Sanchez.* New York: Random House, 1961.

96. LIKERT, R. *New patterns of management.* New York: Mc-Graw-Hill, 1961.

97. LIPPITT, R. *Training in community relations.* New York: Harper, 1949.

98. LIPSET, S. M. *Political man.* Garden City, N. Y.: Doubleday, 1960.

99. LITWAK, E., COUNT, G., and HAYDEN, E. M. Group structure and interpersonal creativity as factors which reduce errors in the prediction of marital adjustment. *Soc. Forces,* 1960, 38, 308-315.

100. LOOMIS, J. L. Communication, the development of trust, and cooperative behavior. *Hum. Relat.,* 1959, 12, 305-315.

101. Love in a Marxist climate. *New Statesman,* Sept. 1, 1960, 60, 326.

102. MANN, P. H. The concept of neighborliness. *Amer. J. Sociol.,* 1954, 60, 163-168.

103. MASLOW, A. H. Self-actualizing people: a study in psychological health. *Personality,* 1950, 1, 11-34.

104. MASLOW, A. H. Love in healthy people. In A. Montagu (Ed.) *The meaning of love.* New York: Julian Press, 1953. Pp. 57-93.

105. MAY, R. (Ed.) *Existence; a new dimension in psychiatry and psychology.* New York: Basic Books, 1958.

106. MAYER, J. E. The self-restraint of friends: a mechanism in family transition. *Soc. Forces,* 1957, 35, 230-238.

107. MERRIAM, A. P. and MACK, R. W. The jazz community. *Soc. Forces,* 1960, 38, 211-222.

108. MILLER, D. R. and SWANSON, G. E. *The changing American parent.* New York: Wiley, 1958.

109. MUNSON, B. E. Attitudes toward urban and suburban residence in Indianapolis. *Soc. Forces,* 1956, 35, 76-80.

110. ORWELL, G. *Down and out in Paris and London.* New York: Harcourt, Brace, 1950.

111. OTTO, R. *Mysticism east and west.* New York: Macmillan, 1932.

112. PARSONS, T. Illness and the role of the physician: a sociological perspective. *Amer. J. Orthopsychiat.*, 1951, 21, 452-460.

113. PEPITONE, A. and SHERBERG, J. Intentionality, responsibility, and interpersonal attraction. *J. Pers.*, 1957, 25, 757-766.

114. REDL, F. and WINEMAN, D. *Children who hate.* Glencoe, Ill.: The Free Press, 1951.

115. REDL, F. and WINEMAN, D. *Controls from within.* Glencoe, Ill.: The Free Press, 1952.

116. REISS, A. J., JR. Rural-urban and status differences in interpersonal contacts. *Amer. J. Sociol.*, 1959, 65, 182-195.

117. REISS, I. L. Toward a sociology of the heterosexual love relationship. *Marriage Fam. Living*, 1960, 22, 139-145.

118. REISSMAN, L. Class, leisure, and social participation. *Amer. Socio. Rev.*, 1954, 19, 17-84.

119. ROSENBERG, B. and HUMPHREY, N. D. The secondary nature of the primary group. *Social Research*, 1955, 22, 25-38.

120. SARMA, J. *The social categories of friendship.* Unpublished doctoral dissertation. Department of Sociology, University of Chicago, 1946.

121. SCHEIN, E. W., SCHNEIER, I. and BARKER, C. H. *Coercive persuasion: a socio-psychological analysis of the "brainwashing" of American civilian prisoners by the Chinese communists.* New York: Norton, 1961.

122. SCHWARTZ, R. D. Functional alternatives to inequality. *Amer. Socio. Rev.*, 1955, 20, 424-430.

123. SCOTT, J. C., JR. Membership and participation in voluntary associations. *Amer. Socio. Rev.*, 1957, 22, 315-326.

124. SHILS, E. A. The study of the primary group. In D. Lerner and H. D. Lasswell (Eds.) *The policy sciences.* Stanford: Stanford University, 1951. Pp. 44-69.

125. SHILS, E. A. *The torment of secrecy, the background and consequences of American security policies.* Glencoe, Ill.: The Free Press, 1956.

126. SHUVAL, J. T. Class and ethic correlates of casual neighboring. *Amer. Sociol. Rev.*, 1956, 21, 453-458.

127. SMITH, J., FORM, W. H., and STONE, G. P. Local intimacy in a middle-sized city. *Amer. J. Sociol.*, 1954, 60, 276-284.

128. SOLOMON, L. The influence of some types of power relationships and game strategies upon the development of interpersonal trust. *J. Abnorm. Soc. Psychol.*, 1960, 61, 223-230.

129. SPIRO, M. E. *Kibbutz: venture in utopia.* Cambridge: Harvard, 1956.

130. STEVENSON, C. L. *Ethics and language.* New Haven: Yale University, 1944.

131. STOUFFER, S. A. An analysis of conflicting social norms. *Amer. Sociol. Rev.*, 1949, 14, 707-717.

132. STOUFFER, S. A., *et al.* (Eds.) *The American Soldier,* Vols. I & II. Princeton: Princeton University, 1950.

133. STOUFFER, S. A. and TOBY, J. Role conflict and personality. *Amer. J. Sociol.*, 1951, 56, 395-406.

134. SWANSON, G. E. The effectiveness of decision-making groups, effects of constitutional arrangements on group efficiency. *Adult Leadership,* 1959, 8, 48-52.

135. SWANSON, G. E. *The birth of the gods, origins of primitive beliefs,* Ann Arbor, Mich.: University of Michigan, 1960.

136. SWANSON, G. E. Determinants of the individual's defenses against inner conflict: review and reformulation. In J. C. Glidewell (Ed.) *Parental attitudes and child behavior.* Springfield, Ill.: Charles C. Thomas, 1961. Pp. 5-41.

137. TAGIURI, R. and PETRULLO, L. (Eds.) *Person perception and interpersonal behavior.* Stanford: Stanford University, 1958.

138. TETTMER, J. *I was a monk.* New York: Knopf, 1951.

139. THIBAUT, J. W. and RIECKEN, H. W. Some determinants and consequences of the perception of social causality. *J. Pers.*, 1955, 24, 113-133.

140. THOMAS, E. J. Effects of facilitative role interdependence on group functioning. *Hum. Relat.*, 1957, 10, 347-366.

141. TILLICH, P. *The courage to be.* New Haven: Yale University, 1952.

142. TILLICH, P. *Love, power, and justice.* Gloucester, Mass.: Peter Smith, 1960.

143. TURNER, R. H. Self and other in moral judgment. *Amer. Sociol. Rev.*, 1954, 19, 249-259.

144. UNDERHILL, E. *Mysticism.* New York: Meridian Books, 1955.

145. WALLIN, P. A. Guttman scale for measuring women's neighborliness. *Amer. J. Sociol.*, 1953, 59, 243-246.

146. WATSON, J. A formal analysis of sociable interaction. *Sociometry,* 1958, 21, 269-280.

147. WEEKS, H. A. *Youthful offenders at Highfields.* Ann Arbor, Mich.: University of Michigan, 1958.

148. WEINBERG, S. K. *Incest behavior.* New York: Citadel Press, 1955.

149. WESTLEY, W. A. Secrecy and the police. *Soc. Forces,* 1956, 34, 254-257.

150. WHITING, J. W. M., KLUCKHOHN, R. and ANTHONY, A. The function of male initiation ceremonies at puberty. In E. E. Maccoby, T. M. Newcomb, and E. L. Hartley (Eds.) *Readings in social psychology.* New York: Henry Holt, 1958, Pp. 359-370.

151. WILENSKY, H. L. Orderly careers and social participation:

the impact of work history on social integration in the middle mass. *Amer. Sociol. Rev.*, 1961, 26, 521-539.

152. WILLIAMS, J. H. Close friendship relations of housewives residing in an urban community. *Soc. Forces,* 1958, 36, 358-362.

153. WILLIAMS, R. M., JR. Friendship and social values in a sub-urban community: an exploratory study. *Pacific Sociol. Rev.,* 1959, 2, 3-10.

154. WILSON, A. T. M., TRIST, E. L., and CURLE, A. Transitional communities and social reconnection: a study of the civil resettlement of British prisoners of war. In G. E. Swanson, T. M. Newcomb, and E. L. Hartley (Eds.) *Readings in social psychology.* New York: Henry Holt, 1952. Pp. 561-579.

155. WINCH, R. F. Mate-selection, a study of complementary needs. New York: Harper, 1958.

156. WORKMAN, H. B. *The evolution of the monastic ideal from the earliest times down to the coming of the friars.* London: Epworth Press, 1927.

157. WRIGHT, C. R. and HYMAN, H. H. Voluntary memberships of American adults: evidence from national sample surveys. *Amer. Sociol. Rev.,* 1958, 23, 284-294.

158. ZBOROWSKI, M. and HERZOG, E. *Life is with people.* New York: International Universities Press, 1952.

159. ZIMMER, B. G. and HAWLEY, A. H. The significance of membership in associations. *Amer. J. Sociol.,* 1959, 65, 196-201.

PART THREE {
SELF-CONTROL
IN
PSYCHOLOGICAL
PERSPECTIVE

Introduction

Behavior may be characterized as a complex interaction of the individual and the environment. The individual enters this interaction on every occasion with a unique selectivity and response repertoire reflecting the cumulative effects of inheritance of species and strain characteristics and of maturation, adaptation, and learning in a specific set of environmental circumstances. The environment exercises both cumulative effects on development and specific influences on behavior in situations in its differential facilitation and obstruction of the alternative responses that it permits. Behavior further represents the integrated action of the organism, although it is convenient for psychologists to identify modification through practices as learning, interpretation of sensory input as perception, and activation and direction toward alternative objects as emotion and motivation.

Basically, this formulation embraces much of what psychologists can say about human and animal responses to stress. The level of abstraction of the statement speaks not of responses to stress per se, but of all of behavior. Thus, it implies that the phenomena of stress behavior are not, as is often implied, somehow different and separate, but rather integral to the lawful principles of animal and human behavior. The study of responses to stress must therefore be concerned with the study of behavior in situational circumstances defined as involving stress.

The three distinguished papers in this session can be conceptualized within the foregoing frame of reference. However, each of the contributors, focusing on particular categories of stressful situations, adds extensive detail to the general formulation for the types of subjects, threats, and environmental circumstances studied. Dr. Janis focuses attention on the threatening situations experienced by wartime populations subjected to aerial bombing, persons in natural and man-made disasters, cancer and surgery patients, pregnant women, combat pilots, and the wives of combat personnel. His elucidation of the role of reality orientation and preparatory communication in "emotional inoculation" and of the dynamics of *the work of* worrying, grief, and mourning, clarify the adaptive mechanics in such stressful situations, and add meaning to the concepts of stress tolerance.

Dr. Korchin, whose experimental studies have included paratroopers, combat personnel and astronauts, as well as more conventional laboratory subjects, directs attention to the diversity found over the range of stress situations, which he analyzes into seven basic categories, and emphasizes temporal ordering of events in the attentional field and the interplay of perceptive (evaluative) acts, motivation, and social context as essential to the understanding of behavior under stress. Dr. Liddell, the eminent representative of the Pavlovian school, presents a provocative analysis of principles derived from Pavlovian conditioning of sheep and goats which he applies to the understanding of self-control under stressful conditions in both Soviet man and men working under organizational restraints.

IRVING L. JANIS

Psychodynamic Aspects of Stress Tolerance

In order to elucidate some of the important aspects of adjustment to threat and danger, this paper will focus on theoretical concepts and observations which bear on unconscious processes that enable people to assimilate distressing life experiences.[1] First we shall examine the extraordinarily pervasive reaction of "obsessional staring," which seems to occur among survivors of every major disaster. Then we shall turn to some parallel phenomena which occur when warnings and other preparatory communications arouse vigilance reactions during periods when people are concerned about impending danger. In this connection, findings will be cited from a number of different investigations which suggest that under certain conditions the arousal of vigilance before actual exposure to stress stimuli tends to enhance subsequent stress tolerance. The final section of this paper will discuss a theoretical construct, "the work of worrying," which helps to explain basic features of adaptation to stress. Some of the main implications of this construct will be presented, bearing especially on the conditions under which preparatory communications can be expected to provide a successful form of "emotional inoculation" against the disruptive impact of stressful events.

This paper is based on material in the author's forthcoming book, which presents a more extensive analysis of research on stress tolerance: *Contours of fear: Psychological studies of war, disaster, illness, and experimentally induced stress,* New York: Wiley & Sons, in press.

Obsessional Staring Following
a Small Scale Disaster

Some important clues concerning the emotional impact of threat stimuli can be obtained from a detailed study of post-disaster staring reactions. The obsessional character of such reactions first became apparent to me ten years ago, when I had the opportunity to investigate at first hand the psychological effects of an unexpected disaster in the community where I live (20).

Early in the morning of February 1, 1954, in a middle-class residential section of New Haven, there was a bomb-like explosion which completely demolished a three-story house, killing four of the occupants and injuring three others. The blast shook hundreds of homes and shattered windows throughout the surrounding neighborhood. Twenty minutes later, a second blast occurred which knocked the house next door off its foundation. Both explosions resulted from an accumulation of gas fumes in the basements of the two houses, following the rupture of a nearby gas main located deep under the frozen ground.

During the three days following the disaster, thousands of curious spectators stood at the periphery of the disaster site, inspecting the damage and watching the activities of emergency rescue and repair crews. Most spectators were in an animated, highly talkative mood and remained for only one or two hours. But there were also some who stood there grimly, hour after hour, without speaking a word to anyone. On inquiry, I learned that many of these silent spectators lived in the immediate neighborhood. They spent the greater part of their waking hours, day after day, standing outside in the bitter winter cold, staring fixedly at the black hole containing the charred debris from the demolished building. From four such persons whom I interviewed individually on the third day after the explosion, some leads were obtained concerning the motivations underlying their obsessional staring.

Initially, upon being violently awakened, these individuals, like the others in their families, had hurried outside to see what was happening and to find out whether their own homes were endangered. This alert vigilant reaction proved to be highly adaptive in some instances, most notably in the case of a family that had decided to pack up and evacuate before the second blast damaged their home.

At the time of the interviews, the respondents' need for information about the disaster had long since been satiated, and yet they continued to be somewhat perplexed. Several respondents at first were reluctant about being interviewed, merely repeating over and over again "I just can't understand it." Later on, however, after they began to verbalize their morose thoughts and feelings, it became apparent that they were trying to comprehend the significance of the disaster, not in terms of its physical causes, which had been explained to them on the first day, but in relation to their own personal concepts of life and death. For example, one man said:

I just stand here all day long looking across the street, I don't know why. I can't get over it. To think that they could be so alive the night before, playing cards, talking to us. Then all of a sudden, for no reason, they are wiped out. A big house is there one minute and the next minute nothing is left of it at all. I just can't understand it.

This man spoke at great length about the shocked surprise created by the explosions. He had been jolted out of his sleep by the first blast and had run to the shattered window of his bedroom to discover what was going on. He was appalled to see the house across the street crumbling to the ground, enveloped in gigantic flames. When the outer wall came crashing down, he thought for a moment that it might hit his own house. In a somewhat dazed state, he got dressed, went outside, and talked with the firemen who were arriving from the firehouse only a block away. From that time on, this man kept a silent vigil, standing outside all day long, staring at the destroyed house. He avoided speaking to anyone in the crowd of curious "outsiders," toward whom he expressed resentful feelings ("The police ought to keep them out"). The affective tone of the interview as a whole, however, was clearly depressive in character, and most of his comments, like the one quoted earlier, indicated an inner struggle to assimilate the personal implications of the distressing disaster events he had witnessed.

In the interviews with three others who lived in the same neighborhood there were similar indications that their staring behavior was part of a general preoccupation with the disaster as a distressing demonstration of the uncertainty of life. In none of the four was there any indication of positive pleasure or subtle release of sadistic impulses, although it is conceivable that such motivations could be operating at a deeply unconscious level. Their depressive tone and their quasi-philosophical expressions of perplexity about man's vulnerability to sudden disaster indicated an effort to "work through" a painful aspect of reality that could no longer be ignored.

Additional interviews were conducted with men and women who lived in the immediate neighborhood of the disaster site but who had not continued to participate in the staring reaction. Several of these respondents spoke about having deliberately stayed away from the area as much as possible in order to avoid being reminded about the nightmarish events they had witnessed on the morning of the explosions. Nevertheless, these respondents gave many indications that they, too, were deeply preoccupied with the disaster. They complained about not being able to get their minds off it and expressed the same type of philosophical ruminations about life and death that were encountered among those who displayed the staring reaction. And the non-starers expressed just as much resentment against the hordes of spectators from outside the neighborhood who had "no right to hang around at a time like this." Most of the respondents, whether starers or nonstarers, spoke as though the disaster belonged only to those few people who were closely touched by it, regarding it as something very personal—a fragile possession that somehow needed to be protected from the unsympathetic scrutiny of calloused outsiders.

The preoccupied reactions observed following the New Haven disaster were almost identical with those described in a report by the National Opinion Research Center on reactions to the large series of gas explosions in 1953 at Brighton, New York (36). Many housewives in the neighborhood of the destroyed homes complained that they could not get the hideous image of the disaster out of their minds even though they wanted to avoid being reminded of it. One woman who made this complaint placed the blame on her surroundings, asserting that the destruction would not stop staring her in the face and that the constant presence of sightseers kept attracting her attention to the disaster site.

You're never left alone long enough to forget it, especially with the shell across the street staring you in the face every time you get up in the morning and go to bed at night. I think as soon as they could . . . get some of these things torn down . . . and filled in—if you can erase the scars you know—that'll help—if they would just get that mess out of there and the sightseers would stop going around (36, p. 145).

Others who acknowledged that they deliberately stared at the destruction made comments from which one can again detect an effort to "work through" the significance of the disaster in personal terms. For example, one respondent said: "I was over watching them hunt for the M——— children who had been trapped in the basement of the house when it exploded—The kids had just been over to our house the day before—I still keep thinking about those two poor innocent children. It could just as easily have been mine" (36, p. 145).

Just as in the New Haven disaster, some of the neighbors deliberately stayed away from the destroyed area of Brighton in an attempt to avoid being confronted with any reminders of the disaster; but they, nevertheless, remained preoccupied with it. One woman, for example, said she was unable to sleep for three nights because, "You'd close your eyes and see a house blowing up in front of you. You could see it every time you closed your eyes" (36, p. 143).

These reactions seem to be only one step removed from the repetitive daydreams and nightmares about disastrous events which occur in people who are suffering from acute traumatic neurosis (28). Freud's hypothesis about recurrent nightmares in chronic war neurosis states that the imaginative reliving of a disaster long after the traumatic events have occurred involves a "belated attempt at mastery" (11), and the same hypothesis might be extended to the milder forms of preoccupation. Later on we shall see that the latter might often prove to be more punctual and more successful attempts at mastery.

The interview comments made by people who displayed obsessional staring in the two gas explosion disasters closely resemble the comments by Londoners who stared gloomily at destroyed buildings during the air war against Britain. According to Matte (34), the subjective thoughts of the silent, staring spectators following the London air raids were centered on the possibilities of injury or death and tended to be a "working through" of the personal meaning of a threat that up to that time they had been trying to deny. Matte believes this thought process serves an important adjustive function among survivors, enabling them to assimilate new and disturbing information about their vulnerability to a threat without becoming panic-stricken or neurotic.

One of his [Matte's] hypotheses is that viewing the destruction stimulates a *gradual* realization of the possibilities of one's own death and thereby minimizes the traumatic effects of a *sudden* confrontation with the realities of air raid dangers. At the same time, the heightened awareness of the danger may have enhanced self-respect ("I am able to take it"). Among those who were initially inclined to ignore or to deny the existence of danger, the adjustment process described by

Matte might be expected to have considerable value as a form of
psychological preparation for withstanding the emotional impact of
increasingly severe air attacks. Some of the persons who were initially
apprehensive might also have benefitted from viewing bomb damage.
Numerous observers mention that there was considerable relief among
the British when they discovered what the raids were really like. They
had expected the attacks to be far more devastating than they actually turned out to be [14, 32, 42, 46]. The satisfaction of curiosity
about the destruction produced by a raid is probably one of the ways
in which grossly exaggerated expectations and fantasies are brought
into line with reality (19, pp. 155-156).

This passage suggests that somewhat different adjustive functions may be involved for people who are near-miss survivors
than for those who are remote-misses. The latter constituted a
sizeable proportion, if not the vast majority, of the curious spectator from remote neighborhoods who came to view the air raid
destruction. For them, the sight of destruction probably served
mainly as a source of information that supplemented whatever
warning communications they had already received. Under conditions where the spectators do not see injured people or maimed
corpses, the expected effect of their scrutiny of the damage would
be a comparatively slight increase or decrease in the level of
emotional tension, depending upon whether their direct observations of the devastation show it to be greater or smaller than they
had originally surmised.

A much more profound type of psychological change would
be expected in those persons who have been emotionally shocked
either by a personal narrow escape from death or by witnessing
the full destructive impact of a disaster on others. According to
numerous studies of wartime and peacetime disasters, direct personal involvement in danger gives rise to acute emotional shock,
traumatic neurosis, and allied forms of emotional disturbance (9,
14, 19, 23, 32, 35, 50). These studies indicate that the symptoms
usually subside within a few days, particularly among clinically
normal persons who have no prior history of neurotic disturbance.
Perhaps when such persons engage in obsessional staring or in
other forms of mental preoccupation with painful reminiscences
about a disaster to which they have recently been exposed, they
sooner or later work out new conceptions of the danger and of
their resources for coping with it, resulting in the development of
more effective self-delivered reassurances. Thus, they might regain
their emotional equanimity and increase their capacity for facing
threats of a recurrence of the disaster without becoming disor-

ganized or hypervigilant. In contrast, the "near miss" cases who succeed in escaping from reminders of the harrowing disaster and who constantly avoid the painful subjective process of working it through may be left with damaging emotional scars. These are probably the people who are most adversely sensitized by their disaster experience, becoming predisposed to overreact to new threats and to suffer from sustained traumatic neurosis.

The foregoing hypotheses are based on the assumption that inner mastery following exposure to stress involves essentially the same type of readjustive function as the "work of morning," which Freud (10) described as essential for accepting the loss of a loved one without becoming pathologically depressed. Studies of grief among the relatives of disaster victims (4, 31) suggest that there are pathologic consequences if the loss is denied and the work of mourning is postponed. On the basis of his investigations of the Worcester tornado and other large-scale disasters, Wallace (47, 48) has noted similar phenomena and has suggested that there is an unconscious process of assimilation which is identical with the work of mourning. His main thesis is that even when a survivor has not lost any loved ones in a disaster, he perceives "cultural damage" which can be just as "shocking" as private loss. Wallace points out that many uninjured survivors "will suffer 'shock' and the subsequent characteristics of the disaster syndrome, partly or wholly as a result of the perception that *a part of their culture is ineffective or has been rendered inoperative.*" And he goes on to say that they react to this perception *"as if a beloved object were dead"* (48, p. 24). The "disaster syndrome" consists of dazed, shocked, preoccupied reactions, including the obsessional staring reactions described earlier in this chapter. Wallace states that:

Again and again in the interviews [of tornado disaster victims at Worcester, Mass.] the phrase 'the end of the world' occurs to describe the phantasy of the survivors; the sight of block after block of ruined houses, of maimed and bleeding people, fallen trees, scarred and lifeless lawns, bedraggled wires, and everything covered with mud, aroused momentarily in many the thought that this was the earth's last hour, or that an atomic bomb had fallen, or that the whole city of Worcester was in ruins (47, pp. 62-63).

But he asserts that the dominant reaction during the initial stage is "stunned disbelief, inability to express emotion, [and] random movement" (48, p. 24). Later on, according to Wallace, there are two further stages, which closely parallel the pattern observed in people who are mourning for a lost loved object:

A stage of passivity, dependence, acceptance of sympathy and help from family and friends; and finally a stage of joining with the community in burying the dead and of taking up a new life more or less free of disabling grief over the deceased (48, p. 24).

We would expect the disaster syndrome and the subsequent stages of recovery to occur mainly among persons who were "near misses." But Wallace implies that the same reactions might occur, at least in attenuated form, among many of the curious spectators who come into the stricken area from places that were untouched by the disaster. Wolfenstein (50), however, suggests other motivations that may enter into spectator behavior. She mentions the spectators' desire to observe forbidden things and calls attention to some indications of unconscious gratification of sadistic impulses, which may occur even though they consciously feel sympathy toward victims and volunteer for rescue work in order to assuage their guilt. Fritz and Mathewson (13) acknowledge that a variety of motives may impel sightseers to converge on disaster sites but point out that there is little evidence to support the charge, often leveled in a resentful way by disaster victims, that the main motive is morbid glee at the sad plight of others. These authors believe that the dominant motivation is more likely to be ". . . the need to assimilate happenings which lie outside the viewer's frame of reference or realm of experience and which may affect his future safety" (13, p. 49). Thus, as these authors suggest, the working through process is not necessarily limited to "near miss" cases who are emotionally shocked by direct exposure to disaster events, but may also occur among outsiders, who become distressed when they learn about the disaster long after it has happened. Like the disaster survivors who engage in obsessional staring, many of the outsiders who converge on a disaster site are likely to be preoccupied with thoughts and fantasies about what *might* have happened during the disaster and about what *could* happen to them in the future.

The "Working Through" Process in Cancer Victims

When suffering and the threat of annihilation extends over a period of many months, as in the case of a protracted illness, the process of working through may go on more gradually and entail a much more profound change in attitudes than when the threat lasts only a short time. Shands (43) has described marked changes in attitudes among those cancer patients who are able to overcome the initially traumatic information about their disease and eventually go about their business again. When a person is given the bad news that he has a malignant tumor, his initial reaction pattern usually resembles the disaster syndrome—dazed emotional shock, apathetic numbness, feelings of depersonalization, and inhibition of action. Shands points out that the patient feels "empty" of purpose and unable to make plans for the future as a consequence of his alien, "doomed" status. After a short time, however, a second phase begins, characterized by intense preoccupation with the disease combined with unsuccessful attempts to alleviate emotional tension by projecting the blame onto doctors or nurses and by denying obvious implications of the malignant illness. According to Shands, these unsuccessful attempts are followed by a third phase in which the person *grieves* over his condition and then gradually readapts, overcoming the sense of emptiness by a new conception of himself which is facilitated by a process of identification. More specifically, the patient identifies himself with someone in the role of a good helper or a good child and in this adopted role he no longer shies away from people. The new identification provides a way of obtaining satisfaction from his interaction not only with doctors and nurses, but also with his family, friends, and fellow patients. The crucial phase in this development, Shands asserts, is the *grieving* reaction which is essential for replacing the initial alien outlook with a more constructive one:

. . . grieving is a response to the loss of a whole system of assumptions and expectations upon which human beings build a view of the world. In some manner the weeping reaction . . . serves to 'dissolve' the old system in such a way that it can be replaced by a new. Where the grieving is blocked for any reason, the patient has to adopt some precarious defensive sort of adaptation rather than attempting, after clearing the site, to make a new construction with the materials at hand (43).

This reorientation is regarded as "adaptive" in the sense that it enables the patient once again to take an interest in the social world around him, to plan his actions in a realistic way that maximizes his chances for survival, and to take account of various limitations imposed by his illness. Shands points out that certain situational factors, such as the availability of a sympathetic listener, can greatly facilitate the reorientation process, provided that the personality of the patient is sufficiently "mature."

Research Findings From Studies
of Surgical Patients

My own studies of surgical patients (22) provide considerable evidence of a "working through" process that closely resembles the reorientation process delineated by Shands for cancer patients and that also has many features in common with the post-disaster process of "working-through," as described earlier in this paper. The surgery studies indicate that when anticipatory fear is stimulated by warnings about an impending danger situation, the working through process can be initiated *before* actual exposure to danger stimuli and can play an important role in enabling the person to cope effectively with subsequent stressful episodes.

The psychological investigations of surgical patients were designed primarily to help answer a number of preliminary questions which are pertinent for developing a general theory of stress tolerance: How do people who display different degrees of anticipatory fear or anxiety react when they subsequently undergo the acute pains, the stressful bodily discomforts, and the severe deprivations of the postoperative period? Does the type of information the patients had been given beforehand by the medical or nursing staff bear any relationship to postoperative emotional reactions?

From the outset, the author assumed that the relationship between preoperative fear and postoperative emotional disturbances would not prove to be a simple one but would, rather, depend upon a number of complex interacting psychological factors. It was felt to be a useful first step, however, to examine critically a questionable assumption which seems to be held by many psychologists and psychiatrists; namely, that the *more anxious* a person becomes when he is confronted with the threat of impending danger, the *poorer* will be his adjustment to the actual impact of the stress when the danger is actually encountered. This assumption is sometimes made by personnel specialists in military and industrial organization, for example when military draftees are being screened for combat duty or when skilled industrial workers are being selected for certain types of dangerous occupations. The same assumption is often invoked when physicians, public health officials, and government leaders decide to withhold realistic information about impending dangers on the grounds that if the recipients' anxiety were stimulated by direful warnings, their emotional stability would be weakened and they would be less able to "take" subsequent adversity.

The notion of a simple one-to-one correspondence between the magnitude of anticipatory fear reactions and the probability of developing maladjustive stress reactions could be said to contain at least a kernel of empirical truth. Many observations indicate that those persons who become excessively apprehensive when they learn about the threat of impending danger are more likely than others to display acute emotional disturbances when they subsequently encounter the actual danger stimuli. For example, systematic data in Stouffer et al. (44) show that there was a relatively high incidence of refusals to jump from an airplane among volunteer paratroopers who had displayed overt fear symptoms on their first day of preliminary tower-jump training. Clinical psychoanalytic reports also suggest that there are certain types of neurotically predisposed persons who consistently overreact to environmental threats and dangers (5, 8, 12, 37, 39). In such persons, repressed infantile anxieties or various displaced fears concerning body integrity appear to be reactivated whenever they perceive either the remote or imminent possibility of suffering actual body damage. As will be seen shortly, the study of surgical patients also confirms the fact that there is a certain type of hyperanxious personality who characteristically reacts with neurotic anxiety to any sign of potential body damage, displaying excessive apprehensiveness before the operation and again afterwards. Such persons seem to react as though they were facing an enormous danger whenever they are told about (or directly confronted with) even very minor threats (e.g., penicillin injections). Because the underlying source of their anxiety remains unconscious, they fail to show the usual decrease in anticipatory fear when given reassuring communications by physicians or other authoritative persons.

The above clinical considerations do not imply, however, that the persons who are best able to cope with actual danger and deprivation are those who experience little or no anticipatory fear beforehand. That other crucial factors may enter into the picture is indicated by evidence from my study of the postoperative emotional behavior of surgical patients in relation to the magnitude and quality of their preoperative fear reactions. On the surgical ward of a large community hospital, 23 typical surgical patients were interviewed intensively before and after undergoing major surgery. Hospital records, including the physicians' and nurses'

226   IRVING L. JANIS

daily notes on each patient's behavior, were also used. Then, later on, as a separate source of systematic evidence on the same general problems, a questionnaire survey was conducted with about 200 male adolescents who had recently undergone a major or minor surgical operation.

The first step in analyzing the case study material consisted of classifying the patients into the following three descriptive categories, according to the available interview data and behavioral records concerning their preoperative emotional status:

1. Extremely high preoperative fear—constantly worried and agitated; has marked sleep disturbances; seeks reassurances from authoritative figures but is only momentarily relieved by them; attempts to avoid or postpone the operation.

2. Moderate anticipatory fear—occasionally tense or agitated; worries about specific features of the operative procedure or anesthesia but is relieved when given authoritative reassurances; able to maintain outward calm most of the time.

3. Extremely low anticipatory fear—constantly cheerful and optimistic; completely denies feeling any concern or worry; no observable agitation or tension in overt behavior; sleeps well and is able to keep self well occupied with reading, socializing, etc.

The following are the main conclusions that emerged from the case study series all of which were supported by correlational data from the survey research.[2]

1. Persons who were *extremely fearful* before the operation were *more* likely than others to be *anxiety-ridden* again afterwards, and their excessive fears of body damage were linked with numerous clinical signs of chronic neurotic disturbance.

2. Persons who displayed a *moderate* degree of preoperative fear were significantly *less* likely than others to display *any form of emotional disturbance* during the stressful period of postoperative convalesence.

3. Persons who showed a relative *absence* of preoperative fear were *more* likely than others to display disturbed reactions of *anger and intense resentment* during postoperative convalescence.

1. In the book on *Psychological Stress* (22), I have described in detail the supporting evidence from the case studies and the correlational data obtained from the survey research. In addition, evidence is described which shows that the observed relationships cannot be attributed to differences in the patients' background characteristics (e.g., age, socioeconomic status, ethnic or religious background) nor to differences in medical status (e.g., type of illness, severity of pain, postoperative prognosis).

Many additional observations contribute evidence in support of the following general theoretical proposition: *The arousal of anticipatory fear prior to exposure to a stressful life situation is one of the necessary conditions for developing effective inner defenses that enable the person to cope psychologically with stress stimuli.* There is considerable supplementary evidence, to be discussed shortly, which indicates that the effectiveness of the inner defenses that are erected depends upon the degree to which the person can overcome the powerful spontaneous tendency to *deny* the possibility of being personally affected by an impending source of danger. The evidence strongly suggests that if certain (nondenial) types of inner attitudes are formed before the danger materializes, the chances of developing traumatic or disorganized emotional symptoms are greatly reduced.

When we investigate those cases in whom anticipatory fear had been aroused before the operation, we find that they had fantasied or mentally rehearsed various unpleasant occurrences which they had thought would be in store for them. Their anticipatory fears seem to have motivated them to seek out and to take account of realistic information about the painful and distressing experiences they would be likely to undergo after awakening from the anesthesia and during the period of convalescence. In these persons, the conceptions developed prior to the operation often turn out to be essentially correct so that when unpleasant episodes occur they are not only relatively unsurprised, but feel reassured that events during the recovery phase are proceeding in the expected fashion.

Some individuals, notably those who displayed excessively high anxiety before the operation, appeared to benefit relatively little from having mentally rehearsed the dangers in advance. Most of these cases, as already stated, were persons who chronically suffered from neurotic anxiety, and their postoperative emotional reactions can be regarded as a continuation of their neuroses. Both before and after the operation they seemed to be unable to develop any effective inner defenses to cope with the threat of body damage. Evidently their fears were grounded not so much in the external dangers of surgery as in long-standing unconscious conflicts that were ready to be touched off by any such environmental provocation.

The psychological situation appears to have been quite different among the patients in the "moderate anticipatory fear" group. These people appeared to be highly responsive to authoritative reassurances from the hospital staff and seemed to have developed a variety of means of reassuring themselves at moments when their fears were strongly aroused. Such patients would frequently report instances of self-reassurance in their postoperative interviews: for example, "I knew that there might be some bad pains and so when my side started to ache I told myself that this doesn't mean anything has gone wrong."

Such self-reassurances appeared to be rare among the patients who had been relatively free from anticipatory fears before the operation. These persons remained emotionally calm during the period when they were able to deny the possibility of danger and suffering, but they reacted quite differently as soon as they began to experience the pains and other harassments that accompany the usual recovery from a major surgical operation. They became extremely agitated and tended to assume that the hospital authorities must be to blame for their suffering. In a few such cases, it seemed quite probable that this way of reacting to external dangers was a manifestation of a characteristic personality tendency and might be quite unrelated to any specific occurrence either before or after the operation. In most of the other cases, however, it seemed extremely likely that the individual's lack of worry beforehand—and the consequent lack of inner preparation for coping with the stresses of surgery—was a consequence of the *lack of adequate preparatory communications.*

In several cases, the interview data and the hospital records indicated that, on the occasion of an earlier operation, their reactions had been of a markedly different character, so that neither the preoperative lack of fear nor the postoperative agitation and resentment could be regarded as typical for these personalities. For instance, before an earlier abdominal operation (appendectomy) one patient, a 21-year old woman, had been given realistic information and reassurances by the physician. At that time she had been moderately worried beforehand but showed excellent emotional adjustment after the operation. About two years later, she came to the same hospital for another abdominal operation (cholecystectomy), but this time without having learned anything from her physician other than "there's really nothing to it; it's a less serious operation than the previous one." On this occasion the patient remained wholly unconcerned about the operation beforehand, apparently anticipating complete invulnerability. But after the operation she became markedly upset, negativistic, and resentful toward the nursing staff. In cases such as this one, it seems that chronic personality predispositions do not fully account for the use of pathogenic denial defenses; rather, adjustment to the fear-producing situation appears to be highly dependent upon the type of preparatory communications that the patients are given during the preoperative period.

Some relevant correlational evidence on this point was obtained from the survey of a large sample of male surgery cases (22, pp. 352-360). The results showed that the postoperative reactions of men who had been informed beforehand about specific unpleasant experiences that were in store for them differed significantly from those of men who were uninformed. The informed cases were more likely than the uninformed to be worried or fearful before the operation, but then were less likely to become angry or emotionally upset during the postoperative convalescent period. A significantly smaller percentage of the informed men subsequently expressed feelings of resentment or developed sustained changes of attitude in the negative direction toward the staff physicians or nurses.

Although these correlational data are based on retrospective reports and therefore cannot be accepted as conclusively valid evidence, they nevertheless add some weight to the following conclusion derived from the parallel findings from the intensive case studies: If no authorative communications are given and if other circumstances are such that fear is *not* aroused beforehand, the person will lack the motivation to undergo the learning process that enables him to build up effective self-delivered reassurances before the onset of the danger situation and therefore he will have relatively low stress tolerance when the crisis is actually at hand.

Additional Studies Bearing on Stress Tolerance

A search of the literature on psychological effects of surgical operations, severe illness, community disasters, and combat dangers revealed many bits of evidence that are consistent with the same general conclusion. For example, parallel findings were reported by Titchener and his associates (45) in a study of 200 randomly selected surgical patients who were given psychiatric interviews before the operation and again from three to six months after discharge from the hospital. These authors found that "increased anxiety and/or fear appearing preoperatively were associated with the maintenance of a good or an improved personality adjustment." From the data they present, however, it is not clear whether their results bear out the curvilinear relationship found in my studies of surgical patients or whether they found a linear inverse relationship such that the higher the level of preoperative fear, the better the postoperative adjustment. In either case, however, their findings clearly bear out the implication that low preoperative fear is *not* associated with good postoperative adjustment. It is also noteworthy that they found anxiety or depression during the week immediately following the operation to be predictive of poor adjustment after convalesence, several months later.

Some systematic observations bearing on the relationship between anticipatory fear and subsequent reactions during a stressful crisis are presented by Cramond and Aberd (6). These authors compared 50 women who had undergone normal labor with 50 who had developed severe uterine dysfunction during labor, a type of dysfunction which in most instances is assumed to be a somatic manifestation of acute anxiety in response to the stresses of childbirth. The women in the dysfunctional group were found to be much more likely to have a history of "suppression or repression of feelings of tension." This antecedent characteristic was found in 54 per cent of the dysfunctional group as compared with only 12 per cent of the normal control group. Thus, once again, a relative absence of fear or anxiety during the pre-crisis period was found to be associated with high emotional disturbance during the crisis period.

Beatrix Cobb and her coworkers (3) compared a group of cancer patients who had delayed coming to a clinic for a medical diagnosis with a comparable group who had come in promptly. They found that the delayers, who had tended to deny the threatening implications of their symptoms before being hospitalized, were more likely than the nondelayers to become resistant and hostile —refusing essential treatments, rejecting the hospital regimen, and creating management problems in the wards. Their description of the subsequent aggressive reactions of the delayers corresponds in exact detail to my own observations of the postoperative aggressive reactions of surgical patients who had denied the threat and had manifested little or no preoperative fear.

A parallel relationship is suggested by the findings from a study of reactions to air raids in England during World War II. Wilson (49) gave a psychiatric examination to 63 people who became psychiatric casualties after a heavy air attack and compared their present and past reactions with those of 102 controls who had been physically injured. He found that the psychiatric casualties were much more likely to have denied their fear beforehand than the control cases, which led him to conclude that "the admission and acceptance of fear is a safeguard against breakdown in conditions of acute stress." Wilson's observations, however, like those of several of the other studies just cited, cannot be regarded as definitive evidence in support of this conclusion since they were based entirely upon retrospective accounts rather than on a followup of people whose level of fear was directly observed before the onset of the acute stress episode.

A study by F. Romalis (40) provides suggestive evidence bearing on quite a different type of wartime stress. In this study, interviews were conducted during World War II with American women who became emotionally upset when their husbands or sons were drafted into military service. The author reports that the most extreme reactions of emotional shock occurred in those women who had been unworried about the impending separation and who had clung to unrealistic fantasies about the man being continually deferred or being allowed to live at home after entering the service. These denial reactions, according to Romalis, were followed by surprise, resentment, and depression when the actual separation subsequently took place.

Grinker and his collaborators (16) report correlational data from combat flying personnel that are in line with the foregoing studies. These investigators administered a questionnaire to 284 air crew officers who had been hospitalized because of anxiety or depression following a tour of combat flying duty. Their responses were compared with those obtained from a control group of 260 officers who had had air combat experience without developing neurotic symptoms. From their retrospective reports, the psychiatric casualties were more likely than the controls to be characterized by: a) unrealistic enthusiasm for combat flying during the early period of their tour of duty and b) marked loss of feelings of personal invulnerability after experiencing the actual stresses of combat. Although not conclusive, these findings, and the other correlational results, are consistent with the findings from the surgery studies. Together with other studies of military combat, they strongly suggest that those men who remained relatively free from fear by denying the danger at the outset of their tour of combat duty were more likely than others to lose their feelings of invulnerability when actually confronted with danger stimuli, developing symptoms of extreme irritability, depression or anxiety, which persisted after they had been removed from combat duty.

Case Studies of the Breakdown
of Denial Defenses

The transformation of an attitude of blanket denial into one of hypervigilance in combat flying personnel is documented by numerous case studies described by Grinker and Spiegel (15) and Bond (2). One case reported by the latter author, for example, illustrates how a minor accident can have a shattering effect on a man who had primarily relied on a blanket immunity type of defense. This man was proud of being a "hot" pilot and had denied experiencing any fear concerning the hazards of combat flying. He was always eager to fly at any time of the day or night. One day, on a routine, non-combat flight, his plane developed an oil leak, which at first he ignored. When he finally realized that something was seriously wrong, he became so apprehensive that he almost collided with another plane over the landing field. Immediately after that he made a second error of judgment which resulted in his hitting a high tension wire, seriously damaging his plane and setting it afire. After ten days in the hospital he had recovered from his burns and was able to return to duty. But from then on he became extremely apprehensive every time he entered a plane. In an effort to control his fear he obtained permission to fly another type of plane, but his emotional tension nevertheless increased, especially after he witnessed a fatal accident involving several of his friends.

In all such cases of a recently acquired phobia toward flying, according to Bond, the onset of symptoms can be ascribed to an event which demonstrates the realities of the danger situation, producing a pendulum-swing from the formula "nothing can happen to me" to "some disaster *must* happen to me" (2, p. 81).

A number of case studies presented by Grinker and Spiegel (15) show how the breakdown of an attitude of blanket immunity leads to a sudden upsurge of intense resentment combined with hypervigilance. They describe a 25-year-old air crew gunner, for example, who was always in a carefree mood on his first few missions, enjoying the sight of flak bursts around him. After several missions, however, he began to realize that the game was being played "for keeps"; thereafter, he became extremely irritable and developed a variety of acute neurotic symptoms including severe headaches, vomiting, loss of appetite, insomnia, and diffuse apprehensiveness. During a sodium pentathol interview, he displayed an acute abreaction, reliving some of his combat experiences and expressing intense hostility toward superior officers: "Damn armchair Generals think you can fly forever . . . I didn't want to fly this one, you s—o—b—." He also expressed a fearful, hopeless outlook: "I've never puked in a g-d- airplane but I think I'm going to . . . Get me out of here . . . *I'll fly but I know better —they will get me sooner or later.*" Grinker and Spiegel state that when this man abreacted his intense fear and hostility, his acute somatic symptoms of gagging and retching reappeared but, later on in his treatment, as he became more aware of his hostility, these visceral reactions subsided.

Similar reactions of irritability and resentment were noted in my study of surgical patients. After awakening from the anesthetic, many unexpectedly found themselves in a state of incapacitation and pain, with the result that they could no longer maintain an attitude of blanket denial. In some cases, patients who had formerly been free from fear suddenly felt helpless in the operating room when confronted with inescapable signs that the surgeon, assisted by the nurses, was about to drug them and cut open their abdomen. Their feelings of helplessness were immediately followed by intense fear and fantasies of hostile intentions on the part of those responsible for carrying out the operation (e.g., a 25-year-old social worker, in her post-operative account of what happened in the operating room, reported: "I felt he could be sadistic if he wanted to . . . I was afraid he might do a hysterectomy instead of the scheduled appendectomy").

At a moment of grave crisis, there seems to be a tendency to project blame upon the authorities for unexpected stress or suffering. Many case observations of the surgical patients suggest that the psychological sequence just noted in the two cases of the combat flyers is a typical reaction among persons who display a relative absence of anticipatory fear: absence of mental rehearsal of the impending danger, then feelings of helplessness when the danger materializes, then disappointment in protective authorities and finally increased expectations of vulnerability.

This psychological sequence, together with various auxiliary propositions to be presented shortly, is put forth as a tentative explanation for the high frequency of disturbances in the post-impact behavior of those people who had managed to ward off anticipatory fear most completely beforehand. It is important to note, however, that the same psychological factors also seem to account for isolated instances of fright and rage behavior among persons who experienced a moderate or high level of anticipatory fear. This is well illustrated by the case of a 29-year-old housewife who manifested a moderate level of anticipatory fear before her operation (lung lobectomy), and then postoperatively was uncomplaining, cooperative, and relatively free from emotional disturbances. Having had a similar operation once before, she expected that there would be acute incision pains and various unpleasant postoperative treatments. But she was caught completely by surprise when, shortly after awaking from the anesthetic, a physician asked her to swallow a drainage tube. On this occasion, she could not get herself to relax and begged the physician to let her alone. She described herself as having been terribly upset because she had not been told there would be any such treatment and felt that something must have gone wrong. During this brief postoperative episode she was unable to dispel unfavorable thoughts about the physician—either he was withholding information about the seriousness of her condition or he was unnecessarily imposing the "hideous" drainage treatment and was carrying it out "so badly it was practically killing me." At no other time during her long and painful convalescence did she entertain any similar doubts about this physician or any other member of the hospital staff; nor did she display any other instance of overt resistance behavior (22, p. 361-363).

The Work of Worrying

The observed relationship between low anticipatory fear and subsequent emotional disturbance forms part of the empirical basis for a theoretical analysis of the consequences of reality-oriented "worrying." A central postulate suggested by the case studies and the correlational findings cited in the preceding sections is that there is a "work of worrying," which, like the "work of mourning," enables the person to cope more effectively in the long run with a painful reality situation (21, 22). "Grief work" instigated by object loss usually does not begin until *after* a blow has struck (10). "Worry work," on the other hand, is assumed to begin as soon as one becomes aware of an *impending danger* that is perceived as threatening the self and therefore occurs *before* a blow strikes.

In order to specify functional properties of the work of worrying, it is necessary to delineate what occurs in its absence. What happens when, because of lack of opportunity or inadequate motivation, a person remains unworried about an impending danger experience and fails to undergo any inner preparation before it materializes? At the moment when inescapable signs of danger or actual suffering are encountered, efforts at intellectual denial (by minimizing or discounting the likelihood of being personally affected by the danger) will no longer succeed. The person then suddenly finds himself unable to ward off intense fear or fright (which sometimes is experienced as anger or other affects), especially because he has not developed any means for actively protecting himself from the danger. Moreover, the crisis seems to be augmented by the fact that when more danger or suffering is encountered than had been expected beforehand, feelings of helplessness are likely to occur which drastically interfere with normal reassurance mechanisms.

One of the most important sources of reassurance, markedly impaired under these conditions, is the anticipation of being protected from the full impact of the danger by the danger-control authorities or other benevolent parent surrogates. The greater the positive disparity between the magnitude of external stress and the magnitude of stress which was anticipated beforehand, the higher the probability that the person will be disappointed in those authority figures who were expected to protect him from danger. For example, in surgical patients and combat soldiers who initially succeed in warding off anticipatory fears by intellectually denying that the danger situation will have any serious effect, a great disparity arises between the low amount of suffering expected beforehand and the great amount of deprivation and suffering subsequently encountered. This disparity gives rise to an acute aggrievement reaction, consisting of a mixture of rage and depressive grief (22). There are some indications, from psychoanalytic case observations, that if one undergoes more suffering than had been expected, the ensuing aggrievement reactions derive their intensity from the *reactivation of childhood disappointments in one's parents* (7, 14, 22, 29). According to this hypothesis, any unexpectedly severe stress experience in adult life will tend to be unconsciously assimilated to early experiences during which the child had felt keenly disappointed in one or both parents. The reactivated childhood experiences may include not only instances of exceptionally harsh punishment at the hands of the parents,

but also accidents, illnesses, and other such unavoidable episodes
of suffering which had been interpreted by the child as being
caused by parental anger or parental neglect. When such emotional
experiences are reactivated in adult life, intense feelings of resentment and/or depression are likely to occur.

The preceding theoretical statements should not be construed
as implying that the only basis for stress-induced resentment (or
depression) is the reactivation of childhood disappointments.
Rather, the reactivation concept is intended to help explain irrational or unprovoked reactions of rage and depression which are
frequently noted among adults at times when they are exposed
to sudden disasters, severe illness, and other such situations of
danger or prolonged deprivation (1, 14, 18, 31, 38).

It is assumed that when an intense aggrievement reaction is
aroused by an adult stress experience, it will be either: a) externally directed toward authorities (resentment and retaliation
against parent surrogates) or b) inwardly directed toward the
self (loss of self-esteem, feelings of hopelessness, and other
symptoms of depression). The degree to which the reaction will
take the form of hostile resentment or depression depends upon
a variety of factors, including personality predispositions as well
as environmental factors. Among the latter are those actions or
inactions on the part of "danger-control authorities" which are
perceived as *deficient* behavior and which resemble the apparent
deficiencies of the parents at times when the child felt neglected
or victimized by unfair punishment. (The term "danger-control
authorities" refers to persons in a dominant role—such as the
government leaders who take charge in a disaster-stricken area
or the commanding officers in a military organization—who are
perceived as having the power to help or hinder one's chances of
escaping intact from current external threats.)

We would predict that when the danger-control authorities
fail to give advance warnings about the magnitude of the suffering
to be expected, the intensity of the disappointment reactions will
be increased, and the aggrievement reactions that are reactivated
will tend to take the form of resentment (from the reactivation of
childhood episodes of "undeserved" punishment) rather than
guilt and docility (from the reactivation of childhood episodes of
"deserved" punishment). For example, when a combat soldier
or flyer receives a slightly misleading communication from his
superiors before going on a harrowing bombing mission, one of
the predicted consequences will be a marked overreaction, which

is out of all proportion to the perceived magnitude of loss. This would be the consequence of a reactivation of affective responses and aggressive action tendencies which the man had developed during childhood experiences, at times when he had been intensely disappointed in his parents' deficient behavior. When neglected or overseverely punished by his parents, a child is likely to protest against the maltreatment and struggle against the incipient guilt feelings evoked by their rejection (e.g., "I don't deserve this; why don't you take better care of me?") An attitude of childlike protest seems to characterize the disproportionately intense anger, resentment, and resistant behavior evoked by seemingly minor frustrations in combat personnel, disaster victims and surgical patients who, in the absence of authoritative preparatory communications, had remained overoptimistic and relatively free from worry before the danger materialized.

Taking account of the available evidence bearing on the dynamics of stress behavior, I have formulated a number of interrelated adverse effects that are to be expected whenever a person has failed to do the work of worrying in advance of being exposed to actual danger or loss (21):

1. The normal tendency to ward off fear by means of blanket reassurances remains dominant and the person therefore does not engage in the mental rehearsing essential for developing two types of self-delivered reassurances that are capable of reducing the probability of subsequent hypervigilance and disappointment in response to severe stress stimuli: (*a*) reality-based expectations about ways and means of surviving the impending danger, the subsequent contemplation of which can function as a source of hope and optimism; and (*b*) reality-based plans for taking effective actions in case various contingencies arise, the subsequent execution of which can reduce feelings of passive helplessness.

2. The person's denial fantasies and overoptimistic expectations remain uncorrected and hence the chances are increased that there will be a marked disparity between the amount of victimization expected beforehand and the amount that is actually experienced, thus increasing the probability of regressive aggrievement reactions (childlike rage or depression).

3. When the person subsequently realizes that the danger-control authorities had failed to predict or give warnings about the dangers that were going to arise, childhood episodes of resentment against the parents (for unfair or unprotective treatment) are especially likely to be reactivated, thus increasing the likelihood that the danger-control authorities will lose their capacity to give reassurances and will be irrationally blamed for inflicting suffering and deprivations.

All three reactions to objective danger situations would be expected whenever a person fails to engage in adequate work of worrying beforehand, whether the failure is attributable primarily to the pre-danger environmental conditions or to exceptionally strong personality needs which predisposed the person to deny clear-cut signs of impending danger.

Thus the work of worrying is conceived as increasing the level of tolerance for subsequent threat or danger stimuli. The more thorough the work of worrying, the more reality-tested the person's self-delivered reassurances are likely to be and hence the more emotional control he will have under conditions of subsequent danger or deprivation. The acute emotional disturbances of hypervigilance and resentment against protective authorities are to be expected whenever there has been a total failure to carry out any work of worrying. These negative reactions can be regarded as being at an extreme end-point of a continuum, which ranges from none at all to the opposite extreme of complete working-through of all sources of stress before the onset of the crisis. Similar negative effects, but of less severity, are expected if the person does only a part of the work of worrying, as in the case of the female patient who had worried about postoperative pains and discomfort but was temporarily upset when she unexpectedly was asked to swallow a drainage tube.

In general, the adequacy of the work of worrying depends on both situational events and personality predispositions. The latter are emphasized by Marmor (33) in his analysis of realistic worrying. This author regards worry over realistic threat as "a defensive function of the ego" which serves to ward off an anticipated trauma or to overcome the painful effects of a trauma that had recently been experienced. Neurotic worriers, according to Marmor, are unable to attain emotional mastery of the anticipated threat situation. These are the people whose reactions to warnings and to subsequent danger stimuli take the form of obsessional preoccupation with the danger, anxiety states, phobias, and other acute neurotic symptoms.

Among less severe neurotics and normal personalities, we would expect the adequacy of the work of worrying to depend largely on the signs of threat to which they are exposed, the type of preparatory communications available to them, and other situational events. Sometimes absence of the work of worrying is caused by the sudden onset of an unpredictable event (e.g., a precipitant disaster caused by an undetected source of danger, as in the Brighton and New Haven gas explosions). Here the essential factor may be that the anticipatory period is too short to allow the person time to prepare himself for the emergency. Often, however, people fail to carry out adequate inner preparation even though there is ample time between an initial warning stimulus and the onset of the crisis. In such instances, one of the major causal factors responsible for the incompleteness of the work of worrying is likely to be *lack of unambiguous warnings about the magnitude of the impending danger.* Some physicians, public health officials and governmental authorities intentionally foster denial of the unpleasant consequences of an impending crisis by asserting that "everything is going to be all right, just leave the worrying to me" (41). And, of course, at the opposite extreme are some danger-control authorities who severely frighten people long in advance of a crisis, giving alarming information before it can properly be evaluated and assimilated, stimulating defensive reactions which preclude the normal work of worrying. Thus, it may often happen that the adequacy of a person's emotional preparation for danger will depend, among other things, upon the *adequacy and timing of the preparatory communications* to which he has been exposed.

Implications for Preparatory Communications

The findings and theoretical analysis presented in the preceding sections have a number of important implications concerning the way in which preparatory communications can produce an increase in stress tolerance. The term "preparatory communications" refers to those messages which are intended to prepare people to resist being adversely affected by the impact of subsequent events. Government agencies and mental health organizations put forth many such communications in an effort to reduce the total national incidence of preventable emotional disturbances and industrial absenteeism, usually employing the resources of the mass media—television, radio, films, pamphlets, magazines and newspapers. There are also other sources of preparatory communications which may sometimes prove to be much more effective, notably those given in face-to-face situations by physicians,

employee counselors, teachers, attorneys, social workers, clergy-
men, and others in similar professional roles who are in a position
to give authoritative communications that are "hand tailored" to
meet the special needs of their clients.

In the theoretical analysis of the "work of worrying" I have
attempted to specify the psychological functions that can be fulfilled by preparatory communications in order to achieve successful emotional inoculation (21).

First of all, authoritative information or warnings about impending
stressful events are needed in order to counteract the person's tendency
to discount the potential danger situation, and, thus to modify the
person's attitude of complete personal invulnerability. By interfering
with spontaneous denial tendencies, realistic information can evoke
some degree of anticipatory fear, with a consequent stimulation of
spontaneous efforts to develop reality-based defenses against fright.

A second function of successful preparatory communication is to
supplement the person's spontaneous protective measures by teaching
him: (a) what he can do to help ward off or minimize the objective
danger (e.g., who he can call upon for help); and (b) what reassurances he can dependably count upon for reducing his fears at the
times when the danger is actually at hand (e.g., information about the
short duration of intense pains, what will be done to alleviate persisting pains, how body damage will be prevented or repaired). By
giving the person a correct cognitive appraisal of the danger situation,
a preparatory communication can help to build an attitude of self-
confidence that can be maintained if the crisis actually arises (e.g.,
"I know what it's all about; I can predict what will happen next")
and at the same time, can help the person to develop realistic expectations that will have a reassuring effect (e.g., "If the pain doesn't
stop soon, I will be given something to relieve it"). For such purposes,
it is probably essential that the preparatory communications focus
attention on the danger signs and events that will actually be perceived by the person. It would be unnecessary, however, and perhaps
even detrimental, to give a vivid picture of disquieting aspects of the
danger situation which will ordinarily remain outside the person's
conscious perceptual or anticipatory experiences (e.g., details about
physiological complications that can cause death while one is unconscious on the operating table).

A third general function of authoritative preparatory communications is to facilitate reliance on the danger-control authorities. This is
perhaps the most difficult effect to achieve because it requires a delicate
balance between conveying unpleasant, fear-arousing information about
impending dangers and offering explicit or implicit reassurances that
will help to reduce anticipatory fears. If the authority figures say things
that stimulate considerable fear, they are apt to be aggressively dis-

missed as alarmists and may even be unconsciously regarded as punitive parental figures whose predictions are tantamount to hostile threats. On the other hand, if the authorities follow up their warnings with elaborate reassurances, their communication may be regarded as a promise of complete (magical) protection from the impact of danger, with a consequent restoration, in a new edition, of a pathogenic attitude of complete personal invulnerability.

There are, of course, many problems concerning the content and timing of effective preparatory communications that will probably not be solved until carefully controlled experiments are carried out. One important set of problems involves the *dosage* of fear-arousing information. In order to stimulate the work of worrying it is necessary to arouse anticipatory fear, but how can this be done without running the risk of provoking either hypervigilance or adverse defensive reactions such as counterphobic indifference and denial? Some preliminary answers are beginning to emerge from systematic communication studies which compare the effects of different dosages of fear-producing material.

A series of experimental studies by the author and his co-workers provide some pertinent results concerning the conditions under which fear-arousing communications tend to stimulate defensive reactions that interfere with the acceptance of the communicator's conclusions and recommendations (24, 25, 26, 27). In general, the findings are consistent with the hypothesis that the relationship between the degree of fear aroused by a communication and the degree to which the communicator's recommendations are accepted is *curvilinear:* as the level of fear is increased from zero to some minimal level, acceptance tends to *increase;* but as the level of fear mounts higher, psychological resistances tend to predominate and unless counteracted by special techniques which prevent defensive avoidance of the message, acceptance will tend to *decrease.* In several studies, involving different age groups, we found that a strong fear version of a communication was significantly less effective than a minimal fear version of the same message in producing adherence to the communicator's recommendation.

The research findings have a number of direct implications for the dosage of fear-arousing statements in preparatory communications. A successful program designed to increase stress tolerance for any impending danger situation would presumably require a series of preparatory communications containing three different types of contents: (*1*) *Fear-arousing statements* which provide accurate information describing the most probable dangers that are likely to be directly experienced by the recipient; (2) *reassuring statements* which indicate how the potential dangers will be kept under control or mitigated; and (3) *recommendations* as to what can be done to protect oneself or to reduce the damaging impact of the potential dangers.

One major implication of the research on fear-arousing communications is that the three types of content should be selected and spaced in such a way as to stimulate a low or moderate degree of fear. Thus, it probably would be advantageous to use a series of separate preparatory communications which will provide a gradual, stepwise increase in the amount and intensity of threat material. Moreover, in order to prevent fear from mounting to such a high level that denial and other avoidance reactions will become dominant, it might be essential to combine fear-arousing statements with reassuring statements. For example, our prediction is that it will prove to be relatively ineffective to give one preparatory communication devoted entirely to describing the threatening aspects of an approaching danger situation and then, sometime later, a second communication which gives the reassuring material. We would expect more favorable results if both types of statements are combined within each communication, so that whenever anticipatory fear is stimulated, the reassurances can help to keep the intensity of fear at a tolerable level.

At present we are able to formulate only a few such tentative generalizations (as yet only partially tested) on how to select and organize the content of preparatory communications that are designed to produce emotional inoculation. As more evidence becomes available from communication research, it should be possible to formulate dependable rubrics that can be applied to the average recipient within our society or within various sub-cultures. It is conceivable, however, that individual differences in sensitivity to fear-arousing material may prove to be so great that very few rubrics will hold true for "people in general." From what is already known about differences in personality predispositions, for example, it is apparent that different persons may require quite different forms of preparatory communications. In fact, one of the direct implications of the research findings on fear-arousing communications is that in order to attain a positive motivating effect, the threat content of a preparatory communication given to chronically anxious persons should be somewhat different from that given to relatively unanxious persons (25). The latter, in contrast to the former, may require a much more dramatic account of the threat (including vivid examples which explicitly point out the ways in which the individual can be personally affected by the impending dangers) in order to overcome their higher threshold of responsiveness to fear stimuli. With such persons, the communicator probably can successfully employ a moderate or fairly strong fear appeal, whereas among persons who are exceptionally apprehensive about body damage, the dosage of fear material might have to be kept to a minimum in order to prevent the arousal of interfering responses. Moreover, hyperanxious persons are less likely to be receptive to certain types of reassurances. For example, their fears might remain unabated or increase when they are given reassuring recommendations that merely provide a means for cutting down on the amount of potential damage without offering a guarantee of complete escape from all sources of danger. Thus, many problems concerning the selection and dosage of fear-arousing and fear-reducing contents will probably require different solutions which take into account personality differences among those for whom the preparatory communications are intended. In any case, a great many more systematic research studies will have to be carried out on predispositional factors as well as content variables before we can expect to have a dependable set of specific guiding principles concerning the effective use of preparatory communications for increasing stress tolerance.

BIBLIOGRAPHY

1. BIBRING, E. The mechanism of depression. In P. Greenacre (Ed.) *Affective disorders.* New York: International Univer. Press, 1953. Pp. 13-46.

2. BOND, D. *The love and fear of flying.* New York: International Univer. Press, 1952.

3. COBB, B., CLARK, R., CARSON, M. & HOWE, C. Patient-responsible delay of treatment in cancer. *Cancer,* 1954, 7, 920-926.

4. COBB, S. & LINDEMANN, E. Neuropsychiatric observations (following the Cocoanut Grove fire). *Ann. Surg.,* 1943, 117, 814-824.

5. CORIAT. I. Dental anxiety: Fear of going to the dentist. *Psychoanal. Rev.,* 1946, 33, 365-367.

6. CRAMOND, W. & ABERD, D. Psychological aspects of uterine dysfunction. *Lancet,* 1954, 2, 1241-1245.

7. DEUTSCH, H. Some psychoanalytic observations in surgery. *Psychosomat. Med.*, 1942, 4, 105-115.

8. FENICHEL, O. *The psychoanalytic theory of neurosis.* New York: W. W. Norton, 1945.

9. FRASER, R., LESLIE, I. & PHELPS, D. Psychiatric effects of severe personal experiences during bombing. *Proc. Roy. Soc. Med.*, 1943, 36, 119-123.

10. FREUD, S. Mourning and melancholia. (1917) *Collected Papers*, Vol. IV. London: Hogarth Press, 1950.

11. FREUD, S. Psychoanalysis and war neuroses. (1919) *Collected Papers*, Vol. V. London: Hogarth Press, 1950.

12. FREUD, S. *The problem of anxiety.* New York: W. W. Norton, 1936.

13. FRITZ, C. & MATHEWSON, J. *Convergence behavior in disaster: A problem in social control.* Committee on Disaster Studies, National Academy of Sciences—National Research Council, 1957.

14. GLOVER, E. Notes on the psychological effects of war conditions on the civilian population, Part III: The blitz. *Intern. J. Psychoanal.*, 1942, 23, 17-37.

15. GRINKER, R. & SPEIGEL, J. *Men under stress.* Philadelphia: Blakiston, 1945.

16. GRINKER, R., BRADLEY, A., FASTOVSKY, A., & WILLERMAN, B. A study of psychological predisposition to the development of operational fatigue, I and II. *Amer. J. Orthopsychiat.*, 1946, 16, 191-214.

17. Institute of Community Studies. *The great London blackout: A report to the Committee on Disaster Studies, National Academy of Sciences—National Research Council.* London: Institute of Community Studies. (Mimeo), 1955.

18. JACOBSON, E. Contribution to the metapsychology of cyclothymic depression. In Phyllis Greenacre (Ed.) *Affective disorders*, New York: International Univer. Press, 1953, 49-83.

19. JANIS, I. *Air war and emotional stress.* New York: McGraw-Hill, 1951.

20. JANIS, I. Reactions to a gas explosion in New Haven, Conn. Unpublished report submitted to the Committee on Disaster Studies, National Academy of Sciences—National Research Council, 1954.

21. JANIS, I. Emotional inoculation: Theory and research on effects of preparatory communications. *Psychoanalysis and the social sciences.* Vol. V. New York: International Univer. Press, 1958.

22. JANIS, I. *Psychological stress.* New York: J. Wiley and Sons, 1958.

23. JANIS, I. *Contours of Fear: Psychological Studies of War, Disaster and Illness.* New York: J. Wiley and Sons, in press.

24. JANIS, I. & FESHBACH, S. Effects of fear-arousing communications. *J. abnorm. soc. Psychol.*, 1953, 48, 78-92.

25. JANIS, I. & FESHBACH, S. Personality differences associated

with responsiveness to fear-arousing communications. *J. Pers.*, 1954, 23, 154-166.

26. JANIS, I. & MILHOLLAND, H. The influence of threat appeals on selective learning of the content of a persuasive communication. *J. Psychol.*, 1954, 37, 75-80.

27. JANIS, I. & TERWILLIGER, R. An experimental study of psychological resistances to fear-arousing communications. *J. abnorm. soc. Psychol.*, 1962, 65, 403-410.

28. KARDINER, A. & SPIEGEL, H. *War stress and neurotic illness.* New York: P. B. Hoeber, 1947.

29. LEWIN, B. *The psychoanalysis of elation.* New York: W. W. Norton, 1950.

30. LINDEMANN, E. Observations on psychiatric sequelae to surgical operations in women. *Amer. J. Psychiat.*, 1941, 98, 132-139.

31. LINDEMANN, E. Symptomatology and management of acute grief. *Amer. J. Psychiat.*, 1944, 101, 141-146.

32. MACCURDY, J. *The structure of morale.* New York: Macmillan, 1943.

33. MARMOR, J. The psychodynamics of realistic worry. *Psychoanalysis and the social sciences.* Vol. V. New York: International Univer. Press, 1958.

34. MATTE, I. Observations of the English in wartime. *J. nerv. ment. Dis.*, 1943, 97, 447-463.

35. MOORE, H. *Tornadoes over Texas.* Austin: University of Texas Press, 1957.

36. National Opinion Research Center. *Human reactions in disaster situations.* Chicago: University of Chicago. (Mimeo.), 1954.

37. NUNBERG, H. *Problems of bisexuality as reflected in circumcision.* London: Imago, 1949.

38. RADO, S. Pathodynamics and treatment of traumatic war neurosis (traumatophobia). *Psychosomat. Med.*, 1942, 4, 362-368.

39. RADO, S. Emergency behavior. In P. Hoch & J. Zubin (Eds.) *Anxiety.* NewYork: Grune & Stratton, 1950. Pp. 150-175.

40. ROMALIS, F. The impact of the war on family life. Part I: Reactions to change and crisis. *The Family*, 1942, 23, 219-224.

41. ROSEN, V. Role of denial in acute postoperative affective reactions following removal of body parts. *Psychosomat. Med.*, 1950, 12, 356-361.

42. SCHMIDEBERG, M. Some observations on individual reactions to air raids. *Internat. J. Psychoanal.*, 1942, 23, 146-176.

43. SHANDS, H. An outline of the process of recovery from severe trauma. *A.M.A. Arch. Neurol. Psychiat.*, 1955, 73, 403-409.

44. STOUFFER, S., LUMSDAINE, A., LUMSDAINE, M., WILLIAMS, R., SMITH, M., JANIS, I., STAR, S. & COTTRELL, L., JR. *The American soldier, Vol. II: Combat and its aftermath.* Princeton: Princeton Univer. Press, 1949b.

45. TITCHENER, J., ZWERLING, I., GOTTSCHALK, L., LEVINE, M., SILVER, H., COWETT, A., COHEN, S., & CULBERSON, W. Consequences of surgical illness and treatment. *A.M.A. Arch. Neurol. Psychiat.*, 1957, 77, 623-634.

46. VERNON, P. Psychological effects of air raids. *J. abnorm. soc. Psychol.*, 1941, 36, 457-476.

47. WALLACE, A. *Tornado in Worcester.* Committee on Disaster Studies, National Academy of Sciences—National Research Council, 1956.

48. WALLACE, A. Mazeway disintegration: The individual's perception of socio-cultural disorganization. *Human Organ.*, 1957, 16, 23-27.

49. WILSON, A. Reactive emotional disorders. *The Practitioner*, 1941, 146, 254-258.

50. WOLFENSTEIN, M. *Disaster.* Glencoe: The Free Press, 1957.

SHELDON J. KORCHIN

Some Psychological Determinants of Stress Behavior

I

In this presentation I would like to consider with you some general ideas about the nature of stress, particularly in relation to psychological functioning, drawing on some studies of laboratory, clinical and life stress. Important in this domain is an understanding of the conditions under which stress situations organize and under which they disorganize behavior. Lastly, I should like to raise some questions about the meaning of "stress resistance," frustration tolerance and cognate concepts which describe individual differences in persons' capacities to function, at all or effectively, under stress.

The use of the term "stress" in behavioral and biological sciences derives from the physical sciences, where *stress* is a force which is exerted on some system in such fashion as to deform, alter or damage the structure of that system, while the resulting deformation is described as *strain*. The stress-strain concepts are thus related in stimulus-response fashion. In our fields, there is no ready agreement on formal definition, but a common sense emerges as to the phenomena under consideration. There are statements which define stress in terms of stimulus properties, others in terms of particular responses, and other definitions in interactional terms. Perhaps the simplest way out of a definitional conflict is to assert that stress—as noun—describes an organismic state. Those events which provoke it are stress situations; the resulting behavioral alterations which occur are stress reactions. Moving the term stress from noun to adjective is consonant with the usage of Janis (1958) and Selye (1950, 1956).

In the stress state there is sufficiently potent danger (actual or anticipated) to the organism's well-being as to require extraordinary measures for the maintenance of organized functioning or, these failing, which may lead to behavioral disorganization, anxiety or other emotional tension. Obviously, there are many threats to well-being, differing in type, intensity, extensity, locus and duration. Some have greater representation in consciousness, others less. Vital danger to life itself can exist without conscious alarm, although physiological stress reactions may be evoked. Such, it is often noted, is the case in carbon monoxide poisoning. But suffocation through other causes leads immediately to anxiety, struggle, and escape. Possibly conscious alarm reactions arose in evolution to signal oncoming danger in those cases where self-initiated actions could avoid its noxious effects.

It was to the great credit of Freud, in his later anxiety theory (Freud, 1936), to recognize the dual function of anxiety in regulatory and pathological behavior. Obviously a symptom of disordered psychological functioning, anxiety serves as the signal of danger in the psychological realm leading to anticipatory and defensive actions designed to restore adaptive functioning and to avert further, more intense anxiety. In its signal function, anxiety may lead to more directed and organized problem-solving behaviors as well as to ego-defensive maneuvers. These failing, either because the stress is too intense or long-standing, or because the coping mechanisms are inadequate to their onslaught, greater anxiety appears as a symptom of a disintegrative state in which the capacity for integrative actions are further reduced. In the psychoanalytic thesis (Fenichel, 1945), anxiety in its signal function is differentiated out of the original primitive emotional state as part of the general story of ego development. Obviously, to feel oneself threatened, there must be a sense of self and sufficiently developed cognitive mechanisms for differentiating not only self and not-self, but the objects of the environment as safe and unsafe. Memory of past dangers and anticipation of future are involved. As anxiety intensifies, there tends to be regression of these ego mechanisms to more primitive forms. The continuity from originally diffuse emotional state, to adaptive use of the painful affect, to pathological breakdown and resulting traumatic anxiety state is well described by Kurt Goldstein (e.g., Goldstein, 1951). In his view, fear (i.e., painful affect directed toward an object and capable of instigating adaptive behavior) is differentiated out of a more primitive emotional matrix. Ultimately, the object of fear is the catastrophic state in which capacity for organized behavior disappears and all that is left, so to speak, is the enveloping anxiety. There are, of course, many important differences in these theories; in their views of the locus and historical development of affects, the role of psychodynamic and unconscious factors, and the like. But I would like to note the common elements: first, the developmental continuum from primitive to focused to disintegrative anxiety (in Fenichel's terms "trauma" to "danger" to "panic"); and second, the relation between such an emotional continuum and more general dimension of behavioral organization-disorganization.

The problem of anxiety is central to the problem of stress. Indeed, stress might be defined as that stimulus condition likely to arouse anxiety, as Basowitz, Persky, Grinker, and I (1955) once suggested, noting at the same time that such stimuli might be more idiosyncratic or universalistic. We noted:

. . . any stimulus may in principle arouse an anxiety response because of the particular meaning of threat it may have acquired for the particular individual. However, we distinguish a class of stimuli which are *more likely* to produce disturbance in most individuals. The term *stress* has been applied to this class of conditions. Thus we can conceive a continuum of stimuli differing in meaning to the organism and in their anxiety-producing consequences. At one end are such stimuli or cues, often highly symbolic which have meaning only to single or limited numbers of persons and which to the observer may appear as innocuous or trivial. At the other end are such stimuli, here called stress, which by their explicit threat to vital functioning and their intensity are likely to overload the capacity of most organisms' coping mechanisms.

. . . Ultimately we can truly speak of a *stress situation* only when a given response occurs, but for schematic purposes as well as consistency with common usage, we may use the term stress to designate certain kinds of stimulating conditions without regard for response. Such stimuli are called stress because of their assumed or potential effect, although we well know that in any given case the organisms adaptive capacity, threshold, or previous learning may preclude any disturbance of behavior. (Basowitz, *et al.,* 1955, p. 7).

Thus, in this statement, the stress state was described in stress-anxiety terms, where 'stress' describes the stimulus conditions and anxiety the defining response. Critics (e.g., Janis, 1958) pointed out two problems in this statement; first, that 'anxiety' defined too narrowly the potential range of disturbed affect, and that perhaps a term like "emotional tension" might be preferable; and that, second, there are logical and methodological problems inherent in an interactional definition which might be avoided by using stress as an adjective describing 'situations', on the one hand, and 'reactions' on the other. These are sensible criticisms and have been built into the definition earlier proposed. Still, have we avoided the interactional problem? Is it not built into the very definition of a "stimulus?"

II

If we turn now to consideration of the range of stress situations, even limiting ourselves to those used in human psychological research, it seems as if any stimulus can be a stressor if it is sufficiently intense, threatening and the proper organismic conditions exist. There have been a number of good reviews of the conditions and effects of stress, and it is hardly necessary to repeat their listing here (see, e.g., Haggard, 1949; Hanfman, 1950; Himmelweit, 1950; Lazarus, et al., 1952; Holtzman & Bitterman, 1952; Miller, et al., 1953; Basowitz, et al., 1955). Various classes (empirical groupings) of stress conditions have been suggested to summarize the variety of situations studied. Thus, Holtzman and Bitterman (1952) have catalogued the following groups of conditions which have been used in order to induce stress experimentally: (1) Disruption of physiological homeostasis. This would include the many studies of hypoxia, severe temperature and humidity, drugs, sleep deprivation, starvation and the like. (2) Unpleasant or physically painful stimuli. Here are included the administration of electric shocks, loud sounds, air blasts, thermal stimulation and similar noxious stimuli. (3) Distractions, razzing, and time pressures. The effectiveness of such agents depends in large measure on the degree to which the subject is ego-involved in the primary task. (4) Real, contrived, or anticipated failure. Utilizing primarily intellectual tasks, this has been a favored method in psychological research. The same comment just made about distractions holds as well for these stress conditions. (5) Social conflict and related procedures. An example of these is the quasi-cooperative construction task used by the OSS assessment staff (OSS Assessment Staff, 1948). (6) Conflicting perceptual cues. This category includes such tasks as mirror-drawing and the Stroop color-word test. (7) Realistic situations threatening the individual's safety, such as simulated battle-fire, parachute jumping, submarine escape training. And not included in such a listing are the many life and laboratory conditions which might engender shame, guilt, anger, feelings of worthlessness, rejection, fear of harm, or loss of love, which are more closely related to clinically important stress.

There is not much to be gained in cataloguing all the possible forms and varieties of stress situations into loosely assembled empirical groups. It begins to be an intellectual exercise of the same sort as the older game of classifying emotions—which once led the exasperated, but always expressive, William James to say, ". . . I should as lief read verbal descriptions of the shapes of the rocks on a New Hampshire farm as toil through them again. They give one nowhere a central point of view, or a deductive or generative principle. They distinguish and refine and specify *in infinitum* without ever getting on to another logical level" (James, 1890, p. 448).

Still, there might be some value in reconsidering the types of stress situations which have or might be studied, to see whether grouping in some more abstract categories might not disclose more about the nature of the stress process.

1. Uncertainty. The ambiguous and vague situation, particularly if action is required and/or the organism is already highly motivated or anxious, is a powerful source of stress. Entrance into a novel situation, whether or not danger actually exists, has been described as an ubiquitous agent in the activation of the adrenocortical system (e.g., see review by Mason, 1959). The importance of novelty as an generic stress suggests the concepts which have been put forth by workers within the Pavlovian tradition. Thus, Liddell (1950) suggests that a prototype of anxiety might be the animal's vigilance response, akin to Pavlov's "What-is-it?" reflex, to a new and strange stimulus. Perhaps the extreme of uncertainty consists of the complete absence of information which exists under conditions of sensory deprivation. Inspired by Hebb's thinking (Hebb, 1955) and the McGill studies (Bexton, et al., 1954), a burgeoning literature has grown demonstrating that sharp reduction of sensory input can lead to gross emotional and behavioral disorganization (for reviews, see: Solomon, et al., 1961; Fiske & Maddi, 1961; and Miller, 1962). The evidence of disturbance, even when in womb-like comfort, points up the important fact that a level of environmental stimulation is necessary for the maintenance of optimal comfort and function, and probably for its development in the first place.

2. Information overload. James Miller has used this phrase to describe the reverse situation; the case where the organism is flooded with competing and demanding stimuli. However large, man's capacity as an information processing system is still finite. All conditions of distraction, excessive stimulation, time pressure, and the like share in being informational overloads. In the psychoanalytic schema, the prototypic trauma is the overwhelming flood of excitation which the infant can neither avoid nor master; and the prototypic defense from which all later ego functions are seen as developing is the effort to block this flood (Reizschutz).

3. Danger. Danger, existing or anticipated, to physical wellbeing or to the satisfaction of central needs, is an obvious source of stress. Properly included here are conditions of frustration. We should recall Maslow's (1943) caution that need deprivation, as such, does not constitute frustration, unless it connotes a threat to self-esteem as well.

4. Ego-control failure. An important function of the self and ego systems lies in the control of infantile and unsocialized impulses which are antipathetic to the self-concept and to internalized social values. The potential failure of controls is therefore stress, for example, in the common instances of temptation. We made use of this in one of our studies to induce some anxiety for experimental study (Korchin, et al., 1958). Subjects were shown a picture tachistoscopically and asked to describe it as carefully as possible. Following this, a subject was again shown the same picture (or so he thought) ostensibly to validate his original description. The picture, however, was changed, and in such a way as to impugn the subject's reality-testing by suggesting the intrusion of ordinarily-denied impulses. Thus, the first pair of pictures consisted of a man with a gun to his head, looking somewhat depressed; the "same" picture shown the second time had a pipe in place of the gun. In one study, it was found that this "ego-disintegrative threat" resulted in greater adrenocortical activation than did an induced failure in a quasi-intellectual test, of the sort more commonly used in psychological stress experiments, though both situations functioned as stress (Korchin & Herz, 1960). The procedure developed by Asch for the study of independence and conformity of judgment is of a conceptually similar sort (Asch, 1952).

5. *Ego-mastery failure.* In discussing personality functioning, the term "control" somehow suggests holding the line, while "mastery" connotes moving forward. Hence, even though these are distinctly overlapping concepts, I would like to distinguish the more positive from the more negative aspects of the problem, as Robert W. White does in his important concept of "competence" motivation (White, 1959; 1960). Being blocked from mastering new goals, developing and exercising new talents, even though there is no danger to present control or need-satisfaction, can be an important source of stress. I am sure that Dr. Goldstein will develop this thesis at length, as he has in previous discussions of self-realization.

6. *Self-esteem danger.* Though related to the points just made, the centrality of the self and the importance of the sentiment of self-esteem in the understanding of stress behavior should be separately emphasized. Situations which lower the subject's feeling of worth have been used in experimental studies; the term "ego-involved" to characterize some of these (as, e.g., in the work of Alper, 1946; 1948) refers not only to the fact that the subject is highly motivated, but that success or failure is vital to his self-esteem.

7. *"Other"-esteem danger.* A parallel source of stress is the danger of losing the esteem of others, losing face, status or love, being rejected or thought unworthy. This may, in large measure, be the outward face of self-esteem, as is suggested in the classic theory of George Herbert Mead (1934). But operationally these are of different order, and their role in stress situations clearly distinguishable.

III

Thus far, I have considered some definitional problems and reviewed some of the general qualities of stress situations which seem important to the understanding of their effects on psychological functioning. To continue this survey, I should like to comment now on those factors within the individual which affect resistance or receptivity to stress and finally to look at the effects of stress on psychological and physiological behaviors (stress reactions). As a map of the terrain, which might have some heuristic value, Figure 1 indicates the areas which seem relevant in the study of stress.

Table 1
Schema of Factors Involved in the Study of Stress

STRESS—STIMULUS		STRESS—RESPONSE
Stress	*Person*	*Experience*
A. Type and intensity of threat	A. Personality traits	A. "Cognitive structure"
B. Social context	B. Ego strength	B. Affective experience
	C. Defenses	C. Somatic experience
	D. Cognitive modes	*Behavior*
	E. Motivation	A. Psychological functions
	F. Somatic compliance	B. Somatic functions

The chart consists of stimulus factors, on the left, and the organism's reactions, on the right. Intervening between them are factors within the person. Overall, then, this is little more than Woodworth's old S-O-R formula, applicable to any behavior sequence, in this case, stress.

Types of stress situations have already been discussed. I should like now to consider three factors which are important at the interface between the stimulus and the person: *perceptive (evaluative) acts, motivation,* and the *social context* within which stress occurs.

When said, it seems self-evident, but we sometimes overlook the fact that the stress situation is part of the "behavioral environment" (Koffka, 1935) not the actual, and that its psychological import for the subject depends on a perceptual (evaluative) act. Recall Koffka's anecdote:

On a winter evening amidst a driving snowstorm a man on horseback arrived at an inn, happy to have reached a shelter after hours of riding over the wind-swept plain on which the blanket of snow had covered all paths and landmarks. The landlord who came to the door viewed the stranger with surprise and asked him whence he came. The man pointed in the direction straight away from the inn, whereupon the landlord in a tone of awe and wonder, said: 'Do you know that you have ridden across the Lake of Constance?' At which the rider dropped stone dead at his feet (Koffka, 1935, pp. 27-28).

Perhaps dropping "stone dead" is a bit excessive—though studies of voodoo death give it credence—but the psychological point is well made. Even such an apparently uniform noxious stimulus as electric shock has been shown by Tomkins (1943) to have quite different meanings, and hence effects, on different people. I should add one cautionary note to this discussion. The importance of the subject's interpretation of the stress situation should not be taken to suppose that everything that affects him is known to him, consciously experienced and interpreted. Stimuli may be subliminally experienced and mesh into unconscious psychological functions. Just as a barely detectible fragrance can evoka a *déjà vu* experience, another can cue an anxiety attack. Certainly, the mechanisms of "behavior without awareness" are still unknown (Eriksen, 1962), but the fact of its operation is demonstrable in many realms of personality functioning and psychopathology.

Related to the matter of perceptual interpretation is the fact that the stress situation occurs within a larger social context which contributes to the interpretative meaning of the stress. Particularly in experimental situations, of short duration and laboratory construction, one can, but should not, lose sight of this fact. Perhaps a person a short distance away from the game of psychological experimentation can better see our faults, and Joan Criswell (1959) points out that we often deceive ourselves into thinking that the subject understands the situation as we intended him to.

A study was done at a large midwestern University to test the hypothesis that subjects in a hypnotic trance could be made to harm themselves. The subject was instructed to reach into a cage which visibly contained live rattlesnakes. Most subjects did so. Fortunately, they were protected by a sheet of "invisible" glass; the subject was not harmed, but the hypothesis was supported. But is this the only explanation? Does a sophomore at a state university, when he has voluntarily come to a professor's laboratory, really expect that he might be killed or even harmed? Is it not as likely that, in some sense, he "knew" that there was no real danger, and that he could carry through the role of "cooperative subject" without any genuine fear of harm befalling him?

Another example arises in one of our experiments (Grinker, et al., 1957). Anxious patients were subjected to stressful interviews. The interviews were designed to explore and confront the patient with potentially painful material of unresolved conflicts. At the same time, the interviewer adopted attitudes which might conflict with the particular patient's needs, and attempted also to distort the flow of communication as a further source of discomfort. For all this, the amount of anxiety aroused by this procedure was relatively small. Many subjects interpreted the meaning of this "stress situation" in terms of their conception of the hospital and their role in it. The hospital was a benevolent place; the staff competent and sympathetic; it was a place for treatment and cure. Hence, this procedure might seem strange and perhaps somewhat annoying, but one could believe that it was some therapeutic device intended for his good. Indeed, an occasional subject commented later on the value of having an emotional problem brought forcibly to his attention, which his therapist had approached so gingerly.

Another factor of the same order is the motivational state of the subject and his more enduring personality traits. The more highly motivated the subject and the more relevant the stress situation to the achievement or frustration of that motive, the more likely are stress reactions to ensue. Similarly, stress effects are greater the more central the frustrated motive or threatened value; that is, the more the subject's identity and self-esteem depend on it. Mahl (1949) studied gastric function in college students at the time of examinations and found some who showed little or none of the predicted changes. On closer investigation, these men turned out to be "gentlemen-C" students, for whom academic achievement was relatively unimportant. We found significant effects of induced failure in a test of "abstract intelligence" on later perceptual performance, when the subjects were young, male psychiatric residents (Korchin, et al., 1951). But in a later study, involving female social service students, the identical task had virtually no effect. In the self-concept (and, I believe, role-concept) of these girls, "abstract intelligence" did not figure prominently. If anyone was frustrated, it was the experimenter! It is easy but not necessary to multiply such examples. In Lazarus' view of stress, the motivational construct is given a central position (e.g., Lazarus & Baker, 1956).

At the conceptual center of the chart (Figure 1) are those factors in the personality structure which describe vulnerability or susceptibility to stress in general. Over and above issues concerned with the nature of the stress stimulus, or its relevance to the subject's values or motives, terms like ego strength, stress resistance, frustration tolerance and the like call attention to qualities in the structure of personality which determine the threshold for stress arousal or the capacity of the individual to maintain organized functioning under stress. Older, and perhaps unnecessarily rejected, terms like "strength of character" or "will power" carry the same connotation. Presumably ego strength arises, in part at least, out of the individual's history of earlier stress adaptations.

Within the same conceptual realm are those ego-defense mechanisms which allow some, if limited, adaptive behavior and protect against the more destructive effects of anxiety. Although of central importance to the understanding of stress behavior, in the present context I want only to note the existence and importance of these factors in personality structure and functioning. We should note, however, that the role of defenses is often entered in the formulation of stress behavior as a sort of filter factor mediating between input and output—if the stress is sufficiently strong and/or the defenses weak, then stress reactions will be enhanced. What is less commonly emphasized is the possibility that psychological and physiological changes may occur as a direct consequence of the defensive processes, although Hanfmann (1950) suggests this hypothesis in an excellent review over a dozen years ago. Moreover, the specific nature of stress reactions may vary with the type of defense utilized, not only with its effectiveness. Mention is made of cognitive modes and somatic compliance on the chart to call attention to other personalistic dimensions which figure in determining the specificity of psychological and somatic response, respectively.

The right hand portion of Figure 1 sketches the main categories of stress reactions. These are separated into two major groups— the experiential and the behavioral—to call attention to the two realms of phenomena which need separate considerations in the study of the stress state. On the one hand, there are the affective and somatic experiences of the subject, properly part of his "private experience," but which become available for study through introspection, verbalization and the judgment of trained observers. On the other hand, there are those measurable aspects of psychological and physiological functioning which can be assessed through objective tests and measures. Study of the relation between phenomena of these two realms is important to the understanding of stress behavior generally, but the reduction of the experiential to the behavioral either for ease or precision or measurement or from philosophical bias is dangerous, I believe, to empirical research in this field.

There is a long-standing bias in psychology to regard as more basic and perhaps more "real" that which can be measured physiologically. By contrast, measures of psychological performance are somewhat more suspect and the subject's reported experience is virtually beyond the pale of scientific credibility. This attitude would be less dangerous if there were invariant relationships be-

tween stress stimuli and particular physiological responses, or between phenomenal experience and physiological measurements.
For one thing, the work of Lacey and Malmo has shown individual response specificity in the study of autonomic functions. In
response to stress, people respond in terms of individually-pat-
terned profiles. Thus one person may show a quickening of the
pulse, another more rapid respiration, and these patterns are remarkably constant over years and in response to quite diverse
stimuli. But, equally important, is the fact that affective experience and somatic response may be dissociated as stress reactions.
Anxiety may be experienced without parallel physiological change,
and vice versa. For these reasons, I would plead for considering
both the physiological and the psychological, and for treating with
equal respect the phenomenal and the behavioral in both realms.
Each of these is a datum in its own right: "I feel apprehensive,"
"I am confused," "I have butterflies in my stomach," failure on
a problem-solving test, and increase in muscle tonicity. Detailed
studies of the relationships among these realms of functioning are
needed, not reductionism.

The term "somatic experience" is suggested to describe the
fact that, as part of the emotional state, we all experience characteristic bodily alterations. When anxious, for example, some of
us feel our hearts beating faster, others constriction of the chest,
others cold extremities. There is no simple relationship between
the type or intensity of such reported symptoms and their measurable physiological counterparts, as Mandler and his associates
have shown (Mandler & Kremen, 1958; Mandler, et al., 1958),
although they and we (Korchin & Heath, 1960) have found that
subjects who report more numerous or intense symptoms are, by
psychological measures, more anxious. Equally interesting is the
consistency in individual experience. Basowitz, et al. (1956), interviewed a group of young physicians and asked them to describe
their characteristic symptoms in emotionally difficult situations.
Later, the men were given a quite small dose of adrenalin. For
some this roused anxiety and somatic symptoms, for others somatic
experience without free anxiety, but in the great majority of cases
the reported experiences were identical with those described as
typical of past life stress. Thus, the "cold-feet" man, got cold feet,
and the "heart-palpitation" man developed heart palpitations.

There is not sufficient time to consider in greater detail the
affective state in stress, except to note again the centrality of the
problem of anxiety. Certainly, stress situations differ in the kinds

of affect aroused, and these in turn may specify the types of psychological and physiological reactions observed. Thus, Ax, Funkenstein, and their coworkers (Ax, 1953; Funkenstein, et al., 1957) have shown that anger-producing situations are more likely to lead to norepinephrine-like responses, whereas those conditions which lead to anxiety or self-directed anger produce epinephrine-like autonomic reactions. In our study of paratroopers in training (Basowitz, et al., 1955), we found evidence that when the focal threat involved fear of failure there was more effective functioning and less extreme physiological reactions than when the focal threat involved concern with bodily harm. We suggested that failure-anxiety (viewed as related to shame) is more likely to organize and facilitate behavior, while harm-anxiety (dynamically related to guilt) is more likely to lead to disorganization. Terms like "emotional arousal" mask the possibility of discovering more specific relationships between the type of emotion and other aspects of behavior under stress.

The schema thus far discussed is entirely contemporaneous. It pictures the action of variables as of a conceptual moment in time. For this presentation, the historical aspect, describing emergence of these personality structures and modes of stress response in the development of the individual has been ignored. Questions as to what conditions lead to greater ego strength, to particular stress susceptibilities, or to one rather than another mode of stress reaction, have been intentionally put aside. But I have neglected also to note another time-related issue—the temporal dimension involved in the ordering of response. The situation we have been discussing describes the acute stress condition, which is typical of much psychological and physiological experimental research. In life stress of a more chronic sort, both the stress situation and stress reactions occur over time, and as Janis (1954) and others have pointed out, may involve distinct phases.

One aspect of the temporal ordering of stress reactions is worth special comment, since it suggests psychobiological mechanisms of considerable importance in stress adaptation. Wartime studies of men under combat stress showed incubation effects of such sort that maximal anxiety might not occur until after men have left the battle scene (Grinker & Spiegel, 1945). We have all had the more common experience of being involved in an actual or near-miss auto accident. We may have functioned appropriately through the crisis, only to find ourselves overwhelmed by anxiety, flooded by somatic symptoms, and unable to drive further when in objective safety minutes and miles later. This delay of maximal anxiety response would seem to have great adaptive value, since it allows appropriate function at the crucial time, even if incapacitating later. In our study of paratroopers, a similar phenomenon was described (Basowitz, et al., 1955). We followed groups of young, healthy men through three weeks of their program, making measures of anxiety, perceptual test performance, and various biochemical functions each day as they made their various tower and airplane jumps. Although these measures moved in more or less sensible ways in response to the events of training, an unexpected finding was a significant increase in stress indicators three days after graduation. It seemed to us that this might represent a release phenomenon from the control of feelings and associated stress behaviors which had been necessary for adaptive behavior during training. Support for this interpretation was also given by the finding that the group which had functioned best, and had the least evidences of disturbed affect or behavior, showed the greatest post-graduation rise.

IV

In the preceding pages, I have tried to schematize and discuss, at least in broad outline, some general issues of stress research and to distinguish some factors which seem important in understanding the interplay of stress situations, qualities of the person and stress reactions. Because of special concern, I have saved for last consideration of the relation between stress and cognitive functioning.

From many theoretical quarters there has been convergence on a construct of activation or arousal as a general dimension which energizes behavior from a state of unorganization, at the one end, through conditions for optimal functioning to states of disorganization, at the other end. Workers concerned with neuropsychology, EEG correlates of behavior, autonomic processes, and the theory of emotion have contributed to this generalization about the curvilinear relation between activation and performance. Optimal functioning exists neither at the minimum nor maximum stimulus inputs, but at intermediate levels. In the context of present concern, it is proposed that increased stress leads to more organized behavior when occurring against a background of low order arousal and to disturbed behavior when imposed on a higher level.[1]

The dual role of anxiety, as organizing signal and disruptive symptom, has already been commented on. As stress mounts, from initially low levels, the organism experiences alertness, excitement and apprehension, all of which can actuate appropriately defensive actions. At still higher levels, with continued stress, there is greater anxiety and eventually panic. The organism becomes less capable of functioning effectively, particularly if such function requires the handling of new, complex, abstract or otherwise demanding tasks. At extreme levels of stress, organized behavior breaks down and not even simple psychological performance is possible.

The life-space, or experiential field, of the subject changes in parallel fashion. At lower levels, attention becomes more focussed and the individual is more attentive to his surround. Irrelevant stimuli are ignored and there is centration on possible sources of threat. The time perspective of the individual tends to contract toward the immediate present; the past is irrelevant and the future vague and uncertain. At the extreme, boundaries become diffused and there is a general state of confusion within which the individual is unable to distinguish the relevant and irrelevant or even the real and unreal. While at lower levels of threat there is heightened awareness of self, at more intense levels there is greater uncertainty as cognitive disorganization mounts.

Review of the formidable literature on psychological functioning under conditions of stress and anxiety suggests certain generalizations. Performance decrement is more likely to occur if the subject is operating at or close to his limit of performance, i.e., if the task requires all available skill, concentration, or effort. Moreover, the more complex the task, the more it involves competing stimuli, the more stress-sensitive it is likely to be. The acquisition of new learning is more difficult than the practice of older. Operating against established habits is difficult. For example, inadequate performance on a mirror-tracing task has been described as pathognomic of anxiety by Wechsler and Hartogs (1945). Tasks requiring a narrow focusing of attention (e.g., digit-span) or wide ranging attention (as in incidental learning) suffer.

Recently, I have suggested that some unity might be given the diverse findings on the effects of stress on cognitive organization and psychological performance by viewing the problem in terms of alteration of the attentional field (Korchin, 1964).

Prior to the more extreme levels of breakdown, there is a narrowing of the attentional field—Tolman (1948) once noted that cognitive maps are narrowed in states of intense emotion. This reduces the flexibility of performance, but whether it facilitates or disturbs performance depends on the nature of the task. For example, it is predictable that where behavior involves "doing two things at once," where there are focal and peripheral functions being assessed simultaneously, there will be relatively more decrement measurable in the peripheral than focal tasks. Vigilance experiments involving a broad field and studies of incidental learning support such a view. Recently, Easterbrook (1959) has proposed a similar interpretation phrased in terms of a reduction in the "range of cues utilized" under emotional arousal.

V

Before concluding, I should like to add a final comment about stress resistance in general, mainly to raise an issue for discussion. By now, I am sure that I have conveyed the complexity of the problem of stress, as I see it. The nature of stress behavior depends on qualities of the threat, its locus, intensity and duration, how it is viewed by the person, his motives, values, defenses, the demands of the task confronting him, and still other factors. All this would suggest considerable specificity in predicting stress resistance or responsivity in a particular man. Yet common sense and clinical knowledge indicate pervasive and consistent differences among individuals in the load they can take. Freeman (1939) once suggested the term "psychiatric plimsoll mark" to characterize individual differences in stress tolerance, drawing for analogy on the mark on the side of a ship to indicate the point to which it could safely be loaded and still withstand the rigors of storm and high sea. This is an expressive phrase, though our earlier analysis would suggest that each of us has many rather than one such mark. However, what is implied in the phrase, and many others like it, is that each man has his "breaking point"; some at a lower and some at a higher level of stress. Corollary to this are the added implications that more stress resistance is better than less, and that having high stress tolerance is part of the general state of personality adequacy. Psychiatrically-ill is often made synonymous with stress-sensitive; mentally-healthy with stress-tolerant. Surely, these are acceptable generalizations and we use them commonly in lay and professional discussions but we should note some unwonted implications.

In opening another conference on stress, Sir Geoffrey Vickers (1960) quoted Field-Marshal Lord Wavell as saying that one should not be surprised at discovering stupidity in generals, for they are selected from the extremely small group of humans who are tough enough to be generals at all. Neither cleverness nor sensitivity are parts of their essential qualifications, but rather that they should be able to function, even if poorly, in situations in which cleverer and more sensitive men would have ceased functioning altogether. Stress resistance may be bought at the cost of other desirable qualities.

The intellectually-dull, the unmotivated, the uninvested may be able to stand frustration better than the more clever and committed man. Stress resistance may result from an insensitivity to the range of experience, which misses potential threat along with other aspects of the world. It is interesting that the word sensitivity carries both good and bad connotations. On the one hand, it suggests finer discrimination and fuller understanding, and on the other hand greater readiness to feel personal hurt, which is perhaps a cost of being more discriminating. I would be hesitant to predict whether the more creative person should be more or less stress resistant.

BIBLIOGRAPHY

1. ALPER, THELMA G. Memory for completed and incompleted tasks as a function of personality: Analysis of group data. *J. abnorm. soc. Psychol.*, 1946, *41*, 403-420.

2. ALPER, THELMA G. Memory for completed and incompleted tasks as a function of personality: Correlation between experimental and personality data. *J. Pers.*, 1948, *17*, 104-137.

3. ASCH, S. E. *Social Psychology*, New York: Prentice Hall, 1952.

4. AX, A. The physiological differentiation between fear and anger in humans. *Psychosom. Med.*, 1953, *15*, 433-442.

5. BASOWITZ, H., KORCHIN, S. J., OKEN, D., GOLDSTEIN, M. S., & GUSSACK, H. Anxiety and performance changes with a minimal dose of epinephrine. *Arch. Neurol. Psychiat.*, 1956, *76*, 98-108.

6. BASOWITZ, H., PERSKY, H., KORCHIN, S. J., & GRINKER, R. R. *Anxiety and stress*. New York: McGraw-Hill, 1955.

7. BEXTON, W. H., HERON, W., & SCOTT, T. H. Effects of decreased variation in the sensory environment. *Canad. J. Psychol.,* 1954, *8,* 70-76.

8. CRISWELL, JOAN H. The psychologist as perceiver. In R. Tagiuri & L. Petrullo. (Eds.), *Person perception and interpersonal behavior.* Stanford: Stanford University Press, 1958. Pp. 95-109.

9. EASTERBROOK, J. A. The effect of emotion on cue utilization and the organization of behavior. *Psychol. Rev.,* 1959, *66,* 183-201.

10. ERIKSEN, C. W. (Ed.) *Behavior and awareness.* Durham, North Carolina: Duke University Press, 1962.

11. FENICHEL, O. *The psychoanalytic theory of neurosis.* New York: W. W. Norton, 1945.

12. FISKE, D. W., & MADDI, S. *The effects of varied experience.* Homewood, Illinois: Dorsey Press, 1961.

13. FREEMAN, G. L. Toward a psychiatric plimsoll mark; physiological recovery quotients in experimentally induced frustration. *J. Psychol.,* 1939, *8,* 247-252.

14. FREUD, S. *The problem of anxiety.* New York: W. W. Norton, 1936.

15. GOLDSTEIN, K. On emotions: Considerations from the organismic point of view. *J. Psychol.,* 1951, *31,* 27-50.

16. GRINKER, R., & SPIEGEL, J. *Men under stress.* Philadelphia: Blakiston, 1945.

17. HAGGARD, E. A. Psychological causes and results of stress. In *Human factors in undersea warfare.* Washington: National Research Council, 1949, Pp. 441-461.

18. HANFMANN, EUGENIA. Psychological approaches to the study of anxiety. In P. H. Hoch & J. Zubin (Eds.), *Anxiety.* New York: Grune & Stratton, 1950. Pp. 51-69.

19. HIMMELWEIT, H. Frustration and aggression. In T. H. Pears (Ed.), *Psychological factors of peace and war.* London: Hutchinson, 1950. Pp. 161-191.

20. HOLTZMAN, W. H., & BITTERMAN, M. E. *Psychiatric screening of flying personnel. VI. Anxiety and reactions to stress.* Randolph Field, Texas: USAF School of Aviation Medicine, 1952.

21. JAMES, W. *The principles of psychology.* Vol. II. New York: Henry Holt, 1890.

22. JANIS, I. Problems of theory in the analysis of stress behavior. *J. soc. Issues,* 1954, *10,* 12-25.

23. JANIS, I. L. *Psychological stress.* New York: John Wiley & Sons, 1958.

24. KOFFKA, K. *Principles of Gestalt psychology.* New York: Harcourt, Brace, 1935.

25. KORCHIN, S. J. Anxiety and cognition. In Constance Scheerer (Ed.) *Cognition: Theory, research, promise.* New York: Harper &

Row, 1964. Pp. 58-78. (Paper presented at the Martin Scheerer Memorial Symposium, University of Kansas, May 7, 1962).

26. KORCHIN, S. J., BASOWITZ, H., GRINKER, R. R., HAMBURG, D. A., PERSKY, H. SABSHIN, J., HEATH, H., & BOARD, F. A. Experience of perceptual distortion as a source of anxiety. *Arch. Neurol. Psychiat.*, 1958, *80*, 98-113.

27. KORCHIN, S. J., & HERZ, M. Differential effects of "shame" and "disintegrative" threats on emotional and adrenocortical functioning. *Arch. gen. Psychiat.*, 1960, *2*, 640-651.

28. KORCHIN, S. J., SINGER, J. L., & BALLARD, R. G. The effect of frustration on the reproduction of visually-perceived forms. *Pers.*, 1951, *1*, 54-66.

29. LAZARUS, R. S., & BAKER, R. W. Personality and psychological stress—A theoretical and methodological framework. *Psychol. Newsltr.*, NYU, 1956, *8*, 21-32.

30. LAZARUS, R. S., DEESE, J., & OSLER, S. F. The effects of psychological stress upon performance. *Psychol. Bull.*, 1952, *49*, 292-317.

31. LIDDELL, H. S. The role of vigilance in the development of animal neurosis. In P. H. Hoch & Zubin (Eds.), *Anxiety*. New York: Grune & Stratton, 1950. Pp. 183-196.

32. MAHL, G. F. Anxiety, HCL excretion, and peptic ulcer etiology. *Psychosom. Med.*, 1949, *11*, 30-44.

33. MANDLER, G., & KREMEN, I. Autonomic feedback: A correlational study. *J. Pers.*, 1958, *26*, 388-399.

34. MANDLER, G., MANDLER, JEAN M., & UVILLER, ELLEN, T. Autonomic feedback: The perception of autonomic activity. *J. abnorm. soc. Psychol.*, 1958, *56*, 367-373.

35. MASLOW, A. H. Conflict, frustration, and the theory of threat. *J. abnorm. soc. Psychol.*, 1943, *38*, 81-86.

36. MASON, J. W. Visceral functions of the nervous system. *Ann. Rev. Physiol.*, 1959, *21*, 353-380.

37. MEAD, G. H. *Mind, self and society from the standpoint of a social behaviorist.* Chicago, Illinois: University of Chicago Press, 1934.

38. MILLER, J. G., BOUTHILET, LORRAINE, & ELDRIDGE, CARMEN. A bibliography for the development of stress-sensitive tests. *PRA Research Note 22.* Army Proj. #29452000, October, 1953.

39. MILLER, S. C. Ego-autonomy in sensory deprivation, isolation, and stress. *Internat. J. Psychoanal.*, 1962, *4*, 1-20.

40. OSS Assessment Staff. *Assessment of men.* New York: Rinehart, 1948.

41. SELYE, H. *The physiology and pathology of exposure to stress.* Montreal: Acta, 1950.

42. SELYE, H. *The stress of life.* New York: McGraw-Hill, 1956.

43. P. SOLOMON, P. E. KUBZANSKY, P. H. LEIDERMAN, J. I. MENDELSON, R. TRUMBULL, D. WEXLER (Eds.), *Sensory deprivation.* Cambridge, Massachusetts: Harvard University Press, 1961.

44. TOLMAN, E. C. Cognitive maps in rats and men. *Psychol. Rev.*, 1948, *55*, 189-208.

45. TOMKINS, S. S. An analysis of the use of electric shock with human subjects. *J. Psychol.*, 1943, *15*, 285-297.

46. VICKERS, G. The concept of stress in relation to the disorganization of human behavior. In J. M. Tanner (Ed.), *Stress and psychiatric disorder*. Great Britain: Adlard & Son, 1960. Pp. 3-12.

47. WECHSLER, D., & HARTOGS, R. The clinical measurement of anxiety. *Psychiat. Quart.*, 1945, *17*, 618-635.

48. WHITE, R. W. Motivation reconsidered: The concept of competence. *Psychol. Rev.*, 1959, *66*, 297-333.

49. WHITE, R. W. Competence and the psychosexual stages of development. In M. R. Jones (Ed.), *Nebraska symposium on motivation, 1960*, Lincoln, Nebraska: University of Nebraska Press, 1960.

NOTE

1. For references and further discussions of these concepts: see, Korchin, 1964.

HOWARD LIDDELL

Experimental Analysis of Stress and Individual Self-Control In Animal Behavior

During the past 40 years two social images of man have emerged. In Russia, since 1921, the communist image of "soviet man" has been a dominant agent in social control. In America, "organization man" has played a similar role. What are the biological origins of these differing but similar practical notions of the individual in his daily round of social activities? Both involve self-control under stressful conditions.

We shall attempt to show that Pavlovian conditioning of sheep and goat has contributed to our understanding of the nature of human self-control under stresses both physical and social. Pavlov began his address on "Experimental Psychology and Psychopathology in Animals" in 1903 (1) with the words:

Esteeming the language of facts as the most eloquent, I ask your attention to the experimental material which gives me the right to speak on today's subject.

I now follow his example. The acute and chronic consequences of stress are most effectively disclosed by employing

Professor Liddell passed away without having had an opportunity to revise his paper. It is reproduced here as he presented it at the conference.

Pavlov's method of the conditioned reflex. Among domesticated animals sheep, goat, and pig have been our animals for conditioning; although we have systematically confirmed Pavlov's findings on conditioned reflexes and experimental neuroses in the dog.

The dog is too eager to please his master and the behavior of the monkey is too complex to justify the cost of its maintenance and the rigors of experimental control. Coldly considered, man himself is the cheapest experimental animal for the study of the extremes of stress and self-control. Moreover, the subject can communicate verbally with the experimenter. Our recurring wars, cold and hot, provide an inexhaustible supply of victims of excessive stresses and loss of self-control. But back to the safety and tranquility of the barnyard.

We have found self-control to be the *sine qua non* of Pavlovian conditioning with its inevitable accumulation of stresses leading to emotional bankruptcy (or experimental neurosis).

All that is to follow began with Pavlov as an eager young physiologist and travelling fellow visiting the laboratories of Heidenhain and Ludwig. There he was imbued with the mechanistic spirit of the physiology of the day. But as a realistic, clinically oriented biologist, what was he to do about his lifelong preference for the dog as an experimental animal—"this faithful and friendly representative of the animal world?"

The dog has a passionate longing for food. He wants to go for a walk with his master. He wants to understand him, to communicate with him. An emotional bond inevitably exists between dog and master. Transference, of which the psychoanalysts make so much in the physician-patient relationship, is but a complex biological variant of the everyday transactions between the dog and his master and the family in which he lives.

In the case of the domesticated sheep and goat matters are much simpler, but even a lamb or kid can become a family pet. One pet lamb would go upstairs in the morning to waken its mistress by licking her face. Many of us remember the goat in harness pulling the children's cart about the farm.

Pavlov's dog during conditioning willingly jumps up on the table at his master's request and allows the loops from the overhead beam of the "Pavlov frame" to be adjusted under his limbs. For a sensitive dog it is a punishment for his master to say "Shame!" In fact, when training a seeing-eye dog punishment is never employed.

The sheep or goat, on the other hand, must be forcibly confined by the experimenter in this "Pavlov frame," before conditioning is undertaken. Thus the sheep or goat subjected to Pavlovian conditioning is *the passive recipient of a stressful stimulus load* imposed upon it at the experimenter's pleasure.

If a brief, mild electric shock is applied to the foreleg the animal leaps upward and thrashes about with all four legs— "running in place." When a buzzer sounds for a few seconds always followed by shock it soon begins its struggle to escape before the shock is administered. Gradually, it comes to assume a pose of tense, quiet watchfulness or vigilance (to use Henry Head's term) (1) which is maintained at increasing physiological cost.

The monotony of this situation is punctuated by bouts of anxiety when the experimenter gives the buzzer signal followed by the shock. Thus, in the Pavlovian situation *the anxiety-punctuated monotony* inevitably leads, in the animal indoctrinated to maintain a pose of docile passivity, to emotional bankruptcy (experimental neurosis). The biological basis for the principal emotional hazard of the "organization man" is provided by a similar monotonous, yet stressful social situation punctuated by categorical demands from higher up. It is a reasonable assumption that our inference applies to the situation of "soviet man."

How has it come to pass that the experimental analysis of animal behavior by Pavlov and his many followers in Russia has led to the idealized conception of "soviet man"? Those who saw Koestler's play "Darkness at Noon" will remember the dramatic impact of this conception as it emerged from the dialogue during the trial of the old Bolshevik.

Work in Pavlov's laboratories had continued without interruption through World War I and the Kerensky revolution. Following the Bolshevik revolution the fate of Pavlov's future investigation of conditioned reflexes is recounted by his distinguished pupil, the late Professor B. P. Babkin (2). He writes:

Pavlov knew from personal experience how benevolently the Soviet authorities could be disposed toward science and scientists. Very soon after the accession of the Bolsheviks to power Pavlov's teachings on conditioned reflexes were recognized by them as affirming that the ir.tellectual life of people can be radically reconstructed and that the world-wide proletarian revolution would create a new human society. Even in 1921, when life in Russia was in a state of complete chaos, the Soviet of People's Commissars extended to Pavlov very exceptional advantages for his scientific work and also privileges, as set forth in the following document.

DECREE OF THE SOVIET OF PEOPLE'S COMMISSARS

Taking into consideration the very exceptional scientific services of Academician I. P. Pavlov, which have enormous significance for the workers of the whole world, the Soviet of People's Commissars has decided:

1. To form on the basis of representations of the Petrosoviet [that is, the Soviet of the city of Petrograd] a special committee with broad powers, having the following personnel, Comrade M. Gorky, Comrade Kristi, director of higher educational institutions, and Comrade Kaplun, member of the Board of Direction of the Petrosoviet, and to direct this committee to create as soon as possible the most favorable conditions for safeguarding the scientific work of Academician Pavlov and his collaborators.

2. To direct the government Publishing House to print in the best printing office of the Republic an *edition de luxe* of the scientific work produced by Academician Pavlov, also to vest in I. P. Pavlov the right of property in these publications both in Russia and abroad.

3. To direct the Committee of Provisions for Workers to supply to Academician Pavlov and his wife special rations equal to caloric content to two academic rations.

4. To direct the Petrosoviet to assure to Professor Pavlov and his wife the perpetual use of the apartment occupied by them and to furnish it and Pavlov's laboratory with the maximum conveniences.

> V. Ulianov [Lenin]
> Chairman of the Soviet
> of People's Commissars
> N. Gorbunov
> Director of Affairs of the
> Soviet of People's Commissars
> M. Glaisser
> Pro Secretary

Moscow, The Kremlin, January 24, 1921

Pavlov's attitude to this practical recognition of the importance of his work in reorganizing and reconstructing what the communists regarded as a decadent society for the benefit of the workers of the world is stated in the preface to his collected lectures (3):

As all our work developed out of physiology, so it has continued directly in that path. The methods and the conditions of our experimentation as well as the scheme of the separate problems, the working up of the results and finally their systematization—all this has remained in the realm of the facts, conceptions and terminology of the central nervous system.

And so it remained to the end of his long life. He believed, as a physiologist, that all behavior is rigidly determined. *"All behavior is reflex action* but new, or conditioned reflexes may be established by the experimenter under conditions subject to his control."

It was Lenin's genius, not Pavlov's, that glimpsed the prospect of creating a new—"soviet man"—by patterning his new reflexes according to Marxist principles through strict educational control and communist party discipline.

The origin of our contemporary conception of "organization man" bears a radically different relation to the history of animal behavior research in this country. Pavlov may have been naive as an observer of social processes but his acute estimate of American animal behavior studies shows surprising intuition concerning the contrasting *laboratory habits of thought* in his own investigations and in American psychological laboratories of that period. To quote again from the preface to his lectures written before he had visited this country (3):

Some years after the beginning of the work with our new method I learned that somewhat similar experiments on animals had been performed in America and indeed not by physiologists but by psychologists. Thereupon I studied in more detail the American publications and now I must acknowledge that the honor of having made the first steps along this path belongs to E. L. Thorndike (4). By two or three years his experiments preceded ours, and his book must be considered as a classic, both for its bold outlook on an immense task and for the accuracy of its results. Since the time of Thorndike the American work (Yerkes, Parker, Watson, *et al.*) on our subject has grown. It is purely American in every sense—in collaborators, equipment, laboratories, and publications. The Americans, judged by the book of Thorndike, set out on this new path of investigation in quite a different manner from us. *From a passage in Thorndike one may conjecture that the practical American mind applied to everday life found that it is more important to be acquainted with the exact outward behavior of man than with guesses about his internal states with all their combinations and changes. With these considerations concerning man, the American psychologists proceeded to their laboratory experiments on animals. From the character of the investigations, up to the present, one feels that both the methods and the problems are derived from human interests.*
(The italics are mine.)

In confirmation of Pavlov's intuition concerning the motivation of American psychologists investigating animal behavior, we must remember that both Thorndike and Watson soon abandoned work with animals. Although Thorndike pursued a career of laboratory research it dealt with human learning and the practical aspects of the educative process. Watson formulated his doctrine of behaviorism, or human psychology from the behaviorists' standpoint, based on lectures delivered at Columbia University, while still investigating animal behavior but soon turned to studies of conditioning in babies. Abandoning his academic career, he eventually founded his own successful advertising agency.

I knew both of these eminent psychologists. Thorndike maintained his keen interest in animal learning to the end. He visited our laboratory in his later years and observed with youthful zest our conditioning experiments with sheep and goats.

In an obituary tribute to Pavlov in the Psychological Bulletin I credited Watson with formulating his doctrine of behaviorism quite independently. He wrote me that I was correct. Had he known in detail of Pavlov's work he would not have originated behaviorism but would have been a follower of Pavlov. I think Watson deceived himself. He was too independent a thinker to have been a follower.

The stress of conflict is not the basic emotional hazard, either for the conditioned sheep or goat or for the young employee of a corporation "on his way up." The animal may become neurotic in attempting to make a difficult discrimination between a signal meaning shock and a signal meaning no shock. It will, however, suffer a neurotic breakdown or collapse of self-control when a 10 second signal always followed by shock is repeated over and over every six minutes for an hour a day, week after week—*anxiety-punctuated monotony.* An unsignalled shock every six minutes, however, is tolerated by the animal. It becomes restless about a minute before the shock is due and if the shock is omitted it continues to make tentative movements of the foreleg for a minute or two after shocking time has passed. However, it maintains its equanimity and neurotic collapse of its self-control does not occur. *The 10 second signal preceding the shock provides the anxiety-punctuation mark.*

So it can be with the "organization man." His basic trouble is not necessarily intra-psychic conflict with ambivalent feelings about his boss.

Present day sociology and psychiatry have become saturated

with the subjective, psycho-analytic point of view emphasizing the basic importance of conflict in the maintenance of self-control under stressful conditions. Freud, himself, gives this view its classical formulation:

Goaded by the id, hemmed in by the superego, and rebuffed by reality, the ego struggles to cope with its economic task of reducing the forces and influences which work in it and upon it to some kind of harmony; and we may well understand how it is that we so often cannot repress the cry: 'Life is not easy.' When the ego is forced to acknowledge its weakness, it breaks out into anxiety: reality anxiety in the face of the external world, normal anxiety in the face of the superego, and neurotic anxiety in the face of the strength of the passions in the id (5).

These histrionic fictions may reassure an emotionally disturbed patient on the psychoanalyst's couch but their scientific value is becoming increasingly questionable, particularly for those of us investigating conditioning under stressful conditions in the simpler mammals.

Conflict is a vague and much overworked notion both in mental medicine and sociology. Freud's dramatic portrayal of three warriors—ego, superego, and id engaged in increasing battle within the personality—does credit to his artistic, rather than his scientific genius.

With the aid of Pavlov's method of the conditioned reflex, it is possible to identify the principal emotional hazards common to animals and man. We have found them to be loneliness, anxiety-punctuated monotony, confusion, and over stimulation (6). Moreover, we have information as to their relative potency in menacing the individual's self-control. In sheep or goat, confusion (or conflict) is less emotionally disturbing than the daily grind of a rigid time schedule of positive signals always meaning electric shock to the foreleg.

A flock of sheep does not constitute a "lonely crowd" because the isolated sheep is never lonely. The sheep or goat is, by its nature, incapable of loneliness. This statement seems to contradict the facts of everyday observation. One of my correspondents, Mrs. Mason Berry of Lafayette, N. Y., describes the behavior of a flock of sheep when alarmed:

Sheep undisturbed will spread out and lie down quietly until eating time; then there is a constant baaing of the mothers for their lambs. But if they have been raided by dogs during the night or early morning, they will be bunched, tails together, faces toward the outside of the circle, watching every approach. Mothers will be cooing softly to their lambs and trying to keep them in the center of the circle. A ram occasionally runs around the outside and holds his head up, sniffing. After such a time, sheep will bunt our own dog and resent driving.

However, we discovered in our early experiments that the isolated sheep is not lonely; i.e. it is not under stress because of being alone. On the basis of our assumption of a "gregarious or flock instinct" we tethered a "social sheep" in one corner of the room to keep company with the animal being conditioned. After several months of this routine we removed the companion sheep from the room with only a momentary restlessness of the conditioned animal. The next day it gave no evidence of loss of companionship during the test hour. Thereafter, all of our conditioning tests of sheep and goats were conducted with the animal in a state of loneliness or in the presence of spectators. It made no observable difference in the animal's skilled performance.

A prime advantage of the comparative approach to the problem of self-control under stressful conditions appears in estimating loneliness as an emotional hazard. Unlike sheep and goat, the dog and monkey can become desperately, even lethally lonely.

One of Pavlov's dogs threatened with drowning in his kennel during a flood of the Neva in 1923 became terrified at the sight of water. Later, during a conditioning test as he stood on the table in his restraining harness, a stream of water trickled under the door. When the dog saw the water he was thrown into panic but was calmed when his master entered the room. During subsequent tests when his master's coat hung on a nail in front of the dog where he could sniff at it as he stood in the Pavlov frame, the water trickling across the floor in front of him was no longer disturbing.

However, if a monkey is placed in solitary confinement for a week or two with food and water automatically supplied, the lonely monkey becomes a dead monkey (7).

Overstimulation as an emotional hazard is ubiquitous for the domesticated animal as it is for man. The harried executive arriving home with bulging brief case for an evening of work is matched by the sheep with too heavy a stimulus load of positive and negative conditioned stimuli. Our first experimental neurosis in the sheep resulted from tripling the number of 10 second metronome signals each followed by shock during three successive daily one hour test periods.

On one occasion we were demonstrating our most proficient conditioned sheep to a psychoanalyst friend. This sheep "Robert," in training for three years, possessed an impressive battery of positive and negative motor conditioned reflexes to buzzer, bell, various metronome rates, tones, and tactile stimuli to ankle and thigh. He was accustomed to exhibiting his precise conditioned reflexes to large lecture groups. As the demonstration proceeded our psychoanalyst became more and more eager to discuss the implications of what he was seeing. Robert at first performed perfectly but during the second hour his mistaking of the familiar positive and negative signals rapidly increased and ended in his utter confusion.

The full understanding of self-control involves an examination of the biological origins of prejudice. Through *Pavlovian conditioning the experimenter can, at will, implant prejudices in an animal's mind.*

Our sheep, conditioned to the sound of the buzzer followed by shock is prejudiced against buzzing sounds for life. *All well established conditioned reflexes last for life.* This statement is not based on assumption. It is based upon our repeatedly confirmed observations. In our life-span studies of conditioning in sheep and goat one of our sheep died at 13 and a half years with his youthful conditioned reflexes intact. During the past winter (1962) our oldest goat, "Brown Billy," died in his fifteenth year still retaining all of his conditioned reflexes, both positive and negative. Both animals confirmed our previously well established conclusion that *Pavlovian conditioning, if long enough continued, inevitably leads to chronic nervous breakdown or experimental neurosis.* They had both succumbed to this chronic emotional disorder and displayed their neurotic manifestations until death.

The classical method of the conditioning reflex supplies the investigator with the dissecting instruments necessary to explore *the anatomy of prejudice.* Our exploration begins with an examination of the basic structure of Pavlovian conditioned reflexes from which our life-long prejudices develop.

If, as we believe, Pavlovian conditioning is primarily concerned with the emotional context of behavior, rather than with learning or intelligence in the pedagogical sense, we may define a positive conditioned reflex as follows. It is an emotionally charged episode of behavior bracketed between two primitive, stereotyped, forced reactions. These forced reactions are unconditioned reflexes in Pavlov's sense. The first is the investigatory reflex or "what-is-it" reflex. The second is the forced reaction (or reinforcement) to food or an irritating substance such as bitters or weak hydrochloric acid in the mouth or mild electric shock to the forelimb.

This conditioned reflex is a special case of Cannon's emergency reaction (as when a cat is barked at by a dog or thrown into cold water). The conditioned reflex, then, is an episode of emergency behavior in response to a stressful stimulus in a stressful situation; a situation which arouses a persistent, quiet watchfulness on the animal's part—the homologue of human anxiety.

Do our experimental studies of the sheep and goat's emotional reactions, acute and chronic, help us to dissect the intricate patterning of human prejudice in relation to self-control when the individual confronts a stressful social situation? Our answer is *Yes* and we will attempt to demonstrate why we believe so.

A conditioned reflex, established for life, is essentially *senseless, rigid, and unrealistic—so are many of our prejudices.* In our experiments if the sheep or goat flexes its leg at the signal for shock it gets the shock nevertheless and nothing of benefit to it is accomplished. The response is rigid and unrealistic as shown in the case of our goat, Brown Billy. Following his original conditioning with shock to the foreleg always following a metronome signal he was trained to flex his foreleg to avoid the shock given at the end of 10 seconds of sounding of a door buzzer. If he kept his forefoot off the floor the shock was automatically disconnected. Until he died at 15 years of age he avoided all shocks and his ritualistic flexion of the foreleg continued of its own momentum. Even though all shocks to his foreleg were avoided for most of his long life his stereotyped behavior remained *unrealistic.* At every alarm he was seemingly *compelled* to flex his foreleg. As he stood in the Pavlov frame any incidental stimulus instantly led to a precise flexion of his foreleg. For example, tapping his chest lightly with a wooden pointer, clapping hands (he would thus acknowledge students' applause), turning on the bright lights for the movie camera, always led to compulsive flexion of his trained forelimb. The most striking instance of his unrealistic behavior when alarmed occurred when we installed an electric fence around the barnyard. Brown Billy was observed to approach the unfamiliar strand of wire and leaning forward got an electric shock on his muzzle. He jumped back and dashed away but after a few steps wheeled, and facing the fence, precisely flexed his foreleg.

As old age approached he responded to a shrinking circle of alarms. He would no longer be compelled to flex his leg at bright lights or hand clapping or lightly tapping his chest but his old enemy, the door buzzer, still elicited a sluggish foreleg flexion.

The facts just presented have led us to the following conclusion. In human, as in animal conditioning *if two vivid experiences coincide they become emotionally glued together and thus a prejudice is born.* This *coincidence principle* explains the origin of many senseless rigid and unrealistic manifestations of self-control in social behavior including political, religious, and racial prejudices.

Pavlov's doctrine of the reflex nature of all behavior and his belief that if the environment is completely under the experimenter's control then the illusion of voluntary action vanishes and the animal's every act is rigidly determined. If the animal can thus become a puppet under the skillful manipulations of the experimenter why cannot "soviet man" become a puppet under the benevolent " dictatorship of the proletariat"? Lenin passionately believed this to be true.

But Pavlov's doctrine tells only half the story—*the negative half.* In Pavlovian conditioning *what does the experimental animal wish to do?* In his chapter on the "reflex of freedom" (3) Pavlov describes the behavior of an incorrigible dog who, because of his inborn reflex of freedom, refused with violent struggling to submit to the restraints of the Pavlov frame. When he was released, however, he would lie quietly on the floor by his master, the experimenter. His rebellion was conquered only by giving him his daily food ration in the Pavlov frame.

We have reason to believe that Pavlov was disturbed by other evidences of wishful behavior in his conditioned dogs. One animal conditioned to expect food when an electric bulb suspended in from of him was turned on, or a metronome on the beam over his head began clicking, or when a door buzzer under the edge of his table sounded, expressed his wish for food during the waiting periods between signals. On one occasion he wagged his tail, licked the electric light bulb in front of him, and salivated. Later, he peered over the edge of the table or up at the metronome overhead, licking his chops, salivating, and wagging his tail in anticipation of the buzzing and clicking.

In our experiments we have observed these "hallucinatory" conditioned reflexes to electric shock in sheep, goat, and pig.

Pavlov's eminent pupil and successor, Professor P. S. Kupalov, calls them conditioned reflexes without initiation.

Now we come to the positive half of the story of self-control under stressful conditions—mutual conditioning.

What about happy prejudices? In view of the previous gloomy subject matter it is necessary to broaden our conception of Pavlovian conditioning. We must include *mutual conditioning*. In mutual conditioning between mother and newborn, the mother's presence becomes a conditioned *security signal* to her offspring. This mutual conditioning establishes a stable pleasure organization between mother and newborn which promotes its health, growth, and development.

The intricate details of the dynamics of this brief interrelationship following birth is summarized by Frances Moore. As the result of many months "round-the-clock" observation of the sheep and goats in our laboratory by Dr. A. Ulric Moore and Frances Moore, she writes:

Mutual conditioning in the sheep and goat is accomplished through all the senses: smell, taste, body contact, hearing, seeing, and by the place sense as well. That is, animals become used to where to find their young, and the young to where the mother is. Any disarranging of the population of a group of mothers and young is very disturbing to the orientation of both mother and young.

When mutual conditioning is accomplished in the normal manner, no inhibiting is required of the young by the mother during the first few days of life. When inhibiting is eventually required by the mother not allowing the young to nurse, the process is very gradual and is done in such a way that the young expects satisfaction in the near future. Refusal is indicated by clear cut signals such as a motion of the leg that covers the udder. There is never any confusion as to what is indicated.

Body contacts with the mother are never refused. She at all times permits the young to make contact with her in any way it may desire. It may sleep close to her or in play may jump on her, or after nursing may stand under her head or body.

Termination of the mutual conditioning is very gradual and is effected by a widening circle as the young become less dependent for food upon the nursing process.

The key to this mutual conditioning seems to be an interplay of pleasurable behavior patterns so that mutual pleasurable stimulation is involved throughout. The signals for the food to be offered are consistent and always followed by what they imply. This results in digestive readiness.

Resting periods are completely relaxed since no ambivalence has been aroused.

The play of the little animal is protected by the mother so that its adventurous activities are encouraged. *Its passivity is thereby counterbalanced by the development of initiative.*

Mutual conditioning discloses the biological origins of operant conditioning, so widely employed by psychologists and neurophysiologists at the present time. Here the animal reaches out and presses a lever to secure what it wishes. With micro-electrodes implanted in various locations in the brain the animal can excite pleasurable foci in its brain or shut off an electrical stimulus to a brain center arousing pain or fear. See John Lilly's excellent summary (7).

Contemporary neuro-physiologists and psychologists are disposed to avoid Pavlov's laborious, time consuming and restricted method of the conditioned reflex. This, of course, is not true in the communist countries. The "blind spot" in the contemporary psychology of learning and emotion is, we believe, mainly due to the emphasis on short-term behavior, as John Lilly calls it. This emphasis results from the present day formidable armamentarium of exquisitely precise surgical, electrical, and chemical techniques together with a confusing array of animal training methods. This embarrassment of riches inclines the enthusiastic young investigator to brief spurts of focussed zeal in his observations of behavior. Moreover, the automatic registration of the performance of numerous animals at the same time involves *the anonymity of the experimental animal.*

This anonymity is impossible with Pavlov's tedious method of the conditioned reflex in which, after months or even years of training, the animal emerges as an individual. We still remember our eccentric old friend, the goat Brown Billy.

BIBLIOGRAPHY

1. HEAD, H. Some principles of neurology. *Brain*, 1918, 41, 344.
2. BABKIN, B. P. *Pavlov, a biography.* Chicago: The Univer. of Chicago Press, 1949.
3. PAVLOV, I. P. *Lectures on conditioned reflexes.* H. W. Gantt (Trans.). New York: International Publishers, 1928.

4. THORNDIKE, E. L. *Animal intelligence—an experimental study of the associative processes in animals,* 1898.

5. FREUD, S. *New introductory lectures on psycho-analysis.* J. H. Sprott (Trans.). New York: W. W. Norton & Company, 1933.

6. LIDDELL, H. S. *Emotional hazards in animals and man.* Springfield, Ill.: Charles C. Thomas, 1956.

7. LILLY, J. C. The psycho-psysiological basis for two kinds of instincts. *J. Amer. psychoanal. Assoc.,* 1960, 8, 659.

PART
FOUR } SELF-CONTROL
IN PSYCHIATRIC
PERSPECTIVE

JOHN C. WHITEHORN

Introduction

As I listened to the discussion this morning, and read some of the documents, I noted certain terms which kept reappearing, and I found these recurrent terms familiar to me by reason of my own necessary preoccupation with these concepts in my day-to-day work as a psychiatrist. For instance, in this discussion of self-control and stress, there has been talk of the commitment to a task, the social context involving expectations, ideas of dependability, motivation, and leadership. Little was said directly about morale, but this concept was clearly implied. These are concepts with which a working psychiatrist has to operate; and it becomes obvious from the discussion that they are considered to have relevance for the more general study of self-control under stress.

I emphasize the word *study* because we are concerned here with the goal of building a reliable body of knowledge, which involves the scientific problem of formulating and testing concepts and propositions, to establish measurable reliability. Elsewhere than in this conference much talk about self-control is exhortative, referring to ideas of sin and morality, but these concepts are not readily susceptible to scientific study, except as part of the matrix of cultural formulation and social expectation.

The psychiatrist, as a clinical scientist, shares this goal with those working in other behavioral sciences, that is, he wishes to establish reliable propositions, and therefore he shares in the need to establish behavioral concepts, and criteria, and terms, whose denotations are sufficiently definable to facilitate reliable observation, public report, and systematic, logical inference. Yet the psychiatrist is committed, also, to the individual therapeutic task. In his employment of words, in interviewing, and in other uses of his talents, skills, and personal qualities, for their influence upon the patient, he is vitally concerned to establish, within the patient, a new and healthier social context, while studying that already existent. While studying existent patterns, he works to produce change, as well as to understand the process of change. His language skills must outrun his logical skills, if he would be effective. His work involves him in an evocative role comparable to that of the poet or artist. He uses language as an instrument of influence, as well as for thinking and recording. It is not surprising, then, if his efforts at scientific communication manifest, at times, strong connotative fringe effects, which may impair their denotative reliability. In compensation for this risk of fuzziness, the psychiatrist, when successful in his therapeutic role, has some justification for feeling that he is dealing with what really counts, in the living person, rather than mere logical abstractions. The strength of his convictions may exceed the weight of his evidence, but he is not alone in this risk.

The psychiatrist often speaks of himself as "helping the patient to find himself." Yet, in actual operation, this is not so highly egocentric or so individualistic a search as it might sound, because the social context gets into the thinking of even the most individualistically-oriented working psychiatrist. The psychiatrist has an interest in situations, an interest which is first of all diagnostic. He judges neurotic and psychotic behavior and feelings by their inappropriateness, which means that he makes implicit judgments about the situation, since it is an evaluation of the situation which enables him to judge the inappropriateness of the patient's behavior or feelings.

In the actual work of the psychiatrist these concepts of situations, expectations, social context, etc., have very immediate and practical relevance, since what the doctor is trying to help the patient to do is to work out a mode of dealing with situations involving others in some manner which is mutually understandable, in a workable measure. It requires a considerable exercise of the imagination and communicative art to establish partnership with the patient so that both can understand the situation in terms of the patient's experience. And then comes the task, how to arrive with the patient, relative, boss, and others, at some consensus of viewing the situation so that it makes sense, both from the common-sense point of view and the patient's peculiar point of view, in a pattern wherein everybody concerned can find some acceptable way of dealing with the others. This is, in part, a conceptual problem in social theory; but also, in part, an emotional problem of establishing workable "we feelings." This is one of the major problems of the psychiatrist; and it has some relevance for much of the discussion. It has relevance for "the psychological preparation for stress," as it was formulated by Dr. Janis in informational terms. Yet, in Dr. Rioch's comment, attention will also be directed to the point that there is an establishment of rapport, in the process thought of as information-giving, which subsequently may be of more importance than the specific items of information in maintaining good steady self-controlled behavior.

Psychological Factors Maximizing Resistance to Stress: With Special Reference to Hypnosis

Introduction

In this paper we shall discuss the potential use of hypnosis as a means of maximizing the individual's capacity to withstand stress. We shall also consider other relevant psychological techniques which must be taken into account in any attempt to evaluate the effectiveness of hypnosis in this area.

The literature on hypnosis does not deal explicitly with the generic topic of maximizing an individual's resistance to stress. There are, however, clinical and experimental reports dealing with specific problems which can be viewed as stressors. In attempting to determine how effective hypnosis is in increasing the individual's

The substantive research reported in this paper was supported in part by contract AF 49 (638)-728 from the Air Force Office of Scientific Research.

I wish to thank my associates, Ronald E. Shor, Donald N. O'Connell, Lawrence A. Gustafson, Peter B. Field, Emily C. Orne, and Frederick J. Evans, for their comments and criticisms in the preparation of this manuscript. Special acknowledgment for editorial assistance is also given to Elizabeth Watson.

self-control, we must therefore extrapolate from evidence which did not originally intend to deal with the particular problem. The objective of our discussion is not only to outline the present state of knowledge but to highlight significant issues which will require further clarification.

In view of the broad meaning of the concept of stress, it seems advisable to define the type of stress with which this paper will be principally concerned.

Stress is considered to mean any physical or psychological environmental pressure which, if continued for a sufficient period at a sufficient intensity, would disrupt the functioning of the individual. In this context successful functioning means the continuation of activities in order to carry out the purposes and intentions of the individual as they existed prior to, and independent of, the stress. It does not refer to the individual's maximizing his comfort or security if such efforts interfere with the optimal behavior indicated in the interest of the realization of his purposes and intentions.[1] Successful resistance to stress could, therefore, be (1) continued activity regardless of environmental pressures or (2) alterations of activity designed to cope with the environment without, however, any change in the purposes, aims, or ideals of the individual. Failure to resist stress would be a change of ultimate purposes and aims in response to environmental pressure, or some form of breakdown.

In order to evaluate the potential utility of hypnosis as a means of maximizing an individual's resistance to stress, one must consider several aspects of this technique.

1. The specific effects of hypnosis which might prove valuable as resources in resisting stress: (*a*) the ability of the hypnotized subject to tolerate intense pain without apparent discomfort, (*b*) an apparent increase in physical capacity, (*c*) the ability to develop a high degree of motivation which can be maintained over a long period, and (*d*) the ability to selectively control knowledge available to consciousness.

2. The conditions most suitable for attaining the hypnotic state and the probability that any given individual will be able to be hypnotized.

3. The availability of the phenomenon during the time of stress. This can be achieved in two ways: (*a*) posthypnotic suggestion, and (*b*) training in self-hypnosis.

Hypnotically Induced
Anaesthesia and Analgesia

It has long been recognized that the deeply hypnotized subject is able to undergo exceedingly painful procedures without reporting discomfort and with little external evidence of pain. Prior to the discovery of anaesthetic agents, much of the interest in hypnosis focused on anaesthesia. Esdaile (1846) conducted a large series of operations employing hypnosis as the only anaesthetic agent. With the discovery of ether and chloroform, the interest in this aspect of hypnosis waned, to be revived within the last 15 years. There have been reports within recent years of major surgery (Caesarean sections, thyroidectomies, a variety of other major procedures, including even cardiac operations) performed without any anaesthetic other than deep hypnosis. Nonetheless the use of hypnosis in major surgery has been extremely limited, so that we may consider the available case histories primarily as demonstrations of its feasibility. However, hypnosis has been widely used to control the pain of dental procedures as well as childbirth. From a clinical point of view there is no question that in suitable subjects hypnosis can induce a degree of anaesthesia which will completely block the subjective appreciation of pain. According to many clinical reports (e.g., Moss, 1952; Shaw, 1958; Winkelstein, 1958), this procedure reduces the morbidity which normally accompanies the operation. However, no controlled data are available to substantiate this claim.

Recently there has been considerable interest in the use of hypnotic techniques to suppress intractable pain such as severe burns, shingles, trigeminal neuralgia and, in particular, incurable malignancies. Striking success in providing comfort to patients with severe pain has been reported (Crasilneck & Hall, 1962; Crasilneck, McCranie, & Jenkins, 1956; Crasilneck, Stirman, Wilson, McCranie, & Fogelman, 1955; Erickson, Hershman, Secter, 1961). This application suggests that hypnotic techniques may be used effectively to suppress not only acute pain for limited time periods (such as is the case when hypnosis is used in operative procedures) but also chronic pain, giving relief over long periods of time. It should be noted, however, that in these clinical instances, it is primarily painful events of a similar nature that are relieved; there are no data indicating that the appreciation of a new and different pain of sudden onset would be prevented. (Morphine, for example, is extremely effective in relieving an existing pain, but while it raises the pain threshold, it will not prevent the appreciation of a new pain.) Whether hypnotic procedures operate much in the way morphine does, or whether they can act to confer a relative immunity from new and different painful stimuli remains to be established.

The experimental work dealing with hypnotically induced anaesthesia has been less convincing. Sears (1932), West, Niell, and Hardy (1952), and others (Brown & Vogel, 1938; Doupe, Miller, & Keller, 1939; Dynes, 1932; Levine, 1930) have tried to show that autonomic responses to painful stimuli are diminished in the individual who is hypnotically anaesthetized. Recently in an exhaustive review of the literature, Shor (1962a) has re-analyzed previous studies and has come to the conclusion that little evidence exists which would support this assertion. It appears then that, in a laboratory situation at least, the autonomic correlates of pain are not significantly reduced by hypnosis; however, the subjective appreciation of pain can readily be affected and apparantly eliminated by hypnotic techniques.

In a recent empirical study, Shor (1962b) reinvestigated the effect of a highly painful electric shock on the autonomic responsivity of a subject in hypnosis, compared with his responsivity to the shock in the waking state.

In his experimental design Shor purposively minimized subjects' anxiety during the experiment in order to investigate the response to the painful stimulus rather than to a complex anxiety-evoking situation. Under these circumstances he found a remarkably low level of autonomic responsivity both in hypnosis and in the waking state. While Shor found no significant differences in the subjects' autonomic responses to electric shock in hypnosis and in the waking state, there was uniform agreement among the subjects that they did not experience discomfort with hypnotic analgesia but did experience considerable pain in the other conditions. Shor suggests that hypnosis probably affects the anxiety component of pain as well as the subjective appreciation of the sensation. Thus, one might well find marked differences in some clinical situations or even in a laboratory situation designed to maximize rather than minimize the anxiety component. Unfortunately, no experimental test of this hypothesis is available.

Thus, the available experimental evidence shows agreement among investigators that the subjective appreciation of pain can be reduced or eliminated by hypnosis. It is doubtful whether the autonomic response to the painful stimulus itself can be affected.

It is highly probable, however, that the autonomic response to an anxiety-provoking situation could be reduced (Barber, 1959).

The clinical observation by dentists that highly anxious patients show the most dramatic relief from hypnotic analgesia would also suggest that hypnosis affects the anxiety component. The observation that after several sessions many of these patients no longer require hypnosis in the dental situation would confirm Shor's experimental evidence. In these instances the patients apparently cease to be anxious and are then able to tolerate the dental procedures with minimal discomfort (Erickson et al., 1961).

Although we still do not know how hypnosis affects the appreciation of pain and reduces the anxiety accompanying painful situations, the technique has proved to be useful in actual practice. It should be pointed out that it is considerably easier to reduce anxiety than to induce actual analgesia; again dentists report that over 90 per cent of their patients benefit from hypnotic procedures while only some 25 per cent are able to develop complete analgesia (Burgess, 1952; Moss, 1952).

A considerable amount of research is needed to clarify these relationships. As we have already suggested, systematic studies which vary the degree of incidental anxiety are particularly needed, since in the clinical context the fear of pain is probably more significant than the pain itself. Anaesthesiologists working with hypnosis and chemical agents have reported that even a minimal degree of hypnotic response by a patient markedly reduces the need for chemical anaesthetic agents. This observation is not strange since it has long been recognized that an anxious patient requires far greater amounts of chemical anaesthesia than one who is relaxed. Finally, the mechanism of hypnotic analgesia itself is by no means clear. It is perhaps relevant that, at least in the lighter stages of barbiturate anaesthesia, the patient's autonomic responses to pain remain preserved. Thus, it would seem most worthwhile to study the parallels between hypnotic analgesia and that induced by barbiturates.

Physical Capacity in Hypnosis and the Waking State

It is commonly believed that hypnotized individuals are capable of performing feats of strength and endurance beyond the capabilities of the normal waking individual. Two kinds of evidence have been used to support this assertion: (1) the apparently superhuman feats of strength that individuals sometimes demonstrate during stage performances of hypnosis, such as supporting the weight of another person on their abdomen while they themselves are rigidly supported only by their head and their toes on two chairs which are as far apart as possible; and (2) the results of controlled laboratory studies.

Elsewhere the author (1954) has discussed this aspect of hypnosis in more detail. It was found that all the apparently superhuman feats ascribed to hypnosis and demonstrated by stage performance are well within the capabilities of the normal waking individual.

In order to understand the laboratory studies it is necessary to consider their generic design. Thus, Nicholson (1920), Roush (1951), and Williams (1929) have demonstrated that hypnosis increases physical capacity. In each of these studies subjects were asked to perform fatiguing tasks such as pulling an ergograph in the waking state and in hypnosis. Order effects were carefully controlled and insofar as possible the same instructions were given in hypnosis as in the waking state. An increment of performance in the hypnotic state was used as evidence for increased capacity in hypnosis.

Thus, while we accept the empirical finding that under the reported experimental conditions there is an increased performance under hypnosis as compared with the waking control condition, we do not feel that this demonstrates an increased physical capacity. In other words, hypnosis may increase performance because it provides increased motivation. As we pointed out, such a conclusion is not warranted because increased performance might well be a function of motivation rather than of actual capacity.

This interpretation was tested in a study (Orne, 1959) which compared the maximal hypnotic performance of individuals with the performance which the same individuals gave when highly motivated in the waking state. With the use of ego-involving motivation, it was demonstrated that all subjects were capable of exceeding their hypnotic performance in the waking state. It was concluded that there is no evidence to suggest that hypnosis leads to an increase in physical capacity over that present in the waking state. Rather, depending upon the level of motivation present during waking control periods, there may or may not be positive increments of performance in the hypnotic state.

Thus, hypnosis can be seen as one of many motivational techniques which will induce an individual to exert himself more than usual. When the results of hypnotic suggestion are compared with far simpler motivating procedures appealing to competition and the individual's view of himself as a man, hypnosis appears less effective. It should be pointed out, however, that the findings discussed above are obtained by studying physical exertion for short periods. Whether the same results would hold true for tasks involving physical endurance over longer periods remains to be established.

The Effect of Hypnosis
On Attitudes and Motivation

In the preceding section we have interpreted the apparent increase in physical capacity observed in hypnotized subjects as being due to an increased motivation of the hypnotized individual to respond to the requests of the hypnotist. While there is a general consensus among workers in this area that such an increase in motivation exists, it is exceedingly difficult to demonstrate such an increase in studies that do not involve physical endurance or painful stimuli.

In brief, it would be necessary to demonstrate that the hypnotized subject is willing to carry out actions that he would refuse to undertake in the waking state or that he will carry out behavioral patterns longer or better in response to hypnotic requests than in response to waking requests. While at first sight this test of an increase in motivation in hypnosis would seem a simple task, we have thus far been unable to devise a successful experimental procedure. The principal problem encountered is the remarkable compliance of the unhypnotized individual in an experimental or quasi-experimental setting. To illustrate this point I often begin lectures on hypnosis to undergraduates as follows:

I will ask a student in the front row for his wallet, another for his watch, while still a third for his shoe. Two students elsewhere in the room may be asked to exchange ties while another is asked to change his seat. After all students have complied with these meaningless and somewhat embarrassing requests, I point out that if I had previously hypnotized them, everyone would have assumed that they were willing to carry out these embarrassing behaviors because they had been hypnotized. In point of fact the simple request to do so in this quasi-experimental context, emanating from an instructor, is quite sufficient to elicit the behavior.

Elsewhere the author (1962a) has discussed in detail the problems of empirically testing this proposition. In brief, waking experimental subjects are willing to carry out any task which an experimenter might conceivably request of them, thus making it impossible to demonstrate an increment in the range of behavior which will be carried out by hypnotized subjects.

In a clinical context situations are encountered which would indicate that in some instances at least, patients will carry out behaviors in response to hypnotic suggestion that they are unwilling or unable to undertake when simply requested to do so. All of the literature on symptom removal is relevant in this regard. For the purposes of our discussion here, the indications, counter-indications, and permanence of direct hypnotic symptom removal are not relevant. The significant observation is that patients show alterations of behavior in response to hypnotic suggestions, which could not be elicited by instructions given in the waking state.

Of equal and perhaps even greater relevance is the clinical observation that habit patterns can be materially affected by requests given in the hypnotic state. In particular, over-eating and smoking, both habits notoriously resistant to change in response to requests, have been radically affected by hypnotic suggestion. Thus, the range of behavior that patients are willing to carry out as well as the motivation to comply with instructions appears more affected by requests received in hypnosis than by requests in the absence of hypnosis.

In addition to the behavioral evidence cited above, many psychiatrists employing hypnosis have observed that their patients tend to develop remarkably intense transference feelings very rapidly. Recently Gill and Brenman (1959) have discussed the ways in which the transference observed during hypnosis differs from the transference seen in usual psychoanalytic treatment. In more general terms these observations would indicate that hypnosis leads to a more rapid development of motivation to follow the instructions of the hypnotist than would be encountered if the technique were not employed.

A related question is whether hypnosis can cause significant and enduring alterations in the basic attitudes of the individual. Early work with suggestive therapy soon focused on the use of hypnosis as a means of affecting attitudes underlying undesirable behavior patterns (Bernheim, 1889; Prince & Coriat, 1907; Sidis, 1902). According to these authors, significant and enduring changes of attitudes could be effected by suggestive techniques.

Fairly recently there has been a resurgent interest in this type of approach with favorable results being reported (Erickson,1954; Haley, 1961; Rose, 1962). Unfortunately, in a therapeutic situation a large number of variables are involved, and there is no way to be certain that the specific suggestions concerning changes in attitudes were the only or even the principal factors which caused the patients to change their attitudes.

Several experimental studies of hypnotically-suggested attitude changes have been conducted by Rosenberg (1959; 1960). He presents evidence that attitudes can be significantly altered by direct suggestion and that the changes will persist at least for several weeks.

Neither experimental nor clinical data are available on the persistence of hypnotically induced attitudes under situations of stress. In the absence of any empirical data there is no *a priori* reason to assume that hypnotically induced attitudes are more resistant to modification by stress than attitudes acquired in a more conventional manner.

In summing up, it would seem that in a medical context at least, hypnosis appears to be an unusually powerful technique capable of altering behavior which had resisted previous attempts at modification. On the other hand, largely due to limitations of the experimental technique itself, there is no convincing experimental evidence that hypnosis is more effective than other simple techniques designed to increase motivation.

It may be important that the hypnotic suggestions given in a medical context are believed by the patient to be beneficial and thus are personally meaningful to him while in other contexts requests lack such personal relevance. Hence, it is not enough to ask whether hypnosis increases the probability of compliance with a request more than other motivational techniques do; rather, the question should be, how effective is hypnosis in eliciting certain specific categories of behavior, i.e., behavior beneficial to the individual which he might be disinclined to carry out versus behavior of no personal relevance?

Selectivity Induced
Amnesia and Hypnosis

One of the more striking phenomena of hypnosis is the inability of the subject to recall information that he has been instructed to forget. Thus, deeply hypnotized individuals who are given a set of instructions which they are then told to forget will be apparently incapable of recall. It is equally possible to cause a subject to forget information normally available, including thoroughly overlearned material, such as his name, a number, color, etc. Despite much urging, the subject will be unable to remember the material for which amnesia was induced. If, for example, the suggestion was to forget the number 3, the subject typically will count, "1, 2, 4, 5." He will continue to count, "10, 11, 12, 14, etc." Again the count will go, "28, 29, 40, etc." When the subject is asked to do simple arithmetic, such as subtracting 7 from 10, he will tend to look confused and answer, "2," or "4." If his response is, let us say, "2," he may then be asked, "What is 8 from 10?" and he will again respond, "2." By this time the subject usually shows considerable discomfort and confusion. It will be clear to him that something is the matter, but he will be unable to specify what and why.

It is easy to see how this phenomenon might be useful in certain stressful situations, such as capture and interrogation, where an individual has information available to him which must be protected. However, the feasibility of this approach must be considered in terms of the technical problems involved. First and foremost, only about 25 per cent of the normal population would be able to reach the depth of hypnosis required for this phenomenon (LeCron & Bordeaux, 1949) and probably the percentage may be even lower (Hilgard, Weitzenhoffer, Landes, & Moore, 1961; Mason, 1960). Further, this type of experimental demonstration, while dramatic, does not really approximate a stress situation in life. For example, we have found that when the hypnotist himself does the prodding, the subject is less apt to report the material for which he is supposed to be amnesic than if another experimenter tries to elicit the information. There is an even higher probability that the subject will recall the material in a discussion with someone whom he does not view as related to the experiment at all. Because of the potential complications inherent in leaving the subject with a suggestion to forget, let us say, the number three, no data are available on the persistence of this type of suggestion. Carefully conducted research with proper safeguards for the subject will be required. At this point, however, it is our impression that in most instances the amnesia will rapidly disappear.

Some data are available on the persistence of amnesia over

a period of a week. In another study conducted in our laboratory, it was necessary that subjects retain their amnesia for long periods. Thus, subjects who manifested complete amnesia for the hypnotic session were asked to return one week later, and at that time the subjects were interviewed by another experimenter about their previous hypnotic experience. Over half of the subjects who initially reported complete amnesia had remembered considerable amounts of the material during the week's time.

These experimental findings indicate that the large-scale use of hypnotically induced amnesia is not feasible. However, there is a small percentage of individuals who are capable of developing true amnesia for prolonged periods. Most subjects who maintain amnesia for one week continue to manifest the phenomenon for longer periods as well. However, only a small percentage of the total population is able to develop this type of amnesia.

Although this phenomenon occurs in relatively few people, it is nontheless worthwhile to investigate the nature of the amnesia involved. As Sutcliffe (1958) has pointed out, the most striking characteristic of posthypnotic amnesia is that the subject is unable to verbalize his knowledge directly. He is not aware that he knows the material which he has been told to forget, or alternatively the subject may remain unaware of how he acquired certain information, taught during hypnosis, which he retains in the subsequent waking state (Evans, 1965; Thorn, 1960). Thus, if amnesia for certain information has been induced and if the amnesic individual is then asked directly to recall the information in the waking state, he will be unable to do so. However, if the individual is asked to solve problems, the solution of which requires use of the information in question, he is able to solve the problems. In other words, if one asks for the material directly, the subject is unable to verbalize it, but when the subject is asked subtly, the presence of the knowledge can be demonstrated (Orne, 1951).

Strickler (1929) in studying the recall of nonsense syllables has shown that nonsense syllables learned under hypnosis for which the subject has amnesia are relearned considerably faster than other nonsense syllables which the subject had never learned at all. Orne and Fisher (1960) have demonstrated that hypnotic amnesia does not prevent retroactive inhibition.

Summing up the evidence, it would seem that hypnotically induced amnesia for important information would not prove particularly useful to an individual under stress. Only few individuals are capable of achieving complete amnesia and even in those individuals the material is far more readily available than is commonly recognized. There is reason to believe that it may be even more difficult for an individual to protect information which is not fully available to him in consciousness. Thus, he might well become aware of fragments which are critically important although he cannot readily identify their significance. Some of the problems inherent in this approach have been discussed by the author elsewhere (1961).

Despite our essentially negative evaluation of the utility of selective amnesia, it should be clear that many unresolved questions remain. Thus, the persistence of amnesia despite strong immediate rewards for recall over time has never been explored. Further, our assertions concerning the potential complications that such a procedure might entail for the subject are extrapolations from the available experimental and clinical evidence. Specific work directed toward evaluating the ability to withhold information consciously available, versus information not available to consciousness, would be highly desirable.

Hypnotizability

It is generally recognized that individuals differ in the ease with which they are able to enter hypnosis. Individuals further differ in the extent to which they can experience the various hypnotic phenomena.[2] Of a volunteer population of college age, less than 10 per cent fail to experience any hypnotic phenomena when they cooperate with the hypnotist. However, only 20 to 25 per cent are able to enter fairly deep hypnosis and only a portion of these are the "really good" hypnotic subjects who can easily manifest all the classic phenomena. The remaining 65 per cent are able to manifest varying degrees of hypnotic phenomena. (Our experience closely approximates that of others; cf. LeCron & Bordeaux, 1949; Mason, 1960.) Practice will tend to increase the depth of hypnosis only to a moderate degree. While in exceptional instances dramatic increases in achieving hypnotic depth can take place, subjects as a rule reach a plateau of depth within two or three sessions. The major effect of practice is that it enables the subject to reach his particular level of hypnosis more rapidly.

The above comments apply to volunteer subjects participating in hypnotic research, who are not being treated for psychological problems. In some clinical situations it is possible to demonstrate marked changes in hypnotizability, but these occur most commonly in individuals who at first fail to show any response. Rarely have we found that the depth (as indicated by the type and intensity of phenomena which can be experienced in response to appropriate suggestion) varies after the first few sessions. Gill and Brenman (1959) report similar findings.

Some authors, notably Erickson (1952) in recent years, have insisted that all individuals can be deeply hypnotized. While Erickson has been able to demonstrate in isolated instances that deep hypnosis can be induced in apparently difficult subjects, there is no available systematic evidence to substantiate his statement. Whenever systematic efforts have been made, the findings have been consistent with the view previously stated.

Certain evidence would suggest that circumstances of high anxiety may increase hypnotizability. Some dentists report remarkably high percentages of results (Burgess, 1952); similarly, some obstetricians find that during pregnancy hypnotizability is increased (August, 1959; Michael, 1952). Beecher's (1956) findings on the effectiveness of the placebo in a battlefield situation versus its effectiveness in a civilian hospital indicate that the placebo reaction is also augmented by high levels of anxiety. Unfortunately, no investigation has been specifically designed to study hypnotizability under anxiety-provoking conditions.

Considerable work is needed to determine whether hypnotizability could be increased by appropriate modifications of the situation. The use of long periods of time, high anxiety situations, mechanical aids, appropriate drugs, etc., have been suggested but have not been systematically studied. In the absence of further progress, however, it is necessary to recognize the limitations presently inherent in any proposed use of hypnosis.

The Phenomenon of
Posthypnotic Suggestion

In many ways the most intriguing aspect of hypnosis is that in appropriate subjects, a suggestion given during hypnosis will be carried out at a later date even in the absence of the hypnotist.

It is possible to give a suggestion so as to elicit the specified behavior at some specified future time in response to a specified future event or in response to a specified future experience. The discussion below will deal with posthypnotic behavior as it is observed in good hypnotic subjects. It should be clear that our discussion concerns a phenomenon which can at present be elicited in less than 25 per cent of the population. Nonetheless, as a paradigm for understanding how a significant interaction at one point in time may determine future experience and behavior, it is of extreme interest.

To describe a typical posthypnotic response: I suggest to an excellent subject in deep hypnosis that when I remove my glasses he will remove his watch. On awakening the subject appears perfectly normal and has no recollection of his hypnotic experience. Some minutes later I remove my glasses and the subject continues to talk with me, but can be seen shifting his watch from one hand to the other. When asked why he changed the position of his watch, he may report that the strap felt tight or perhaps that he experienced a mild discomfort (itching or the like) and wanted to gain relief from this sensation. When I inquire whether the watch is now comfortable, he will assure me that it is. However, when I again remove my glasses, the watch leaves the other wrist. I again question him about the removal of the watch and am told that for some reason it again felt uncomfortable. I comment that this seems peculiar and suggest that the subject put on his watch and cease fidgeting. When he does so, I will be informed on inquiring that the watch now feels comfortable. However, as soon as I again remove my glasses, the subject will look at me strangely and say with obvious discomfort, "I am sorry, but for some reason my watch feels uncomfortable again."

At this point, the subject, and particularly the intelligent subject, will conclude that the peculiar feeling of the watch must somehow be related to a prior hypnotic suggestion. He may ask quite directly whether this is the case. If I evade answering directly and ask the subject to figure it out, he will become ill at ease and exhibit obvious conflict. Finally, he will remove his watch and conclude, "You must have given me a suggestion that I take off my watch." My response may now be that if this is the case he might like to try to keep his watch on, and he will readily agree, replacing it at this time on his wrist and reporting that it now feels comfortable. When in the course of further conversation, I again remove my glasses, the subject will smile and observe, "Ah, that's it; I am supposed to remove my watch whenever you remove your glasses. Well, I won't this time!" As we continue to talk, however, the subject's hand will be seen moving slowly toward his watch, but in the process of undoing the clasp, the subject may start, as if becoming aware of his behavior, and say firmly, "No, I won't." He will in a determined manner keep his left hand at his side and continue in conversation with a set expression. Within a minute or two, however, the hand will again approach the watch, and after one or more repetitions of this sequence, the subject finally may exclaim, "Ah, the heck with it!" and take off his watch.

In the above illustration of the typical posthypnotic response of an excellent hypnotic subject, two conceptually distinct attributes of the phenomenon may be observed: (1) a lack of awareness of the source of motivation for an item of behavior, and (2) a compulsion to carry out an item of behavior. It should be noted that the lack of awareness is not a necessary and essential feature. It can be observed above that even after the subject had become aware that removing the watch was due to a posthypnotic suggestion and even after he had decided at one level to "fight" the suggestion, he nonetheless found himself responding to it. Indeed it was only when the subject became aware that his removing the watch was a posthypnotic suggestion that the compulsion aspect of the suggestion became apparent.

When the same posthypnotic suggestion is given to different subjects, it is possible to observe widely dissimilar patterns of response. Some subjects will not rationalize their behavior; they will merely remove the watch, and if asked why, they may reply that they felt an urge to do so. Other subjects will remove their watch without any apparent awareness of their behavior; they may actually seem surprised to find the watch in their hands. Still other subjects will show considerable conflict, apparently resisting an impulse; ultimately, they may or may not remove the watch.

Not all individuals who respond to posthypnotic suggestions develop amnesia for the actual suggestion. It is often difficult to determine to what extent their compliance with a suggestion is accompanied by a compulsion to do so. Thus, subjects may describe their experience in terms ranging from an irresistible impulse to carry out the suggested behavior to a rather bland statement, "I did what you told me to, because you asked me to do it."

When it is made difficult for subjects to carry out post-hypnotic suggestions, the differences in the hypnotic experiences of different subjects as reflected in the descriptions given by the subjects emerge in a more objective light. Thus, subjects will differ markedly in their determination to carry out suggestions in the face of obstacles. When circumstances make it impossible to carry out the suggested activity, a variety of behavior patterns can be observed. Some subjects exhibit serious disturbances, ranging from symptom formation (e.g., Wolberg, 1947) to transient confusion and spontaneous reentry of hypnosis (J. R. Hilgard, E. R. Hilgard, & Newman, 1961). Others, after an initial attempt to carry out the action, do not show any signs of disturbance nor will efforts to elicit subjective discomfort meet with success. It is by no means clear whether the differences in responses to posthypnotic suggestions are entirely due to differences in the "depth of hypnosis" at the time the suggestion was given. While this view is implicit in much of the literature, few attempts have been made to study different types of reactions to posthypnotic suggestions. It is our impression that some of the differences discussed above may be related to personality variables, i.e., they may be more than just differences in degree of response.

The mechanism of posthypnotic behavior is not as yet fully understood. Not only are satisfactory theoretical formulations lacking, but even simple observational data describing the conditions under which certain events will or will not take place have not been systematically produced.

One aspect of posthypnotic behavior is relevant to this discussion. While demonstrations usually deal with simple motor behavior, it is possible to elicit in some subjects, during the waking state in response to posthypnotic suggestion, any and all phenomena which can be elicited in deep hypnosis.

It is well to recall that *no differences* have as yet been demonstrated in the *range of behavior* that individuals will carry out in response to posthypnotic suggestion from that which can be elicited by simple requests in an experimental situation. However, the subjective experience of the individual while carrying out posthypnotic suggestions is markedly different from that of the individual carrying out a simple waking request.

It is not intended in this paper to evaluate the theoretical formulations which have been set forth to explain the posthypnotic phenomenon or hypnosis in general. Rather the discussion will be confined to clinical and experimental observations in order to pinpoint areas where further systematic observation is imperative before an adequate theoretical formulation is possible. The emphasis here will be on those aspects of the phenomenon which bear on the central theme of this conference.

PERSISTENCE OF POSTHYPNOTIC BEHAVIOR

Erickson (1939; M. H. Erickson & E. M. Erickson, 1941) in a number of highly imaginative studies has investigated the nature of the posthypnotic phenomenon. He reports cases in which posthypnotic behavior persisted over several years. Unfortunately, these clinical observations are not compared with the effect of simple instructions. Furthermore, they were obtained by using subjects who were in a quasi-therapeutic relationship with the investigator.

A recent report by Crasilneck and Hall (1962) illustrates a unique type of persistence of posthypnotic response. Working with terminal cancer patients in an attempt to suppress intractable pain, Crasilneck and Hall suggested that in response to the hypnotist's voice the patient would move his forefinger. When these patients became moribund and ceased to respond to any instructions from the medical or nursing personnel, they continued to raise their forefinger in response to suggestions from the hypnotist. What is most striking in this report is that the response of the forefinger was the only sign of life persisting in a number of moribund patients. Reality factors prevented the investigators from obtaining controlled data; however, their study raises basic issues about the mechanism which triggers posthypnotic behavior.

Two experiments have been devised specifically to study the persistence of posthypnotic behavior. In both instances the authors compared persistence of behavior in response to posthypnotic suggestion with the persistence of the same behavior when waking control subjects are asked to carry out the behavior as part of their experimental instructions.

Kellogg (1929) instructed hypnotized subjects to read certain sonnets and suggested to them that as they were reading, they would breathe twice as fast on even-numbered pages. The same instruction was given to waking control subjects. All subjects were tested immediately after receiving instructions, the following day, and then at one- or two-week intervals, up to 90 days.

Kellogg reports that the posthypnotic response declined during the first three weeks and then leveled off and continued without further decrement. The waking control subjects in contrast showed an initial rise in their response and then maintained a consistently high level of response throughout the duration of the experiment. Kellogg's experimental design necessitated the repetitive testing of each subject; hence no conclusions could be drawn about the persistence of posthypnotic behavior in the absence of practice effects.

Patten (1930) addressed himself specifically to testing the persistence of posthypnotic behavior while at the same time avoiding the confounding effect of practice. Experimental and control subjects (in hypnosis and the waking state, respectively) were instructed that at some later time a series of words would be read to them. They were further instructed to press their right forefinger whenever the name of an animal was read. A sufficient number of subjects were run so that each subject was tested only once. Time intervals ranged from zero to 33 days after the initial instructions. At the time of the test, the experimenter distracted the subjects from the initial instruction by telling them to note whether any words were presented twice. Pressing of the right forefinger was recorded.

Patten found that the response to the posthypnotic suggestion showed some decline; however, it endured for the duration of the study. In the waking control group the strength of the response declined less than it did in the experimental group.

EFFECTIVENESS OF POSTHYPNOTIC SUGGESTION

Both Patten's and Kellogg's studies conclude that posthypnotic suggestion was less effective than simple instruction. These findings are clearly contrary to the popularly held view that posthypnotic suggestion is a powerful technique for controlling behavior. They demonstrate that behavior can be affected for varying periods of time but that experimental instructions given to a cooperative subject are actually more effective.

Elsewhere the author (1962b) has discussed the very special form of social interaction which constitutes an experimental situation. As we have pointed out earlier, subjects will in such situations carry out a remarkable range of activities and show a surprising degree of motivation in following them through. It would seem that the findings of Kellogg and Patten could be considered as much a study of the motivation of experimental subjects as an investigation of posthypnotic behavior. Since the hypnotic subjects also are participants in an experiment, one might conclude that either hypnosis somehow interferes with the motivation or that it appeals to a different set of motives.

In order to clarify some of the issues raised by Patten and Kellogg, work is currently being conducted in our laboratory by Damaser (1964). In designing this present study, it was considered important to use a measure of posthypnotic response where the behavior is carried out in the absence of the hypnotist.

The behavioral item which was chosen was that subjects be instructed to mail business reply cards daily for a period of 83 days; however, subjects are given 150 postcards and are not told the duration of the experiment. On the 70th day they receive a letter from the project director, who is *not* the hypnotist, telling them that the experiment is over. (This was intended to establish whether hypnotized subjects would continue sending postcards since the instructions to discontinue sending the postcards did *not* stem from the hypnotist.)

A number of other technical problems were controlled in this study such as the hypnotizability of controls and depth of hypnosis. The major comparisons were between three groups: deeply hypnotized subjects who received a posthypnotic suggestion to send postcards; a second group also deeply hypnotized but not given any posthypnotic suggestion, who were subsequently asked in the waking state to send postcards; and a third group who were given both the posthypnotic suggestion and the waking request. The study is as yet incomplete, and a full discussion of its implications would take us beyond the scope of this paper; however, the preliminary analysis clearly supports the findings of Patten and Kellogg. Thus, the posthypnotic suggestion group sent significantly fewer postcards than the waking request group.

These findings are difficult to interpret. They cannot be ascribed to differences in hypnotizability. It seems likely that we are dealing with two different kinds of motivations in the two groups. Thus, the subject who is responding to a posthypnotic suggestion would perceive the experiment as a test of the strength of the posthypnotic suggestion. He would carry out the posthypnotically suggested behavior as long as he felt a compulsion to do so; however, he would view that his role was either to stay neutral and allow the impulse to elicit the behavior or, in some instances that he should actively fight what he would perceive to be an alien impulse. In other words, in this particular kind of experiment the posthypnotically instructed subject would consider it inappropriate to respond without some form of compelling impulse. The control subject, on the other hand, is in a totally different situation. He feels that it is his task to make himself respond as long and as regularly as possible. He is motivated to perform the experimentally-given task successfully and he will typically arrange to remind himself to perform the task regularly.

One might thus well ask: Is the use of a control group appropriate at all or do the results obtained with controls merely detract from or obfuscate the significant finding that subjects will indeed carry out posthypnotic suggestions? Regardless of the answer given to this question, we feel that great care is necessary in evaluating the effectiveness of posthypnotic suggestion. Thus in the kind of experimental situation described above, the cooperative experimental subject is characteristically so strongly motivated that the motivation due to posthypnotic suggestion appears slight by comparison. However, before we draw any conclusion, we must remember that we seem to be dealing with a different type of motivation, as is borne out by the very fact that the posthypnotic-suggestion groups consistently perform worse in situations of this kind. Nonetheless, there are quite a few clinical studies and reports which indicate that in clinical situations posthypnotic suggestion appears to be a considerably more potent tool.

The clinical literature (e.g., Erickson et al., 1961; LeCron, 1961; Mason, 1960; Schneck, 1953) provides a large number of reports indicating that posthypnotic suggestion can be significantly more effective than instructions given to the waking individual in such situations as weight reduction, the elimination of undesirable habits or symptoms, such as smoking, nail biting, enuresis, conversion symptoms, etc. While no control studies on the effectiveness of simple requests are available, one can be certain that the patients in these instances had all failed to respond to simple requests instructing them to alter their behavior and sought professional help only when other means were ineffective. However, it must be recognized that clinical reports do not indicate whether the behavioral changes could not have just as readily been brought about by a waking suggestion given by a prestigeful and convincing authority figure, or whether the induction of hypnosis did indeed facilitate the process. While this issue is an interesting research problem, it seems relatively unimportant in the context of our present discussion since the type of motivation produced by prestige suggestion and that produced by hypnosis appear qualitatively the same.

In clinical situations posthypnotic suggestion is reported to be effective in altering behavior which had previously resisted attempts at change. Why is it that in a clinical situation where individuals are attempting to change their own behavior in a fashion more satisfactory to themselves, posthypnotic suggestion facilitates change? In these situations posthypnotic suggestion appears to add to their motivation whereas in experimental studies such an effect has been difficult to demonstrate. This might be understood, in part at least, in terms of the individual's attitude toward his own behavior. Thus the individual who seeks treatment in order to alter his behavior is not interested in testing the effectiveness of the posthypnotic suggestion, but welcomes it as an ally in his struggles to change his behavior. This attitude is considerably different from that of the experimental subject which we have discussed earlier. Simple instructions cannot be expected to change the patient's behavior since he is already consciously motivated to do so. Thus, it is not surprising that in clinical situations posthypnotic suggestion turns out to be relatively effective.

There is evidence then that posthypnotic suggestion may elicit behavior which is relatively trivial to the individual. It would seem that the motivation to carry out this behavior and the subjective experience of so doing are different depending on whether they occur in response to a posthypnotic suggestion or in response to a simple request; however, there is in any event abundant evidence that in the experimental situation the waking request is more effective. On the other hand, a posthypnotic suggestion given to help an individual who wishes to carry out desirable behavior but finds his task difficult or impossible is an effective instrument. No specific data are available that would permit one to conclude that hypnosis, in itself, is capable of increasing self-control or resistance to stress. However, such an effect seems to be indicated in the clinical situations described in the literature. Empirical studies directed at this issue will need to be undertaken.

THE EFFECT OF CHANGING REALITY CONDITIONS
ON THE PERFORMANCE OF POSTHYPNOTIC BEHAVIOR

Erickson in some of his experimental and quasi-experimental work with posthypnotic suggestion makes the point that post-hypnotic behavior can best be viewed as a reinstatement of the original hypnotic state lasting only for the duration of the response. He further implies that the posthypnotic suggestion once given becomes isolated from explicit or implicit instructions subsequently given in the waking state. Waking reality is important only to the extent that it provides the cue which triggers the effect of the posthypnotic suggestion. Thus, the posthypnotic suggestion once given is viewed as an isolated subsystem which will affect thoughts, attitudes, and behaviors when triggered by predetermined cues; however, this subsystem cannot be altered except by re-induction of hypnosis. Erickson also describes a curious effect when it becomes impossible for the individual to execute a posthypnotic suggestion; for example, a subject is told in hypnosis to place a certain pencil in his pocket in response to a cue word, but the pencil is surreptitiously removed before the subject can carry out the response. When the cue word is given, the subject will become confused and then lapse into deep hypnosis.

In this context we shall not try to examine the evidence for and against Erickson's formulation of the mechanism of post-hypnotic behavior. The clarification of the mechanism is necessary and remains an important research task; however, we are more concerned here with a different aspect, i.e., whether posthypnotic suggestions are independent of significant alterations in the subject's environment. All of Erickson's research demonstrating the fixed nature of the posthypnotic response involves observation by Erickson himself. Thus, it would be possible that Erickson communicated to the subject in the waking state the precise nature of the activity expected. A study by S. Fisher (1954) strongly suggests this possibility.

Fisher gave a number of subjects the posthypnotic suggestion that they would scratch their right ear each time that they heard the word "psychology." On awakening he tested for this response and found it present. At that point he was interrupted by one of his colleagues who dropped into his office for a visit. By his general behavior Fisher indicated that the experiment was terminated, and he, the colleague, and the subject engaged in casual conversation. In the course of this conversation the word "psychology" was mentioned. The overwhelming majority of subjects no longer responded to the word by scratching their ear, despite the fact that the suggestion had not been removed. After a while the colleague excused himself and Fisher turned to the subject, bcame somewhat more formal and by his behavior indicated that the experiment was still in progress. In this situation the word "psychology" again evoked the response of scratching the right ear.

Fisher concluded that the posthypnotic suggestion is not merely the effect of an isolated subsystem triggered by a specific cue. Rather the individual gives posthypnotic responses on the basis of what he believes to be appropriate. Thus, the context might determine whether or not the word "psychology" would elicit the posthypnotic response.

Two aspects are particularly interesting in the Fisher experiment: (*1*) that a number of subjects insisted that they had carried out the suggested behavior throughout, while others gave very superficial rationalizations, suggesting that in retrospect they felt that they should always have responded to the word "psychology," (*2*) three subjects did always respond to the word "psychology" even during casual conversation.

Fisher's study, though very suggestive, does not fully resolve the issue. Perhaps subjects perceived the posthypnotic suggestion to mean that they should scratch their right ear only when "psychology" was mentioned during the *experiment,* and assuming the experiment terminated, they no longer believed it necessary to respond. However, the fact that three subjects did respond consistently requires further investigation. It is possible that these subjects assumed that it was their task to respond even when the situation was not obviously "experimental." A different possibility is that there are two different mechanisms of posthypnotic response: one illustrated by these three subjects, the other by the rest of the subject population. This experiment ought to be repeated with explicit instructions to the subjects to respond to the word "psychology" for a specified period of time, such as the next three days.

Regarding the use of posthypnotic suggestion as protection against stress, data are needed that will establish whether an individual will carry out suggested behavior even though he knows that the hypnotist does not have any way of checking his behavior and/or that the hypnotist does not appear to care whether the subject continues to respond. (The clinical situation does not offer us any data on this question since therapists are always presumed to care whether their patients respond favorably. Further, the patient usually returns to tell the therapist the results of the suggestion.) This lack of definitive data may be due to two factors: (*1*) imprecise formulation of the question, and (*2*) technical difficulties in monitoring private behavior. Yet it would appear that in situations of this kind we might well observe a difference between requested behavior and posthypnotic suggestion. It would seem likely that subjects would not carry out behavior which they believe cannot possibly be verified by the experimenter, while posthypnotic suggestion might be effective even though the hypnotist is known to have no apparent way of checking whether the suggestion is followed.

A closely related problem of considerable practical and theoretical interest is the connection between a positive relationship of subject to hypnotist and the performance of posthypnotic behavior. It is known that a subject who had previously entered hypnosis with a particular hypnotist may refuse to do so if problems arise in the relationship. However, we have no data on how a deteriorating relationship with the hypnotist influences the effectiveness of a posthypnotic suggestion. Broadly stated the issue is, to what extent does the posthypnotic suggestion come to function as a quasi-autonomous unconscious wish that has become a part of the individual, and to what extent does its effectiveness depend on a continuing positive relationship with the original hypnotist? An analogue to this question is the issue of how permanent the changes are that are achieved in psychotherapy. In theory, at least, definitive psychotherapy yields results independent of the relationship between therapist and patient while transference cures depend upon a continuing positive relationship with the therapist. Lest, however, we infer from this formulation an answer to the question raised above, it should be pointed out that no empirical test of the proposition regarding psychotherapy is available. The technical problems engendered in a rigorous test of this widely accepted proposition are such that it may never actually be carried out.

In summarizing our discussion of the posthypnotic phenomenon, we believe that it presents an extemely useful paradigm for studying the effect of a variety of motivating techniques on behavior. The widely held assumption that posthypnotic suggestion is uniquely effective in eliciting compliance with simple requests is not justified by the experimental evidence. On the contrary, waking requests are considerably more effective, i.e., experimental subjects who have received waking requests have been found to perform simple tasks for longer periods and more consistently than have subjects responding to posthypnotic suggestions. On the other hand, in certain clinical situations, it would appear that posthypnotic suggestion is remarkably effective. The paradox between clinical and experimental data requires explanation.

Regarding the mechanism of posthypnotic behavior, we have formulated two questions which appear central and for which data are totally lacking: (*1*) Will a subject carry out a posthypnotic suggestion irrespective of whether he believes that the hypnotist will know or care about his compliance, and (2) Is a continuing positive relationship with the hypnotist necessary for the subject to continue to carry out posthypnotic behavior? Empirical research designed to answer both of these questions will be technically difficult but indispensable if we wish to evaluate the possible utility of hypnotic suggestion in situations of stress.

Self-Hypnosis

An alternative to using posthypnotic suggestion as a means of making certain hypnotic phenomena available to the individual when needed is training in self-hypnosis. Despite widespread interest in this phenomenon there has been little systematic or well-controlled research. Further, the differences between self-hypnosis and posthypnotic phenomena may not be as great as is commonly believed.

The very term "self-hypnosis" implies that an individual enters hypnosis without a hypnotist. Various methods have been developed to enable individuals to accomplish this goal and depending upon the purpose of the procedure, different aspects of hypnosis have been emphasized. Thus, religious and mystical as well as therapeutic aims have prompted individuals to explore procedures of self-hypnosis.

The most common medical way in which this technique is currently used in the United States is exemplified in the work of Erickson (1954) who induces hypnosis in a patient and then suggests that the patient, by thinking about it, will be able to bring about the same experience in the hypnotist's absence. For example, in cases of terminal cancer, anaesthesia may be suggested, and, once the patient has been able to respond to this suggestion, he will be "taught" to think about the idea of feeling no pain, thus inducing anaesthesia in himself subsequently. The teaching takes place in hypnosis and the ideas are presented to the patient as posthypnotic suggestions. Clearly, in this instance, it is difficult to determine whether the mechanism involved is a peculiar form of posthypnotic suggestion or whether it is more properly a self-induced hypnotic state. At the very least, it must be recognized that the self-induced hypnotic experience has very direct roots in the original hypnotic session. One of the interesting aspects of this technique is that it can be "taught" to a suitable subject very rapidly and that the skill may persist for a long period of time. From a clinical point of view, it is irrelevant whether this skill is posthypnotic behavior or truly self-induced hypnosis. It seems to have some of the properties of both. Until more is known empirically about the characteristics of posthypnotic behavior, it will be difficult to evaluate what kind of effect is involved.

The best known Western advocate of self-hypnosis or auto-suggestion was Coué (1922). However, despite his famous edict that all suggestion is auto-suggestion and all hypnosis is self-hypnosis, his actual procedure differed little from practitioners of different persuasions. Thus, when doing a classic postural sway test, instead of saying to the subject, "Imagine yourself falling backward; you are falling backward," he would say "Say to your-self, 'I am falling backward; I am falling farther and farther backward.'" Despite this variation introduced in the more classi-cal hypnotic procedure, the net result was the same, and in his own practice and that of his followers the patient was taught "self-hypnosis" by the hypnotist. Again it is difficult to determine the extent to which we are dealing here with a more classic post-hypnotic phenomenon.

The relationship between hypnosis and the various yoga sys-tems has been subject to considerable commentary. All the classical hypnotic phenomena have in one way or another been described in the context of yoga. It is outside of the framework of this paper to discuss in detail the relationship between the two states. We wish to comment only that the avowed purpose of yoga is to enable the individual to become independent of his external world and his physical wants. For these reasons control of pain and pleasure are important in the attainment of the yogi's goals. The training of yoga emphasizes many aspects typical of the hypnotic experience, such as concentration on relatively limited stimuli, quasi-rituals, and the relationship to a teacher. In this context it is relevant to note that yoga training is almost always undertaken with a "master." Thus, the development of yoga meditation encompasses many of the conditions of hypnosis (Das, 1963).

The most systematically developed medical application of self-hypnosis has been the technique of autogenic training developed by Schultz (1932; Schultz & Luthe, 1959). This approach is avowedly derived from yoga, but has been stripped of its mystical roots and adapted to treatment purposes. The term "autogenic training" emphasizes the training and learning aspects of this

technique. In brief, Schultz begins by asking the patient to learn
a basic exercise. The individual is asked to be seated in a comfortable chair, focus his thoughts on his right hand, and say to
himself, "My right hand and arm are growing heavy; my right
arm is growing relaxed. My right hand is growing heavy." This
exercise is first undertaken in the presence of the physician but
subsequently practiced by the patient at home. One of the significant differences between this technique and the approach of
Erickson described above is that as a result of the practice sessions
at home the patient learns to become more proficient in the absence
of his doctor than in his presence.

Once the patient is able to induce the subjective experience
of heaviness in the right arm, he proceeds to add another idea.
He is taught to begin by making his arm heavy and then adding
the idea of warmth. Thus he now concentrates, "My right arm is
heavy; I am quiet and relaxed. My right arm is warm and comfortable." Once the patient has achieved the point where he is
able to induce heaviness and warmth, he goes on to develop
regular deep breathing and then subsequently may learn to induce
total relaxation of his body, subjective experiences of calm, the
experience of relaxing internal organs, etc. According to Schultz,
patients can be trained to slow their pulse, selectively increase
circulation in various limbs, etc.; they may further be instructed
to utilize this technique for the purposes of inducing sleep, temporary analgesia, etc.

This technique has been widely used throughout central
Europe and is currently considered one of the basic psycho-
therapeutic tools. It has been taught to large numbers of individuals
not merely as part of therapeutic treatment but also as a prophy-
lactic measure. As with many procedures of this kind a considerable body of very impressive clinical material is available.
One of the most interesting examples of this kind is a case
reported by Schultz: An individual who had been trained by him
in the past became trapped in an avalanche while skiing and was
totally immobilized in the snow for several hours. However, during
this time he selectively concentrated on each of his four limbs
in rotation. On being rescued, he did not have any significant frostbite in contrast to the other members of the party. Further
anecdotal evidence relevant to this discussion is the reports of
patients who were inmates of concentration camps and who felt
that their training was a major factor in their survival because

it enabled them to withstand the physical and mental rigors of this situation.

It should be emphasized that despite the popularity of this technique in some parts of Europe (especially those under German influence) no rigorous experimental evaluation has yet been undertaken. Thus, the reported changes of physiological function by trained individuals have not been compared with the capabilities of highly motivated untrained individuals. Anecdotal evidence, no matter how impressive, is at best suggestive. However, it would appear fruitful to examine rigorously the potential usefulness of autogenic training.

From a theoretical viewpoint several aspects of this technique are particularly interesting. Thus, in their practice sessions, individuals characteristically exceed the performance attained in the presence of the doctor. Further, many individuals who have considerable difficulties in entering hypnosis are able to develop considerable skill in autogenic training, and it appears that these skills once thoroughly learned are available to the individual without further instruction. It should be noted that the training itself can be undertaken in a group situation, apparently with success equal to that of the individual one.

Much information, however, is still needed. Little is known about the relative ease with which different types of individuals acquire the skill of autogenic training. Even less is known (1) about the effectiveness of autogenic training as a tool enabling individuals to resist stressful situations and (2) the degree of physiological response that the individual can produce at will compared with his capabilities prior to training.

The relationship between hypnosis as we know it and the type of training proposed by Schultz is quite close. Thus, autogenic training has been called by Kretschmer (1949), in recent years one of its more ardent proponents, "active hypnosis" in contradistinction to passive or classical hypnosis. Kretschmer has pointed out that individuals who have been trained in "active hypnosis" may easily enter classical hypnosis. Further, the classical phenomena of hypnosis can be induced during "active hypnosis."

One of the interesting aspects of autogenic training is that individuals very rarely acquire considerable competence in this technique in the absence of active supervision by another person. Thus, although much of the training, i.e., the practicing, takes place in the absence of the hypnotist, a positive relationship with some professional individual appears to be an indispensable aspect of the training. Probably the implied presence of this individual during private practice sessions is necessary. Some of the questions that we raised regarding the posthypnotic phenomenon are also relevant here; namely, is a continued positive relationship with one's teacher necessary in order to retain one's skills in autogenic training? If such a relationship is not necessary in the case of autogenic training, would it also not be necessary for self-hypnosis taught via posthypnotic suggestion, as discussed earlier?

In the absence of relevant experimental evidence we are forced to extrapolate from anecdotal material. Thus, in the writings of many mystics, it is reported that when they doubted either the Divinity itself or the interpretation of their teachers, they found it impossible to attain experiences which they had been able to achieve in the past. To the extent that the mystical experience can be understood as a form of self-hypnosis, these anecdotal reports allow us to make the tenuous inference that a positive relationship with one's "teacher" may be of considerable importance in self-hypnosis. Whether such a relationship is essential only during the learning phases of these skills or continues to be a prerequisite for the retention and practice of self-hypnosis is not clear.

In summarizing the work on auto-hypnosis in the context of this symposium, it would seem that this method is preferable to a simple posthypnotic suggestion. A greater number of individuals can be taught auto-hypnosis than are able to benefit maximally by posthypnotic suggestion. While posthypnotic behavior appears to become less effective without periodic renewal of the suggestion, skills attained by self-hypnosis can be maintained and augmented by the individual himself. Further, whereas posthypnotic behavior may be experienced by the individual as something alien and outside of his control, self-hypnosis can make available to the individual the same skills, but they are now experienced as being under his control.

On the other hand, it should be emphasized that almost no experimental evidence is available on self-hypnosis; the data available are all derived from a clinical or quasi-clinical context. It should be remembered that in these situations posthypnotic suggestion has proved to be extremely effective. Thus some of the apparent advantages of self-hypnosis may not be real insofar as they may merely reflect a lack of evidence about self-hypnosis.

The mechanism of action of self-hypnosis is totally unclear, and all of the issues raised in the previous section on posthypnotic behavior need to be explored in relation to self-hypnosis. Finally, it is possible that the distinction between self-hypnosis and post-hypnotic behavior is artificial. A great many of the necessary and sufficient conditions are the same for both phenomena. Thus, hypnosis has been conceptualized as self-hypnosis, and self-hypnosis may just as well be conceptualized as hypnosis. It remains to be established whether any essential differences exist between these two phenomena. It is clear, however, that a great many individuals find it more acceptable to be trained in self-hypnosis than to "be hypnotized." If for no other reason, this alone strongly suggests that the potential of self-hypnosis as a useful technique should be explored.

General Considerations

Some of the major problems and unresolved issues connected with the use of hypnosis as a means of protecting the individual from stress have been discussed; however, the use of a specialized technique such as hypnosis can be meaningfully considered only in the more general framework of psychological variables affecting an individual's tolerance to stress. While other papers will consider these problems in more detail it seems appropriate to sketch here briefly the general issues that need to be considered in any program of empirical research.

In the introduction of this paper we defined stress as a stimulus which, if continued for a sufficient period of time at a sufficient intensity, will bring about breakdown of the individual. This defines a stimulus as a stress not by its objective qualities but rather by its effect on the individual. We have chosen this definition because it avoids the difficult, if not impossible, task of specifying in objective terms the stimulus properties of a stressor, the difficulty being that many stimuli may be stressors for some individuals but not for others. Except in the extreme ranges the past experience of the individual with the stimulus will determine the extent to which it is a stressor for him. This observation suggests that one way of enabling an individual to become resistant to a stress is to allow him to have appropriate prior experience with the stimulus involved. The biological notion of immunization provides a model for this approach. If an individual is given the opportunity to deal with a stimulus that is mildly stressful and he is able to do so successfully (mastering it in a psychological sense or again achieving homeostasis in a physical sense), he will tend to be able to tolerate a similar stimulus of somewhat greater intensity in the future. By exposure to stimuli of gradually increasing intensity the individual will eventually be able to tolerate stimuli which initially would have caused breakdown of functioning. Training is the behavioral corollary to the immunization model. Such a procedure alters the individual in that a given stimulus ceases to be a stressor. Strictly speaking, however, it does not enable an individual to tolerate a given stress better; rather, it alters the range of stimuli which are stressors.

In considering the question of what enables an individual to tolerate stimuli which are stressors *for him,* we encounter marked individual differences. The notion of ego strength is the construct that is used to account for these differences clinically. While this term has wide clinical usage, there is no consensus either about what determines a given individual's ego strength or how it can be measured. It is generally agreed that early childhood experiences play a crucial role and that the availability of significant positive relationships during this time is essential. Further it is often conceived of as a generalization derived from a variety of mastery experiences and the relative absence of significant failures. Identification with positively cathected models is assumed to play a role. However, the relative weighting of these factors as well as the significance of later life experiences and constitutional variables is the subject of much controversy. It is beyond the scope of this paper to delineate this concept. Rather, we wish to emphasize that wide individual differences exist in abilities to withstand stimuli that are stressors. Since the ego strength of an individual is, to a large part at least, a function of his early life experience and is augmented in adulthood only by significant emotional corrective experiences such as therapy, we can assume ego strength as a given for the purposes of this discussion.

Over and above the specific past experiences with certain classes of stimuli which tend to define stressors for the individual and the general ego strength at the individual's disposal, there are numerous different situational factors which will determine his resistance to stress. These factors related to specific motivational variables are subject to environmental manipulations and tend to raise an individual's tolerance to stress generally. One might facetiously think of these as ego-strength substitutes. A few of these variables are particularly relevant to this paper and are discussed below.

An example of a situational variable which affects an individual's tolerance for discomfort is his perception of normative behavior. Within a wide range individuals govern their willingness to work and also to endure discomfort, even pain, by what they believe to be the behavior of individuals seen as their peers. Work norms are well known in industry; however, they also seem to apply in tests of human endurance such as athletics. The four-minute mile is a case in point. Until the four-minute mile was actually run, it was assumed to exceed the capabilities of human endurance; however, once this record had been established a number of runners surpassed it within a remarkably short period. The same may be said for all record performances of athletic endurance. The average athlete in today's Olympic competitions far exceeds the performance of the outstanding athlete a generation ago. It seems unwarranted to assume that we are witnessing dramatic changes in human endurance; rather the goals of individuals in competition have changed as the norms of outstanding athletic performances have risen. One would wonder why no resourceful coach has hit upon the plan of informing athletes under his care of plausible but fictitious unofficial performances by their future opponents.

In our laboratory, this mechanism was clearly seen to operate when we were attempting to devise a safe but highly noxious stimulus in the form of an electric shock to the hand. Equipment was built intended to deliver shock of an intensity well beyond that tolerable to anyone in the laboratory. However, experimental subjects soon demonstrated that what our staff had considered to be the greatest possible intensity was still tolerable. Subsequent to this performance the members of the laboratory team found that the shock level could indeed be tolerated, and the machine was modified to provide further intensity, again well beyond what was viewed as tolerable by the members of the laboratory. To our chagrin, it was necessary to modify the equipment yet a third time before it delivered shocks of sufficient intensity that no experimental subject wished to go to the very top of the scale. The subjective experience of the laboratory personnel is essentially similar to that of the athletes discussed previously. Once it was demonstrated by an experimental subject that the stimulus was tolerable, it did become so, at least for some members of the staff.

Another illustration of how effective norms might be in modifying the subjective experience of a situation as stressful is given in a recent experiment on "meaning deprivation" (Orne & Scheibe, in press). It was felt that one of the major variables which affected subjects' behavior in sensory deprivation situations was the accoutrements of the situation which defined the task as stressful and potentially dangerous. These include a physical examination and history, a subject release form which absolves the experimenter and institution of all responsibility of undue consequences, an aura of concern, continuous observation, and above all, the presence of an emergency "release" button. It was felt that these variables rather than sensory deprivation itself accounted for many of the reported phenomena. Accordingly, 10 subjects were treated in a manner identical to previous experiments in sensory deprivation but then placed in a well lighted experimental cubicle with food and water and an optional task. These subjects were not informed of the four-hour duration of the experiment.

The control group was treated in the same manner but the subjects were placed in the cubicle without previously signing a release form, a physical examination, nor was there a panic button present in the cubicle. These subjects were told that they were control subjects for a sensory deprivation experiment.

The experimental subjects found the experiment quite unpleasant and reported a wide variety of subjective experiences and discomfort not found in the control group as well as showing differences on "objective" pre- and post-experimental tests. Thus, it is quite evident that the identical objective conditions resulted in very different experiences for the two groups of subjects depending upon the social definition of the situation. Were we to conduct this type of an experiment again, I suspect that we could keep the total procedure constant and yet achieve significant differences between a group which is told in advance that they are controls from a group in which the subjects perceive themselves as experimental.

It would seem thus that one can markedly affect an individual's tolerance of stress by manipulating his beliefs about his own performance in the situation. If he expects the situation to be stressful, he will experience it as stressful. If he feels that we expect him to be capable of mastering the stress, it will maximize the probability that he will do so.

Thus far, we have discussed stresses which can fairly readily be investigated in the laboratory. One kind of stress which plays a major role in life, particularly during such situations as war, captivity, illness, etc., is extremely difficult to manipulate in experimental contexts. This is the absence of meaning as defined by the individual. We have tried to devise an experimental situation where individuals would discontinue following instructions because they did not view their behavior as meaningful. For example, subjects would be placed in a small room and asked to do simple addition problems. Each sheet of paper would take about 10 minutes to complete and they faced a stack of some 2,000 sheets of paper. They were deprived of their watch and told to work, that the experimenter would eventually return. Under these circumstances subjects worked for many hours. Even when the task was not only to complete each page but upon completion of each page to tear it into many pieces and throw it away, subjects carried out their task faithfully. Despite the fact that they had to destroy their work they tended to work accurately. The experiment had been intended to be a psychologically-stressful situation insofar as it created a meaningless task for the subject. However, when the subjects were interviewed, it became clear that they had ascribed meaning to their experiences because they performed their task in the context of an experiment. Thus, some subjects (correctly) surmised that their performance was being monitored although all the appearances indicated that a monitoring arrangement would be impossible. Others felt that the experiment was designed to test their endurance, etc.[3]

Unfortunately, within the context of an experimental situation it is impossible—with the techniques presently available—to investigate the stress of futility and of being in a meaningless situation. Yet it is the feeling that one's performance is without meaning that can be extremely destructive in life situations. The very fact that an experimental situation provides sufficient purpose for the experimental subject to undertake, with relative comfort, tasks which would otherwise be excessively boring and frustrating indicates that it is the mental set more than the objective properties of the task which defines a situation as stressful for an individual. One might conceive of the experimental situation as providing a mental set which successfully protects the individual from this type of stress. Hence, it may be meaningful to view the experimental context as one of several powerful mental sets which will enable an individual to successfully perform tasks which in other contexts would interfere with his functioning.

Closely related to the need for viewing one's behavior as purposive and meaningful is the individual's feeling that he can control his own behavior. For example, a recent review of the effects of sensory deprivation discusses patients' reactions to confinement in an iron lung (Solomon, Leiderman, Mendelson, & Wexler, 1957). The loss of control over one's motor functions is viewed as a significant stress. Schein (1956) points to the significance of physical confinement in "brainwashing" situations. From both reports it is obvious that the individual feels powerless to control his behavior. However, in both instances some individuals are able to focus upon mental processes that remain under their control; these individuals are able to use whatever restricted range of behavior that remains available to them and maintain their ability to function. The attitudes and mental set of the individual may well determine to what extent he can find meaning in the situation and tolerate the loss of physical autonomy.

We should hypothesize that many individuals would be protected to a considerable degree from the stress of these situations if they perceived themselves as carrying out a purposive task. This hypothesis is supported by descriptions of concentration camp experiences (Frankl, 1946). Appropriate instruction might well facilitate the individual's efforts to maintain autonomy.

In this connection one aspect of self-hypnosis is particularly relevant. The anecdote about the individual caught in an avalanche was discussed earlier. Schultz (1932) ascribed the individual's successful resistance to frostbite to judicious and successful control of the bloodflow to his extremities. An alternate hypothesis would be that the very activity of controlling the flow of blood allowed the individual to retain a measure of control over his autonomy, and thus to avoid an anxiety reaction which would have decreased the bloodflow to the extremities. Perhaps the illusion of autonomy can effectively protect the individual from stress. This assumption is subject to empirical test. The hypothesis would be that individuals who had learned "autogenic training" would have a greater ability to resist a stress, such as being in a tank-type respirator, than individuals without such training.

A different psychological situation which can markedly affect an individual's ability to tolerate stress is illustrated in our laboratory research. Subjects are placed in a peculiar psychological situation in order to serve as controls for the performance of hypnotized individuals. The technical advantages and reasons for the use of this group have been described elsewhere (Orne, 1959). In brief, this is a group of subjects who are instructed to simulate hypnosis in order to deceive the experimenter. They understand clearly that the experimenter does not know which subjects are simulating and will discontinue the experiment if he recognizes that they belong to the simulating group. When we began to experiment with simulating subjects, we were surprised to find that, contrary to views reported in the literature, this group of subjects could not be distinguished from deeply hypnotized individuals by their response to tasks involving painful stimulation. On the contrary, in an experiment by Shor (1959) it was found that this group of subjects chose to tolerate a significantly higher level of painful stimulation than the hypnotized group. We have been unable thus far to find any behavior or task that would be carried out by hypnotized subjects but which this group would fail to undertake in a laboratory situation. This includes a replication of the classic studies by Rowland (1939) and Young (1952) who attempted to demonstrate that subjects in hypnosis would carry out self-destructive or anti-social behavior. In these experiments subjects were requested to handle a poisonous snake, remove a penny dissolving in fuming nitric acid with their bare fingers, and throw the acid at a laboratory assistant. In our replication, five out of six deeply hypnotized subjects could be induced to carry out all these tasks, while six out of six simulating (waking) subjects did the same (Orne & Evans, 1961).

We believe that the situation where a subject is requested to simulate hypnotic behavior warrants in itself further investigation. Once the subject is committed to playing this role, it appears that he is willing to exert himself to the utmost, including the toleration of considerable anxiety and actual pain, in order to continue with this task successfully. In our situation the motivation for the initial commitment by the subject seems intuitively clear. The subject is given the opportunity of playing an important part in the experiment and at the same time of "Putting one over on the experimenter." Legitimately making a fool of an authority figure is, to most college students, a very appealing task. In this context, it is interesting to note that difficulties arose with this type of control group only when the experimenters were younger graduate students, particularly female students. In these circumstances, some subjects felt quite guilty about deceiving the experimenter. The subjects' feelings in this regard were typically phrased as "I felt so badly about fooling that nice girl." Significantly though, subjects did not experience guilt in deceiving senior investigators.

That an individual's commitment to a certain role protects him from stress has long been recognized intuitively and this fact may well form the basis for a wide variety of social institutions. For example, a military organization with a high *esprit de corps* tends to create a feeling among its members that they are committed to belonging to a special group of individuals. Because of their membership in this group, they are expected to and indeed are able to tolerate stresses above the capabilities of the average individual. The training of the marine corps and the parachutists are particularly good examples in our own military establishment.

Thus far, we have used the term commitment rather loosely; however, it seems advisable to specify the antecedent conditions which might cause an individual to become committed to a role which then, in and of itself, becomes a useful prop against conditions of stress. There appear to be at least three conceptually distinct factors involved.

(*1*) The individual must find the role congenial, desirable, and appropriate to himself. (*2*) The role must be legitimately ascribed to the individual by significant figures whom he accepts as qualified to ascribe the role to him. Who the significant figures are varies with the role to be ascribed. Thus, peers might ascribe the role of leader while university authorities would ascribe the role of Ph.D. (*3*) It appears that commitment to a role is markedly enhanced by a legitimized, arduous, training period involving recognized *rites de passage*.

Concluding Remarks

If one summarizes the general problem of using psychological techniques to maximize the individual's resistance to stress, it appears that over and above the individual's ego strength, his specific experience with stimuli closely related to the stressors is subject to systematic change, and further, that the individual's own tolerance will be affected by his beliefs concerning the tolerance shown by his peers with regard to the same stress. We have pointed out that one of the stresses frequently encountered in life is the feeling that one's own behavior is meaningless, and we have described certain aspects of the experimental setting which make it impossible to investigate this stress within a laboratory context. Finally, we have suggested that certain roles, once they are assumed by the individual, will be maintained at great cost and that in order to maintain them individuals appear willing to tolerate stress which they would otherwise avoid or perhaps be unable to tolerate.

Hypnosis as a specific technique of maximizing an individual's tolerance to stress needs to be viewed in the light of these considerations. Certain hypnotic phenomena, such as control over the appreciation of pain and fatigue, may prove to be useful in this respect. However, one should recognize that the total hypnotic situation embodies a number of the situational qualities discussed above. Thus, having learned to enter hypnosis and having successfully tolerated stimuli which would otherwise seem intolerable inevitably give the individual the experience of successful mastery of stimuli similar to those which might subsequently be stressors. Being a hypnotized subject itself involves assuming a role which the individual may be highly motivated to maintain. Beliefs shared by the hypnotist and subject about a hypnotized individual's tolerance of certain stresses redefine the norms by which the individual judges his own behavior. Finally, in a situation where an individual is robbed of his ability to control his environment or even his own body, hypnotic phenomena may provide a form of self-control of which the individual cannot be deprived.

A great number of unanswered questions prevent us from definitively evaluating the potential utility of hypnosis as a means of increasing the individual's self-control. The use of posthypnotic suggestion or, perhaps what might be even more effective, systematic training in self-hypnosis may provide a useful tool capable of increasing the individual's tolerance for stress. On the other hand, the increased tolerance could also be a function of a number of other independent psychological factors incidental to, but unavoidably associated with, the hypnotic situation. The relative utility of hypnotic phenomena (versus these incidentally-associated psychological factors), i.e., the entire question of which factors contribute more to the individual's ability to tolerate stress, requires empirical clarification.

REFERENCES

Ås, A., & Lauer, Lillian W. A factor-analytic study of hypnotizability and related personal experiences. *Int. J. clin. exp. Hypnosis*, 1962, 10, 169-181.

AUGUST, R. V. The obstetrician and hypnosis. *Amer. J. clin. Hypnosis*, 1959, 1, 151-154.

BARBER, T. X. Toward a theory of pain: Relief of chronic pain by prefrontal leucotomy, opiates, placebos, and hypnosis. *Psychol. Bull.*, 1959, 56, 430-460.

BEECHER, H. K. Evidence for increased effectiveness of placebos with increased stress. *Amer. J. Physiol.*, 1956, 187, 163-169.

BERNHEIM, H. *Suggestive therapeutics.* (C. A. Herter, Tr.) New York: London Book, 1889.

BROWN, R. R., & VOGEL, V. H. Psycho-physiological reactions following painful stimuli under hypnotic analgesia contrasted with gas anesthesia and Novocain block. *J. appl. Psychol.*, 1938, 22, 408-420.

BURGESS, T. O. Hypnosis in dentistry. In L. M. LeCron (Ed.), *Experimental hypnosis.* New York: Macmillan, 1952. Pp. 322-359.

COUÉ, E. *Self mastery through conscious auto-suggestion.* New York: American Library Service, 1922.

CRASILNECK, H. B., & HALL, H. A. The use of hypnosis with unconscious patients. *Int. J. clin. exp. Hypnosis*, 1962, 10, 141-144.

CRASILNECK, H. B., McCRANIE, E. J., & JENKINS, M. T. Special indications for hypnosis as a method of anesthesia. *J. Amer. med. Ass.*, 1956, 162, 1606-1608.

CRASILNECK, H. B., STIRMAN, J. A., WILSON, B. J., McCRANIE, E. J., & FOGELMAN, M. J. Use of hypnosis in the management of patients with burns. *J. Amer. med. Ass.*, 1955, 158, 102-106.

DAMASER, ESTHER. An experimental study of long-term post-hypnotic suggestion. Unpublished doctoral dissertation, Harvard Univer., 1964.

DAS, J. P. Yoga and hypnosis. *Int. J. clin. exp. Hypnosis*, 1963, 11, 31-37.

DOUPE, J., MILLER, W. R., & KELLER, W. K. Vasomotor reactions in the hypnotic state. *J. Neurol. Psychiat.*, 1939, 2, 97-106.

DYNES, J. B. An experimental study in hypnotic anaesthesia. *J. abnorm. soc. Psychol.*, 1932, 27, 79-88.

ERICKSON, M. H. Experimental demonstrations of the psychopathology of everyday life. *Psychoanal. Quart.*, 1939, 8, 338-353.

ERICKSON, M. H. Deep hypnosis and its induction. In L. M. LeCron (Ed.), *Experimental hypnosis.* New York: Macmillan, 1952. Pp. 70-112.

ERICKSON, M. H. Special techniques of brief psychotherapy. *J. clin. exp. Hypnosis*, 1954, 2, 109-129.

ERICKSON, M. H., & ERICKSON, ELIZABETH M. Concerning the nature and character of post hypnotic behavior. *J. gen. Psychol.*, 1941, 24, 95-133.

ERICKSON, M. H., HERSHMAN, S., & SECTER, I. I. *The practical application of medical and dental hypnosis.* New York: Julian Press, 1961.

ESDAILE, J. *Mesmerism in India, and its practical application in surgery and medicine.* London: Longman's, 1846.

EVANS, F. J. The structure of hypnotic phenomena—a factor analytic investigation. Unpublished doctoral dissertation, Univer. of Sydney, submitted 1965.

FISHER, S. The role of expectancy in the performance of posthypnotic behavior. *J. abnorm. soc. Psychol.*, 1954, 49, 503-507.

FRANKL, V. *Und doch zum Leben Ja sagen!* Vienna: Deuticke, 1946.

GILL, M. M., & BRENMAN, MARGARET. *Hypnosis and related states.* New York: Int. Univer. Press, 1959.

HALEY, J. Control in brief psychotherapy. *Arch. gen. Psychiat.*, 1961, 4, 139-153.

HILGARD, E. R., & LAUER, LILLIAN W. Lack of correlation between the California psychological inventory and hypnotic susceptibility. *J. consult. Psychol.*, 1962, 26, 331-335.

HILGARD, E. R., WEITZENHOFFER, A. M., LANDES, J., & MOORE, ROSEMARIE K. The distribution of susceptibility to hypnosis in a student population: A study using the Stanford Hypnotic Susceptibility Scale. *Psychol. Monogr.*, 1961, 75, No. 8 (Whole No. 512).

HILGARD, JOSEPHINE R., HILGARD, E. R., & NEWMAN, MARTHA. Sequelae to hypnotic induction with special reference to earlier chemical anesthesia. *J. nerv. ment. Dis.*, 1961, 133, 461-478.

KELLOGG, E. R. Duration of the effects of post-hypnotic suggestions. *J. exp. Psychol.*, 1929, 12, 502-514.

KRETSCHMER, E. *Psychotherapeutische Studien.* Stuttgart: G. Thieme, 1949.

LECRON, L. M. *Techniques of hypnotherapy.* New York: Julian Press, 1961.

LECRON, L. M., & BORDEAUX, J. *Hypnotism today.* New York: Grune & Stratton, 1949.

LEVINE, M. Psychogalvanic reaction to painful stimuli in hypnotic and hysterical anesthesia. *Bull. Johns Hopkins Hosp.*, 1930, 46, 311-339.

MASON, A. A. *Medical hypnosis.* New York: Paul B. Hoeber, 1960.

MICHAEL, A. M. Hypnosis in childbirth. *Brit. med. J.*, 1952, 1, 734-737.

MOSS, A. A. *Hypnodontics: Hypnosis in dentistry.* Brooklyn, New York: Dental Items of Interest Publishing Co., 1952.

NICHOLSON, N. C. Notes on muscular work during hypnosis. *Bull. Johns Hopkins Hosp.*, 1920, 31, 89-91.

ORNE, M. T. The mechanisms of hypnotic age regression: An experimental study. *J. abnorm. soc. Psychol.*, 1951, 46, 213-225.

ORNE, M. T. Die Leistungsfaehigkeit in Hypnose und in Wachzustand. *Psychol. Rdsch.*, 1954, 5, 291-297.

ORNE, M. T. The nature of hypnosis: Artifact and essence. *J. abnorm. soc. Psychol.*, 1959, 58, 277-299.

ORNE, M. T. The potential use of hypnosis in interrogation. In A. D. Biderman, & H. Zimmer (Eds.), *The manipulation of human behavior*. New York: John Wiley & Sons, 1961. Pp. 169-215.

ORNE, M. T. Antisocial behavior and hypnosis: Problems of control and validation in empirical studies. In G. H. Estabrooks (Ed.), *Hypnosis: Current problems*. New York: Harper & Row, 1962. Pp. 137-192 (a).

ORNE, M. T. On the social psychology of the psychological experiment: With particular reference to demand characteristics and their implications. *Amer. Psychologist*, 1962, 17, 776-783 (b).

ORNE, M. T., & EVANS, F. J. Antisocial behavior and hypnosis. Paper read at XVII Annual Conference of the British Psychol. Soc., (Australian Overseas Branch) Sydney, August, 1961.

ORNE, M. T., & FISHER, R. Retroactive inhibition in hypnosis. Unpublished study, Boston: Mass. Mental Health Center, 1960.

ORNE, M. T., & SCHEIBE, K. The contribution of non-deprivation factors in the production of sensory deprivation effects. *J. abnorm. soc. Psychol.*, in press.

PATTEN, E. F. The duration of post-hypnotic suggestion. *J. abnorm. soc. Psychol.*, 1930, 25, 319-334.

PRINCE, M., & CORIAT, I. Cases illustrating the educational treatment of the psychoneuroses. *J. abnorm. Psychol.*, 1907, 2, 166-177.

ROSE, J. T. The use of relevant life experiences as the basis for suggestive therapy. *Int. J. clin. exp. Hypnosis*, 1962, 10, 221-229.

ROSENBERG, M. J. A disconfirmation of the description of hypnosis as a dissociated state. *Int. J. clin. exp. Hypnosis*, 1959, 7, 187-204.

ROSENBERG, M. J. Cognitive reorganization in response to the hypnotic reversal of attitudinal affect. *J. Pers.*, 1960, 28, 39-63.

ROUSH, ELSIE S. Strength and endurance in the waking and hypnotic states. *J. appl. Physiol.*, 1951, 3, 404-410.

ROWLAND, L. W. Will hypnotized persons try to harm themselves or others? *J. abnorm. soc. Psychol.*, 1939, 34, 114-117.

SARASON, S., & ROSENZWEIG, S. An experimental study of the triadic hypothesis: Reaction to frustration, ego-defense and hypnotizability. II. Thematic apperception approach. *Charact. & Pers.*, 1942, 11, 150-165.

SCHEIN, E. H. The Chinese indoctrination program for prisoners of war: A study of attempted "brainwashing." *Psychiatry*, 1956, 19, 149-172.

SCHNECK, J. M. *Hypnosis in modern medicine*. Springfield, Ill.: Charles C Thomas, 1953.

SCHULTZ, J. H. *Das Autogene Training*. Stuttgart: G. Thieme, 1932.

SCHULTZ, J. H., & LUTHE, W. *Autogenic training*. New York: Grune & Stratton, 1959.

SEARS, R. R. Experimental study of hypnotic anesthesia. *J. exp. Psychol.*, 1932, 15, 1-22.

SHAW, S. I. *Clinical applications of hypnosis in dentistry.* Philadelphia: Saunders, 1958.

SHOR, R. E. Explorations in hypnosis: A theoretical and experimental study. Unpublished doctoral dissertation, Brandeis Univer., 1959.

SHOR, R. E. The frequency of naturally occurring 'hypnotic-like' experiences in the normal college population. *Int. J. clin. exp. Hypnosis*, 1960, 8, 151-163.

SHOR, R. E. On the physiological effects of painful stimulation during hypnotic analgesia: Basic issues for further research. In G. H. Estabrooks (Ed.), *Hypnosis: Current problems.* New York: Harper & Row, 1962 (a).

SHOR, R. E. Physiological effects of painful stimulation during hypnotic analgesia under conditions designed to minimize anxiety. *Int. J. clin. exp. Hypnosis*, 1962, 10, 183-202 (b).

SHOR, R. E., ORNE, M. T., & O'CONNELL, D. N. Validation and cross-validation of a scale of self-reported personal experiences which predicts hypnotizability. *J. Psychol.*, 1962, 53, 55-75.

SHOR, R. E., ORNE, M. T., & O'CONNELL, D. N. A study of the psychological correlates of hypnotizability. Unpublished paper, Boston: Mass. Mental Health Center, 1963.

SIDIS, B. *Psychopathological researches.* New York: G. E. Stechert, 1902.

SOLOMON, P., LEIDERMAN, P. H., MENDELSON, J., & WEXLER, D. Sensory deprivation; a review. *Amer. J. Psychiat.*, 1957, 114, 357-363.

STRICKLER, C. B. A quantitative study of post-hypnotic amnesia. *J. abnorm. soc. Psychol.*, 1929, 24, 108-119.

SUTCLIFFE, J. P. Hypnotic behaviour: Fantasy or simulation? Unpublished doctoral dissertation, Univer. of Sydney, 1958.

THORN, WENDY A. F. A study of the correlates of dissociation as measured by hypnotic amnesia. Unpublished B. A. thesis, Dept. of Psychol., Univer. of Sydney, 1960.

WEST, L. J., NIELL, KARLEEN C., & HARDY, J. D. Effects of hypnotic suggestions on pain perception and galvanic skin response. *Arch. Neurol. Psychiat.*, 1952, 68, 549-560.

WHITE, R. W. A preface to the theory of hypnotism. In S. S. Tomkins (Ed.), *Contemporary psychopathology.* Cambridge, Mass.: Harvard Univer. Press, 1943. Pp. 479-502.

WILLIAMS, G. W. The effect of hypnosis on muscular fatigue. *J. abnorm. soc. Psychol.*, 1929, 24, 318-329.

WINKELSTEIN, L. B. Routine hypnosis for obstetrical delivery: An evaluation of hypnosuggestion in 200 consecutive cases. *Amer. J. Obst. Gynecol.*, 1958, 76, 152-160.

WOLBERG, L. R. Hypnotic experiments in psychosomatic medicine. *Psychosom. Med.,* 1947, 9, 337-342.

YOUNG, P. C. Antisocial uses of hypnosis. In L. M. LeCron (Ed.), *Experimental hypnosis.* New York: Macmillan, 1952. Pp. 376-409.

NOTES

1. It should be clear that we are departing from the more usual psychological or psychiatric view of adaptation. Successful resistance to stress in certain situations, such as captivity, may lead to the destruction of the individual—behavior which would be viewed as self-destructive in a psychiatric context. In this paper, adaptation to stress does not include engaging in behavior which alters the individual's purpose.

2. Although many investigators using a variety of clinical instruments have tried to shed light on the subject, the personality variables determining hypnotizability have remained obscure. Indeed hypnotizability is an attribute of individuals which has not been successfully related to such tests as the MMPI, CPI, etc. (Hilgard & Lauer, 1962; Shor, Orne, & O'Connell, 1963). Hypnotizability does show a relationship to subjects' attitudes towards hypnosis (Sarason & Rosenzweig, 1942; Shor et al., 1963; White, 1943).

As measured by questionnaires or interviews, there is also a demonstrable, but relatively low, relationship between hypnotizability and the tendency of individuals to experience spontaneously trance-like phenomena (As & Lauer, 1962; Shor, 1960; Shor, Orne, & O'Connell, 1962). However, these measures cut across the usual kinds of personality variables employed in psychology.

3. These experimental studies were conducted by Mr. Thomas Menaker.

DAVID McK. RIOCH

A Behavioral Approach to
the Problem of Self-Control

Ordinary, everyday uses of the terms "I" and "myself" seem to vary widely, although it also seems that one can identify common symbolic aspects of these uses. Certain persons who have suffered amputation of a hand are very clear that "the hand" and, consequently, certain behavior is lost. There is no suggestion that part of "the I," "the me," or "the self" is lost. In contrast, other persons separated from a loved companion—or even from a loved landscape—express the loss as "it is as though I had lost part of myself" or, "part of me is gone."

Of course, if one defines "the I" and "the me," in contradistinction to "the not I" and "the not me," as bounded by the skin (and possibly by the respiratory, gastro-intestinal and genito-urinary mucuous membranes) then in both the cases mentioned one can say the terms "I" and "me" are being used metaphorically or analogically. The introduction of such a subsidiary hypothesis hardly helps unless one agrees to operate in the frame of reference of the ancient humors[1]—where "the I" is in a good, or bad, or what-not humor. It is probably more economical to assume that language is a part of social behavior and has overt and covert aspects. The overt is interpersonal or intrasocial, the covert is symbolic behavior. The necessary, but possibly not sufficient, mechanisms which mediate symbolic behavior are intracerebral. Although we know virtually nothing of the detailed mechanisms through which this comes about, we may not be too wrong if we speak of language behavior as a class of nervous system activity which has the capacity for orienting large amounts of other nervous system activity in the pattern similar or closely related to that in which the language activity was learned. Hortatorily, language behavior may orient the activity of the nervous systems of other persons in a similar manner, i.e., by evoking similarly their symbolic behavior to the extent that the coding system is mutually shared. Thus, the concept referred to as "the I" or "the self" in the problem of the self-control of behavior must be expanded to the set of social roles which are regarded as preferable by the reference group involved, including the probability that these patterns of interaction with the environment will be maintained. Sullivan dealt with this problem in his development of the concept of "the self-system." It is also of interest that insofar as late European royalty were considered to be "the law" or to be above "the law" they were referred to in the third person, not in the first.

In the social realm the coding system of symbolic behavior is a critical problem. Since symbols are digital, are arbitrary, and are independent of real time and space, their manipulability—within the limits imposed by the symbols themselves—is a function of the capacities of the "thinker" (whether man, machine or combination). For the same reasons the extent to which predefined behavior (overt or covert) can be evoked reliably by symbols in a wide variety of circumstances is very limited, unless ample time for learning the code is available. Not only the data to be operated on, but also instructions to start, the operations to perform, their sequence and instructions to stop must be symbolically given. Since living organisms cannot merely be turned on and off like machines, the transition states preceding and succeeding the required behavior also need attention. In everyday life most of these problems are met and instructions are given in what Jurgen Ruesch has called "the silent assumptions of communication." In this conference, however, we have to deal with situations in which the usual social assumptions may not apply and these sequences at least need to be mentioned.

For a considerable period preceding the modern era small, face-to-face groups and even larger socio-economic and national systems were relatively stable. Under these conditions a person knew who he was, who he could rely on and what was expected of him. He had a "soul" and was committed to his fellows in the "normal human" value system. Under these conditions the doctrines of the will and of self-control were generally accepted along with the doctrines of reality and of normal *vs.* abnormal. In other words, in our earlier, stable social structure it was economic to postulate "the will," "reality," "normal *vs.* abnormal," etc. for purposes of communication, since the connotations of these terms were generally well known. It was not necessary to question the operations the postulates represented. In retrospect these doctrines are hardly surprising, since events which could not be dealt with in these terms were the exception rather than the rule. With the social and technological revolutions of the modern era, and the enormously increased vertical and horizontal social mobility, this situation no longer pertains. Simmel (11) was the first to point out in this century that a human person (in distinction to his anatomy, chemistry, etc.) can only be defined in terms of his social group and of his role, status, function, etc. in that group. George H. Mead (5) later developed the concept of "the self" as the learned set of accepted or recognized social roles. Harry Stack Sullivan (9) extended this concept to his "self-system" and pointed out the relation of this system to his concept of anxiety and also to the concept of "reality" as social consensus. Sullivan's "self-system" is an admittedly difficult concept to grasp. It lays emphasis on behavior rather than on "feelings," although the latter accompany the former. In very general terms the "self-system" may be thought of as that set of behavioral roles which have been found through trial and error to most likely avoid humiliations, anxiety or more serious social isolation. Sullivan arrived at these conclusions by detailed observations of the course of behavior, noting what patterns were related to concepts of the self as good or bad and what patterns were rejected as "not-I." The most important aspect of the concept is that the "self-system" is developed in relation to the social group and continues to develop or change throughout life.

Simmel, Mead, and Sullivan were important pioneers in developing an operational approach to the study of behavior and in initiating the formulation of behavioral data in operational terms. It was not possible, however, to deal with such concepts rigorously in even the simplest biological systems until the development of the concepts of cybernetics and of communication as the flow of information in under-specified situations (i.e., in situations in which the system may be in one or other state and must therefore be dealt with probabilistically.) The importance of the modern concepts for the problems of self-control of behavior under stress lies not in the direction of providing a better "explanation" of the phenomena, but rather it consists in providing a frame of reference which facilitates differentiating the phenomena into smaller segments, some of which may be independently manipulable.

In an informal seminar Harry Stack Sullivan discussed the doctrine of "the will" roughly as follows. He said he had not been able to find behavioral or operational criteria to define any force or power driving behavior to which the term "will" might be applied. Rather, any specific instance—for example, the "will" to go to an address in Washington—could be divided into "foresight" (based on previous experience) of the location and of the possible routes, comparison of the routes and decision on one or the other.[2] This breakdown is not too dissimilar to the analysis of behavior by Miller, Galanter, and Pribam in "Plans and the Structure of Behavior" (7). Their use of the Image and the Program as a hierarchical system of TOTEs (Test-Operate-Test-Exit) and the analogies they demonstrate between the behavior of organisms and the operations of computers provide a frame of reference of considerable use for the analysis of a variety of patterns of behavior. Such theoretical formulations immediately call attention to several independent functions which must be performed for maintaining the stable organization of behavior. For example, there is the problem of the selection of the objective from the available store of images; there is the necessity for maintaining the objective in mind while developing or selecting a plan for its attainment and also for controlling the course of the plan in action; there are the problems of decision between short plans requiring attention and/or physical effort and longer plans involving periods of waiting and so on.

Such systems for formulating data on behavior are effective mainly in those areas which are reasonably well known and in which the external load on the organism is not unusual. In unusual circumstances, with increase in the external load and with decrease in the efficiency of the data processing mechanisms, it is preferable to formally take the environment into account. This can be done by defining behavior as the temporally structured interaction of the organism with the environment, as in a transactional system. The transaction can be defined as that interaction with the environment which is relevant to the attainment of a predetermined consummatory act or state. The transaction can be differentiated into the cue (environmental or from memory) at its onset, the course, the information controlling its course and the change in input at the termination of the transaction on attainment of the goal. Transactions can be dealt with hierarchically and the interaction with the environment can be formulated in terms of the somatic and cerebral mechanisms and in terms of the number of environmental factors involved which the degree of detail relevant to the problem in hand requires. The efficient use of a transactional system for formulating behavior requires, however, constant recognition that this is a mode of formulation and not in any sense an attempt at "explanation" or a statement of "causation." (Cf. J. Z. Young's comment (12) that "proof" of a proposition is equivalent to "satisfaction of the investigator's curiosity.") Further, and possibly more important, one must recognize that the initiation and termination of transactions are arbitrarily determined. Since the relevant events in the temporal course of the transaction depend on the initial state of the interacting system and on the consummatory act or state terminating the transaction, the definition of these states or the assumptions made with respect to them are of primary significance. The advantage of the transactional system of formulation is that it assists in calling to attention data and operations likely to be occluded in the assumptions underlying classical approaches to behavior.

In considering the problems of the self-control of behavior under stress it is important to note that the aspects of behavior requiring attention vary with the situation and the objective to be accomplished. The training, the information, and the support relevant to maintaining reliable behavior in a rifleman, in an infantry company, in a commando, in a battalion combat commander, in a strategist at division level, and so forth are very different. It is now quite apparent that there is no unitary function such as "self-control" and also no unitary phenomenon such as "stress." In the organism-environment transactional system there is a wide variety of factors which are independent, but which interact in the course of the transaction. To a considerable extent many of these different factors can be expressed in roughly quantitative terms, such as, the temporal duration, the number of sub-transactions into which the whole must be divided, the number of relevant environmental factors involved, the rate of data processing required, the clarity of the criteria for determining the relevance of data for the course of the transaction, the adequacy of the support of the brain by the body, the probability of successful accomplishment of subsidiary steps and the significance of such success to the total course, and so forth.

In most transactions of everyday life the goal virtually defines the course and also defines the probable *subsequent* goal and course—in Miller's terminology (7), the plan is part of the image. In transactions of any degree of complexity or of difficulty of execution it is not possible to maintain the ultimate goal clearly in mind while carrying out subsidiary steps. Here, however, use is made of language in its function of directing behavior and in its function of retrieving orientation in an incomplete transaction. In such sense, language may be regarded as a set of precomputed answers providing a variety of instructions for directing the course of behavior. Since language is arbitrary, but is primarily socially determined, its use in controlling behavior will depend on the characteristics of the group to which the subject owes allegiance, as well as on the nature of his commitment to this group. Thus, in certain social groups there is a silent assumption that the verbal communication is binding for a considerable period of time, particularly when it is part of a contractual interaction. In other groups—or between members of different groups—no such implication may be involved. Memory of a command, agreement or verbal contract will have very different effects in these different situations. I emphasize the importance of the reference group since human symbolic behavior is a function of the social group and man is dependent on his symbolic behavior for maintaining transactions of any degree of complexity or duration.

I should also like to comment briefly on the concept of commitment. In a rigorous discussion of the problem of "person" and "machine" Dr. Donald M. MacKay (2) points out that one "can exercise an option" and *either* commit oneself to a person *or* analyze a mechanism according to pre-determined criteria. In commitment there is necessarily expectancy of adequate response to maintain the interaction, the objectives or purposes being determined by the interaction of the persons involved. In dialogue, thus, the two persons form a single system, maintained by the flow of information. In contrast, study of a biological phenomenon on the basis of behavioral criteria and using operational formulations is the study of mechanisms, with the ultimate purpose of reproducing them deterministically according to logical criteria. Thus, the states of commitment-expectancy and that of analysis-reconstruction are two separate realms of discourse. A person can be in one of them or in the other, but not in both simultaneously. Within limitations which have not been defined, it seems probable that one can retrieve some aspects of the course of a commitment-expectancy interaction from memory and subject them to study. Successive operations of this type, dealing with limited aspects of communication, would appear to be necessary to develop or learn and also to maintain the coding system. This problem will not be considered here further than to call attention to a question raised by Dr. MacKay (2), namely, whether or not the phenomena of commitment to a person and of behavorial analysis of a mechanism are related to or clarify the "I-Thou" and the "I-It" concepts respectively.

In operations involving humans who are banded together to accomplish a mission the realm in which the operations occur is the realm of commitment-expectancy. The more complex the operation the greater the necessity for reliability of the social communication which maintains commitment-expectancy. Such reliability is even more significant in human groups composed of members responsible for different aspects of a joint project, especially when one or more members must be separated from the face-to-face relationship for periods of time.

The organization of behavior (apart from that completely specified by the function-structure of the organism and of the environment) requires a goal, since the goal determines the relevance of information and the course. The possibility of establishing distant goals subsequent to immediate objectives by exercise of "foresight" and of maintaining the retrieval of these goals reliably in decision making, is limited. In situations in which the probabilities of the course of a transaction are too uncertain to be used for anticipatory guidance of behavior, effective control of the organization of behavior may be exercised by limiting attention to the prescribed program, i.e., to performing the prescribed, separate acts without attention to the distant goal. It is routine to make decisions on difficult or insoluble problems-in-living according to the accepted mores and, under stress, according to the accepted verbal formulae of the reference group. Presumably there is the assumption that the social group will provide support or, at least, acceptance if the accepted moral principles are followed, regardless of the consequences. Under extreme stress acceptance as a member of the group—even as a "bad" member—with its capacity to maintain the organization of behavior is preferable for some persons to the threat of "not being a person" and of the catastrophic reaction (the "anxiety," in Sullivan's sense) which is likely to ensue. Anecdotes from combat situations[3] and clinical observations of schizophrenic panics ("*it* took over") give support to this formulation. A considerable variety of formulations —from, let us say, "Valhalla" to "Fate"—have been used to control the structuring of information on the course of events and to occlude ignorance in order to avoid the problem of selection of goals (change of goal) in the course of a stressful transaction.

The concepts of stress and of anxiety have developed in biology and psychiatry as though they were two integrated states of the organism for which single measures could be found. Some authors have treated anxiety as an emotion and practically always the subjective phenomena are emphasized. Such views of stress and of anxiety have been useful in opening up this field, but are proving inadequate. As more data are obtained, it is becoming clear that we will have to define the load on the organism, the organism's response, and the further course of the interaction of the organism with the environment. The state of the art is by no means such that these problems can be dealt with in anything approaching a definitive manner at present. It is proposed here, therefore, only to draw attention to a few phenomena in order to illustrate the nature of the problem.

A cold, external environment appears to have very different effects on men depending on the adequacy of their protective clothing. There are well substantiated anecdotes of men on expeditions who attempted suicide by exposing themselves to the cold in little more than their underwear. In at least two cases about which I have heard, the men suffered severe cold injury of their extremities, nose, ears, etc., but found shivering in the cold so disturbing that they returned to shelter in time to avoid dying. In contrast, it is well known that if a man in adequate protective clothing lies down to "rest" in severe cold he can freeze to death with no shivering or discomfort. The difference in response seems to be due to the effect of the rate of heat loss on the sensory cold transducers. A number of phenomena of this type have been described, demonstrating that under- or over-reaction of one or another system which affects the internal milieu of the body may lead to death (cf. "The Psycho-physiology of Death," (8)). From such observations one may conclude that the term "homeostasis" refers to the general tendency of living organisms to maintain certain intra-somatic functions and states within a relatively narrow range. "Homeostasis," however, does not refer to an integrated neural mechanism or system. The constancy of the internal milieu seems to be achieved by a variety of independent neural and other circuits which are influenced by mid- and fore-brain mechanisms, but not in a manner to maintain the *over-all* constancy of the internal milieu. One or another aspect may "take precedence," as it were, and thus lead to changes in other somatic functions incompatible with life. This area needs much more attention than it has received, both from the standpoint of determining the peripheral circuits and also from the standpoint of the influence of fore-brain mechanisms on these circuits.

It is of course quite apparent in the preceding illustration on the effect of a cold environment that a man's successful response depends on so-called "cognitive" functions, e.g., developing appropriate clothing and appropriately using the clothing. This principle, however, is no different from that applying to other species. Numerous animals can only survive in hot environments, for example, by searching for and finding a cool place to lie down in.

It is important to bear in mind that the range of load that the organism can tolerate without serious disturbance is greatly increased by the ability to recognize and utilize supportive aspects of the environment. For the human, of course, this ability includes construction of artificial environments of various types from clothing to shelters, together with plans and instructions for their appropriate use. Amongst the earliest changes under stress, however, is the decrease in capacity for planning and "thinking," resulting in more and more control of behavior by the immediate environmental contingencies. Plans must, therefore, be made and learned in advance. This is of particular significance under those conditions in which metabolic disturbances result in what Dr. Adolf Meyer used to call "the failure of the body to support the brain." Examples include heavy physical effort, food (calories) deprivation, sleep deprivation, and so forth. Although in these conditions the duration of the stress may be the critical factor, clear formulation of the intermediate and of the ultimate goals and thorough training in the operations to be performed have a potent effect on the maintenance of the control of behavior. Increased frequency of "lapses" of attention was a function of duration of sleep deprivation up to 90 hours in the studies of Williams, Lubin and Goodnow (10). However, most of the subjects who were given a goal of 72 hours could not stay awake at 73 and 74 hours, whereas subjects with a goal of 96 hours showed no unusual difficulty until the goal was reached. Various subjective phenomena seemed to be more related to the approach to achieving the goal than to the actual duration of wakefulness (6). Although adequate data are not available, a few measurements indicate that the prolonged deprivation type of load does not evoke adrenal responses, in spite of the fact that the subject may "feel" seriously uncomfortable. It appears that both adrenal cortical and medullary responses are part of a system called into play by immediate physical involvement with the environment or by anticipation of such involvement.

In the course of studies of emotional disturbance in monkeys, Mason and his associates (4) found that the blood levels of 17 hydroxy-corticosteroids and of nor-epinephrine were elevated routinely following painful stimuli or following a conditional stimulus (light, buzzer, etc.) signalling a painful stimulus. In contrast the blood levels of epinephrine remained unchanged except under particular circumstances. These circumstances included completely novel experiences (such as the first time blood was drawn); presentation of a stimulus which signalled that one or other of several stimuli would be presented, each of which indicated a different ultimate event; and, having trained the monkey to avoid a shock by pressing a lever at appropriate intervals, giving him two or three "free" shocks during a 10-minute test period. Uncertainty or ambiguity concerning the course of events is common to these situations. One may say that they place the monkey in a situation which for him is "open ended." It thus appears that this characteristic is either more strongly alerting or that there are qualitatively different responses evoked by threatening situations depending on whether the course is known (and the subject is, as it were, committed to a known response) or whether the course is not known and it is necessary to wait for further information to direct action. In both cases, the general behavior of the animals has been roughly the same as to movements and automatic manifestations.

In another series of studies Friedman, Mason, and Hamburg (1) have found that humans under prolonged stress show very different patterns of adrenal cortical responses. The 24-hour excretion of 17 hydroxy-corticosteroids has been measured in parents of children during the terminal stages of leukemia. Wide differences in the excretion rates have been found for different people, though the rate for any one person over very long periods stays in the high, intermediate, or low categories. With particularly distressing events, most people tend to excrete increased amounts of 17-hydroxy-corticosteroids. However, some people in the low excretion group may show a paradoxical response and secrete less at the time of events which most people find disturbing. Psychiatric and psychological data being collected have so far shown a remarkably good correlation with the hormonal data, indicating that we are dealing with total patterns of response rather than with merely differences in adrenal functions. How these patterns of response may be related to more or less effective handling of different types of stress still must be determined.

In summary, we may note that for purposes of analysis the concepts expressed as "the will," "self-control" of behavior under "stress," and so forth must be expanded in two directions. Firstly, the behavior referred to needs to be described in terms of the social roles of the reference group and in terms of the reliability of social communication in the group. Secondly, it is necessary to expand these concepts in terms of the characteristics of the load on the organism and in terms of the mechanisms involved in the changing interactions of the organism with the environment in response to the load. There is no single factor such as "the will" or such as "stress." The problems of selecting, training and operating with personnel under unusual circumstances will require study and analysis of the relevant factors in the particular circumstances to which the men are to be subjected. These are no longer academic problems, but call for much closer relationships between scientific analysis of behavior and human operations in the field.

BIBLIOGRAPHY

1. FRIEDMAN, S. B., MASON, J. W. & HAMBURG, D. A. Urinary 17-hydroxycorticosteroid levels in parents of children with neoplastic disease. *Psychosomat. Med.*, 1962, in press.
2. MACKAY, D. M. The use of behavioral language to refer to mechanical processes. *Brit. J. Phil. Sci.*, Vol. XIII No. 50, 1962.
3. MARSHALL, S. L. A. *Men against fire.* New York: William Morrow, 1953.
4. MASON, J. W., MANGAN, G., BRADY, J. V., CONRAD, D. & RIOCH, D. M. Concurrent plasma epinephrine, nor-epinephrine and 17-hydroxycorticosteroid levels during conditioned emotional disturbances in monkeys. *Psychosomat. Med.*, 1961, 23, 344-353.
5. MEAD, G. H. *Mind, self and society.* Chicago: Univer. of Chicago Press, 1934.
6. MORRIS, G. O., WILLIAMS, H. L. & LUBIN, A. Misperception

and disorientation during sleep deprivation. *AMA Arch. Neurol. & Psychiat.*, 1960, 2, 247-254.

7. MILLER, G. A. GALANTER, E. & PRIBAM, K. H. *Plans and the structure of behavior.* New York: Henry Holt & Co., 1960.

8. SIMON, A. *The physiology of emotions.* Springfield, Ill.: Charles C. Thomas, 1961.

9. SULLIVAN, H. S. *The interpersonal theory of psychiatry.* H. S. Perry & M. L. Gavell (Eds.), New York: W. W. Norton, 1953.

10. WILLIAMS, H. L., LUBIN, A. & GOODNOW, J. Impaired performance with acute sleep loss. *Psychol, Monogr.*, 1959, 73(14), 1-26.

11. WOLFF, K. H. *The sociology of Georg Simmel.* Glencoe, Ill.: The Free Press, 1950.

12. YOUNG, J. Z Doubt and certainty in science. London: Oxford Univer. Press, 1953.

NOTES

1. As in the case of the ancient humors, the instincts, motives, inherited factors, natural properties, etc., are frequently used as connoting occult forces to explain the course of behavior, particularly of the goal-directed type. Less commonly they are used as highly condensed symbols to denote extensive patterns of social behavior.

2. It will be noted that in this formulation ordinary concepts of "motivation" are not only omitted, but "the will" is not recognized as a force or drive producing the behavior. The common use of "motives" to describe behavior avoids the need for repetitive, elaborate descriptions of more or less standard cultural patterns and provides an indicator of the probable future course insofar as the behavior is correlated with a cultural pattern shared by the observer and the subject. "Motives" are inferred from a variety of behavioral phenomena, including the verbal, gestural, etc. behavior of the subject, the course of the action, the termination of the particular pattern and the transition to another, and so forth. The subject usually includes his "feelings," "sensations," anticipatory "thoughts," etc. as data for identifying his "motives." Consistency as well as clarity of communication in the system of describing behavior in motivational terms depends on extensive knowledge of the behavior itself, of the social system of which it is a part and of the social system in which the formulation is used. (The importance of the use of the formulation follows from the fact that the social system of communication is changed and a new social situation is created by feeding-back the decision arrived at—i.e., the formulation—into the system.) It will be obvious that the major difficulty in the use of a motivational terminology for formulating the phenomena of behavior is the problem of identifying the criteria on which the terminology is based. This difficulty frequently leads to inferring the subject's "motives" from the "feelings" his behavior evokes in the observer. The mechanisms involved in such analyses are obscure, though the conclusions are frequently very convincing in their over-simplification.

3. S. L. A. Marshall has discussed this problem in detail in *Men Against Fire* (3).

KURT GOLDSTEIN

Stress and the Concept
of Self-Realization

Dr. Klausner has confronted us with a difficult problem. He asks, somewhat puzzled himself, whether the question of self-control under stressful conditions, this enigma of a classic intransigence of civilization, may not be due to an inflexible formulation of the question. I have the feeling he may be right. Is it at all possible to come to a solution concerning this paramount problem of our existence starting out from what one usually calls self? Could it not be that our idea of the self is a misconception and thus starting from the self the reason for our failure? Dr. Klausner gave an excellent survey of the various attempts to solve the problem. Does not the great difference of opinions, even of contradictory viewpoints, already show that there may be something basically wrong in the belief in this intransigence? Dr. Klausner ponders the correctness of the restriction on the scope of our discussion, that the self, the individual, is supposed to exert the control, but he means we have to accept this restriction because without it the distinction between our work and the general theory of human behavior would become unclear. But is this distinction necessary? Is it even possible? Does not what we mean by self represent an essential part of human nature? Are not perhaps the different proposals to control stress an expression of different concepts of human nature? I personally think that the basic reason for the uncertainty in the recommendation

341

of definite means to control stress in a special situation comes from the atomistic interpretation of man's nature which makes us put one or another isolated capacity of man into action.

My viewpoint which I want to communicate to you originated from my criticism of the possibility of understanding human behavior by the atomistic approach, i.e., from the study of isolated phenomena. I came to this critical attitude during my practical work with patients with mental defects. When I tried to improve the patients by studying and retraining the defects in isolation, in the way usual at that time, I saw very soon that this atomistic procedure often was not successful. The results were much better when I started with the observation of the behavior of the individual in its totality in as many different life situations as possible. I called this procedure the organismic approach. I have discussed in detail in my book *The Organism* (2) the difference between the atomistic and the organismic approach for studying biological phenomena. I could show by many examples the essentially greater success of the latter for our practical endeavor to improve the patients and also for the purpose of understanding the structure of the organism and its functioning in general.

When I received Dr. Klausner's friendly invitation to participate in a discussion about the "Self-Control of Stress," I accepted it with pleasure because my practical and scientific work with brain-damaged individuals (7) had given me much occasion to study persons under stress and to observe how they behaved in their abnormal condition. When I pondered what I could contribute to the discussion, I thought it might be useful to refer to my personal experiences with those patients where the correct handling of their conditions was of paramount importance for their existence.

The main result of my studies was that normal functioning of the organism is guaranteed when it is in an adequate relationship with the world in which it has to live, in other words that this relationship is the presupposition of its existence, i.e., the realization of all capacities which are characteristic for its nature. Abnormal behavior is the expression of a disturbance of this adequacy and with that of the organism's self-realization. It was my task as physician to help the patient to restore the adequacy which was disturbed by what we call sickness. Thus we had much occasion to study whether, when, and in what way adequacy could be achieved under this condition; in other words, the functioning of the organism could be guaranteed in spite of severe defects. You will realize the parallel between this task and the attempt to control a stress situation.

I called the severe disturbance of the organismic functioning "catastrophic condition" because of a disturbance of the function of the whole organism. This applies also if the defect concerns only one part of the organism, e.g., only a part of the brain.

I put the study of the disturbances—of the failure of the organism in its totality—into the foreground because I had realized that for understanding the disfunctioning of one defective part the knowledge of the functioning of the organism in its totality is of paramount significance. It was an important purpose of my afore-mentioned book to prove this and to demonstrate the usefulness of the methodological procedure which results from this assumption for therapy, i.e., the attempt to bring the individual into a condition in which he could realize his nature as highly as possible under the given circumstances.

Decades ago when I was faced with the task of treating an enormous number of brain-injured soldiers during and after the first World War, the study of patients which I conducted together with the psychologist, A. Gelb (3), led us to assume that the most severe disturbance in those patients consisted of an impairment of the highest mental capacity of man, the so-called abstract attitude. The observation that the patients could fulfill a great number of tasks which did not require the use of the abstract attitude induced us to distinguish forms of behavior in man: the abstract one and another which we called concrete behavior. Later, together with Martin Scheerer (6), I gave a detailed description of the two attitudes and their influence on definite forms of behavior through the use of many examples as evidence that the defect of the abstract attitude shows equally in all performance fields—in perception, action, thinking, language, etc.

I can give here only briefly some characteristics of the two forms of mental attitude with respect to human behavior. I would like first to emphasize that the effect of the abstract attitude as regards its impairment is of special significance for understanding the problems which our patients present as do normal persons in stress situations. In our concrete behavior we respond unreflectingly, somewhat passively, to claims upon us which are thrust on us as a palpable configuration in the experiential realm. Most of our concrete reactions are determined by the claims of everyday life. I would like to mention further that the concrete attitude exists also in respect to ideas, thoughts, feelings, even to those

KURT GOLDSTEIN

experiences not directly dependent upon the immediate outer world, thus also to recollections. In the abstract attitude our responses show an essentially different character. They imply conscious activity in the sense of reasoning, awareness, and an accounting to oneself of what one is doing. We detach ourselves from the given sense experience and embrace a much greater part of the world than corresponds, in scope, to the present stimulus. We transcend the immediate given situation and consider it from a conceptual aspect.

In normal life we always use both capacities together, whereby now the concrete and now the abstract is in the foreground, corresponding to whichever way the task can best be fulfilled. I wish to emphasize that the results concerning the individual's change of behavior are not considered here with respect to the diseased brain function but simply as material for our study of the behavior of man.

The material from which I set out was particularly useful as I had to do with young and generally healthy individuals and I had occasion to observe them over a long period of time—some even for many years—under very different conditions: in their everyday life, in the hospital, at home, and in controlled experiments in the laboratory. For our problem (control of stress), it was further very important that our studies were focused particularly on how to improve the individual; that our specific problem was to find out how, if the defect could not be totally eliminated, the patient could at least be brought to a condition which made it possible for him to live in some adequacy. In other words, our aim was to so arrange it that he should not too much and too frequently come into "catastrophe," or, to state it positively, to manage the condition in such a way that he, in spite of the persistence of the defect, should come into a state where he could live in a somewhat *ordered* way so that he could be improved by the treatment of his special condition.

We have, in the monograph I mentioned, enumerated a great number of specific behavior forms for which the use of the abstract attitude is necessary and in which, therefore, the patients failed. The helping procedure which we used successfully relied on the possibility of organizing the world in such a way that individuals who have not yet developed the abstract attitude or are unable to use it for any reason and are therefore forced to live on the concrete level can, despite this, exist in adequacy on the concrete level of behavior. I mention this point particularly because, as we shall see, it is very important for helping individuals in some stress condition.

I would like to mention as examples in normal life in this respect the situation of normal infants where the abstract attitude is not yet developed (which does not take place before the beginning of the second year of life); further, of adults employed in many industries who find their working situation continually demands that they function on the concrete level; and in the situation of so-called primitive peoples where there is no doubt that they act mostly on a "lower level," I think on that level which I term concrete. The way these people can manage to live became understandable when the late anthropologist, P. Radin, showed that in all such tribes there exist "thinking people," who organize the tribe's world in such a way that the existence of this living on the concrete level becomes possible. I would like to underscore here that living on a "primitive" level should *not* be interpreted simply as the expression of an inborn reduced (defective) mentality, which does not exist in these people but is still often erroneously assumed.

With respect to the problem of stress, it follows that we have to evaluate the means which we apply to avoid (or overcome) stress from the point of view of the individual's ability to change the condition of his life so that the possibility of self-realization will be improved.

Before I discuss how the patient comes out of his dangerous situation, I would like to insert a few remarks as to why I use pathology in my studies for understanding normal behavior, particularly because I want to avoid a possible misunderstanding, namely, the assumption that behavior in pathology is modified in a way which is essentially different from that of normals. I have shown in *The Organism* (2) how observation of pathological patients makes the analysis of the structure of single performances easier, particularly in relation to the function of the total organism. But what seems to me most important is that I emphasized, on the basis of observation, that using pathological material is in no way dangerous when one considers carefully the modification of behavior by pathology; in other words, what pathology means in comparison with the normal behavior of an organism.

I came in this respect to the conclusion that pathology is determined by the same phenomenon of isolation which also normally plays an essential role in the organization of performances, indeed, a phenomenon often neglected. This isolation is, in pathol-

ogy, only exaggerated and can be evaluated by careful study of
the relationship of the isolated performances to the self-realization of the individual in the situation (see *The Organism* (2),
ff. 133).

When we observe a patient with a severe defect of abstraction
we see that if he is confronted only with tasks which can be performed concretely, he may not appear much disturbed and communication with him may in general be quite possible. On the
other hand, when the task needs abstraction he does not simply
fail but shows severe total disorder. He displays physiological and
psychological phenomena which have the character of what we
call anxiety. Previous analysis of anxiety (10) in general revealed
that its appearance is not simply a consequence of the experience
of failure but rather *belongs intrinsically* to the condition of failure,
i.e., to the condition of *lack of adequacy* between the organism
and the demands made on it. Anxiety is the subjective experience
of the condition in which the organism's existence is in *danger*.
Certainly catastrophe is connected with an event in the external
world and the disorder of behavior can be understood by us in
terms of lack of *objective* coming to terms by the organism with
the world. *The subject, however, is not aware* of the relation to
a definite outer world. Anxiety is not a reaction to an object;
anxiety represents an emotional state in which the individual
cannot come in contact with *anything*. Anxiety is not an emotion
which affects the individual in general and in all conditions in
which he is. It is related to the severe catastrophe which the
patient confronts due to the lack of abstraction.

Now, how does the patient *get rid of the danger* of the severe
shock which goes along with the damage of his power of abstraction? Due to this defect he is unable to extricate himself from the
condition of anxiety. But, on the other hand, we observe that
generally he becomes quieter and more ordered with time. Observation shows that this is *not* an effect of an *improvement* of
the defect or a restoration of the capacity of abstraction. Apparently ordered behavior and adequacy between the organism
and the demands of the world can exist in spite of the continuance
of the defect. The behavior of the patient reveals that this can
happen in two different ways. One is that he reacts only to things
he can handle. He can come into this condition passively. He is
induced by the trend for self-realization to do those things in which
he need act only in a definite way—in the way of concrete behavior, as we call it. He sticks to this because he is not disturbed

and is able to live. He does not do this voluntarily, i.e., by a will to escape catastrophe.

The new situation is the result of an involuntary biological procedure. Indeed, he can come into this situation and live in it only when the people around him have arranged the world in such a way that he is not confronted with tasks which he cannot, with his reduced capacity, fulfill. One could say he is living on a lower level of existence which is guaranteed by the abstract attitude of others.

We mentioned before the significance of this organization of living in different situations of normals. The persons in these situations can act concretely because this attitude and the trend for self-realization are not disturbed and cannot be as long as the organism lives at all; it is simply an expression of living.

However, living on this lower level of existence may not always be satisfying to the patient. There are different states of order, different degrees of self-realization in which the individual is accustomed to live according to his individual nature. Simple survival without being able to live in at least a somewhat "adequate" form of self-realization may bring new anxiety. This does not show in patients with severe defect of abstraction because the defect itself does not permit them to realize the restrictions on their nature. The same may happen in conditions of very severe stress. But it is different in patients who are not so severely disturbed and in individuals who are in a somewhat less severe stress condition. Here a second way must be found for reducing catastrophe: The individual must *accept and bear some restrictions*. The patient has to learn to bear some restrictions if he does not want to live at the lower level of existence. If he is able to learn this he will reach a higher degree of self-realization. But it is not sufficient that the individual is in a situation, an adequate milieu, in which he is able to live undisturbed and in order. There exist different states of order of different value for self-realization, for existence. This way of living may bring more or less restriction, the individual may survive, but not live in a way adequate to his "nature." It is different in patients who are not so severely disturbed (as well as in normal individuals who come into a stress condition).

Here another way must be found if the patient is really to exist. He must bear some restrictions and accept them if he does not want to live on a lower level of existence. If he is able to do so then he will live with a higher degree of self-realization. The main task of therapy is to teach the individual the significance of accepting restrictions. Awareness of the result will help the individual to realize the necessity of restrictions for a better way of living. But even that is not yet sufficient. He has to acknowledge that restriction is not demanded by anyone or anything outside of him, it is not a sacrifice but a necessity which normal human beings also have to accept to a certain degree and in the same way if they want to achieve an adequate degree of self-realization. It is in principle the same as in normal life. The necessity of self-restriction plays a particular role in patients who are not so severely disturbed. When we said before that patients are in a condition of anxiety, we can speak here in principle of a similar emotional state but one very different in its effect on behavior. The "adequacy" is not at all so strongly interrupted, the individual is not so reduced in his judgment, and he even tries by all possible means to come into contact, to find out the reason for his disturbance, and to fight against it. He shows all the characteristics of the condition we call "fear" (10). As a matter of fact, we observe that he considers the situation in its relation to his self-realization and is ready to restrict himself. He thus shows a higher degree of self-realization than one would expect considering his disturbance. The individual more or less understands the significance of self-restriction for general improvement. Our procedure in treating him consists not the least in instructions regarding this point and in helping him to experience how the restriction makes a higher degree of self-realization possible. Here, therefore, the personal relationship between physician and patient acquires an important role. The nature of this relationship will become more understandable later when we shall see how it belongs to a special sphere of human nature.

In the phenomenon of self-restriction we are confronted with a problem which we meet not only in sick people but which is an important problem in normal life as well. It is especially necessary to be sure of its nature because its appearance often goes along with the restriction of other people with whom one is in contact. Far better self-realization of one individual self-restriction of the "other" is necessary. Already the support of the sick individual we mentioned needs some self-restriction on the part of the helper. We can say in general some self-restriction is a phenomenon necessary for any relationship between people. One should be very aware of this; otherwise, the "other," who has to restrict himself, may consider this as an aggressive act in relation to his own better self-realization, and our self-restriction may be considered as an expression of sacrifice demanded from someone or something from the outside.

Both assumptions would do an injustice to "human existence" by making self-restriction an act imposed by demands from the outside and so take away the experience of necessity which belongs to human existence. This would make self-restriction for both partners in this common enterprise an act which loses its important human significance.

The adult in our culture has to learn to take restriction during his life as, for instance, when the situation in industry demands that he work on a concrete level which he himself may experience as restriction.

Restriction belongs to human life. One could say it is an expression of the imperfection of man's nature and should, so evaluated, be accepted as something necessary for man in society without which the individual would not be able to exist. This shows how important the social relationship is for understanding the self-imposed restriction and, on the other hand, what role the correct organization of society plays for the correct behavior of the individual in a difficult situation. We shall see later that the same is particularly valid for understanding the control of stress conditions. In this way, the introduction of a principle of self-imposed restriction manifests a universal recognition on the part of all men of a voluntary limitation of their behavior in such a way as to enhance the existence of man. This principle is not comprehensible through the laws of natural science; it is rather a value and is not determined by any outside fact of religion or philosophy but only by the single realization of what nature is and what it needs in order to exist.

As we said, self-restriction is not an expression of sacrifice. As such it would not be understandable or appear useful in practice. Self-restriction belongs to the realization of human nature and is an expression of man's imperfection which can be accepted only if one understands human behavior, particularly the all-important factor which self-realization represents in man's existence and by which he is seen in relation to all organismic life.

I am fully aware that the assumption that self-restriction and imperfection belong to man's nature and that acknowledging this will make his behavior not only most understandable but guarantee the highest form of performance will be rejected entirely or accepted only with hesitation; it may even appear ridiculous at a time of such great success in certain areas of human endeavor as obtains in our era.

We are confronted here with a very serious problem not only concerning patients or people in stress but in general. Its neglect may lead us to overlook the danger which may arise from an over-valuation of success which, in turn, creates a danger one cannot even foresee but which may menace our existence by defying specific characteristics of man's nature. Not a few people see this but their warning does not get much attention. I see the greatest danger in overlooking the central significance of intimate relation-ships between individuals so basic for human existence and in the neglect or even the loss of recognition of the aforementioned sphere of human nature in which the intimate mutual relationship between individuals becomes manifest, which I call the "sphere of immediacy."

When I emphasized that human behavior can be adequate only by using both abstract and concrete behavior I did not describe the situation in its totality. For the sake of simplicity I did not mention the influence of this sphere of immediacy on man's be-havior which my studies of abnormal behavior have increasingly revealed to be of the greatest significance for doing justice to the condition of disease and stress, for understanding phenomena such as self-restriction, and the necessity for self-realization of simul-taneous self-restriction by the "other."

The assumption of such a sphere is not a mere subjective phychic phenomenon. It is not an irrational assumption, unrelated to the objective world. As a matter of fact, it appears strange only because it corresponds to another, not generally realized, aspect of the world in which we are involved in our totality, while in its so-called object aspect the world is considered from an isolated point of view which we prefer for some special purposes. The sphere of immediacy is also governed by laws like the laws of the objective world, though of a kind different from that which is called logic. It is an inner experience in its own right and occurs particularly in definite situations which cannot be understood by the abstract-concrete attitude alone.

When we try to bring ourselves into this sphere or, better said, when we are on occasion drawn into it by the attractive character in which it presents itself, the words which we use to describe our experiences and which may, from the usual aspect of language, appear somewhat strangely reminiscent of the language which

poets and philosophers use, become not only comprehensible—
they open up a new world to us to which we do not generally give
attention in the course of our practical or scientific endeavors.
More correctly said, we intentionally repress it because we are
afraid its influence may disturb the stability and security of the
world important in our culture. As a matter of fact, these experiences of immediacy originate from the same world in which we
otherwise live. They represent only *another aspect* of this world.
To come into this sphere of immediacy, we must try to ignore
somewhat the "natural science" attitude which, as a matter of fact,
one could also call "unnatural" because it does not comprise the
total human being.

The experience of immediacy cannot be reached by a discur-
sive procedure or by any kind of synthesis; it can be reached only
by, so to say, surrendering ourselves to the world in which we come
into contact, without being afraid of losing the relation with our
"ordered" world. Experience teaches us that we can live in both
spheres. The abstract attitude makes it possible to experience both
separately and to shift from the one to the other. Our existence
is based not only on objectively correct order but at the same time
on comfortableness, well-being, beauty, and joy—all these are
experiences which belong in the sphere of immediacy. Emergence
of the "adequacy" to which we have referred earlier presupposes
a structure of personality which functions not only in the experience of the static condition of the abstract-concrete sphere, but
also tolerates possible *uncertainty* without feeling in danger of
losing its existence. The sphere of immediacy has a dynamic character, which is of particular significance for the possibility of existing in spite of uncertainty and thus reveals the very core of human
nature.

The sphere of immediacy is already present in the first of life
of the human being. It has here even a particular significance because the abstract-concrete attitude is not yet developed. (The
latter does not appear, even in primitive form, prior to the end of
the first or beginning of the second year.) It is an important phenomenon for building up the relationship of the infant with the
mother and the world.[1]

The sphere of immediacy reveals itself in many situations of
everyday life, e.g., in friendship, in love, in the instigation of creative production, in the religious attitude; it is not even missing
as an instigating part of our scientific work. As a characteristic
event, it appears in the situation where we meet an old friend

whom we have not seen for a long time in an unexpected encounter.

The feeling of the unity of both spheres is basic for the experience of well-being and self-realization. This is evident when we feel deeply deceived in an encounter with the "other." We do not have simply a feeling of a mistake—to which we pay much or little attention—but we feel *deeply disappointed, even shocked.* The experience is, so to say, a shaking of our existence; it touches on a central phenomenon of man, the experience of existence, of realizing one's nature, which is possibly only in the real unity with the "other" and the world.

This sphere has a special significance for our understanding of the problem of self-realization in relation to my and the other's self-restriction. Ordered behavior, the basis of self-realization, asks for a balance in the relationship of the self: restriction of the "me" and the self-restriction of the "other." This may be experienced by the other as unjust interference with *his* behavior, with *his* freedom, and this will occur particularly if he considers the demand to restrict himself as aggressive. This feeling can be avoided only if the necessity for self-restriction by the other is accepted by him as belonging to human nature and if he sees my self-realization as the reciprocal of his self-restriction. This will occur in the experience of the phenomenon in the sphere of immediacy. I cannot enter into a detailed discussion of this problem here. I would like to emphasize for clarification of the phenomenon of self-restriction that we should perceive in the sphere of immediacy that the other person does the same so that self-imposed self-restriction appears as belonging to man's nature.

The sphere of immediacy is of the greatest significance for the organization of a social world and for the understanding of others. Its acceptance for the existence of man requires courage which in its final analysis is nothing but an affirmative answer to the imperfect nature of man. But in realizing that he is not alone he can overcome his imperfection in belonging together, in living in a unity with the "other," which gives the individual a special meaning which has largely been lost in our civilization. We repress these experiences more or less because we are afraid to disturb the stability and security of the "world," considered so important in our contemporary culture.

On several occasions I have mentioned stress in relation to what we have observed in patients. Now I want to offer some further clarification of the one or the other occurrence in stress, draw to your attention some differences between behavior in control of stress in sickness and in stress conditions of normal people in abnormal circumstances in which the individual is able to react normally. One can say that stress is objectively disorder in the behavior of an organism which is accompanied by the disagreeable experience of a kind of shock, of a menace more or less to its existence. We see the cause of this disorder in the discrepancy between the available capacities of an individual and the demands made upon him. Stress can be caused by psychic and physical events and has psychic and physical manifestations.

Not every inadequacy produces stress, only that which hinders the individual's ability to realize his essential capacities or those which he considers essential. Hence, disturbance in the relationship of the individual to other people and to society is of particular importance for the occurrence of stress. What is essential is determined by whether or not other persons and society permit self-realization in the situation in which the individual has to live.

Stress can appear in different intensity but we should not evaluate the condition simply from the quantitative point of view. Intensity is only one factor and its degree must be considered in relation to a number of circumstances if one wants to understand why and how stress occurs: the condition of the individual, the effect of the damage on his mental capacity, the place and the time when the incident occurs. Whether a disturbance of some intensity is experienced simply as a disagreeable event as as stress can be understood only by considering the total situation. Observation shows that there is a difference in principle between conditions of stress. In respect of the principal different reaction in both conditions, we should speak of fatal and non-fatal stress, manifested in the fact that in the former the individual is totally out of contact with the world and can in no way contribute to controlling the situation while in the non-fatal condition the individual is in contact, is even very eager to realize what is going on, and how he may be able to fight the dangerous situation. The emotional upset in which he is, corresponds to that which we will call fear and which is essentially different from anxiety (10).

The individual may come into a higher form of self-realization because he may accept what we explain to him in relation to the necessity of self-imposed restriction. In the fatal condition of stress all that could happen would be a sinking down to a lower level of existence, to a concrete behavior, which may bring some relief but which will occur only if the people around him permit it. Otherwise, he will break down. In no way can he do anything himself to control the stress condition. When later, under favorable external circumstances, the cause of stress is eliminated by others, the feeling of stress may sooner or later diminish or disappear but the individual may remain in some danger. One has to be aware that for someone who underwent fatal stress the aftereffects may produce symptoms which have to be treated physically and psychologically in order to avoid hypersensitivity to small incidents or even the beginnings of an anxiety neurosis. An important problem is what we should do in a situation in which we expect that the individual will probably, or with some certainty, be in a severe stress situation. I cannot discuss this problem here, a problem which we shall have to meet more and more in the general and the special dangers with which we have to live in our culture. While I cannot discuss this here I would like to point out its great significance.

While writing this paper, I again reflected especially on the problem which Dr. Klausner has set before us, i.e., self-control in stress situations. I have made some remarks to emphasize its dependence upon the social situation in which it occurs. I came to the general conclusion that all the factors I mentioned concerning the causes, the different characteristics and different handling of stress may not be satisfying in respect of the problem of self-control. Always the help by others is in the foreground and with this we came to the significance of the social situation. Stress will never be totally reduced. It belongs to life and will be diminished the more the social situation makes possible the highest degree of self-realization for all individuals. One of the greatest impediments to reducing stress in our time is the uncertainty and inconsistency of present civilization and the lack of any values which are in accordance with our experiences and which the individual can accept wholeheartedly and which make life worth living in spite of necessary restriction.

My discussion has put self-realization into the foreground. I hope it will be clear that to say that we are concerned by nature to realize ourselves to the fullest possible degree is not to enunciate an egotistic concept. It is not that at all. My concept assumes that man has by nature the will to persist in the essence of his being and that this is not a metaphysical conviction but based on our very experience of how individuals behave in the particular situations which they encounter in life. With this conviction as the basis for a reasonable understanding of our observations, we do not need to assume transcendental values or religious, political, or

philosophical ideas; and we are able to eliminate so many concepts in vogue now, such as the wish for security or the drive to
eliminate tension, the effect of the pleasure principle, the power
or death instinct, which to me all seem to be products of the iso-
lating, atomistic procedure in understanding man and which are
not proven and not necessary to assume. I think that the organismic holistic approach alone makes it possible to understand
human nature and so also to control stress situations.

BIBLIOGRAPHY

1. GOLDSTEIN, KURT. Zur Theorie der Function des Nerven-
system. *Arch. f. Psychiatrie*, 1925.

2. GOLDSTEIN, KURT. *The Organism*. New York: American Book
Co., 1938 (including extensive bibliography).

3. GOLDSTEIN, KURT & GELB, A. *Psychological Analysen von
Hirnpathological Falle*. Leipzig: Barth, 1920.

4. GOLDSTEIN, KURT. *Behandlung, Fursorge der Hirnverletzten*.
Leipzig: Vogel, 1918.

5. GOLDSTEIN, KURT. *Human Nature in the Light of Psychopathology*. Cambridge: Harvard University Press, 1940.

6. GOLDSTEIN, KURT & SCHEERER, M. Abstract and Concrete
Behavior. *Psycholog. Monographs*, Vol. *53*, No. 2, 1941.

7. GOLDSTEIN, KURT. The Modification of Behavior Consequent
to Cerebral Lesions. *Psychiat. Quarterly*, Vol. *10*, 1936.

8. GOLDSTEIN, KURT. Concerning the Concept of Primitivity. In:
Culture in History: Essays in Honor of Paul Radin. New York: Columbia University Press, 1960.

9. GOLDSTEIN, KURT. The Smiling of the Infant and the Problem of Understanding the Other. *J. of Psychology*, Vol. *44*, 1957.

10. GOLDSTEIN, KURT. The Structure of Anxiety. In: *Progress of
Psychotherapy*. New York: Grune & Stratton, 1957.

11. GOLDSTEIN, KURT. The Concept of Health, Disease and Therapy: Basic Ideas of an Organismic Psychotherapy. *J. of Psychotherapy*,
Vol. *8*, 1954.

12. GOLDSTEIN, KURT. Concept of Transference. *Acta Psychothera-
peutica*, 1954.

NOTE

1. My study of the origin of "smiling in the infant" (9) and of the condition
for the appearance of that smiling presents particularly good material for studying the nature of the sphere of immediacy and its significance for man's existence.

PART FIVE } SCIENTIFIC
HERMENEUTICS

SAMUEL Z. KLAUSNER

Scientific Hermeneutics

From Past to Future Research
Through Hermeneutics

INTRODUCTION

We have arrived at a crossroads of research on self-control. The introductory codification of past literature produced a quaternate of concepts of conscious control —the efforts to synergy, conquest, harmony, and transcendence. These efforts were exerted in control of drive, affect, intellect, and performance. Some of the papers which followed dealt with aspects of the control effort and others dealt with the stresses against which the control effort is exerted. Nelson, examining the writings of the historic, especially medieval, religious, and the psychoanalytic elites, showed how the stresses experienced by individuals and the methods of mitigating these stresses have been bound up with the successive "orchestrations" or conscience, casuistry, and the cure of souls. Hadas found the Greek attitude toward self-control reflected in epic poems and artistic relics. Their ethical relativism spared them stresses to which we are subject. Dornbusch described the theme of uplift as a method of control advocated in popular literature. Opler, referring to medical case studies and reports of participant observation, contrasted the phenomena of illness in several contemporary cultures. Swanson re-examined social science literature on primary relations to show how society controls and generates love so that man, through the enhancement of another, may find the strength to act and to endure. Janis described the way people facing medical operations or caught in public disasters manage their anxieties—and thus, themselves—through constructive anticipatory worry. Korchin delineated evidence on the mastery of ego-threats which has accumulated in experimental reports. Liddell presented a paradigm of human vigilance reactions and neurotic breakdowns based on the responses of periodically shocked sheep in harness. Orne used experimental findings to evaluate the role of hypnosis and self-hypnosis in helping people bear trying circumstances. Rioch, relying on clinical and experimental results, dealt with the management of unusual informational inputs. Goldstein examined self-control as self-realization which is endangered by loss of the abstract attitude and which may be discovered through the sphere of immediacy.

Though each paper deals with some aspect of control or of stress, to review them solely in terms of those common themes would sacrifice their uniqueness on the altar of aseptic generalization. Each contribution brings its own legitimate and significant, though different, perspective to the analysis. This final paper asks, "Where do we go from here in research on self-control?" Before asking this question in general, however, let us see where each specific contribution leads us in terms of new research.

THE HERMENEUTIC MAP

In reviewing these papers, we are in the position of the individual researcher who, having converted his original hypothesis into an acceptable proposition, seeks the next step in research. Our contributors have presented a grand array of propositions. A future course for scientific research, in this as in any other area, must be charted on a map of the ground already traversed. From the contours of the familiar we draw inferences about the unfamiliar area still to be traversed. Does this mean that a future course may be sketched only by some creative and so presumably unpredictable process? Does it depend upon a researcher's unique insight into a connection between an established proposition and a new problem or fact? Francis Bacon thought otherwise. He proposed the development of new hypotheses by inductive generalization following scholastic principles. Actually, experience in the scientific community suggests that the move forward relies on some combination of logic and of creativity. Rules of logic may enter as a heuristic directing us from one proposition to a new set of hypotheses, but these rules do not discriminate the salient from the pedestrian hypotheses.

Explicatory heuristics have guided scholars for almost three millennia to the hidden implications of sacred texts. Their problem, though not involving empirical tests, is logically akin to the problem we face in science. Interpretation and exposition of restricted texts is used to develop new propositions to fit a myriad of new situations. By what right does a theologian quote "render unto Caesar" in defense of his stand for separation of church and state and according to what interpretive principle does another theologian deny the validity of the inferred proposition? Justification for these inferences are given in terms of hermeneutic[1] principles, rules which define appropriate ways for understanding holy writ or holy ikons. Since Hermes not only interpreted the gods to man but also doubled as a god of science, his memory is not violated when we follow hermeneutic principles in science. These two applications of hermeneutics differ, however. Theological hermeneutics generate new rational assertions of Truth. Scientific hermeneutics generate new empirical questions about truth.

Biblical exegetes codify their principles of interpretation and exposition. Scientists engaging in hermeneutics have but rarely codified the principles. Such a codification would be useful but would divert us from the purpose of this concluding paper.[2] Hermeneutic principles will be applied implicitly in this exercise to generate testable hypotheses from the propositions presented by our contributors. Following are a few guiding principles in the form of some questions we put to ourselves when we read our colleagues' reports. (1) Would a relationship established between concepts at one level of generalization hold for the derivatives of these concepts at a higher level of generalization? (2) Would a relationship established among more abstract constructs also hold in specific instances of these constructs, or, under conditions differing from those of the original test, or, under different degrees of the phenomenon referred to by the construct? (3) May a new hypothesis be generated by relating several propositions to one another or by relating an established proposition to a new practical problem? These are three ways of generalizing hypotheses by asking "if." We may also ask "why" or "how." When an author indicates a correlation between phenomena, we may ask (4) which mechanisms intervene between the phenomena to account for the correlation. New hypotheses may be generated by exploring these mechanisms.

Only a fraction of the worthwhile research ideas inspired by each author's contribution can be presented here. The research hypotheses to be suggested might not always reflect the author's central theme. A relatively minor point in a study may sometimes produce fruitful successor hypotheses. These successor hypotheses might not be the ones the authors would have recommended. Principles of discrimination or generalization may be applied to a proposition to obtain a new hypothesis. The direction of discrimination or generalization, however, is not dictated by the principle itself. Consequently, the lines of inquiry to be suggested will, in a sense, be personal to the editor. They are a product of the confrontation between the contributor's propositions and the peculiar intellectual apperception of the editor. As such, they will serve the reader as paradigms for his own hermeneutic activity. The reader, with a different intellectual perspective, may derive quite another set of hypotheses from the same contribution.

The suggested hypotheses may not even be "new." In many cases, they are elucidated in other works of the contributor himself. Their statement is then essentially a request for summarizing research already performed with reference to our problem focus. A few of the hypotheses would require the assembling of new data to test them.

New Research in
The Perspective of History

HADAS

Hadas is concerned with man striving to imitate God, and, as a result, neither becoming Godlike nor realizing in himself what is manlike. Man should accept the chthonian urge and divest himself of the villainy of absolutes. Physis, being of nature, is to be accepted as beyond man's control. Nomos, being man-made, appears as a variety of directives among which man may choose.

Hadas tells us that the variety of equally valid nomos spared the Greeks the stress of guilt or self-condemnation. Generalizing, this suggests that a culturally relativistic attitude might lessen the impact of these types of psychological stressors.

This is stated in another way in his discussion of polytheism. Hadas showed that Greek polytheism involved a conception of the relation of human freedom and determinism and, implicitly, of responsibility and guilt, which spared them some stresses in this area from which moderns suffer. Do particular cosmological attitudes expose individuals to characteristic types of stress as well as providing characteristic defenses against stress? Is there a difference in the way stress is managed among members of, for example, a theistic as opposed to a nontheistic system? Are certain stressors more ably encountered through one rather than another religious system?

Now a paradox appears. The hypothesis holds that a culturally relativistic attitude which recognizes several equally valid rights enables man to escape the frustration and sense of injustice attendant upon a failure respecting one of them. Yet, on the other hand, research has shown that the individual is supported in resisting stress by group solidarity and singleness of purpose. The availability of a variety of purposes would, from this point of view, weaken him. Must lack of enthusiasm be the price man pays for freedom from guilt?

The physis-nomos distinction suggests the empirically testable hypothesis that recognition and acceptance of the unavoidability of the unavoidable disaster reduces its stressor potential. Closely associated with the acceptance of Fate is, as Hadas points out, the Greek view of Hope as an evil, an illusion which lulls people to rest. The simple contrast of this observation with the attitude prevalent in our own society reveals that dependence upon hope as a way of managing stress is not culturally universal. The conditions for cultural variation in the attitude toward hope are open to investigation. Rationally-oriented societies might be less likely to invoke hope, while societies which relate to the environment magically might be more likely to do so. If this be true, then the contemporary Western attitudes toward hope could be a medieval inheritance which may be expected to disappear with increasing rationalization. This would presage a change in prevalent Western ideologies of encouragement which are based on the acceptance of hope as a valid attitude.

NELSON

Nelson seeks to link the responses of individuals to the workings of cultural systems and their economies of symbolic resources. He supposes that every individual and every group in society inevitably confront the quandaries associated with the achievement of moral consistency, effective function in relation to prevailing circumstances, and "peace of mind" or "soul." For him, successive phases in the history of East and West have been characterized by different arrangements of the three systems connected with the establishment of the conscience, the elaboration of moral principles in relation to the here and now (casuistry) and the management of the strains and stresses in the program of "cure of souls." Within this framework he is concerned with the "madnesses" of individuals who lose their bearings with respect to the meanings which comprise the *directive* systems. Here he distinguishes six sets of cues: the so-called *percipienda, sentienda, agenda, credenda, miranda,* and *emulanda* cues. The symbolic economy involving these cues is a stage where, through a paradoxical antagonistic cooperation, therapist and patient strive toward a mastery of self and the world and toward overcoming the anguish of the individuated ego.

Nelson suggests some sociocultural conditions under which various systems of spiritual direction emerge. The principal condition is that a discrepancy exist between expectations about the environment and responses of the environment. Each type of schema of spiritual direction is associated with its peculiar discrepancy. New cosmologies and eschatologies emerge in periods of great upheaval, social unpredictability, and anomie. This insight might be pursued. Under what conditions might the philosophical anthropological and the axiological questions inform spiritual direction? Are systems of spiritual direction concerned with philosophical anthropology in periods when man feels overwhelmed by his environment, when there is a demise of the old gods and a need for reassessing man's relation to natural and social order? Do value schemes emerge, for example, when civilizations are re-establishing themselves after a disintegration or when new elites emerge and old elites, the guardians of traditional values, sink into oblivion?

The structures, as well as the cultural schemas of spiritual direction, also seem bound to cultural conditions. Nelson conjectures that psychoanalysis did not originate in Protestant culture areas because the Protestant view of justification by faith does not encourage organized spiritual direction and because Protestant emphasis on self-reliance militated against recourse to other humans for spiritual counsel. Does a group confessional type directive system, with its revelation of personal guilt, emerge only within familistic type social structures? Does charismatic healing require paternalistic and hierarchical structures? In what ways do modern and current programs in the "cure of souls" exhibit the consequences of the postmedieval erosion of the systems of conscience and casuistry?

New Research in a Sociological Perspective

DORNBUSCH

Dornbusch is concerned with what Everyman's secular guides proclaim about self-control. Their assertions and recommendations are cast in the formal categories developed in the introductory "Collocation of Concepts of Self-Control." Dornbusch seeks the content with which the writers of secular inspirational literature fill these categories of manifest objects of and methods of control. Among the methods of control recommended in the popular literature, "positive thinking" is one of the more prominent. "Positive thinking" is recommended not only alone but also in combination with recommendations that the individual control unconscious processes, engage the threat and select an environment to have a desired impact on his self. The content category of "positive thinking" is thus, to use the language of the "Collocation," associated with the formal categories of the efforts to harmony, transcendence, and synergy, respectively. Since "positive thinking" is a value category, it is easy to see how it can occur in association with all the formal categories. Other content categories such as methods of exorcism or meditation might be found to have special affinity for the efforts to conquest. Prayer might tend to be associated with the effort to harmony and participation in a mob as a way of gaining control to be associated with the effort to synergy. The study of these relations between content and formal categories should be pursued as a way of determining the cultural bounds of each of the formal methods.

Dornbusch's analysis of the statements of these popular self-help books leads to the question of to whom the statements are made. These books sell millions of copies, but the buyers are not evenly distributed through all social strata. What is the character of the audiences reached by these books? Does the secular as opposed to the religious self-help literature claim a different audience? Do the culture groups attracted by works that employ references to control of the unconscious differ from those attracted to works referring to selection of environmental stimuli? To what extent are these attractions tied to the symbols or slogans used and to what extent are people attracted by one or another formal approach to self-control? That is, is an urban intellectual audience drawn by the term "unconscious" or is there something in the structure of their situation which makes the effort to harmony appealing? Are there certain groups of individuals who will buy almost every book in this field that comes to their attention, regardless of whether it is secular or religious or whether it stresses the effort to harmony or the selection of environmental stimuli? Is there a class of "true believers" who successively try various types of self-help literature?

What function does reading these books have for the readers' personal programs of self-control? How do those who seek direction through reading differ from those who seek help from friends or from professionals, such as ministers, psychiatrists, or mediums? Might this literature be relevant to a certain stage in the process of seeking help even for those who visit counselors? Might reading provide a preliminary problem-mapping prior to seeking out a counselor, or might it function as an adjunct while visiting one?

Dornbusch, using his sample, tests some of the hypotheses suggested in the introductory collocation. His sample of self-help literature, as did the earlier one, emphasizes the effort to conquest as a method of control but does not stress the effort to harmony and the effort to transcendence. Works written by psychiatrists are an exception to this. Works in his sample also provide examples of the effort to synergy. His comparison of the self-help literature in two time periods suggests that one might study the empirical frequencies in other literatures of the four types of "effort." How are the types of effort advocated related to the types of self-control problems or manifest objects of control which the particular literature sets for itself? Is the type of effort advocated influenced by the culture in which the literature emerges? Experimental work on the relation between type of effort and manifest objects could uncover the mechanisms involved in controlling each object.

Dornbusch's sample of self-help literature emphasizes the control of cognitions and of affects, especially of affects involved in relating to others. The earlier "Collocation" sample noted more interest in the control of drives. Dornbusch points out that this may be due to a broad cultural shift. What determines whether a culture chooses to interpret stress through internal affectual manifestations or to focus upon the external environment as a source of stress? Does interest in controlling the internal as opposed to the external worlds depend upon the position the individual occupies in the hierarchy of power—that is, on his realistic chances of controlling the environment? Might the disenfranchised be concerned with internal control and might the upwardly mobile be concerned with environmental control? Would an individual's religious world view affect his interpretation of the origins of and the way to control stress? Would belonging to a Protestant society produce externally oriented conceptions while belonging to a Buddhist society produce internally oriented conceptions?

OPLER

Opler's individuals work out their cultural destinies as in a Greek tragedy. Their destinies are guided by the microcosm of the family and national culture they carry within themselves. Personal encounters become vehicles for cultural encounter and, as such, potentially conflictual. Cultural anthropological knowledge can prevent these encounters from producing a *Kulturkampf* by deflecting meetings between incompatible cultural elements. Those who carry their culture to another community must consider whether what they bring is acceptable to the community for which it is intended.

Illness, as a culturally related phenomenon, has at once universal and particular aspects. Basically, Opler says, illness is defined as a condition which impairs functioning in any context. Individuals judged schizophrenics in America would not be able to function in African society. Specific cultural contexts, however, affect the frequency of one or another type of impairment by, for example, furnishing guidelines for being ill, exposing individuals to peculiar stresses deriving from their peculiar patterns and producing peculiar susceptibilities in individuals which remain effective even after they have left the core of the culture. It would seem to follow that a program of training for self-control suited to one cultural group might not be suited to another. This would be a particularly serious problem in an American setting where, in groups recruited nationally, such as the military, members are likely to be from culturally divergent backgrounds. We would want to know why, despite this problem, groups such as the military do succeed in training individuals from diverse backgrounds with similar methods. Is it that military tradition has evolved some nearly universal directives? If so, a discovery and a cataloging of these near universals might help reveal the bounds within which cultural considerations are relevant.

Opler's case study of the interdependence of the symptoms of the Italian wife with those of the Irish husband is especially instructive. Individual self-control might be considered in a dyadic context. Perhaps, the self-control of one member of a group is so tied to that of another member that what is good for the goose need not be good for the gander. Suppose two individuals were relatively independent and mutually supportive. Increased control on the part of one might then enhance the self-control of the other. Suppose, however, that two are bound in a dependency relationship of nurturer and nurtured. Then, increased self-control on the part of the nurtured one might increase the stress upon the nurturer by depriving him of his needed dependent. The very success at self-control by one member of a dyad may impair the self-control of the other.

In the husband-wife case, Opler referred to the influence of the patriarchal Italian as opposed to the matriarchal Irish home to account for the contrasting adaptive mechanisms. These family structures would differ in their consequences for their male and female children. These questions may be studied separately. Are females better adapted than males to certain types of stress? To what extent is stress resistance a function of family authority structure? The interaction of these factors could be studied. A study could inquire into the interrelation of sex and the structure of the family of origin as they influence stress resistance on both males and females.

SWANSON

Swanson is concerned with the individual in the perspective of social structure, a complex of relationships between individuals and the norms which regulate these relationships. Much of the inner life of the individual consists of importations of relationships which first existed for him as interpersonal events. To understand certain individual dynamics, one looks at the dynamics of his social experience. Swanson reviews the routinized ways society guides its members to relations of love. The structure encapsulates the members' lives, trains them, controls their hatreds and defines the scope of their love relations. It provides opportunities for them to find one another and to realize love, either spontaneously or through effort. Individuals discover norms as principles inherent in the relations they have with others.

Swanson describes love as a relationship aimed at enhancing the other. For the other, enhancement means increased wisdom in formulating objectives (a cognitive function), security to venture and take risks (a motivational function), and the ability to find and accept forgiveness (principally an evaluative function).

These suggested functions could be empirically investigated. What is the effect of love upon recognition, either in the sense of rational action, as implied in the original proposition, or as an influence upon intellectual performance or abstract thought? Regarding the motivational and evaluative functions, does love generally motivate an individual to take risks and enable him to give and accept forgiveness, or are these consequences restricted to commitment to the relationship in which love is generated?

Love emerges between individuals who are functionally inter-dependent, related by complementary roles, as well as between individuals who are socially homogeneous or bound by common destiny. Do the mechanisms for generating love differ in these two situations and does the nature of the love generated differ?

Sometimes love is spoken of in terms of spontaneous flowering and at other times as something requiring work to give and to receive. Might spontaneity and work assume primacy during different phases in the generation of love? Is there a stage of laying the self open to await illumination, and another stage in which the relationship requires the expenditure of effort? If so, in what sequence would these phases appear?

In the process of deepening love, Swanson suggests that there are periods of withdrawal from intimacy and even hostility. Would this phasing of approach-withdrawal cross-cut the phases of action-waiting hypothesized above, or might they operate separately? On a psychological level, these phases suggest that oscillatory personality processes, in addition to stable traits, are involved in the growth of love. How do social relationships established in an oscillatory fashion differ from those based on more directly established cathexes?

Swanson suggests a connection between the severity of initiatory rites and the strength of the commitment attained by the initiate. Is the mechanism here a social weeding out so that only the most committed pass the initiation or do the rites themselves generate the commitment? Since initiation rites tend to be more severe in closed than in open groups, does it follow that high commitment requires a closed group? Swanson alludes to limits on the strength of commitment or of love which individuals can sustain. What social mechanisms enable individuals to adapt psychologically in relationships where they cannot meet the emotional expectations?

Socially provided opportunities for love to flourish include occasions for candidates to meet, norms which guide their interaction when they do meet, and the denotation of individuals with whom it is permissible to enter a love relationship. Organizations ordered on paternalistic and hierarchical principles provide a different structure of opportunities or rules for encounter between members than organizations ordered on fraternalistic and egalitarian principles. How does the power structure affect the rules defining permitted love relationships and the forms for initiating those relationships? Does one structure provide means for containing love within given strata and another facilitate its crossing between strata?

Swanson suggests that intermember hatred emerges where the group does not provide embracive controls for the love relation. How does this happen? Is it that the relaxing of controls releases the hatred latent in the cathexes which are already ambivalent, or does the relaxation of controls produce an anomic situation which generates frustrations in general? The love object may then be an innocent receiver or absorber of the hostile reactions to this frustration.

Swanson notes that individuals receive different types of love from different sources. What psychological arrangements enable individuals to integrate love experiences from many sources? Consistent with Swanson's proposition about the exclusiveness of love relations, each love partner might be expected to be jealous of others. This proposition may be elucidated through a notion of a love status set. The love status set might be measured by the number of sources from which love is obtained. The degree or type of commitment might be measured by the number of types of love received in a single relationship. Might the scope of the love status set which each particular love partner will tolerate be related inversely to the degree of commitment expected and attainable in that particular relationship? Accepting love in many relationships may well be associated with low commitment to any single relationship.

New Research in
Psychological Perspective

JANIS

Janis' individuals are concerned with maintaining their equilibrium, if not with continuing their tasks, when disaster strikes. Advance information incites "anticipatory fear" which, as it is worked through, helps them prepare inwardly. Failure to work through anxiety in advance may leave individuals with an aggrievement reaction, which is related to the "disaster syndrome," and disable them after the trial.

Disappointment in the "protective authorities" may lead to a feeling of vulnerability and, as a consequence, to reduced self-control. This might be manifested as disturbed behavior in the postimpact period. The intervening and dependent variables of this proposition may be studied further by treating them as the classificatory variables that they are. The feeling of vulnerability may be related curvilinearly to disturbed post-impact behavior. A slight or moderate sense of vulnerability might lead to constructive preparations for defense. A relatively high degree of feeling of vulnerability may well, as Janis suggests, be positively correlated with subsequent disturbed behavior. If individuals feel hopelessly vulnerable, however, their very surrender might function as a coping mechanism. Varying the independent variable, disappointment with the "protective authority," suggests a second line of inquiry. The "protective authorities" may not have to be considered invulnerable in order to be psychologically protective. If they share the victims' fate, the latter may not be disappointed and consequently behave in a disturbed manner in the post-impact period.

The aggrievement reaction, Janis notes, may involve expressing hostility towards the "protective authorities" (extropunitive) or be manifest as depression (intropunitive). Both hostility and depression of this sort would encumber teamwork. The defense, whether hostile or depressive or of some other form, that becomes habitual among members of a group would be a function of the group norms and social structure in which the individual is socialized. By specifying these social conditions affecting the selection of a mode and direction of defense, the group might learn how to harness the victim's bitterness in reconstruction or in attacking the enemy who caused the disaster.

Advance information about a stress situation, Janis says, restructures the perceptual field, permitting individuals to cope with danger. This consequence, as Janis has shown elsewhere, is not uniform for all types of advance information. Advance information of certain types might induce regression or fantasy or denial, which might reduce ability to cope with the danger. What of the timing of advance warning? Might information given too early create tension from the sheer expectancy or if given too late not allow adequate internal preparation for the danger? What is the consequence of advance warning of a disaster which does not materialize? How may a population be prepared to accept "cries of wolf" and still respond each time? Public interpretation of the advance warning may change with each successive repetition. Issues like these have been treated by Janis in some of his other work.

Janis explains staring at a disaster as an attempt to master the directly or vicariously experienced trauma. As opposed to this compulsion to look, what of the situation in which the individual is "unable to look"? Is the latter an attempt at mastery by denying or shutting out the experience? Janis, himself, has worked on this question. Moving the proposition from the psychodynamic to the interpersonal level, we note that society compels looking in some situations (drumming out ceremonies and executions), while in other situations the social norms forbid looking (at an individual's disability or at the Holy). What factors underlie social approval of one or another defense, and what are the social functions of the alternative behaviors?

Further propositions are suggested by varying the sensory mode involved in mastery of stress. Does mastery by looking involve a different type of working-through process than does mastery by retelling as, for example, in the case of a veteran relating his war experiences time and again? Does the process differ again when mastery is achieved by simulating patterns of motility similar to the patterns associated with the traumatic situation as, for example, in the case of the movements of an Indian War dance? Are some stresses better controlled by employing one or another sensory mode?

"Shock" among survivors of a disaster, Janis says, results from the perception that part of their culture has been rendered ineffective. What types of cultural loss precipitate individual "shock"? Does "shock" occur because personality and culture are phylogenetically related, so that the destruction of cultural elements may result in a resonant destruction of the derivative elements internalized in the personality? May this "shock" be attenuated through ritual demonstrations which reaffirm the integrality of the culture? To what extent is the impact on the personality due to its ontogenetic relations with culture? Does the destruction of parts of the culture remove functionally interrelated props from the personality? The answer to these questions would help in establishing a priority of efforts to assure cultural protection in disaster.

Janis raises the problem of learning to manage fear. Fear itself, however, may act as an extrinsic motive and increase subject matter learning when it is kept at a low level. High levels of fear may disorganize the individual rendering him unable to learn. These propositions, combined with Janis' propositions about psychological inoculation, suggest that if fear is but gradually increased, each time an individual works through fear at one level, he would be prepared to face an objectively more threatening situation. He would be able to manage increasing amounts of fear. A traumatizing overdose of fear, however, could reduce rather than increase ability to handle the next fear experience. Turning back, now, from the management of fear to fear as a motive, it seems that increasing ability to manage fear may reduce its value as a motive in learning subject matter. An instructor training persons in managing fear who is also responsible for teaching performance might be drawn into a vicious circle of increasing threats in order to assure learning.

KORCHIN

Korchin deals with the problem of remaining calm and getting on with the job in the face of adversity. Adversity may take the form of a severe stimulus which cannot be handled, such as that due to a threat which hits at the individual's self-esteem or sense of identity. Such a condition may cause loss of equilibrium or of ego mastery. One way the self may protect itself would be by avoiding "arousal," that is, by not caring or by being insensitive to experience. Another protective device would be to hold back the response or "incubate" it. A failure to handle "arousal" may result in a somatic experience especially when the response is not manifested.

Korchin discusses the relations among three factors: sensitivity to experience, performance, and stress resistance. Performance varies directly with sensitivity to experience (at least certain performances and types of experience). On the other hand, stress resistance varies inversely with sensitivity to experience. If we combine these two relationships, we might hypothesize that reducing sensitivity to experience in order to increase stress resistance would result in a reduced performance level. Thus, training for performance under stress faces a paradox. The trainer, it would seem, would have to settle for optimizing rather than maximizing stress resistance and performance. In a graph of these two relationships, the abcissa through the lowest acceptable performance level would intersect the sensitivity to experience curve at the minimum sensitivity that could be tolerated for that level of performance. This would set a limit for training for stress resistance by reducing sensitivity.

A similar problem arises in the interrelations of performance, stress and arousal. Performance would be best when arousal, as expressed in motivation or commitment to a situation, is relatively high. Korchin points out, however, that stress with high arousal leads to disorganized behavior. One could determine optimum levels of arousal so that adequate performance could be obtained without producing behavioral disorganization of such a magnitude that it would cancel the gain from arousal. The proposition may be further specified by thinking in terms of different degrees of stress and arousal. What, for example, are the effects upon the organization of behavior of high or low stress coupled respectively with high or low arousal?

Korchin's notion of the "incubation" of the anxiety response, its failure to appear for some time after a trauma, opens several issues. Is individual activity during the impact, the instance cited by Korchin, the only basis for "incubation"? How does the probability of "incubation" vary when we vary suddenness or severity of impact and previous training of the individual for the situation? Assuming that "incubation" of response is a form of inhibition of response, then its practical effect would depend upon the breadth of the spectrum of responses required. "Incubation" or inhibition of a sector of the organism could be dysfunctional for a performance requiring a rather holistic commitment of the organism. Blocking out a response might restrict the level of integration upon which the organism could operate. Other studies by Korchin and his associates provide information on these issues.

Throughout, there is the question of when a stress passes the individual tolerance level. When is there information overload? The information overload equation is not likely to be linear for any of the types of input, whether physical, sensory, or symbolic. The degree of reduction in tolerance for a given increment of input is likely to be more marked near the upper limit, as Korchin has shown elsewhere. Thus, aside from the absolute quantity of input, we would want to consider the rate of change in stimulus input which an organism can tolerate. Slowly increased or decreased input might be more tolerable to the organism than suddenly increased or decreased input.

Stress induces, Korchin says, a regression of ego mechanisms.

This regression might be adaptive if restricted to the duration of stress or until other coping mechanisms take over. What of points of no return in this regression? How would these differ for various personalities? Could training push points of no return further back? Much good work on these issues has already been accomplished under such rubrics as "breaking point" and "experimental neurosis."

LIDDELL

Liddell sets himself the problem of man surveying a dangerous world, anticipating a blow and preparing to duck it when it comes. The worst dangers are anxiety-punctuated monotony, being over-burdened or being lonely. Man's gestures to ward off the inevitable blow fail because, in part, he is a prisoner of an "emotional glue" implanted within him. Despite apparent hopelessness, man's independent spirit will assert itself in the end.

Liddell draws the implications for symbolic stimuli from his work with sensory stimuli. With regularly spaced and painful stimuli, tension rises before and drops after the stimulus. The stimulus may be a regular but unfulfillable demand for performance—perhaps even an expectation that an individual endure a stressful situation. The "Chinese water torture" situations with which Liddell is concerned are such that the individual is neither able to affect the source of the stimulus nor is he able to develop a defense against it. He must survive it. These environmental "inevitables" are the conditions of existence. One is reminded of the types of environmental conditions which guide evolutionary selection. Organisms with certain types of endowments can exist under conditions which exceed the adaptive capacity of other organisms. Might a process of social selection appoint individuals endowed with the capacity to encounter certain unusual conditions for the community? Could this be consciously planned so that, aside from training individuals to master stress, criteria might be established for selecting individuals to assume stressful roles?

Self-control is defined by Liddell to include any factor which directs behavior. Thus, prejudice is treated not only attitudinally but as a behavioral guide, as a form of self-control. A prejudice is established through the "coincidence principle." Many events, however, occur coincidentally and yet few remain emotionally glued together. What determines whether a coincidental occurrence will remain implanted as a prejudice guiding future behavior? Is this a matter of repetition or of significant traumas? Well-known principles from learning theory may be brought to bear here upon the problem of self-control.

Not all responses to stress are guided consciously. Liddell discusses alertness or vigilance as one type of response to anxiety-punctuated monotony. Under what conditions will vigilance, rather than other mechanisms, such as fainting or aggressive striking out, emerge in anticipation of a painful stimulus?

Some responses obtain the character of a reflex. Persistence in responses to pain which do not relieve pain, such as leg flexion in response to shock, seem stamped-in because they are vestiges of previous normal ways, perhaps paleological ways, of withdrawing from pain. These reflexes to stress which show resistance to extinction would have to be taken into account in training for self-control. The repertoire of such reflexes might be mapped.

Another caveat for the trainer is implied in Liddell's work. He notes that Pavlovian conditioning inevitably leads to a "nervous breakdown" if continued for a long time. This suggests a curvilinear relationship between conditioning and self-control. A moderate amount of conditioning builds in self-control, but overearning may disorganize the organism.

New Research in Psychiatric Perspective

ORNE

Orne studies the case of a man facing his task with grim determination. Forces barring the path to his goal are effective, in large measure, insofar as the individual considers them effective. Objective success is partially contingent upon the individual's conception of his ability. Each time an obstacle is overcome, greater strength is gained for tackling the next one. Ability to control behavior and overcome obstacles may be increased through training. The instructor in self-control may be a higher authority whose power the trainee comes to share. Though respecting this authority, the individual is not a buffeted automaton, since he has the ability to outwit the authority.

Orne's discussion of self-hypnosis and its relation to an original hypnosis raises several practical questions. Does practice influence the ability to attain self-hypnosis? What is the affect of removal in time from the original hypnosis? Is periodic renewal of the original hypnosis required to maintain self-hypnotic ability? Would the frequency with which such renewal is required depend upon the personality of the subject or of the hypnotist or upon some peculiarities of their relationship?

Orne raises the problem of differentiating hypnotic from normal conforming behavior for purposes of experiment. Hypnotic and conforming behaviors both arise in the context of authority relationships. Hypnotic authority rests upon unconscious transference mechanisms, while conforming tends to be understood in terms of conscious mechanisms. The type of authority which supports the ability to control behavior, either through conscious conformity or through self-hypnosis, may determine the type of stress response that can be controlled. Would charismatic authority better prepare an individual to face uncertainty, while the conscious expectation of sanctions better prepare him to face a known danger? The traditional concept of discipline includes both of these dimensions. What may be learned by studying the forms of discipline or authority traditionally associated with groups organized for encountering stress such as the military or heretical religious sects?

Orne suggests that commitment to a task, once established, becomes a relatively independent motive for continuing with the task regardless of the cost. This lack of regard for cost implies a shift from what Max Weber called "responsible action" to what he termed "action oriented to absolute ends." Does a viable society require a differentiation between members who assume socially protective or "responsible" roles and those who assume roles of high goal commitment?

Orne discusses the influence of the meaning of stress upon ability to tolerate stress. Does the meaning of stress derive from the significance of the act which the stressor is frustrating, from the goals not attained or from the experienced painfulness of a disequilibrated physiological or personality system? The factor of meaning distinguishes inherent painfulness from the perception of pain. Prior experience with pain would have differing consequences in these two cases. To the extent that stress is rooted in a perception, prior experience might reduce its pain potential. The individual would know what to expect, have learned how to handle the situation and be able to face his ordeal with less anxiety. On the other hand, prior experience with inherent painfulness may well increase its pain potential as happened with Liddell's sheep subjected to intermittent shock.

This distinction between perceptually induced stress or pain and inherent painfulness suggests additional hypotheses. Perception is a function of the social situation of the perceiver. The definition of the situation as painful would be a function of the social norms of the membership group or of the reference group to which the individual looks for evaluative standards. Does the tolerance for discomfort differ among individuals who occupy different positions in the group structure, corresponding, for example, to the differential institutionalization of a norm of affective neutrality? If so, does the ability to tolerate discomfort channel individuals into one or another social position or is the tolerance a product of the exigencies imposed upon the occupants of each position? The group itself has an ethos regarding response to pain. Under what conditions will a stoic attitude toward pain arise? Does it depend on the way power is organized in the group, or upon the security the group enjoys or upon whether the group is in a pioneering or a consolidating stage?

RIOCH

Rioch deals with the type of stress which might be encountered by a young man in a hurry to attain a goal despite obstacles in his way. These obstacles are tackled by processing data and managing informational overloads when they occur.

In this spirit, Rioch relates the loss of capacity for judgment under stress to decreased ability to store and retrieve information in the course of the transaction. Reference to mechanisms of storing and retrieving suggests that it might be fruitful to bring past research on the relation of anxiety to learning and memory to bear on the problem at this point. Such research would help distinguish between stress which restricts informational storage and a trauma which accounts for almost immutable informational storage.

Reduction in the capacity for data processing, says Rioch, reduces the load that an organism can tolerate. Combining this and the previous proposition suggests that stress tolerance decreases with increasing stress. The more the organism is under stress, the less stressful increment it is able to handle. The rate at which stress tolerance decreases might be more rapid under extreme stress than it would be within the range of mild stress. Thus, the boundaries of stress tolerance would be approached rather rapidly under more extreme conditions. We again arrive at the question of determining the upper and lower limits of environmental conditions in which an organism can survive.

In reality, the organism would not encounter isolated stressors. Do the limits for one type of stressor change when the organism is at the same time or sequentially subject to another stressor? The organism's responses also are not isolated but are systemic. Rioch notes that each system which controls the organism-environment interaction has its own peculiar homeostatic limits for each stressor. The propositions stated above in isolated variable language may be restated in system language. What are the limits of stress tolerance for various systems? How does the condition of one system, for example, that of heat exchange, affect the homeostatic balance of another system, for example, the system of symbolic interaction?

Let us turn to some more specific propositions. Rioch suggests that formulations such as Fate relieve the individual of the problem of goal change under stress by structuring information during the course of the event. The way the information is structured may influence the course of the event. Fate may be dysfunctional in some situations requiring an instrumental orientation. Further, various symbols may differ in efficacy. Would a formulation such as "have faith" have a different implication for the course of the transaction than a formulation such as "we have superior strength and will win"?

Rioch refers to the control of one's own behavior under conditions of uncertainty by limiting attention to a "prescribed program," a plan of action. Such "programs" exist as part of the "wisdom of the race." An examination of traditional "programs" would be instructive for devising new ones. "Banks" of such "programs" might be established for use in various situations of stress. This would involve "action research" on such topics as training for performance in sports and training programs for desert survival.

Several propositions about stress management and group behavior emerge from Rioch's work. Rioch finds that decisions made under stress tend to follow the mores of the reference group. This suggests that some behavior under stress which appears disorganized may actually be organized in terms of the norms of another group. The group whose norms are followed in stressful situations might differ from the group whose norms guide nonstress behavior. What determines the reference group which will be selected as a source of norms for stressful situations? Rioch suggests that the individual will follow norms of that group from which he anticipates support. The implied hypothesis is that under stress an individual may shift allegiance, perhaps temporarily, to that group which can offer a program for handling stress or to that group which supports him in his hour of need.

Predictability of behavior in a group, a safeguard against group disorganization, rests, in part, on what Rioch terms commitment-expectancy. This concept links individual self-control with the context provided by the behavior of others. In a complex group, the maintenance of commitment-expectancy turns upon the reliability of communication. This suggests studies of the communications network and of the types of institutionalized communications codes which help maintain commitment-expectancy.

GOLDSTEIN

Goldstein writes of man subject to immutable suffering but determined to affirm life. Suffering may come from loss of the abstract attitude. An individual's strength to affirm himself is born in the sphere of immediacy, in the camaraderie of those locked with him in his suffering. Others in his environment may use their abstract attitude to protect him from catastrophe. Consideration of the situation of these others suggests some questions. What is the impact upon those who protect an individual who has lost his abstract attitude? The individual who has lost the abstract attitude may choose to live on a lower level of existence by engaging the environment in less demanding ways. Must those who interact with him lower their levels of existence to maintain the relationship? The loss of self-control on the part of an individual may affect the organization of those about him. How does the protective group reorganize itself or reallocate tasks to adapt to a member who is operating at a lower level? What forms of social reorganization encourage the afflicted individual to raise his level of existence and what forms encourage him to sink to an even lower level? Which forms of protective organization least impair group functioning?

Mastery of a situation, Goldstein says, transforms the personality in relation to that situation. The individual's nature is realized at a higher level and he is ready for a more severe test. In this way, stress mastery would grow cumulatively as the individual realizes his potential. How may an individual assess his maximally realizable nature? What determines the level to which one may reasonably aspire? Would this have to be assessed externally by others?

The relationship between "self-realization" and "level of aspiration" may well be curvilinear. A low level of aspiration denies the individual the opportunity to realize his nature. A high level of aspiration may involve failure to accept reality or, as Goldstein says, to accept restrictions. Under this condition he also will not realize his nature. May an optimum level of aspiration for an individual be determined in view of some objective assessment of the individual's nature?

A relation in the sphere of immediacy would contribute to the control of self under stress. How, though, does one arrive at the sphere of immediacy? Goldstein says surrender may be a way-station. Surrender of self, then, becomes a factor in control of self. Yet, if the individual surrenders, he may not be able to influence the environmental source of stress (unless that source responds psychologically to the act of surrender). Does this imply an inherent contradiction between the attitude which will enable an individual to eliminate environmental stress and the attitude that will enable him to bear the restrictions imposed by severe stress? This question stands at the juncture between Eastern and Western thought on self-control.

Toward a Program of Research on Self-Control

Reviewing each contributor's work individually has helped preserve their distinctive suggestiveness. The time has come to summarize these suggestions in a recommendation for a program of research in self-control. Organizing them around a "natural" partitioning of the concrete phenomenon of self-control reduces their heterogeneity. The phenomenon of self-control may be partitioned with reference to three principal substantive issues: (1) stressor conditions impinging upon the organism, (2) the tolerance capabilities of the organism in the face of these conditions, and (3) the ways the individual is enabled to manage stress or to exert self-control.[3] As noted with reference to individual discussions above, this will not be an exhaustive set of research recommendations nor the only set that follows from the contributors' propositions. The research questions to be raised here are, as above, not necessarily the ones the contributors would raise but are those which come to the mind of the editor of this volume as a result of having studied the various contributions. As before, some of the recommendations will simply require that research already available, some by our contributors themselves, be summarized with respect to our problem. Other recommendations will inform new inquiries.

Research on stressor conditions might engage in further specifying the stressors and in differentiating them from similar conditions which are not stressors. The stressor condition which encumbers the organism in its attempt to store information should be distinguished from anxiety which motivates learning and from the trauma which imprints information (R). What of stressors peculiar to a given culture? Does guilt appear as a stressor only in cultures having certain types of religious systems, such as the monotheistic, and not in others, such as the polytheistic (H)? May the numerous fears cited as stressors be substructured to produce a small list of empirically determined ultimate objects of fear, and may these be compared with the "ultimate objects" of fear delineated in some well-known theological and psychological writing (K)? Might we specify those parts of a culture the loss of which is most likely to traumatize the individual? Why are certain cultural vacua more frightening than others (J)? Further information is needed about the role of cultural definitions in the experience of pain and about the way perceptual processes enter into the definition of a stressor (Or). What are the possibilities and limitations in generalizing from the effects of sensory to the effects of symbolic stressors (L)?

The state of the organism in response to the stressor is the second research area. Reflex responses to stressors which may be adaptive with respect to certain functions may disable the organism for complex action. Such reflexes should be studied as secondary stressors for the organism in its attempt to manage stress (K). Studies are needed on stress tolerance under differing rates of stimulus input, under differing absolute quantities of input, and on the effect of increments of input at different levels of stress (K, R). Parameters of stress tolerance should be determined for various types of stressors and for the various organismic systems involved (K, R). Changes in tolerance levels for a given stressor due to the simultaneous or sequential input of another stressor might also be investigated (R). In what ways do males and females differ in their tolerance for given stressors (Op)?

Individual management of stress, the ability of the individual consciously to control his acts despite pressure, is the central concern of this book. Hypotheses have been suggested regarding some personality mechanisms involved in anxiety reduction or in warding off the consequences of stress. Mechanisms which are essentially unconscious or automatic enter as conditions affecting the implementation of conscious means of self-control and merit study in this light. How do personality and social factors influence the selection of the relatively conscious aspects of mechanisms of defense? When, for instance, will the individual stare and when will he refuse to look? When will he become vigilant and when might he faint? Factors influencing the employment of one or another sensory mode—sight, hearing, motility—in the defense and the implications of the sensory mode involved for conscious control should also be investigated (L, J). How is the perception of the stressor related to the type of defense selected (Or)? What are the mechanisms by which conscious activities interpenetrate unconscious processes in phenomena such as the incubation of anxiety (K)? How does mastery of one stressful situation affect mastery of successive situations of that or other types? When does the ability to control the self under stress grow cumulatively with each experience (G, J)? Do some forms of mastery leave the organism helpless before an ensuing threat? What factors of constitutional endowment or socialization influence levels of potential stress mastery? How may an individual assess his potentially realizable nature (G)? If an individual calls upon several external supports in order to master stress, how does his personality integrate aid from these various sources (S)?

Ability to manage stress is also a function of the social context. Group norms influence the decision to try to manage stress (H) as well as the selection of responses to stress. The way stress is to be managed differs from one national group to the other and among subgroups within each nation. How may training for self-control be fitted to specific cultural contexts (D, Op)? What aspects of the broad culture of a group direct the use of one or another defense (J)? What determines the suitability of internally or externally oriented techniques (D)? What aspects of stress management are nearly universal (Op)? Data should be collected on the groups which an individual uses as reference groups for norms for meeting a stressful situation? What characteristics make one group more efficacious than another in this respect? How may allegiance be shifted temporarily to a reference group which provides support in the face of stress without disrupting an individual's primary allegiance (R)? What are the implications for self-control of various patterns of communication in the group (R), the type of authority which assures order in the group (Or),

the type of power structures or the form of stratification in the
group (S)? Group support for managing stress is, in part, a derivative of intermember solidarity. A group may be solidary for
one situation and not for another. How do organizational factors
determine the extent of solidarity for stress management in the
group, and the relative positions of members who may become
solidary for this purpose (S)? How are different patterns of fa-
milial authority related to ways of controlling the self (Op)?
What organizational characteristics allow the individual to adapt
to stress by lowering his level of existence and what characteristics
encourage him to adapt with greater self-realization (G)? Looked
at in reverse, what is the effect of the type of protection afforded
on group functioning and how do various types of protective activities affect the ability of other group members to manage their
stresses (G)?

Aside from the normative and the structural influences, groups
help individuals master stress through ritual activities. What mechanisms are involved in developing self-control through rituals such
as initiatory rites? Are these mechanisms of social selection or
do they generate control (S)? What is the effect of removal in
time from the original ritual or, in the case of a hypnotic experience, from an original hypnosis (Or)? What determines the scope
of control generated by group processes? Is self-control limited to
mastery of stresses arising in the specific relations in which that
control is generated, or is the control ability generalized and, if
so, under what conditions (S)? Work is needed on the formal
aspects of the process by which the ability to control the self is
generated. Are these processes phased in alternate periods of
activity and waiting and of approach and withdrawal (S)? Relationships established in an oscillatory fashion, such as through
alternate approach and withdrawal, may tend to involve a degree
of ambivalence. What accounts for stability among the partners
to such an ambivalent relationship when the relationship itself is
subjected to a stressor (S)? How does a relationship adapt when
it generates more love than the individual personality can sustain
(S)? A group has the possibility of a division of labor for stressful situations. How may a group identify its more resilient individuals and recruit them for particular stressful roles? What group
factors determine the proportion of resilient individuals which it
contains (L, Or)?

Learned techniques or "programs" of action may increase the
individual's ability to act under stress in a controlled manner.

"Banks" of programs for action in stressful situations should be made available (R). The methods of training or the directive systems depend not only on the character of the stress to be managed, but also on the societal and institutional ethos and the stage of development of the group (N, Op). What are the implications of this fact for adapting "programs" of self-control such as yoga or Zen meditation, from other cultures to our own? What types of groups tend to employ particular symbols such as "hope" or "faith" in the management of stress, and what is the consequence for self-control of these and other symbols (H)? Are various religious orientations equal alternatives in the management of stress, or is each religious form especially suited for meeting a particular class of stressful situations (N)?

Two types of paradoxes arise in relation to self-control. The first paradox is that a factor which, in a certain quantity or under certain conditions, may increase control may, in another quantity or under other conditions, decrease it. One type of advance information about a disaster may lead to preparation for coping with the disaster, and another type of information may lead to regression or fantasy behavior (J). A moderate sense of vulnerability may encourage individuals to prepare for and rationally meet a disaster, a greater sense of vulnerability may produce disturbed postimpact behavior, while a complete sense of vulnerability or surrender may again provide a coping mechanism (H, J). Moderate conditioning may implant self-control, but overconditioning may produce behavioral disorganization (L). Regression may be adaptive as a way of handling stress, but one may regress so far that the personality cannot return to normal functioning when the pressure is off (K). Too low a level of aspiration may lead to reluctance to try, but too high a level may lead to frustration and loss of control (G). Research is needed on the affect of differing degrees of the same factor upon control or loss of control and on various external conditions which turn the same factor once into a source of strength and one into a source of weakness.

A second type of paradox is that the very nature of the mechanisms, which are involved to enable performance under stress, themselves introduce a new disturbance in the situation. The paradoxes referred to in the paragraph above are resolved when we realize that the various factors are related to self-control in a curvilinear fashion. The solution is to determine optimal degrees of these factors. The second type of paradox tends to be an inherent dilemma of the control situation and not given to resolution by control of a single variable. The very factor which, on the one hand, engenders self-control, on the other hand, undermines the act for which the control was originally sought. Simplification of communication patterns and of the communication codes may increase reliability of behavior and so increase the self-control of group members. At the same time, this simplification may reduce the flexibility of the group's operation in the face of novel situations (R). Fear may act as a motive encouraging learning, but in learning to manage fear, the individual may become so inured to it that it is robbed of its motivating potential (J). Reduced sensitivity to experience may protect an individual from disturbing environmental input but, at the same time, reduced sensitivity lowers the acuity of performance (K). Arousal operates as a motive enabling individuals to perform, but stress under a condition of arousal may induce disorganized behavior (K). Inhibition of an anxiety response may help behavioral control, but inhibition of the response of a segment of the personality may prevent the broad integration required for holistic execution of complex tasks (K). Surrender may be a way of controlling the internal response to stress, but it reduces the persons' ability to control the environmental forces generating the stress (G). Research here would have to specify the conditions for optimum functioning in a balance between maximizing control and minimizing performance decrement. Resolution requires a study of the relation of the controlling factor, simultaneously, to two variables, stress resistance and performance.

Scholars like those who advanced the propositions from which these new hypotheses were hermeneutically derived may carry this work forward. The end of this book is the beginning of new research.

The art of progress is to preserve order amid change, and to preserve change amid order. Life refuses to be embalmed alive. The more prolonged the halt in some unrelieved system of order, the greater the crash of the dead society.

Alfred North Whitehead in
Process and Reality

NOTES

1. I have been reminded of this hoary term by my colleague Professor Jacob Taubes who, for some years, has been leading a faculty seminar in hermeneutics at Columbia University.

2. Hopefully, another worker will pause to make this codification for us. Fragmental statements from a scientific hermeneutics would include Goode's work on "specification of the concept" in which the dimensions of a relatively vague notion are specified by collecting the contexts in a given work in which it is found and comparing its varied meanings. Goode's "reconceptualization" is also a hermeneutical device which explains the findings of a study through constructs not employed by the original researcher. The axiomatization of sociology and psychology in Homans' *The Human Group* and Zetterberg's *On Theory and Verification in Sociology* shows how established concepts and propositions are ordered in patterns of theorems and corollaries from which one may deduce new theorems and corollaries for testing. Merton's paradigm of functional analysis is a hermeneutical outline of questions to guide analysis of a substantive area. His principle of multiple function, for example, is a generic statement which leads the student to seek additional functions for an observed phenomenon by examining its relation to other elements in the same system or by studying its impact on other systems.

3. The letters in parentheses in the following text indicate whether the summary suggestions are based on hypotheses derived from contributions of D-Dornbusch, G-Goldstein, H-Hadas, J-Janis, K-Korchin, L-Liddell, N-Nelson, Op-Opler, Or-Orne, R-Rioch, or S-Swanson.

NAME INDEX

389

SUBJECT INDEX